Chartered Institute of
Management Accountants

This book comes with free EN-gage online resources so that you can study anytime, anywhere. This free online resource is not sold separately and is included in the price of the book.

How to access your on-line resources

You can access additional online resources associated with this CIMA Official book via the EN-gage website at: **www.EN-gage.co.uk**.

Existing users

If you are an **existing EN-gage user**, simply log-in to your account, click on the 'add a book' link at the top of your homepage and enter the ISBN of this book and the unique pass key number contained above.

New users

If you are a new EN-gage user then you first need to register at: **www.EN-gage.co.uk**. Once registered, Kaplan Publishing will send you an email containing a link to activate your account - please check your junk mail if you do not receive this or contact us using the phone number or email address printed on the back cover of this book. Click on the link to activate your account. To unlock your additional resources, click on the 'add a book' link at the top of your home page. You will then need to enter the ISBN of this book (found on page ii) and the unique pass key number contained in the scratch panel below:

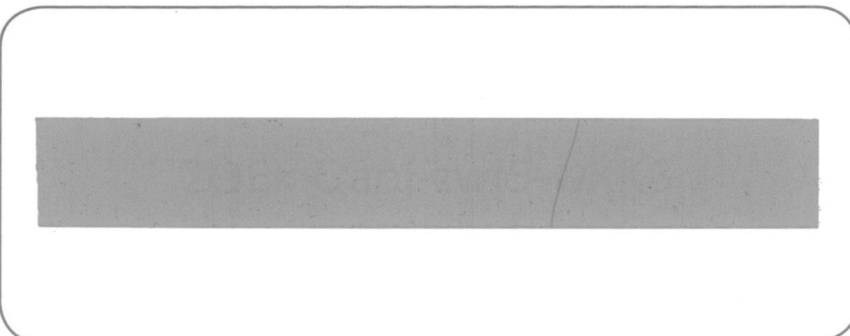

Then click 'finished' or 'add another book'.

Please allow 24 hours from the time you submit your book details for the content to appear in the My Learning and Testing area of your account.

Your code and information

This code can only be used once for the registration of one book online. This registration will expire when this edition of the book is no longer current - please see the back cover of this book for the expiry date.

Existing users

If you are an **existing EN-gage user**, simply log-in to your account, click on the 'add a book' link at the top of your homepage and enter the ISBN of this book and the unique pass key number contained above.

CIMA

Paper C04

Fundamentals of Business Economics

Study Text

CIMA Certificate in Business Accounting

Published by: Kaplan Publishing UK

Unit 2 The Business Centre, Molly Millars Lane, Wokingham, Berkshire RG41 2QZ

Acknowledgements

The CIMA Publishing trade mark is reproduced with kind permission of CIMA.

British Library Cataloguing in Publication Data

A catalogue record for this book is available from the British Library.

ISBN: 978-1-78415-284-0

Printed and bound in Great Britain.

Contents

Paper Introduction

Acknowledgements

Every effort has been made to contact the holders of copyright material, but if any here have been inadvertently overlooked the publishers will be pleased to make the necessary arrangements at the first opportunity.

How to Use the Materials

These Official CIMA learning materials brought to you by CIMA Publishing and Kaplan Publishing have been carefully designed to make your learning experience as easy as possible and to give you the best chances of success in your *Fundamentals of Business Economics* computer based assessments.

The product range contains a number of features to help you in the study process. They include:

- a detailed explanation of all syllabus areas;
- extensive 'practical' materials, including readings from relevant journals;
- generous question practice, together with full solutions;
- a computer based assessments preparation section, complete with computer based assessments standard questions and solutions.

This Study Text has been designed with the needs of home-study and distance-learning candidates in mind. Such students require very full coverage of the syllabus topics, and also the facility to undertake extensive question practice. However, the Study Text is also ideal for fully taught courses.

The main body of the text is divided into a number of chapters, each of which is organised on the following pattern:

- *Detailed learning outcomes.* You should assimilate these before beginning detailed work on the chapter, so that you can appreciate where your studies are leading.
- *Step-by-step topic coverage.* This is the heart of each chapter, containing detailed explanatory text supported where appropriate by worked examples and exercises. You should work carefully through this section, ensuring that you understand the material being explained and can tackle the examples and exercises successfully. Remember that in many cases knowledge is cumulative; if you fail to digest earlier material thoroughly, you may struggle to understand later chapters.
- *Readings and activities.* Most chapters are illustrated by more practical elements, such as relevant journal articles or other readings, together with comments and questions designed to stimulate discussion.

- *Question practice.* The test of how well you have learned the material is your ability to tackle computer based standard questions. Make a serious attempt at producing your own answers, but at this stage don't be too concerned about attempting the questions in computer based assessments conditions. In particular, it is more important to absorb the material thoroughly by completing a full solution than to observe the time limits that would apply in the actual computer based assessments.
- *Solutions.* Avoid the temptation merely to 'audit' the solutions provided. It is an illusion to think that this provides the same benefits as you would gain from a serious attempt of your own. However, if you are struggling to get started on a question you should read the introductory guidance provided at the beginning of the solution, and then make your own attempt before referring back to the full solution.

Having worked through the chapters you are ready to begin your final preparations for the examination. The final section of this Study Text provides you with the guidance you need. It includes the following features:

- A brief guide to revision technique.
- A note on the format of the computer based assessments. You should know what to expect when you tackle the real computer based assessments and in particular the number of questions to attempt.
- Guidance on how to tackle the computer based assessment itself.
- A table mapping revision questions to the syllabus learning outcomes allowing you to quickly identify questions by subject area.
- Revision questions. These are of computer based assessments standard and should be tackled in computer based assessments conditions, especially as regards the time allocation.
- Solutions to the revision questions.
- Two mock computer based assessments.

You should plan to attempt the mock tests just before the date of the real computer based assessments. By this stage your revision should be complete and you should be able to attempt the mock computer based assessments within the time constraints of the real computer based assessments.

If you work conscientiously through this official CIMA Study Text according to the guidelines above you will be giving yourself an excellent chance of exam success. Good luck with your studies!

Quality and accuracy are of the utmost importance to us so if you spot an error in any of our products, please send an email to mykaplanreporting@kaplan.com with full details, or follow the link to the feedback form in MyKaplan.

Our Quality Co-ordinator will work with our technical team to verify the error and take action to ensure it is corrected in future editions.

Icon Explanations

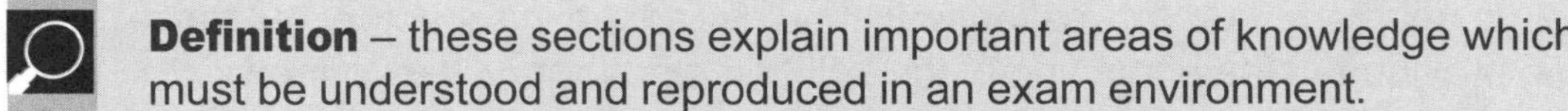

Definition – these sections explain important areas of knowledge which must be understood and reproduced in an exam environment.

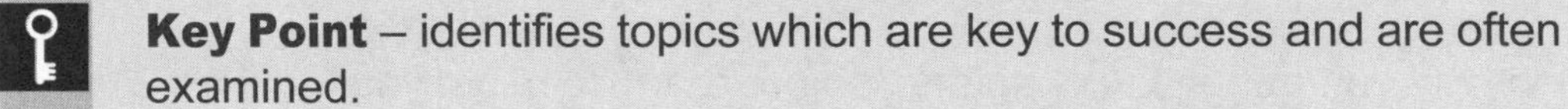

Key Point – identifies topics which are key to success and are often examined.

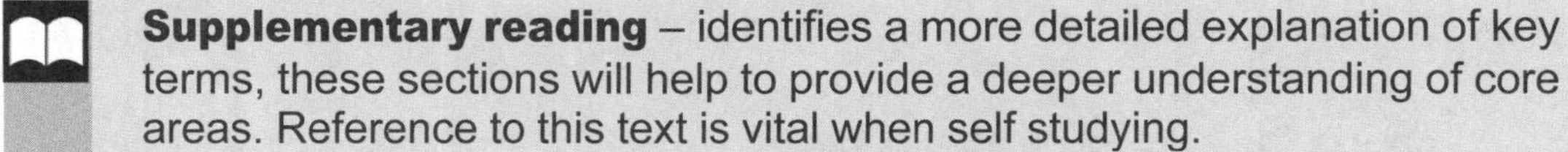

Supplementary reading – identifies a more detailed explanation of key terms, these sections will help to provide a deeper understanding of core areas. Reference to this text is vital when self studying.

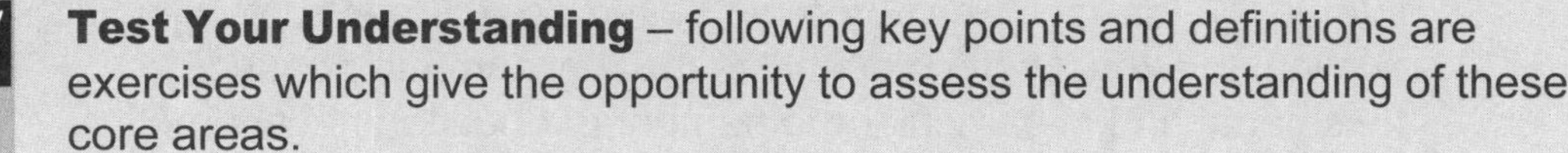

Test Your Understanding – following key points and definitions are exercises which give the opportunity to assess the understanding of these core areas.

Illustration – to help develop an understanding of particular topics. The illustrative examples are useful in preparing for the Test Your Understanding exercises.

Exclamation Mark – this symbol signifies a topic which can be more difficult to understand, when reviewing these areas care should be taken.

Study technique

Passing exams is partly a matter of intellectual ability, but however accomplished you are in that respect you can improve your chances significantly by the use of appropriate study and revision techniques. In this section we briefly outline some tips for effective study during the earlier stages of your approach to the exam. Later in the text we mention some techniques that you will find useful at the revision stage.

Planning

To begin with, formal planning is essential to get the best return from the time you spend studying. Estimate how much time in total you are going to need for each subject you are studying for the Certificate in Business Accounting. Remember that you need to allow time for revision as well as for initial study of the material. You may find it helpful to read 'Pass First Time!' second edition by David R. Harris, ISBN 9781856177986. This book will provide you with proven study techniques. Chapter by chapter it covers the building blocks of successful learning and examination techniques. This is the ultimate guide to passing your CIMA exams, written by a past CIMA examiner and shows you how to earn all the marks you deserve, and explains how to avoid the most common pitfalls. You may also find "The E Word: Kaplan's Guide to Passing Exams" by Stuart Pedley-Smith ISBN: 9780857322050 helpful. Stuart Pedley-Smith is a senior lecturer at Kaplan Financial and a qualified accountant specialising in financial management. His natural curiosity and wider interests have led him to look beyond the technical content of financial management to the processes and journey that we call education. He has become fascinated by the whole process of learning and the exam skills and techniques that contribute towards success in the classroom. This book is for anyone who has to sit an exam and wants to give themselves a better chance of passing. It is easy to read, written in a common sense style and full of anecdotes, facts, and practical tips. It also contains synopses of interviews with people involved in the learning and examining process.

With your study material before you, decide which chapters you are going to study in each week, and which weeks you will devote to revision and final question practice.

Prepare a written schedule summarising the above and stick to it!

It is essential to know your syllabus. As your studies progress, you will become more familiar with how long it takes to cover topics in sufficient depth. Your timetable may need to be adapted to allocate enough time for the whole syllabus.

Students are advised to refer to the notice of examinable legislation published regularly in CIMA's magazine (Financial Management), the students e-newsletter (Velocity) and on the CIMA website, to ensure they are up-to-date.

Tips for effective studying

(1) Aim to find a quiet and undisturbed location for your study, and plan as far as possible to use the same period of time each day. Getting into a routine helps to avoid wasting time. Make sure that you have all the materials you need before you begin so as to minimise interruptions.

(2) Store all your materials in one place, so that you do not waste time searching for items around the house. If you have to pack everything away after each study period, keep them in a box, or even a suitcase, which will not be disturbed until the next time.

(3) Limit distractions. To make the most effective use of your study periods you should be able to apply total concentration, so turn off the TV, set your phones to message mode, and put up your 'do not disturb' sign.

(4) Your timetable will tell you which topic to study. However, before diving in and becoming engrossed in the finer points, make sure you have an overall picture of all the areas that need to be covered by the end of that session. After an hour, allow yourself a short break and move away from your books. With experience, you will learn to assess the pace you need to work at. You should also allow enough time to read relevant articles from newspapers and journals, which will supplement your knowledge and demonstrate a wider perspective.

(5) Work carefully through a chapter, making notes as you go. When you have covered a suitable amount of material, vary the pattern by attempting a practice question. Preparing an answer plan is a good habit to get into, while you are both studying and revising, and also in the examination room. It helps to impose a structure on your solutions, and avoids rambling. When you have finished your attempt, make notes of any mistakes you made, or any areas that you failed to cover or covered more briefly.

(6) Make notes as you study, and discover the techniques that work best for you. Your notes may be in the form of lists, bullet points, diagrams, summaries, 'mind maps' or the written word, but remember that you will need to refer back to them at a later date, so they must be intelligible. If you are on a taught course, make sure you highlight any issues you would like to follow up with your lecturer.

(7) Organise your notes. Make sure that all your notes, calculations etc., can be effectively filed and easily retrieved later.

Computer based assessments

CIMA uses objective test questions in the computer based assessments. The most common types are:

- Multiple choice, where you have to choose the correct answer from a list of four possible answers. This could either be numbers or text.
- Multiple choice with more choices and answers, for example, choosing two correct answers from a list of eight possible answers. This could either be numbers or text.
- Single numeric entry, where you give your numeric answer, for example, profit is $10,000.
- Multiple entry, where you give several numeric answers.
- True/false questions, where you state whether a statement is true or false.
- Matching pairs of text, for example, matching a technical term with the correct definition.
- Other types could be matching text with graphs and labelling graphs/diagrams.

In every chapter of this Study Text we have introduced these types of questions but obviously we have to label answers A, B, C etc rather than using click boxes. For convenience we have retained quite a lot of questions where an initial scenario leads to a number of sub-questions. There will be questions of this type in the CBA but they will rarely have more than three sub-questions.

Guidance re CIMA online calculator

As part of the CIMA Certificate level computer based assessment software, candidates are now provided with a calculator. This calculator is onscreen and is available for the duration of the assessment. The calculator is available in each of the five Certificate level assessments and is accessed by clicking the calculator button in the top left hand corner of the screen at any time during the assessment.

All candidates must complete a 15 minute tutorial before the assessment begins and will have the opportunity to familiarise themselves with the calculator and practice using it.

Candidates may practise using the calculator by downloading and installing the practice exam at http://www.vue.com/athena/ . The calculator can be accessed from the fourth sample question (of 12).

Please note that the practice exam and tutorial provided by Pearson VUE at http://www.vue.com/athena/ is not specific to CIMA and includes the full range of question types the Pearson VUE software supports, some of which CIMA does not currently use.

Fundamentals of Business Economics Syllabus

The computer based assessments for *Fundamentals of Business Economics* are 2 hour assessments comprising 75 compulsory questions, with one or more parts. Single part questions are generally worth 1–2 marks each, but two and three part questions may be worth 4 or 6 marks. There will be no choice and all questions should be attempted.

Additional CBA resources, including sample assessment questions are available online at www.cimaglobal.com/cba2011

Structure of subjects and learning outcomes

Each subject within the syllabus is divided into a number of broad syllabus topics. The topics contain one or more lead learning outcomes, related component learning outcomes and indicative knowledge content.

A learning outcome has two main purposes:

(a) To define the skill or ability that a well prepared candidate should be able to exhibit in the examination

(b) To demonstrate the approach likely to be taken in examination questions

The learning outcomes are part of a hierarchy of learning objectives. The verbs used at the beginning of each learning outcome relate to a specific learning objective e.g.

Calculate the break-even point, profit target, margin of safety and profit/volume ratio for a single product or service

The verb **'calculate'** indicates a level three learning objective. The following table lists the learning objectives and the verbs that appear in the syllabus learning outcomes and examination questions.

Certificate level verbs

CIMA VERB HIERARCHY

CIMA place great importance on the choice of verbs in exam question requirements. It is thus critical that you answer the question according to the definition of the verb used.

In Certificate exams you will meet verbs from levels 1, 2, and 3. These are as follows:

Level 1: KNOWLEDGE

What you are expected to know

VERBS USED	DEFINITION
List	Make a list of.
State	Express, fully or clearly, the details of/facts of.
Define	Give the exact meaning of.

Level 2: COMPREHENSION

What you are expected to understand

VERBS USED	DEFINITION
Describe	Communicate the key features of.
Distinguish	Highlight the differences between.
Explain	Make clear or intelligible/state the meaning or purpose of.
Identify	Recognise, establish or select after consideration.
Illustrate	Use an example to describe or explain something.

Level 3: APPLICATION

How you are expected to apply your knowledge

VERBS USED	DEFINITION
Apply	Put to practical use.
Calculate	Ascertain or reckon mathematically.
Demonstrate	Prove with certainty or exhibit by practical means.
Prepare	Make or get ready for use.
Reconcile	Make or prove consistent/compatible.
Solve	Find an answer to.
Tabulate	Arrange in a table.

PAPER C04
FUNDAMENTALS OF BUSINESS ECONOMICS

Syllabus overview

This paper primarily deals with the economic context of business and how competition, the behaviour of financial markets, and government economic policy can influence an organisation. It also provides the key microeconomic techniques underlying price determination and profit maximisation decisions.

The focus of this syllabus is on providing candidates with an understanding of the areas of economic activity relevant to an organisation's decisions.

Syllabus structure

The syllabus comprises the following topics and study weightings:

A	The macroeconomic context of organisations	25%
B	The goals and decisions of organisations	25%
C	The market system and the competitive process	25%
D	The financial system	25%

Assessment strategy

There will be a two hour computer based assessment, comprising 75 compulsory questions, each with one or more parts.

A variety of objective test question styles and types will be used within the assessment.

C04 – A. THE MACROECONOMIC CONTEXT OF ORGANISATIONS. (25%)

Learning outcomes On completion of their studies students should be able to:			Indicative syllabus content
Lead	**Component**	**Level**	
1. explain the factors affecting the level of a country's national income and the impact of changing growth rates on organisations.	(a) explain determination of macroeconomic phenomena, including equilibrium national income, growth in national income, price inflation, unemployment, and trade deficits and surpluses; (b) explain the stages of the trade cycle, its causes and consequences for the policy choices of government; (c) explain the consequences of the trade cycle for organisations; (d) explain the main principles of public finance (i.e. deficit financing, forms of taxation) and macroeconomic policy; (e) describe the impacts on organisations of potential policy responses of government, to each stage of the trade cycle.	2 2 2 2 2	• Changes to equilibrium level of national income using an aggregate demand and supply analysis. [5] • Types and consequences of unemployment, inflation and balance of payments deficits. [5] • The circular flow of income, the main injections and withdrawals and their determinants. [5] • The trade cycle and the implications for unemployment, inflation and trade balance of each stage (recession, depression, recovery, boom). [5] • Government macroeconomic policy goals: low unemployment, inflation, external equilibrium and growth. [5] • Government policy for each stage of the trade cycle. [5] • Impacts of recession and boom on forecast sales of capital and consumption goods, industry profitability and employment levels in the firm. [5] • The main principles of public finance: the central government budget and forms of direct and indirect taxation, incidence of taxation (progressive, regressive) and potential impact of high taxation on incentives and avoidance. [5] • The main principles of public finance: fiscal, monetary and supply side policies, including relative merits of each. [5] • The effects on organisations of changes to interest rates, government expenditure and taxation. [5] • The effects on organisations of direct government macroeconomic policies including prices and incomes policies, labour market regulation, regulation on trade and policies to encourage investment. [5]

Learning outcomes On completion of their studies students should be able to:			Indicative syllabus content
Lead	**Component**	**Level**	
2. explain the factors affecting the trade of a country with the rest of the World and its impact on business.	(a) explain the concept of the balance of payments and its implications for government policy; (b) identify the main elements of national policy with respect to trade; (c) explain the impacts of exchange rate policies on business.	2 2 2	• The main flows measured in the balance of payments accounts and the causes and effects of fundamental imbalances in the balance of payments. [6] • Arguments for and against free trade and policies to encourage free trade (e.g. bi-lateral trade agreements, multi-lateral agreements, free trade areas, economic communities and economic unions), and protectionist instruments (tariffs, quotas, administrative controls, embargoes). [6] • The effect of changing exchange rates on the profits of firms and international competitiveness of national industry. [6]
3. explain the influences on economic development of countries and its effect on business.	(a) explain the concept of globalisation and the consequences for businesses and national economies; (b) explain the role of major institutions promoting global trade and development.	2 2	• The nature of globalisation and factors driving it (improved communications, political realignments, growth of global industries and institutions, cost differentials). [6] • The main trade agreements and trading blocks. [6] • The social and political impacts of globalisation (e.g. widening economic divisions between countries) and its influence on business (e.g. off-shoring), industrial relocation, emergence of growth markets, enhanced competition, cross-national business alliances and mergers). [6] • The impacts of modern information and communication technologies on international trade and patterns of development. [6] • The principal institutions encouraging international trade (e.g. WTO/GATT, EU, G8). [6]

C04 – B. THE GOALS AND DECISIONS OF ORGANISATIONS (25%)

Learning outcomes On completion of their studies students should be able to:			Indicative syllabus content
Lead	**Component**	**Level**	
1. distinguish between the economic goals of various stakeholders and organisations.	(a) distinguish between the goals of profit seeking organisations, not-for-profit organisations (NPOs) and governmental organisations;	2	• The forms of public, private and mutual ownership of organisations and their goals. [1] • Concept of returns to shareholder investment in the short run (ROCE and EPS) and long run (NPV of free cash flows) and the need for firms to provide rates of return to shareholders at least equal to the firm's cost of capital. [1] • Impact on share price of changes to a company's forecast cash flows or its required rate using perpetual annuity valuations with constant annual free cash flows, or NPV calculations with variable cash flows over three years. [1] • Role of stakeholders in setting goals and influencing decisions in organisations. [1] • Types of not-for-profit organisations. [1] • The status of economic considerations as constraints rather than primary objectives of not-for-profit organisations. [1] • The potential difference in objectives between management and shareholders. [1] • The principal-agent problem, its likely effect on decision making in profit seeking organisations. [1]
	(b) explain shareholder wealth, the variables affecting shareholder wealth, and its application in management decision making;	2	
	(c) identify stakeholders and their likely impact on the goals of organisations and the decisions of management;	2	
	(d) distinguish between the potential objectives of management and those of shareholders, and the effects of this principal-agent problem on decisions concerning price, output and growth of the firm.	2	

Learning outcomes On completion of their studies students should be able to:			**Indicative syllabus content**
Lead	**Component**	**Level**	
2. describe the behaviour of the costs of a product and service provider as volume changes and the implications for prices, competition and industry structure.	(a) distinguish between the likely behaviour of a firm's unit costs in the short run and long run; (b) illustrate the potential effects of long run cost behaviour on prices, the size of the organisation and the number of competitors in the industry; (c) illustrate the potential impact on prices and competition of e-business and globalisation.	2 2 2	• Changing efficiency in the short run (eventually diminishing marginal returns) and the long run (increasing and diminishing returns to scale). [2] • Graphical treatment of short run cost and revenue behaviour as output increases using curvilinear and total cost curves. [2] • Long run cost behaviour and the long run average cost curve. [2] • Increased competition and lower prices from the impact of e-business on costs of information search and by enabling low or zero variable cost. [2] • Impact on competition of the ability of business to source products and services from low cost emerging economies. [2]
3. calculate the level of output and price to maximise profits.	(a) demonstrate the point of profit maximisation graphically using total cost and total revenue curves; (b) calculate the point of profit maximisation for a single product firm in the short run using data.	3 3	• Short-run profit maximisation using graphical techniques. [2] • Profit maximising output using data on price, quantity and unit costs. [2]

C04 – C. THE MARKET SYSTEM AND THE COMPETITIVE PROCESS (25%)

Learning outcomes On completion of their studies students should be able to:			Indicative syllabus content
Lead	**Component**	**Level**	
1. demonstrate the determination of prices by market forces and the impact of price changes on revenue from sales.	(a) identify the equilibrium price in a product or factor markets likely to result from specified changes in conditions of demand or supply; (b) calculate the price elasticity of demand and the price elasticity of supply; (c) explain the determinants of the price elasticities of demand and supply; (d) identify the effects of price elasticity of demand on a firm's revenues following a change in prices.	2 3 2 2	• The price mechanism, determinants of supply and demand and their interaction to form and change equilibrium price. [4] • The price elasticity of demand and supply. ***Note:*** calculate using arc and point methods. [4] • Influences on the price elasticities of demand and supply. [4] • Consequences of different price elasticities of demand for total revenue, following price changes. [4]
2. explain the reasons for and effects of government intervention to stabilise prices.	(a) identify causes of instability of prices in markets for primary goods; (b) explain the impact of instability of prices on incomes of producers and the stability of the industry; (c) explain the effects on prices, producer revenues and market equilibrium, of government policies to influence prices in markets; (d) illustrate the impacts of price regulation in goods and factor markets.	2 2 2 2	• Impact of periodic variations in output, short run inelasticity of supply, inelastic demand and the cobweb (or hog cycle) on price stability in primary markets. [4] • Implications of price fluctuations for producer incomes, industry stability and supply. [4] • Government price stabilisation policies; deficiency payments, set-aside, subsidies. [4] • Impact of employment costs. [4] • Impact of minimum price (minimum wage) and maximum price policies in goods and factor markets. [4]

Learning outcomes **On completion of their studies students should be able to:**			**Indicative syllabus content**
Lead	**Component**	**Level**	
3. explain the main sources of market failures and the policies available to deal with them.	(a) explain market concentration and the factors giving rise to differing levels of concentration between markets, including acquisitions and combinations;	2	• Measures of market concentration and the impacts of market concentration on efficiency, innovation and competitive behaviour. [5] • Business integration including mergers, vertical integration and conglomerates. [5]
	(b) identify the impacts of the different forms of competition on prices, output and profitability;	2	• Effect of monopolies and collusive practices on prices and output, and profitability. [5]
	(c) explain the main policies to prevent abuses of monopoly power by firms;	2	• Competition policy and fair trading regulations. [5]
	(d) explain market failures and their effects on prices, efficiency of market operation and economic welfare;	2	• Positive and negative externalities in goods markets, merit good and demerit goods. [5]
	(e) explain the likely responses of government to market failures.	2	• Government response to market failure: indirect taxes, subsidies, polluter pays policies and regulation. [5] • Government response to market failure: Public assurance of access to public goods, healthcare, education and housing. [5] • Government response to market failure: Public versus private provision of services (nationalisation, privatisation, contracting out, public private partnerships). [5]

C04 – D. THE FINANCIAL SYSTEM (25%)

Learning outcomes On completion of their studies students should be able to:			Indicative syllabus content
Lead	**Component**	**Level**	
1. explain the causes of demand for finance and the assets used for borrowing.	(a) identify the factors leading to liquidity surpluses and deficits in the short, medium and long run in households, firms and governments; (b) explain the role of various financial assets, markets and institutions in assisting organisations to manage their liquidity position and to provide an economic return to holders of liquidity.	2 2	• Finance for households: month to month cash flow management; short-term saving and borrowing; home buying; pension provision. [7] • Finance for firms: cash flow management; finance of working capital and short-term assets; long term permanent capital. [7] • Finance for government: cash flow management; finance of public projects; long term management of the national debt. [7] • Role of financial assets, markets and institutions: credit agreements, mortgages, bills of exchange, bonds, certificates of deposit, equities. [7]
2. explain the functions of the main financial markets and institutions in facilitating commerce and development.	(a) explain the financial and economic functions of financial intermediaries; [7] (b) explain the role of commercial banks in the process of credit creation and in determining the structure of interest rates; [7] (c) explain the role of the 'central bank' in ensuring liquidity and in prudential regulation; [7] (d) explain the origins of the 2008 banking crisis and credit crunch; [7] (e) explain the role of the foreign exchange market and the factors influencing it, in setting exchange rates; [7] (f) explain the role of national and international governmental organisations in regulating and influencing the financial system; [8] (g) explain the role of supra-national financial institutions in stabilising economies and encouraging growth. [8]	2 2 2 2 2 2 2	• Role and functions of financial intermediaries: maturity transformation, risk management, aggregation, matching borrowers and lenders. [7] • Role and influence of commercial banks on the supply of liquidity to the financial system through their activities in credit creation. [7] • Yield on financial instruments (i.e. bill rate, running yield on bonds, net dividend yield on equity), relation between rates, role of risk, the yield curve. [7] • Role and common functions of central banks: banker to government, banker to banks, lender of last resort, prudential regulation. [7] • Influence of central banks on yield rates through market activity and as providers of liquidity to the financial system as lenders of last resort, including by quantitative easing. [7] • The 2008 banking crisis and credit crunch: exposure to sub-prime debt, poor regulation, excessive lending. [7] • Role of foreign exchange markets in facilitating international trade and in determining the exchange rate. [8]

Learning outcomes **On completion of their studies students should be able to:**			**Indicative syllabus content**
Lead	**Component**	**Level**	
			• Influences on exchange rates: interest rates, inflation rates, trade balance, currency speculation. [8] • Governmental and international policies on exchange rates (exchange rate management, fixed and floating rate systems, single currency zones). [8] • Role of major institutions (e.g. World Bank Group, International Monetary Fund, European Central Bank) in fostering international development and economic stabilisation. [8]

chapter

1

The Goals and Decisions of Organisations

Chapter learning objectives

Upon completion of this chapter you will be able to:

- distinguish between the goals of profit-seeking organisations, not-for-profit organisations (NPOs) and governmental organisations
- explain shareholder wealth, the variables affecting shareholder wealth, and its application in management decision making
- identify stakeholders and their likely impact on the goals of organisations and the decisions of management
- distinguish between the potential objectives of management and those of shareholders, and the effects of this principal-agent problem on decisions concerning price, output and growth of the firm.

1 The nature of organisations

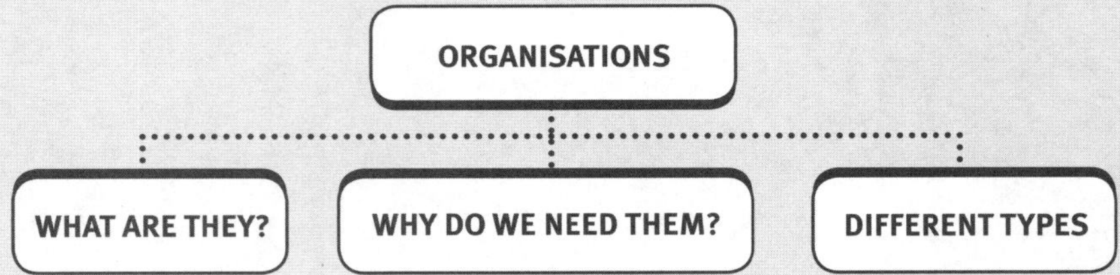

1.1 What is an organisation?

'Organisations are social arrangements for the controlled performance of collective goals.' (**Buchanan and Huczynski**)

The key aspects of this definition are as follows:

(a) 'Collective goals' – organisations are defined primarily by their goals. A school has the main goal of educating pupils and will be organised differently from a company where the main objective is to make profits.

(b) 'Social arrangements' – someone working on his own does not constitute an organisation. Organisations have structure to enable people to work together towards the common goals. Larger organisations tend to have more formal structures in place but even small organisations will divide up responsibilities between the people concerned.

(c) 'Controlled performance' – organisations have systems and procedures to ensure that goals are achieved. These could vary from ad-hoc informal reviews to complex weekly targets and performance review.

Illustration 1 – Definition of organisations

For example, a football team can be described as an organisation because:

- It has a number of players who have come together to play a game.
- The team has an objective (to score more goals than its opponent).
- To do their job properly, the members have to maintain an internal system of control to get the team to work together. In training they work out tactics so that in play they can rely on the ball being passed to those who can score goals.

- Each member of the team is part of the organisational structure and is skilled in a different task: the goalkeeper has more experience in stopping goals being scored than those in the forward line of the team.
- In addition, there must be team spirit, so that everyone works together. Players are encouraged to do their best, both on and off the field.

Test Your Understanding 1

A queue of people standing at a bus stop is an example of an organisation if they all want to travel to the same place.

True/False.

Supplementary reading – Defining organisations

As yet there is no widely accepted definition of an organisation. This is because the term can be used broadly in two ways:

- It can refer to a group or institution arranged for efficient work.
- Organisation can also refer to a process, i.e. structuring and arranging the activities of the enterprise or institution to achieve the stated objectives.

There are many types of organisations, which are set up to serve a number of different purposes and to meet a variety of needs, including companies, clubs, schools, hospitals, charities, political parties, governments and the armed forces.

What they all have in common is summarised in the definition given.

1.2 Why do we need organisations?

Organisations enable people to:

- share skills and knowledge
- specialise and
- pool resources.

The resulting synergy allows organisations to achieve more than the individuals could on their own.

As the organisation grows it will reach a size where goals, structures and control procedures need to be formalised to ensure that objectives are achieved.

These issues are discussed in further detail below.

Illustration 2 – The nature of organisations

When families set up and run a chain of restaurants, they usually do not have to consider formalising the organisation of their business until they have five restaurants.

After this stage responsibilities have to be clarified and greater delegation is often required.

1.3 Classifying organisations by profit orientation

Organisations can be classified in many different ways, including the following:

Profit seeking organisations

Some organisations, such as companies and partnerships, see their main objective as maximising the wealth of their owners. Such organisations are often referred to as 'profit seeking'.

The objective of wealth maximisation is usually expanded into three primary objectives:

- to continue in existence (survival)
- to maintain growth and development
- to make a profit.

Not-for-profit organisations

Other organisations do not see profitability as their main objective. Such not-for-profit organisations ('NFPs or NPOs') are unlikely to have financial objectives as primary.

Instead they are seeking to satisfy particular needs of their members or the sectors of society that they have been set up to benefit.

Illustration 3 – NFP organisations

NFPs include the following:

- government departments and agencies (e.g. HM Revenue and Customs)
- schools
- hospitals
- charities (e.g. Oxfam, Red Cross, Red Crescent, Caritas) and
- clubs.

The objectives of NFPs can vary tremendously:

- Hospitals could be said to exist to treat patients.
- Councils often state their 'mission' as caring for their communities.
- A charity may have as its main objective 'to provide relief to victims of disasters and help people prevent, prepare for, and respond to emergencies'.
- Government organisations usually exist to implement government policy.

NFPs must stay within their budgets to survive. But their stakeholders are primarily interested in how the organisation contributes to its chosen field. This can frequently lead to tensions between financial constraints and the NFP's objectives.

Test Your Understanding 2

Which of the following best completes the statement 'Financial considerations are a constraint in not-for-profit organisations because.....'

A they have no profits to reinvest

B they meet the needs of people who cannot afford to pay very much

C they don't have much money

D their prime objectives are not financial but they still need money to enable them to reach them

Test Your Understanding 3

Which one of the following is not a key stakeholder group for a charity?

A employees and volunteers

B shareholders

C donors

D beneficiaries

One specific category of NFPs is a mutual organisation. Mutual organisations are voluntary not-for-profit associations formed for the purpose of raising funds by subscriptions of members, out of which common services can be provided to those members.

Mutual organisations include:

- some building societies
- trade unions and
- some social clubs.

Supplementary reading – Financial objectives in NFPs

Many NPOs view financial matters as constraints under which they have to operate, rather than objectives. For example,

- Hospitals seek to offer the best possible care to as many patients as possible, subject to budgetary restrictions imposed upon them.
- Councils organise services such as refuse collection, while trying to achieve value for money with residents' council tax.
- Charities may try to alleviate suffering subject to funds raised.

Test Your Understanding 4

Which one of the following would not be a stakeholder for a mutual society?

A shareholders

B customers

C employees

D managers

Test Your Understanding 5

Some building societies have demutualised and become banks with shareholders. Comment on how this may have affected lenders and borrowers.

1.4 Classifying organisation by ownership/control

Public sector organisations

The public sector is that part of the economy that is concerned with providing basic government services and is thus controlled by government organisations.

Illustration 4 – Public sector organisations

The composition of the public sector varies by country, but in most countries the public sector includes such services as:

- police
- military
- public roads
- public transit
- primary education and
- healthcare for the poor.

Private sector organisations

The private sector, comprising non-government organisations, is that part of a nation's economy that is not controlled by the government.

Illustration 5 – Private sector organisations

Within these will be profit-seeking and not-for-profit organisations.

This sector thus includes:

- businesses
- charities and
- clubs.

Supplementary reading – Co-operatives

A co-operative is an autonomous association of persons united voluntarily to meet their common economic, social and cultural needs and aspirations through a jointly owned and democratically controlled enterprise.

(The International Co-operative Alliance Statement on the Co-operative Identity, Manchester 1995)

Co-operatives are thus businesses with the following characteristics:

- They are owned and democratically controlled by their members – the people who buy their goods or use their services. They are not owned by investors.
- Co-operatives are organised solely to meet the needs of the member-owners, not to accumulate capital for investors.

For example, a retail co-operative could comprise a group of people who join together to increase their buying power to qualify for discounts from retailers when purchasing food.

Co-operatives are similar to mutual organisations in the sense that the organisations are also owned by the members/clients that they exist for. However, they tend to deal in primarily tangible goods and services such as agricultural commodities or utilities rather than intangible products such as financial services.

Test Your Understanding 6

Which of the following are usually seen as the primary objectives of companies?

(i) To maximise the wealth of shareholders

(ii) To protect the environment

(iii) To make a profit

A (i), (ii) and (iii)

B (i) and (ii) only

C (ii) and (iii) only

D (i) and (iii) only

Test Your Understanding 7

Many schools run fund-raising events such as fêtes, where the intention is to make a profit. This makes them 'profit-seeking'.

True or False?

2 Shareholder wealth

2.1 Maximising shareholder wealth

As stated above, companies have the primary objective of maximising shareholder wealth. This should ultimately be reflected in

- higher share prices
- higher dividend payments.

Attempts to measure and increase shareholder value have focussed on incorporating three key issues:

- Cash is preferable to profit

  Cash flows have a higher correlation with shareholder wealth than profits.

- Exceeding the cost of capital

  The return, however measured, must be sufficient to cover not just the cost of debt (for example by exceeding interest payments) but also the cost of equity (the return required by shareholders).

- Managing both long- and short-term perspectives

  Investors are increasingly looking at long-term value. When valuing a company's shares, the stock market places a value on the company's future potential, not only its current profit levels.

Supplementary reading – Profit and shareholder value

Just because a company has made a profit, it does not follow that shareholder wealth has been increased. Consider the following example.

EVA plc has the following financial structure:

- \$100 million debt with an interest rate (pre-tax) of 6%
- \$200 million equity where it is estimated that shareholders want a return of 15%

The company has made a profit before interest and tax of \$36 million and pays tax at 30%.

Comment on whether directors have achieved their objective of increasing shareholder wealth.

Solution

Let us construct a conventional company income statement:

	Working	\$m
Profit before interest and tax		36
Interest	100 × 6%	(6)
Profit before tax		30
Tax @30%		(9)
Profit after tax		21
Minimum profit required by shareholders	200 × 15%	30

The company has made a profit.

However, the way we prepare income statements does not show the return required by shareholders. In this example the profit is not enough to cover the "cost of equity" and the company could be said to have reduced shareholder value.

2.2 Short-term measures of financial performance

It is quite possible that financial performance of a business in the short run could be different to its performance in the long run. Thus measures are needed both of short-run and long-run financial performance.

Two standard measures of short-run performance are:

(1) return on capital employed;

(2) earnings per share.

Return on capital employed (ROCE)

$$\text{ROCE} = \frac{\text{profit before interest and tax}}{\text{average capital employed}} \times 100\%$$

Comments:

- ROCE gives an indication as to how well a business uses its capital (think assets) to generate profits;
- Being a percentage makes it easy to compare the ROCE of different companies.

Another similar measure of the return to shareholders' capital is:

$$\text{Return on net assets RONA)} = \frac{\text{operating profit (before interest and tax)}}{\text{Total assets minus current liabilities}} \times 100\%$$

The higher the figure for ROCE or the return on net assets is, the more profitable the company is. However, ROCE is a measure of the net income generated by the business and not about where that income goes. Shareholders will be more interested in profits after the payment of interest and tax.

Earnings per share (EPS)

As its name suggests, EPS determines the profits available to ordinary shareholders, expressed per share.

$$\text{EPS} = \frac{\text{profits after interest, tax and preference share dividends}}{\text{number of ordinary shares issued}}$$

Of course this figure only gives the earnings per share that each owner of ordinary shares might expect to receive. It is up to the Directors to decide whether / how much to pay out as a dividend.

Furthermore, to calculate a rate of return for the shareholder, the price that the potential shareholder has to pay to acquire a share must be taken into account.

Test Your Understanding 8

The following is an extract from the accounts of EBG.

	$000
Revenue	500
Cost of sales	200
Gross profit	300
Distribution costs	100
Admin. expenses	50
Operating profit	150
Interest	10
Profit before tax	140
Taxation	30
Profit after tax	110
Capital employed	3,000
Share capital (1 million shares @ $1)	1,000

Calculate

(a) ROCE
(b) EPS

Test Your Understanding 9

RGP currently has an eps figure of 10c with 1 million shares in issue. A proposed new project will increase profit after tax by $25,000 per annum and will be financed by the issue of a further 400,000 shares.

Calculate the new eps and indicate how shareholders will perceive the change.

2.3 Long-term measures of financial performance

In addition to measuring current financial performance, companies also need to be able to measure longer-term performance, in particular, in relation to investment. In this case it is important that a business can be sure that returns to shareholders are at least equal to the cost of acquiring the capital required to produce a long-term flow of earnings.

In making these sorts of assessment several problems arise:

- establishing the cost of capital to finance the investment project;
- estimating the flow of income derived from the capital investment over the whole life of the investment;
- valuing that flow of income.

To solve these problems we calculate the present value of future cash flows by a process of discounting. This was covered in C03 but a recap is given here for completeness.

2.4 The concept of discounted cash flows

(1) Decisions should be based on cash flows rather than profits

This is mainly because there is a higher correlation between shareholder value and cash flow than there is with profits. Furthermore, profits can be distorted by accounting policies.

(2) Money has a time value

When considering a decision that affects cash flows over the longer term (here, over one year), managers need to recognise that cash received in the future is less valuable than the same sum received now.

Example

A $1 million receipt anticipated in 5 year's time is not equal in value to $1 million received now.

The reasons for this are as follows:

(a) **Inflation** – Inflation erodes the purchasing power of the money. The $1 million in 5 years' time will not buy as much as £1 million today.

(b) **Risk** – $1 million today is more certain than the estimated $1 million in 5 years' time.

(c) **Interest** – $1 million received today could be invested to earn interest. In 5 years' it will have grown to more than $1 million. Alternatively, the $1 million received today could be used to repay a loan or reduce an overdraft, thus saving interest.

The above factors are usually combined into a 'discount rate' based on the cost of capital.

(3) Discounting

The main implication of the time value of money is that cash flows at different times cannot be compared directly. Instead they need to be converted to their equivalent value at the same time.

The normal convention for this is to 'discount' all future cash flows to give their 'present value' at time zero (now). This is achieved by multiplying each cash flow by an appropriate 'discount factor'.

Present value = future cash flow × discount factor

For a one-off cash flow at time t = n, the discount factor = $1/(1 + r)^n$

For a repeating cash flow at times t = 1 – n, the "annuity" discount factor = $[1 - 1/(1 + r)^n] \times 1/r$

For a perpetuity cash flow at times t = 1 – ∞, the discount factor = 1/r

(4) The net present value (NPV) of a project is the sum of the discounted future cash flows minus the capital cost of the project.

If the NPV >0 then the project will raise shareholder value and should be accepted but rejected if NPV<0 as it would reduce shareholder value.

e.g

Illustration 6 – NPV

AFG has 1 million shares in issue with a current price of $2 per share.

The directors are considering a 3 year project with the following (post tax) cash flows ($):

Timing	t=0	t=1	t=2	t=3
Initial investment	(100,000)			
Sales		90,000	75,000	45,000
Costs		(30,000)	(25,000)	(15,000)
Scrap proceeds				10,000
Net cash flow	(100,000)	60,000	50,000	40,000

The directors have estimated the company cost of capital at 10%

Required:

(a) Calculate the net present value of the project cash flows

(b) Advise whether the project should be accepted

(c) Estimate the impact on the company share price if the project is accepted

Solution

(a) NPV

Timing	t=0	t=1	t=2	t=3
Net cash flow	(100,000)	60,000	50,000	40,000
Discount factors @10% (working)	1	0.909	0.826	0.751
Present values	(100,000)	54,540	41,300	30,040
Net present value (NPV)	**$25,880**			

Working: discount factors can either be taken from the tables or calculated as

DF for t = 1 is given by 1/(1 + 0.1) = 1/1.10 = 0.909

DF for t = 2 is given by $1/(1 + 0.1)^2 = 1/1.10^2 = 0.826$

DF for t = 3 is given by $1/(1 + 0.1)^3 = 1/1.10^3 = 0.751$

(b) The NPV > 0 indicating that the receipts are worth more than the outflows so overall the project should increase shareholder wealth. If we have got the estimates correct, then this project should increase shareholder wealth by $25,880

(c) The company is currently worth $2 million. If the project is undertaken, then the value should rise to $2,025,880 or approximately $2.03 per share.

Note: Our answer to part (c) makes some major assumptions:

- Management will communicate all details of the project to the stock market so investors can factor it into their decisions whether to buy or sell the shares
- The market believes the directors' estimates and that the company can deliver the projected cash flows
- The stock market is efficient enough to process the information so that the change in share price fully reflects the NPV.

Illustration 7 – Further examples of discounted cash flows

The directors of a company are considering a reorganisation that should result in cost savings of $100,000 per annum. Estimate the likely impact on the value of the company assuming that the savings continue

(a) For ten years

(b) Forever

The company has a cost of capital of 15%.

Ignore taxation.

Solution

Increase in value of company = NPV of savings

(a) PV = 100,000 × 10yr annuity factor @15% = 100,000 × 5.019 = $501,900

(b) PV = 100,000 × perpetuity factor @15% = 100,000 × 1/0.15 = $666,667

Test Your Understanding 10

A company is planning to invest in a new project. The information about this project is as follows.

Capital cost of the project	$20,000	
Expected life of the project	3 years	
Scrap value of investment at end	$5,000	
Expected net income streams	Year 1	$10,000
	Year 2	$10,000
	Year 3	$10,000

You are required to:

(a) Calculate the net present value of the project assuming a discount rate of 10%.

(2 marks)

(b) Calculate the net present value of the project assuming that the income stream in the third year is reduced to $7,000.

(2 marks)

(c) Calculate the net present value of the project assuming the original income streams but a discount rate of 5%.

(2 marks)

(d) State whether each of the following would be likely to make the project more or less valuable:

(i) a rise in interest rates — more valuable/less valuable **(1 mark)**

(ii) a fall in labour costs for the company — more valuable/less valuable **(1 mark)**

(iii) an expected fall in the value of scrap machinery — more valuable/less valuable **(1 mark)**

(iv) a higher than expected sales volume from the new project — more valuable/less valuable **(1 mark)**

(Total marks = 10)

Test Your Understanding 11

Discounting a future stream of income means:

A taking into account possible future falls in the stream of income

B ignoring yearly fluctuations in income and taking the average

C reducing the present value of future income streams because future income is worth less than current income

D reducing the present value of future income streams to take account of the effect of inflation

2.5 Share values

The concept of discounted cash flows can be used to explain how press releases and market rumours can affect the share price.

- Suppose the company announces a new project. If the market believes that the project will deliver a positive NPV, then the share price should rise.
- Any information that reaches the market that suggests that future cash flows will be higher than previously forecast should result in a share price rise.

- If bad news reaches the market then as well as revising forecast cash flows downwards, investors may reassess the investment as having higher risk. This will result in a higher cost of capital and thus future receipts will be less valuable than previously estimated. The end result is a fall in the share price.

Many variables will affect the value of shares. These tend to fall into two groups:

(1) factors *external* to the business which may affect a wide range of shares: the onset of a recession would tend to depress share values in general as would a rise in interest rates;

(2) factors *internal* to the business that might affect the future flow of profits such as the failure of a new product, an expected decline in sales or a significant rise in costs.

Illustration 8 – Share values

BP

After the oil spill catastrophe in 2010, BP's share value fell by 47% to their lowest level in 13 years. This fall could be explained as the market revising (downwards!) its estimates over BP's future cash flows, in particular:

- Incorporating potential costs in cleaning up the damage caused
- Possible US government action
- BP's ability to win new contracts in the longer term

In addition the shares would have been seen as a higher risk (effectively resulting in a higher discount rate being applied to the cash flows)

Recovery since 2010

Many UK companies have seen a rise in their share prices since 2010 due to:

- increased confidence that that the worse of the recession is over
- expectations that low interest rates would continue for some time
- prospects that economic growth may resume after 2012

Test Your Understanding 12

A company has released a press statement publicising its plans to develop a new product range in order to enter a high growth market.

Consider how the concept of discounted cash flows could be used to determine the likely impact of the announcement on the company's share price.

3 Stakeholders

Stakeholders are "those persons and organisations that have an interest in the strategy of an organisation". Stakeholders normally include shareholders, customers, staff and the local community.

It is important that an organisation understands the needs of the different stakeholders as they have both an interest in the organisation and may wish to influence its objectives and strategy.

Useful definitions:

(a) **Stakeholder interest** – an interest or concern that a stakeholder has in an organisation's actions, objectives or policies.

(b) **Stakeholder influence** – the level of involvement that a stakeholder has in the functions of an organisation and the ability to bring about a desired change.

The degree of interest and influence of different stakeholder groups can vary considerably:

- A well organised labour force with a strong trade union will be able to exercise considerable influence (e.g. through strike action) over directors' plans and will be particularly interested in any plans that relate to jobs, working conditions and the welfare of staff.
- The residents of a small village might have great interest in the plans of a major supermarket chain to close the local village store but would have little power to influence the decision.

Stakeholders can be broadly categorised into three groups: internal (e.g. employees), connected (e.g. shareholders) and external (e.g. government).

3.1 Internal stakeholders

Internal stakeholders are intimately connected to the organisation, and their objectives are likely to have a strong influence on how it is run.

Internal stakeholders include:

Stakeholder	Need/expectation	Example
Employees	pay, working conditions and job security	If workers are to be given more responsibility, they will expect increased pay.
Managers/directors	status, pay, bonus, job security	If growth is going to occur, the managers will want increased profits, leading to increased bonuses.

3.2 Connected stakeholders

Connected stakeholders can be viewed as having a contractual relationship with the organisation.

The objective of satisfying shareholders is taken as the prime objective which the management of the organisation will need to fulfil, however, customer and financiers objectives must be met if the company is to succeed.

Stakeholder	Need/expectation	Example
Shareholders	steady flow of income, possible capital growth and the continuation of the business	If capital is required for growth, the shareholders will expect a rise in the dividend stream.
Customers	satisfaction of customers' needs will be achieved through providing value-for-money products and services	Any attempt to for example increase the quality and the price, may lead to customer dissatisfaction.
Suppliers	paid promptly	If a decision is made to delay payment to suppliers to ease cash flow, existing suppliers may cease supplying goods.
Finance providers	ability to repay the finance including interest, security of investment	The firm's ability to generate cash.

3.3 External stakeholders

External stakeholders include the government, local authority etc. This group will have quite diverse objectives and have varying ability to ensure that the organisation meets their objectives.

Stakeholder	Need/expectation	Example
Community at large	The general public can be a stakeholder, especially if their lives are affected by an organisation's decisions.	E.g. local residents' attitude towards out-of-town shopping centres.
Environmental pressure groups	The organisation does not harm the external environment.	If an airport wants to build a new runway, the pressure groups may stage a 'sit in'.
Government	Company activities are central to the success of the economy (providing jobs and paying taxes). Legislation (e.g. health and safety) must be met by the company.	Actions by companies could break the law, or damage the environment, and governments therefore control what organisations can do.

Trade unions	Taking an active part in the decision-making process.	If a department is to be closed the union will want to be consulted, and there should be a scheme in place to help employees find alternative employment.

Test Your Understanding 13

Which of the following is not a connected stakeholder?

A Shareholders

B Suppliers

C Employees

D Customers

Test Your Understanding 14

R is a high class hotel situated in a thriving city. It is part of a worldwide hotel group owned by a large number of shareholders. Individuals hold the majority of shares, each holding a small number, and financial institutions own the rest. The hotel provides full amenities, including a heated swimming pool, as well as the normal facilities of bars, restaurants and good quality accommodation. There are many other hotels in the city, all of which compete with R. The city in which R is situated is old and attracts many foreign visitors, especially in the summer season.

Who are the main stakeholders with whom relationships need to be established and maintained by management? Explain why it is important that relationships are maintained with each of these stakeholders.

4 Stakeholder conflict

The needs/expectations of the different stakeholders may conflict. Some of the typical conflicts are shown below:

Stakeholders	Conflict
Employees versus managers	Jobs/wages versus bonus (cost efficiency)
Customers versus shareholders	Product quality/service levels versus profits/dividends
General public versus shareholders	Effect on the environment versus profit/dividends
Managers versus shareholders	Growth versus independence

Solving such conflicts will often involve a mixture of compromise and prioritisation.

Supplementary reading – Resolving stakeholder conflict

To help resolve stakeholder conflict, many firms will try to assess both the degree of interest on stakeholders and their power/influence to affect the business.

For example, the government may have high power but may be relatively uninterested in the affairs of a particular company. On the other hand a major key customer may have both influence and interest and so must be incorporated in any significant decisions as a "key player".

With companies the primary objective of maximising shareholder value should take preference and so decision making is simplified to some degree. However, this does not mean that other stakeholders are ignored. For example,

- If we do not pay employees a fair wage, then quality will suffer, ultimately depressing profits and shareholder wealth

Some firms address this by seeing shareholder wealth generation as their primary objectives and the needs of other stakeholders as constraints within which they have to operate:

- We try to increase profit subject to ensuring good working conditions for employees, not polluting the environment, etc.

Supplementary reading – Stakeholder conflict for NFPs

Unlike firms, NPOs may not have one dominant stakeholder group. Consequently the NPO seeks to satisfy several different groups at once, without having the touchstone of one primary objective, such as profit, to adhere to.

For example, a council may express its mission as 'caring for the community'. Suppose it is considering building a new car park in the city centre where there is currently a small green park. This would affect the community as follows:

- Local businesses would see more trade.
- More jobs would be created for local residents.
- Better parking for shoppers.
- More traffic, congestion and pollution for local residents.
- Loss of a park, thus reducing the quality of life for locals.
- The receipts from the car park could be used to reduce council tax bills and/or fund additional services for the community.

This type of decision is particularly difficult as:

- How do you decide which stakeholder group should take preference?
- Most of the factors being considered are very difficult to quantify (e.g. quality of life) and
- How do you offset different issues measured in different ways (e.g. how many extra jobs justify the extra congestion and pollution?)

Some public sector organisations try to quantify all of the issues financially to see if the benefits outweigh the costs ('cost-benefit analysis').

For example, congestion will delay people, thus adding to journey times. The value of people's time can be estimated by looking at the premium they will pay for quicker methods of transport such as train versus coach.

5 Management objectives

An extremely important stakeholder conflict is that between shareholders and the managers.

5.1 The principal agent problem

In some, usually small, companies the owners also manage the business.

However, companies that are quoted on a stock market are often extremely complex and require a substantial investment in equity to fund them. They therefore often have large numbers of shareholders.

These shareholders delegate control to professional managers – the board of directors – to run the company on their behalf. Thus shareholders normally play a passive role in the day-to-day management of the company.

This separation of ownership and control leads to a potential conflict of interests between directors and shareholders. This conflict is an example of the principal agent problem. The principals (the shareholders) have to find ways of ensuring that their agents (the managers) act in their interests.

Supplementary reading – The principal agent problem

In any organisation there are:

- *principals*: in the case of companies the principals are the legal owners of the organisation – the shareholders;
- *agents*: those appointed by the principals to act on their behalf such as the board of directors and senior managers in a company.

The principal–agent problem is not confined to business and companies, it affects all organisations.

- In the case of public sector industries, the principal is the legal owner, that is the state represented by the government, and the agents are the senior managers placed in charge of the industries.
- The issue may arise for individuals. If an individual wishes to buy a house he or she may well appoint a lawyer to conduct the legal aspects of the transactions. Here the house buyer is the principal, and the lawyer is the agent.

The problem posed by agency theory is how can the principal ensure that the agent will behave in such a way as to achieve the aims and intentions of the principal? There is clearly the possibility of conflict in that the agent may act to achieve a set of objectives reflecting their self interest and objectives rather than those of the principals. In companies the board of directors and/or senior management may pursue objectives that are not the same as those of the shareholders. In effect, the shareholders may lose control of the companies they legally own.

This loss of control by shareholders over their companies is called the *divorce of control from ownership*. How might this loss of control occur?

- organisations may become *too large* for shareholders to effectively control
- organisations may become *too complex* for shareholders to effectively control; this complexity may be in technologically, commercially or structurally

Individual shareholders may lose control especially where they only own a small number of shares or where they own shares in many companies because they lack the time or incentive to exert their control.

Indeed, it is because of these sorts of problems that shareholders face that they appoint agents to act for them in the company.

The problem is less acute for institutional shareholders such as pension funds. Because they have large shareholdings and have time and expertise they find it rather easier to ensure that directors and managers comply with their overall wishes. Nonetheless, shareholders still need to create mechanisms to encourage directors and managers to act in a way that promotes shareholder interest. Since shareholders are primarily interested in the flow of dividends and the share price, it is possible to devise incentive schemes to encourage directors to emphasise the pursuit of profits.

Examples include:

- remuneration and bonuses related to the profit performance of the company
- share distribution schemes to encourage directors and managers to aim for a higher share price for the company
- bonuses related to variables that will indirectly contribute to the maximisation of shareholders wealth such as sales growth or market share.

Even here, however, there is some disquiet. The incentive schemes are often designed by the directors and remuneration committees that in turn often reflect the interests of directors in general. There is thus a feeling that the schemes provide targets that are too easy to achieve and bonuses that are often only very loosely linked to the achievement of those targets. Even worse the bonus system may lead to serious problems. The crisis in the financial systems of many countries in 2008 was partly ascribed to the bonus system. It was claimed that directors and senior managers in banks and other financial institutions adopted excessively risky business policies in the pursuit of generous short-term bonuses at the expense of longer-term financial stability. The result was a wave of banking collapses that was only stemmed by massive government intervention and support. Thus the problem of the agents in a company pursuing a different set of objectives from those of the principals remains.

What sort of objectives might directors and senior managers in companies pursue? It is likely that their objectives will be more complex than those of the shareholders. In the first place, management will face pressures from a wide range of stakeholders, not just the shareholders. Moreover, management will have its own aims and objectives which may differ in important ways from those of the shareholders.

How might the aims and objectives of management differ from those of shareholders?

- Management will have to balance the interests of different stakeholders in the company. Since these stakeholders have a variety of objectives, profit is unlikely to be the sole aim of management.
- Management may have objectives of its own. These may include salaries, non-salary benefits ('perks'), power, status and prestige, safety and security and a 'quiet life'. The problem with these is that they *may conflict* with the objectives of profitability. For example, many of the management's objectives, such as salary, power and prestige, may be related more strongly to the *size* of the company (sales, market share, number of employees) than to the underlying *profitability* of the company (return on capital employed).

- Other common short term objectives include
  - sales maximization (Baumol) – this is often simpler than profit maximisation as it excludes costs. Proponents would argue that higher sales usually results in greater profit
  - growth maximisation (Marris) – in the longer term a larger company is likely to be more profitable due to increased revenue and cost economies of scale
  - "satisfying" (Simon) – for example trying to achieve sales growth subject to a minimum increase in profit of 5%. Such targets are often seen as more practical than "maximise profits", which is seen as unachievable.

Bonuses become the norm for bosses

Only four chief executives in the FTSE 100 went without a bonus last year, as companies increasingly rely on the extra payments to reward their top executives.

The bonuses are more often paid in cash and shares tied to the company's performance than options and long-term incentives. According to a report published today by PricewaterhouseCoopers, they are the one part of executives' pay packages that most effectively motivate them.

PwC argues that traditional compensation can provide 'outstanding rewards' for outstanding performance, but gives rise to anomalies where performance is anything less than stellar. 'Our research shows that commonly used packages are often not hugely successful at aligning pay with how well CEOs perform for shareholders over a sustained period. At the same time, some plans are just too complex, meaning that they can be severely undervalued by executives and, in our experience, often discounted altogether. In many cases, they are not effective in encouraging executives to perform better.'

Source: Fiona Walsh: The Guardian, August 21st 2006

Thus management may have a complex set of objectives. Nonetheless, it is likely that the profitability of the company will remain an important, indeed probably the most important objective. If a company has a poor profitability performance then the board of directors and senior managers may face:

- smaller bonuses and performance related pay
- the possibility of dismissal by shareholders
- the threat of takeovers if the company share price falls significantly.

Thus the relationship between shareholders (the 'principals') and boards of directors ('the agents') is complex one and might differ from company to company. Nonetheless, the belief that there are problems in the process of corporate governance has prompted attempts in many countries at reform of this relationship.

5.2 Possible areas of conflict

The main areas where managers may not act in the shareholders' best interests are as follows:

- 'Fat cat' salaries and benefits – the media regularly highlight cases where directors are paid huge bonuses; despite the company they manage making a loss. Obviously in most cases directors deserve their high salaries but not in all cases.
- Mergers and acquisitions – research suggests that the majority of acquisitions erode shareholder value rather than create it. Some argue that the reasons such takeovers occur is because directors are looking to expand their own spheres of influence rather than focus on shareholder value.
- Poor control of the business – the Enron and WorldCom scandals in the US in 2002 resulted in calls to improve the control that stakeholders can exercise over the board of directors of the company.
- Short-termism – managers may make decisions to maximise short-term profitability to ensure they get bonuses and hit targets, rather than looking at the long-term. For example, a project that creates wealth in the long run but is loss-making in the first two years may be rejected.

Attempts to resolve this conflict can take a number of forms:

- Corporate governance (see below) tries to improve ways companies are run through a mixture of principles and regulation.

- A review of the remuneration and bonus schemes given to directors. For example high bonuses linked to profit may encourage short-termism that ultimately undermines the long-term prospects of the business. Some firms are looking to reward directors using shares (or share options) to ensure goal congruence.

5.3 The objectives of corporate governance

Corporate governance is defined as '*the systems by which companies and other organisations are directed and controlled*'.

As the name suggests, corporate governance is concerned with improving the way companies are governed and run. In particular it seeks to address the principal agent problem outlined above.

The main objectives are as follows:

- to control the managers/directors by increasing the amount of reporting and disclosure
- to increase level of confidence and transparency in company activities for all investors (existing and potential) and thus promote growth in the company
- to increase disclosure to all stakeholders
- to ensure that the company is run in a legal and ethical manner
- to build in control at the top that will 'cascade' down the organisation.

Corporate governance should thus be seen as the system used to direct, manage and monitor an organisation and enable it to relate to its external environment.

Illustration 9 – Corporate Governance principles

Corporate governance is one way of trying to manage the principal agent problem. While rules and principles vary across the world, typical aspects include the following:

- the board of directors should meet on a *regular basis* and that active *responsibilities* at board level should be spread over the board and not concentrated in a few hands; in particular, the roles of *chairperson* and *chief executive* should be kept separate;
- directors should have *limited contracts* (e.g. 3 years) and all director reward and *payments should be publicly disclosed*;
- there should be three *sub-committees* of the board: an *audit* committee, a *nominations* (to the board) committee and a *remunerations* (of board members) committee;

- greater use should be made of *non-executive directors* with no direct financial interest in the company in order to provide some independence within the board especially on the board's sub committees;
- the annual accounts should contain a statement, approved by the auditors, that the business is financially sound and is a *going concern*.

Test Your Understanding 15

Which of the following is not a prime objective of corporate governance:

A to control directors' activities

B to improve the way companies are run

C to improve employee's working conditions

D to protect shareholder interests?

Supplementary reading – The UK Corporate Governance Code

The UK Corporate Governance Code (2010) represents 'best practice' in corporate governance and what may be seen as a model for companies to adopt. The main features of this model are:

- separation of powers especially in relation to roles of the chairman and the chief executive
- board membership to include an appropriate balance especially in relation to executive and non-executive directors
- the adoption of the principles of transparency, openness and fairness
- to adopt an approach which reflects the interest of all stakeholders
- to ensure that the board of directors are fully accountable
- detailed disclosure and reporting requirements
- remuneration committees to determine the pay of directors
- nomination committees to oversee appointments to the board
- arrangements for organising the Annual General Meeting (AGM).

Test Your Understanding 16

Answer the following questions based on the preceding information. You can check your answers below.

(1) What does ROCE mean and what does it measure?

(2) What does the term *discounting* mean?

(3) How is the net present value (NPV) of an investment project calculated?

(4) If the rate of interest used as the discount rate in the calculation of the NPV of a project rose, would the NPV rise or fall?

(5) Identify four different types of not-for-profit organisations.

(6) Explain what is meant by the term *stakeholders*.

(7) Identify five stakeholders for a typical business.

(8) Explain what is meant by the *principal–agent* problem.

(9) Give two reasons why shareholders may lose control of the company they own.

(10) What is meant by the term *corporate governance*?

Test your understanding answers

Test Your Understanding 1

False.

Despite having identical individual goals, there is no collective goal that motivates people to work together in any way. For example, passenger A will not be concerned if they get the last available place on a bus while passenger B has to wait for the next one.

Test Your Understanding 2

D

NFPs are often stopped from realising all their goals by a lack of money. But making money is not their primary goal.

Test Your Understanding 3

B

Charities, unlike companies, do not have shareholders. Charities could not operate without the work of employees and volunteers, or without donations from their donors, so these are both important stakeholder groups. The objective of a charity is to provide help or support for its beneficiaries. so beneficiaries are also an important stakeholder group.

Test Your Understanding 4

A

Response (A) is the correct answer as a mutual society does not have shareholders but is owned collectively by its customers, for example a mutual building society is owned by its depositors.

Test Your Understanding 5

Mutual building societies exist for the benefit of their members. This is reflected in setting:

- interest rates for borrowers as low as possible
- interest rates for savers as high as possible.

The aim is not to make a profit so the borrowing and saving rates are moved as close as possible with a small margin sufficient to cover costs.

Once it becomes a bank the building society must then seek to maximise shareholder wealth and become profit seeking. This is done by increasing borrowing rates and reducing saving rates.

Members will thus find that the terms offered by the building society become less attractive.

However, when demutualising most building societies give their members windfalls of shares so members become shareholders, thus benefiting from dividends and share price increases.

Test Your Understanding 6

D

While protecting the environment is to be encouraged and is reinforced within statute to some degree, it is not a primary objective of the company. Companies exist primarily to maximise the return to their owners.

Test Your Understanding 7

False

Schools run fund-raising activities to help pay for extra books, e.g. to improve the quality of education given to pupils. The primary objective is educational, not profit. The money made at the fête is thus a means not an end.

Test Your Understanding 8

(a) ROCE = operating profit/capital employed = 150/3,000 = 5%

(b) eps = profit after tax/no of shares = 110/1000 = 11 cents per share

Test Your Understanding 9

Existing profit after tax = eps × number of shares = 0.10 × 1 million = $100,000

New profit after tax = 100,000 + 25,000 = $125,000

New number of shares = 1 million + 400,000 = 1.4 million

New eps = 125,000/1,400,000 = $0.089, or 8.9 cents

This is lower than before so shareholder reaction will be negative.

Test Your Understanding 10

(a) NPV

Timing	t=0	t=1	t=2	t=3
Net cash flow	(20,000)	10,000	10,000	15,000
Discount factors @10%	1	0.909	0.826	0.751
Present values	(20,000)	9,090	8,260	11,265
Net present value (NPV)	**$8,615**			

(b) NPV

Timing	t=0	t=1	t=2	t=3
Net cash flow	(20,000)	10,000	10,000	12,000
Discount factors @10%	1	0.909	0.826	0.751
Present values	(20,000)	9,090	8,260	9,012
Net present value (NPV)	**$6,362**			

(c) NPV

Timing	t=0	t=1	t=2	t=3
Net cash flow	(20,000)	10,000	10,000	15,000
Discount factors @5%	1	0.952	0.907	0.864
Present values	(20,000)	9,520	9,070	12,960
Net present value (NPV)	**$11,550**			

(d) 1 *less valuable* as a higher interest rate would increase the cost of capital and raise the discount rate to be used.

2 *more valuable* as lower labour cost would raise the net income stream from the project.

3 *less valuable* as a reduction in the value of scrap machinery reduces the income stream in the final year of the project.

4 *more valuable* as this would raise revenue and it would be expected to raise the net income stream from the project.

Test Your Understanding 11

C

Responses (A) and (B) are concerned with the absolute value of income streams and not discounting those streams. Response (C) is correct since discounting is done because future income is worth less now even in the absence of inflation. Response (D) is a bit more tricky to evaluate as one aspect of the time value of money does relate to incorporating the effects of inflation. However, interest rates and risk are perhaps more important.

Test Your Understanding 12

Future cash flows

Assuming the markets believe, and have confidence in, the directors' claims, then they should revise their estimates of the company's future cash flows upwards.

Cost of capital/discount rate

The new venture is likely to be seen as increasing the company's risk and hence investors will want a higher return to compensate. This will be reflected in a higher discount rate being used to discount the (revised) future cash flows.

Share price

The impact on the share price will depend on the net effect of the above factors. If the shareholders are optimistic about the future growth plans without being overly concerned about the extra risk, then the share price should increase. A fall in share price would indicate more serious concerns over the risks and/or a lack of belief that the high growth in cash flows will materialise.

Test Your Understanding 13

C

Employees are "internal" stakeholders.

Test Your Understanding 14

Internal stakeholders

The employees and managers of the hotel are the main link with the guests and the service they provide is vital to the hotel as the quality of the guests' experience at the hotel will be determined by their attitude and approach.

Managers should ensure that employees achieve the highest levels of service are well trained and committed.

Connected stakeholders (shareholders, guests, suppliers)

The shareholders of the hotel will be concerned with a steady flow of income, possible capital growth and continuation of the business. Relationships should be developed and maintained with the shareholders, especially those operating on behalf of institutions. Management must try to achieve improvements in their return on investment by ensuring that customers are satisfied and willing to return.

Each guest will seek good service and satisfaction. The different types of guest will have different needs (business versus tourist) and management should regularly analyse the customer database to ensure that all customer needs are being met.

Suppliers must be selected very carefully to ensure that services and goods provided (e.g. food/laundry) continue to add to the quality of the hotel and customer satisfaction. They will be concerned with being paid promptly for goods, and maintaining a good relationship with the suppliers will ensure their continued support of the hotel.

External stakeholders (the government and the regulatory authorities)

The management of the hotel must maintain close relationships with the authorities to ensure they comply with all legislation – failure to do so could result in the hotel being closed down.

Test Your Understanding 15

C

While governance would ensure compliance with relevant legislation concerning employee working conditions, the primary focus is not employees per se.

Test Your Understanding 16

(1) ROCE is the *rate of return on capital employed* and is a measure of the flow of profits compared to the capital employed in the business. It is thus a measure of the profitability of that capital.

(2) Discounting is the process by which future streams of income can be given a present value; that is the value is reduced to take account of the factor that income in the future is valued less highly than that income now. This gives the *discounted cash flow*.

(3) The NPV of a project is calculated by adding together the discounted cash flow for each of the years of the lifetime of the investment project and subtracting from this the initial capital cost of the project.

(4) The value of the NVP would fall since a rise in the discount rate would mean giving lower valuations to future streams of income.

(5) Not-for-profit organisations include state-owned (public sector) activities, mutual societies, charities, private clubs, QUANGOs and voluntary organisations.

(6) Stakeholders are those persons and organisations that have an interest in the strategy, aims and behaviour of the organisation.

(7) Stakeholders may include: shareholders, management, employees, suppliers, customers, the suppliers of financial services, the local community.

(8) The principal – agent problem arises when principals (such as shareholders) appoint some agents (such as directors) to act on their behalf (running a company) and cannot be sure that those agents will always act so as to promote the interest of the principals.

(9) *There may a divorce of ownership from control* because:

- companies may become too big for shareholders to effectively control
- companies may become too complex for shareholders to control
- individual shareholders may lack the power, knowledge, interest or time to control the companies they own.

The term *corporate governance* refers to the systems by which companies and other organisations are directed and controlled. For Plc companies this means the role of the Board of Directors and its relationship to the shareholders.

chapter

2

Cost Behaviour and Pricing Decisions

Chapter learning objectives

After completing this chapter you should be able to:

- distinguish between the likely behaviour of a firm's unit costs in the short run and long run
- illustrate the potential effects of long-run cost behaviour on prices, the size of the organisation and the number of competitors in the industry
- illustrate the potential impact on prices and competition of e-business and globalisation
- demonstrate the point of profit maximisation graphically using total cost and total revenue curves
- calculate the point of profit maximisation for a single product firm in the short run using data.

1 Introduction – Increasing shareholder wealth

1.1 Business strategy

If we limit our discussion here to profit-seeking companies, then the primary objective is to maximise (or at least increase) shareholder wealth. We saw in Chapter 1 that this implies that the use of discounted cash flow techniques is the best way of assessing projects as the project NPV should correlate with shareholder wealth generation.

However, before they can estimate future cash flows the managers need to decide on their business strategy:

- which markets should they operate in?
- what should be the basis of their competitive advantage?
- to what extent should they perform all activities in house or should they outsource or be part of some form of joint venture?
- should products be manufactured in the domestic country or made off-shore?
- what should their portfolio of products be and how should they be marketed?

An in-depth discussion of these issues is beyond the scope of this paper but a basic knowledge of some of these will help you understand linkages within the economics syllabus.

1.2 Competitive strategy

Michael Porter stated that a key decision when trying to obtain a sustainable competitive advantage was the choice between 'cost *leadership'* and *'differentiation'*:

- **Cost leadership**

  Here the company seeks to compete by achieving lower costs than its rivals for similar products and services. If can then either undercut competitors on price, or charge similar prices and enjoy superior margins.

  Note that the idea here is not that we sell an inferior product, rather that we match competitors' quality but have the advantage of lower costs.

- **Differentiation**

  Here the company tries to differentiate itself by offering a better product than competitors. The customer is prepared to pay a premium price for the added perceived value in the product.

Note that 'better' in this context could include brand name, reliability, performance, image, technical features, etc. Often the pursuit of these results in higher costs but the firm can charge higher prices. The firm thus enjoys a greater margin than the undifferentiated product.

The significance for C04 is that this forms the basis for understanding decision making regarding costs.

- All firms will look for opportunities to reduce costs, for example by shifting production to China (off-shoring)
- However, for all firms, but particularly differentiators, there is a balance to be gained between cost and quality.
- In many mature industries it can become increasingly difficult to gain an advantage through differentiation as rivals soon copy any product developments. The key focus of many firms is thus to seek cost advantages.

The rest of this chapter looks at costs and cost advantages in more detail before then focussing on decision making to maximise profit.

2 The theory of costs

2.1 Factors of production

Economic resources are referred to as factors of production. These are usually classified as:

- Land

  This is the term used to cover all *natural resources*. Although largely in limited supply it can be improved through technological advances, for example irrigation. The reward accruing to land in the production process is termed *rent*.

- Labour

  This is a specific category of *human resource*. The quality of labour can be raised through education and training. The application of capital, through the use of machinery, will improve labour productivity. The reward of labour is termed *wages.*

- Enterprise

  This is another human resource but refers to the role played by the organiser of production, including *risk*. In return for risk-taking, organising and decision taking, entrepreneurs receive *profit*.

- Capital

  These are man-made resources. Capital may be *fixed*, for example a factory, or *working* capital, for example raw materials and work in progress. The reward accruing to capital in the production process is termed *interest.*

Test Your Understanding 1

Match the following factors of production to their associated rewards:

Factors

- Land
- Capital
- Enterprise
- Labour

Rewards

- Interest
- Wages
- Profits
- Rent

2.2 Cost behaviour

Fixed and variable costs

Fixed costs are costs that do not change with the level of production and include, for example, the rent of premises, the depreciation of a machine and the managing director's salary.

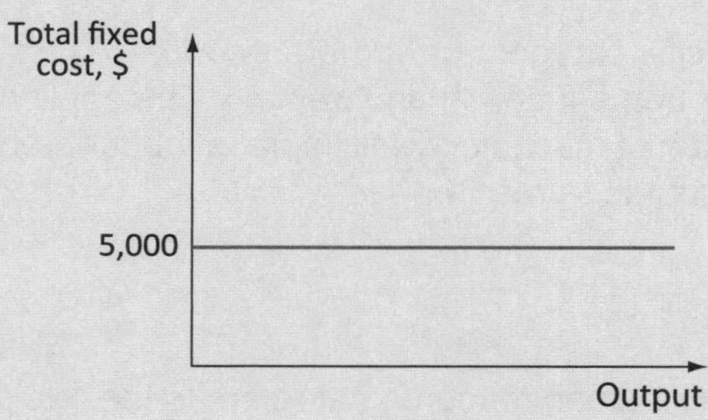

However, the average fixed cost per unit will fall as output increases as the (same) costs are shared over more units.

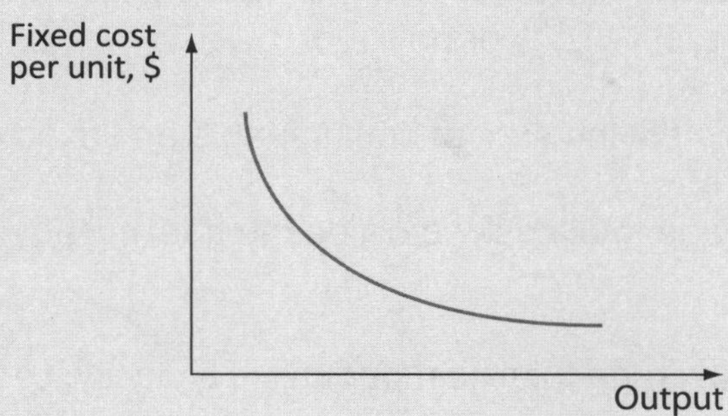

Variable costs are costs which do change with the level of output. For example, more steel is needed for producing 1,000 cars than for making 10 cars. Variable costs arise from using inputs such as labour and raw materials. In practice there are costs such as sales expenses which are semi-variable, but the analysis is simplified by distinguishing only fixed and variable costs.

The average variable cost per unit can vary with output as discussed below.

Short run

The short run, in economics, is defined as a period of time in which at least one factor of production is fixed. Thus it is not a time period which can be measured in days or months.

This fixed-factor definition means that the level of production in the short run can be increased only by adding more variable factors to the fixed factor. For example, we cannot increase the size of the factory but we can ask workers to do overtime.

Long run

In the long run, all factors are considered to be variable. This means that the level of production in the long run can be increased by adding more of all factors to the production process.

However, it is assumed that the quality of the factors stays constant. In the very long run the assumption of fixed technology is removed. Consequently, advances in technology can lead to improvements in the productivity of factors of production.

Efficiency in the short run

One way of discussing efficiency (we will meet others later) is to consider the average total cost (ATC) per unit.

The total cost is simply the sum of both variable and fixed costs.

To derive an average total cost we divide the total cost by the number of units produced.

The graph of the average total cost per unit is typically *'U-shaped'*:

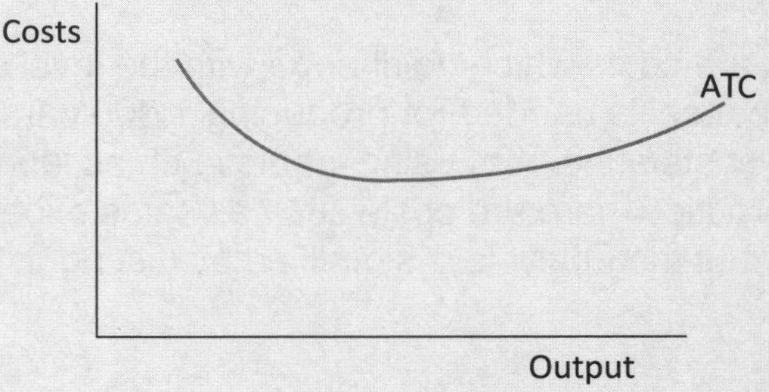

There is thus an optimal level of production which is defined as that which minimises the average total cost of production.

Note that we are only considering costs here so this is not necessarily the level of output that will maximise profit.

To illustrate this consider the following table:

Output (units)	Fixed costs	AFC	Variable costs	AVC	Total Cost	ATC
1	30	30	25	25	55	55
2	30	15	40	20	70	35
3	30	10	54	18	84	28
4	30	7.50	80	20	110	27.50
5	30	6	110	22	140	28
6	30	5	150	25	180	30
7	30	4.29	210	30	240	34.29

Note:

- AFC = average fixed cost per unit
- AVC = average variable cost per unit
- ATC = average total cost per unit = AFC + AVC

For these figures we could argue that the firm is most efficient when it produces 4 units as the average total cost is at a minimum there.

A graph showing each of AFC, AVC and ATC would look as follows:

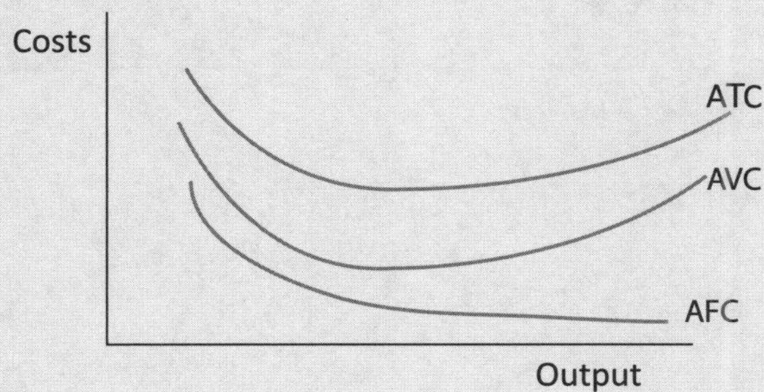

We can see that the AFC will continue to fall as output rises but the AVC curve initially falls and then increases. The combined effect is the 'U' shaped ATC curve.

This 'U' shape can be explained by **the law of diminishing returns**.

This law states that as equal quantities of one variable factor input are added to a fixed factor, output initially increases by a greater proportion (increasing returns), causing average cost to fall. A point will be reached beyond which the resulting addition to output will begin to decrease (diminishing returns), causing average costs to rise.

For example, suppose we increase the number of workers while fixing the number of machines. Initially the extra workers will allow specialisation and greater efficiency. At a later point, however, staff are getting in each other's way and waiting to access machines. The system thus becomes less efficient and what is really needed is more machines rather than more workers.

Cost behaviour in the long run

In the long run all factors of production can be varied – in the above example this would involve buying more machines. If all factors can be varied, then the law of diminishing returns cannot apply.

This means that the firm can move to a different short-run cost curve – in fact the long-run cost curve is essentially a combination of different short-run cost curves. It is thus possible to ensure that the firm always operates near the bottom of the short-run average cost curves.

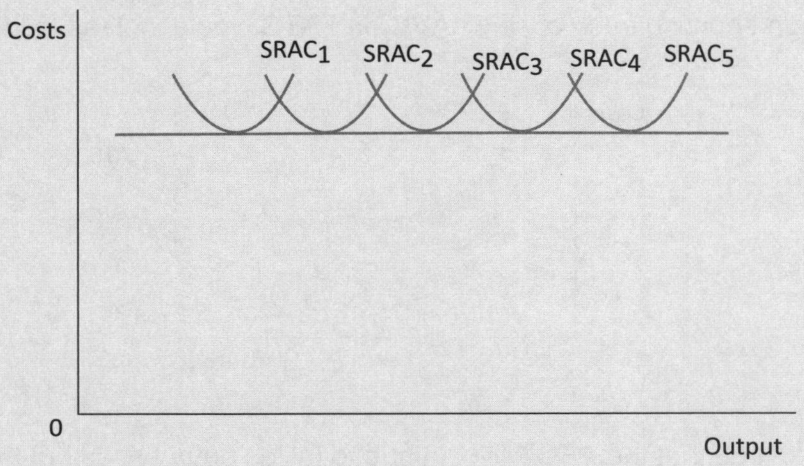

However, the long-run average total cost curve (LRATC) is not flat as economies and diseconomies of scale occur:

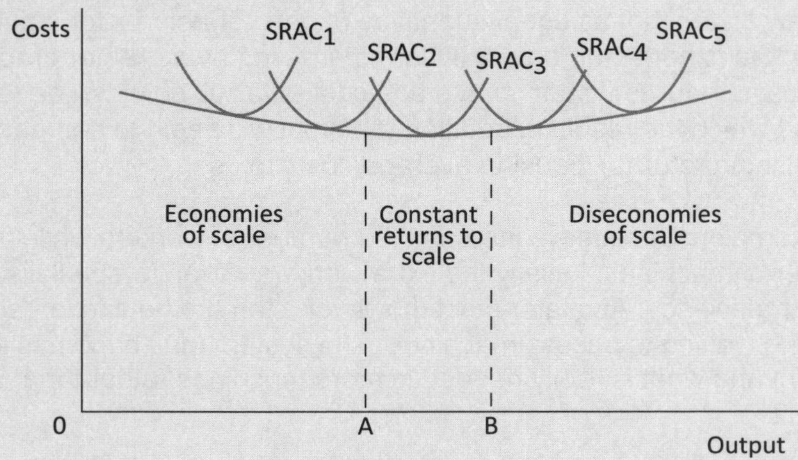

Economies of scale (also known as increasing returns to scale) are defined as reductions in unit average costs caused by increasing the scale of production in the long run.

For example, a larger firm may be able to gain greater discounts when purchasing raw materials.

Diseconomies of scale (also known as decreasing/ diminishing returns to scale) are defined as increases in unit average costs caused by increasing the scale of production in the long run.

Diseconomies can arise as a firm grows very large. These often reflect the difficulty of communicating within a large organisation, together with a decline in management control.

Implications for businesses

- Increasing and diminishing returns

  In the short run all firms should seek to use their assets efficiently to operate at their minimum average cost if possible. To do this may involve work analysis and time and motion studies. Historically many firms found increased role specialisation could help here.

- Economies and diseconomies of scale

  Managers need to understand whether economies of scale exist or are possible in their industry and the extent and nature of such economies.

  If such economies exist, then firms will need to achieve *'critical mass'* in order to be competitive on cost. The low costs that result allow the firm to set its prices below those of smaller competitors and can act as a serious barrier to new firms trying to enter the industry. Obtaining such scale of production can result from organic growth and / or acquisition. While this results in larger firms, it often means fewer as well.

  This explains why many industries are dominated by large players. However, the firm should not simply grow for growth's sake as diseconomies of scale will erode its cost advantage.

  The alternative to competing on cost would be differentiation, perhaps specialising in a market niche, but even here if the price difference between the differentiator and the large cost leader is too great, then customers will be unwilling to pay the premium.

The existence of significant economies of scale can be expected to lead to:

- costs and therefore prices falling as firms increase their scale of output;
- barriers to entry for newer smaller firms; and
- industries dominated by a small number of large firms.

Illustration 1 – Economies of scale

The motor manufacturing industry is dominated by global firms. This is due to significant economies of scale such as

- purchasing discounts – e.g. steel
- use of large automated production lines
- marketing economies
- ability to have global supply chains benefiting from lower costs in certain countries.

However, if you are trying to buy a house, then you will most likely find yourself dealing with small local firms of estate agents. This is because economies of scale are less significant and local expertise and local presence is deemed to be more important.

Supplementary reading – Further detail on economies of scale

Economies of scale

When the advantages of expanding the scale of operation accrue to just one firm, these economies are termed **internal.** They can be obtained in one plant, belonging to a firm, or across the whole company. The main internal economies are as follows:

- **Technical economies.** These relate to the scale of the production and are usually obtained in one plant. Large-scale operations may make greater use of advanced machinery. Some machines are only worth using beyond a minimum level of output which may be beyond the capacity of a small firm, for example, robots used in car assembly. Such equipment may facilitate the division of labour. In addition, more resources can be devoted to research in large firms, because the cost is borne over more units of output, and this may lead to further technical improvements and subsequent cost reductions, for the whole company.
- **Financial economies.** It is usually easier for large firms with household names to borrow money from commercial banks and raise funds on the Stock Exchange. Similarly, their loans and overdrafts will probably be charged at lower interest rates because of their reputation and assets.
- **Trading economies**. Large firms may be able to secure advantages both when buying inputs and selling their outputs. They could employ specialist buyers and, through the quantity of their purchases, gain significant discounts from their suppliers.

Similarly, bulk selling enables a large firm to make savings in distribution costs, the time and cost of salespeople and advertising expenses.

These savings are more marked when many products are sold together in related markets. Thus, one big advantage of Nestle's takeover of Rowntree Mackintosh was that the goods of each could be marketed together, with little extra total cost, thereby reducing the distribution costs of each product sold.

If a large firm produces several products in different markets, then one failure is unlikely to cause the closure of the whole conglomerate. Thus, trading risks can be spread when a wide range of products are sold.

- **Managerial economies.** These are the many administrative gains which can be achieved when the scale of production grows. The need for management and supervision does not increase at the same rate as output. Specialists can be employed and their talents can be fully utilised in personnel, production, selling, accountancy and so on. Such organisational benefits may lower the indirect costs of production and lead to the efficient use of labour resources.

However, it is possible for general advantages to be obtained by all of the firms in an industry, and these are classed as **external economies of scale**. Most of these occur when an industry is heavily concentrated in one area. The area may develop a reputation for success, for example, computers and electronics in Silicon Valley in California. There may be a pool of skilled labour which is available, and this may lower training costs for a firm. Specialised training may be provided locally in accordance with the industry's needs. This might be provided by a training board to which firms contribute to gain access to the available expertise. Furthermore, a localised industry may attract to it specialist suppliers of raw materials, components and services, who gain from a large market and achieve their own economies of scale, which are passed on through lower input prices. Occasionally, firms in an industry share their research and development facilities, because each firm individually could not bear the overheads involved but can fund a joint enterprise.

Diseconomies of scale

These exist when the average cost rises with increased production. If they are specific to one firm they are categorised as internal.

- **Technical diseconomies**. The optimum technical size of plant may create large administrative overheads in its operation, thereby raising ATC, even though the production cost is lowered.
- **Trading diseconomies**. With large-scale production, products may become standardised. This lack of individualism may reduce consumer choice and lead to lower sales. In addition, it may be difficult to quickly adapt mass-produced goods to changing market trends.

- **Managerial diseconomies.** As the chain of command becomes longer in an expanding hierarchy (when productive capacity grows), senior management may become too remote and lose control. This may lead to cross-inefficiency (complacency) in middle management and shop floor hostility. A concomitant of this is the generally poor state of labour relations in large organisations, which are more prone to industrial stoppages than small firms. This is partly because the trade unions are better organised. Other administrative weaknesses faced by increasingly large organisations are the prevalence of red tape and the conflict between departmental managers who have different objectives and priorities.

However, there may also be general disadvantages which afflict all firms as the scale of the industry grows. The main external diseconomy is technical. If a resource is over utilised then shortages may arise. A shortage of labour might lead to higher wages in order to attract new recruits, while a shortage of raw materials might lower output. Both changes would raise the average cost of production.

Test Your Understanding 2

The 'law of diminishing returns' can apply to a business only when:

A all factors of production can be varied.

B at least one factor of production is fixed.

C all factors of production are fixed.

D capital used in production is fixed.

Test Your Understanding 3

A company doubles its input of land, labour and capital and its output more than doubles. This is an example of:

A decreasing returns to scale

B constant returns to scale

C increasing returns to scale

D diminishing returns

Test Your Understanding 4

Which of the following is not a source of economies of scale?

A The introduction of specialist capital equipment.

B Bulk-buying.

C The employment of specialist managers.

D Cost savings resulting from new production techniques.

Test Your Understanding 5

Answer the following questions based on the preceding information. You can check your answers below.

(1) What is the definition of fixed costs?

(2) In what time period are all factors of production variable?

(3) Why do diminishing returns occur in the short run?

(4) Distinguish between internal and external economies of scale.

(5) Give two examples of diseconomies of scale.

2.3 Opportunity costs

Opportunity cost is the value of the benefit sacrificed when one course of action is chosen in preference to an alternative.

In most cases the opportunity cost of a particular course of action is the next best alternative foregone.

For example, suppose I plan to use a machine in a new project and that

- I already own it
- If not used in the project it could be sold for $10,000

You might argue that the cost of using the machine is zero based on the fact that I do not have to spend any money to acquire it. However, by using it in the project I have foregone the opportunity of selling it. I thus have an opportunity cost of $10,000 that needs to be incorporated in my decision as to whether or not to do the project.

All decision making should be based on looking at the net future incremental cash flows involved. For example, in the above example an opportunity cost of (10,000) could be a cash flow in a NPV calculation.

Test Your Understanding 6

Company C is considering whether or not to develop a new range of chocolate bars. This will replace an existing range. The predicted revenue cash flows for the next year are as follows:

Sales from new range – $100,000

Sales from existing range if the new range is not introduced – $30,000

Ignoring production costs, what cash flow figure should be used in a NPV calculation for the first year?

A $100,000

B $70,000

C $30,000

D ($30,000)

Illustration 2 – Normal profit

An important example of an opportunity cost is "normal profit".

Suppose Jaime is currently employed earning $25,000, has money invested earning interest of $1,000 and own some land that is currently rented for an income of $2,000.

Now suppose that Jaime is thinking about giving up his job and setting up his own business. This will use his savings and land. For this to be worthwhile the new business will have to generate profits of at least $28,000. The $28,000 can be interpreted as the opportunity cost of Jaime's income foregone and is known as normal profit.

If the profits are $30,000, say, then Jaime will only be $2,000 better off. This surplus is known as "super-normal" profit.

Note: to be completely accurate we should also add a risk factor to the above figures when determining normal profit as setting up a new business is riskier (usually) than working for someone else.

3 Pricing decisions

Having looked at cost behaviour this section considers how firms should set their prices.

3.1 Pricing considerations

When setting a price businesses will take into account four factors, known collectively as the "4Cs":

- Costs

  In the long run a firm will want to set a price that covers its average total cost per unit.

  Note: In the short run a firm will continue to trade providing its revenue covers variable costs as it would have to pay its fixed costs even if output was zero. If revenue falls below variable costs, then the managers should consider stopping production immediately and avoiding those costs. In the long run it must cover both variable and fixed costs.

- Customers

  A firm will need to set a price that its target customers are willing to pay. Most firms have to reduce prices if they want to sell more units (i.e. they face downward sloping demand curves) so have to balance the link between price and quantity sold.

- Competitors

  The pricing decision needs to be consistent with the competitive strategy chosen, so a cost leader would usually set a price equal to or slightly lower that competitors, whereas a differentiator might set a price at a premium.

- Corporate objectives

  In most exam questions the objective will be to set a price that maximises profit. However in reality there are other objectives including pricing to maximising revenue, dropping prices to penetrate new markets and/or setting high prices to reinforce a high quality image.

3.2 Maximising profit

In the exam you need to be able to use tables and graphs to identify the optimum price. This is best seen through an example:

Illustration 3 – Pricing example

The following table shows the output, price , total revenue (TR) and total cost (TC) figures for a new product.

Output Q	Price	Total Revenue TR	Total Cost TC	Total Profit TP
0	9	0	40	–40
10	8	80	70	10
20	7	140	100	40
30	6	180	140	40
40	5	200	180	20
50	4	200	200	0

From the table we can see the following:

- total revenue (TR) doesn't always keep rising when more units are sold. The price cut to generate the extra business can more than offset the gain in volume obtained.
- the maximum profit appears to be at quantities of 20 and 30 units and we suspect it might lie somewhere between these two.
- maximum revenue and maximum profit do not occur at the same price and quantity.

This can also be seen graphically. Profit maximisation will then occur when total revenue (TR) exceeds total cost (TC) by the greatest amount. The shaded area represents the levels of output within which profits are made. The maximum profit is shown by the greatest difference between total revenue (TR) and total cost (TC), which is at output level 30.

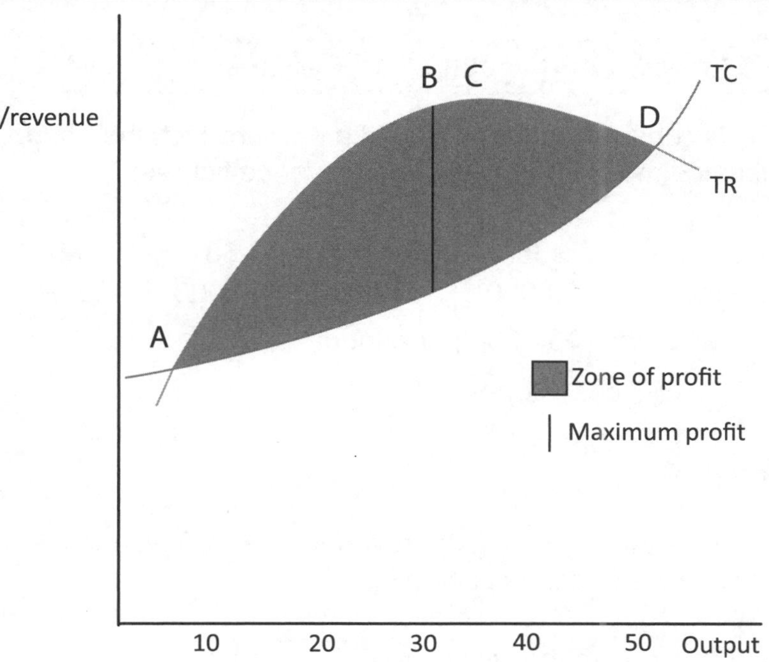

Note that on the graph we can identify the following points:

A A break even point (profit = 0)

B Maximum profit

C Maximum revenue

D A second break even point

Test Your Understanding 7

Zeek is considering the pricing of a new product, the Thripp, and has estimated the following costs and revenue figures:

Price	$6	$7	$8	$9	$10
Demand	50,000	45,000	40,000	35,000	30,000

- Fixed costs $60,000 per annum
- Variable cost $2 per unit

Required:

Produce a table showing the revenue and profit at each level and use it to advise the directors assuming

(a) They wish to maximise profit

(b) They wish to maximise revenue

Supplementary reading – Current trends

There are a number of current trends regarding costs and pricing that you need to be aware of:

Globalisation

Globalisation brings new market opportunities, for example in China, giving scope for higher revenues and even greater economies of scale for multinational firms. These cost reductions bring even greater cost advantages to larger firms.

However, the opening up of markets also exposes those firms to higher competition in their domestic markets from foreign firms (for example Chinese firms expanding into Europe), resulting in downward pressure on prices.

Globalisation has also resulted in greater standardisation of products and the cost advantages that go with that.

Globalisation is discussed in more detail in Chapter 6.

Emerging economies

Four of the fastest growing economies in the world are the so called "BRIC" economies – Brazil, Russia, India and China. In early 2011 China became the second largest economy in the world, overtaking Japan and in March 2012 Brazil overtook the UK to become the 6th largest economy. This presents western firms with both major opportunities and major threats.

Traditionally Western firms have taken advantage of lower costs in emerging economies either through outsourcing or off-shoring. For example, many clothing items are manufactured in Asia. Historically there was seen to be a cost advantage to doing this but now many Chinese firms can offer higher quality and lower costs.

This is having a profound impact on firms in the West who are finding their traditional competitive advantage eroded. While some have been forced out of business, others have moved into more differentiated high-tech market segments and others have outsourced to cut costs.

E-business

The growth in the internet has affected businesses in many ways including

- Cheaper and more efficient procurement. For example, there is greater availability of information upon which to choose suppliers, compare prices and negotiate lower costs. Online ordering gives more efficient procurement allowing lower levels of inventory to be held.
- New businesses might become possible. For example, auction sites and photo album sites.
- The industry structure can be changed. For example, in the music business it can be argued that the large CD publishers have less power because music can be self-published on the internet.
- IS/IT can provide an organisation with competitive advantage by providing new ways of operating. For example, airlines save money by encouraging internet bookings.
- Barriers to entry have been eroded. For example, if you wanted to enter the banking industry twenty years ago you would have had to acquire premises at significant cost. Now you can open an online bank with much lower initial costs.
- Information concerning competitors is much easier to access resulting in greater price transparency.
- Reducing variable costs to near zero – see next section.

Note that many of these trends in e-business have eroded the traditional advantages gained by larger firms.

Impact of E-business on transaction costs

A transaction cost is a cost incurred in making an economic exchange (i.e. the cost of participating in a market).

For example, consider buying a CD from a store. To purchase the CD, your costs will be not only the price of the CD itself, but also:

- the energy and effort it requires to find out which CD you want, where to get the CD and at what price,
- the cost of travelling from your house to the store and back,
- the time waiting in line, and the effort of the paying itself;

Transaction costs are all the costs beyond the cost of the CD.

E-business is driving down the costs of transactions, as it is relatively easy to obtain reviews and customer feedback to decide which CD you want, then to check availability, prices and finally to transact a deal on-line. A more recent trend is now not to buy a physical CD but to download the songs digitally.

The result of this is the restructuring of various retailing sectors such as those for books, CDs, DVDs, software and computer games where online retailers now dominate and high street premises are being closed.

Furthermore, from the seller's perspective the internet has enabled variable costs to be to be reduced dramatically and in some cases to near zero.

Consider how much extra it costs i-tunes, say, if ten additional customers buy and download a particular song – other than royalties to original artists there are no variable costs. Similarly with online booking and check-in, airlines have reduced variable costs per passenger.

A combination of high fixed and low variable costs puts more pressure on firms to win new customers and to dominate markets. Internet marketing is seen as key here.

Test Your Understanding 8

Which of the following is **not** a recognised consequnce of the growth in e-business:

A A reduction in barriers to entry in some industries

B An increase in transaction costs

C Greater price transparency

D More efficient and cheaper procurement.

Test your understanding answers

Test Your Understanding 1

- Land – rent
- Labour – wages
- Enterprise – profit
- Capital – interest

Test Your Understanding 2

B

The law of diminishing returns states that if more units of a variable factor are added to a fixed factor, the increment in output will eventually decline. Responses (A) and (C) are therefore incorrect. Response (D) is also incorrect, since the law applies for any fixed factor, not only capital.

Test Your Understanding 3

C

C is the correct answer because output has increased in percentage terms by more than the increase in inputs.

Test Your Understanding 4

D

Economies of scale are the cost savings resulting from any activity or process which is made possible by increasing the scale of output. This applies to responses (A), (B) and (C), since these are made possible as the size of businesses increases. Response (D), however, is incorrect since it refers to technical change, and this would reduce costs for all producers, large and small.

Test Your Understanding 5

(1) Fixed costs are those which do not change with the level of production.

(2) All factors of production are variable in the long run.

(3) Diminishing returns occur in the short run because one factor of production is fixed. Thus, output can be raised only by adding more units of a variable factor. This adds progressively smaller amounts of extra output and leads to increases in average cost.

(4) Internal economies are achieved by one firm within its own operations, whereas external economies are advantages available to most firms from the operation of the whole industry.

(5) Administrative duplication and conflict of objectives between different departments in a large organisation.

Test Your Understanding 6

B

There are two relevant cash flows:

- The new range will give $100,000
- There is an opportunity cost of ($30,000) relating to sales foregone for the existing range

The net figure is $70,000.

(Alternatively, you could have observed that the incremental sales was an increase of $70,000)

Test Your Understanding 7

Price	**$6**	**$7**	**$8**	**$9**	**$10**
Revenue ($000)	300	315	320	315	300
Variable costs ($000)	(100)	(90)	(80)	(70)	(60)
Fixed costs ($000)	(60)	(60)	(60)	(60)	(60)
Profit ($000)	**140**	**165**	**180**	**185**	**180**

(a) The optimum selling price is $9 per unit, selling 35,000 units with a corresponding profit of $185,000 p.a. (Note: in reality the variable cost per unit might differ from one level of output to another because of the operation of increasing and diminishing returns and this would affect the optimal solution.)

(b) The highest revenue is at a price of $8 with sales of 40,000 units.

Test Your Understanding 8

B

The growth in e-business has decreased transaction costs.

chapter

3

The Market System

Chapter learning objectives

On completion of their studies students should be able to:

- identify the equilibrium price in a product or factor markets likely to result from specified changes in conditions of demand or supply;
- calculate the price elasticity of demand and the price elasticity of supply;
- explain the determinants of the price elasticities of demand and supply;
- identify the effects of price elasticity of demand on a firm's revenues following a change in prices.
- identify causes of instability of prices in markets for primary goods;
- explain the impact of instability of prices on incomes of producers and the stability of the industry;
- explain the effects on prices, producer revenues and market equilibrium, of government policies to influence prices in markets;
- illustrate the impacts of price regulation in goods and factor markets;
- explain market failures and their effects on prices, efficiency of market operation and economic welfare;
- explain the likely responses of government to market failures.

1 Introduction

1.1 Different market systems

Given that resources are limited ('scarce'), it is not possible to make everything everyone would want ('unlimited wants'). All societies are thus faced with a fundamental economic problem:

- What goods and services should be produced?
- In what quantities?
- Who should make them?
- Who gets the output?

There are three main economic systems or approaches to solve this problem:

- **A market economy** – interaction between supply and demand (market forces) determines what is made, in what quantity and who gets the output. Patterns of economic activity are determined by the decisions made by individual consumers and producers.
- **A command economy** – production decisions are controlled by the government.
- **A mixed economy** – in reality most modern economies are a **mix** of free markets and government intervention.

1.2 Market forces

In a free market, the quantity and price of goods supplied in a market are determined by the interaction between supply and demand.

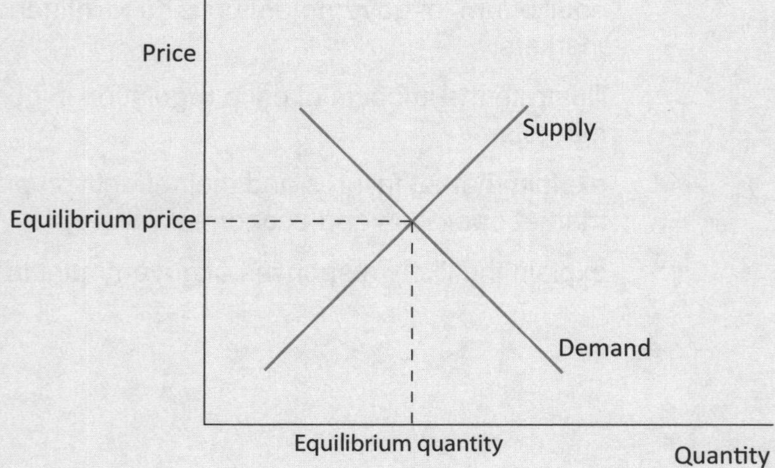

A market price will be set by the *'invisible hand of the market'* through the interaction of supply and demand.

In this chapter we will explore this process by looking at demand and supply in detail and at how the price mechanism sets the price. We will then consider the subject of *'market failure'* and the reasons why governments are not content to leave everything to market forces.

2 Demand

2.1 Individual demand

Individual demand shows how much of a good or service someone intends to buy at different prices.

This demand needs to be effective in that it is backed by available money, rather than just a general desire without the necessary financial backing.

When considering demand at a price, we assume that the conditions of demand (i.e. other variables – see below) are held constant.

- For most goods, the lower the price, the higher will be its demand. This is the result of two processes.
  - **A substitution effect** – this is where a consumer buys more of one good and less of another because of relative price changes. Thus if two goods are substitutes, a fall in the price of the first will lead consumers to switch some demand to the lower-price good, substituting the first good for the second.
  - **An income effect** – this is where a change in the price of good affects the purchasing power of the consumers' income. For example, if the price of a good falls, the consumer experiences a rise in their real income and, as a result, tends to buy more of all normal goods and services. In most cases the income effect is relatively weak. However, if expenditure on the good is a large proportion of consumer income, e.g. in the case of house purchase, the effect will be relatively large.
- When the demand for a good or service changes in response to a change in its price, the change is referred to as:
  - an *expansion* in demand as demand rises when the price falls. (**Note:** older texts refer to this as an *extension* so ensure you are happy with either term)
  - a *contraction* in demand as demand falls when the price rises.

- The relationship between demand and price can be shown in a diagram and is referred to as a *demand curve*. (Note: For such graphs we plot *quantity* along the horizontal axis and *price* on the vertical axis. This may seem the wrong way round to you as we are arguing here that demand depends on price and we normally have the dependent variable on the vertical axis. However, this is the accepted approach for economics.)
- Thus in the diagram below the downward-sloping demand curve D illustrates a normal downward-sloping demand curve and movements along this curve as the price changes would be called a contraction in demand (price is rising) or an expansion in demand (price is falling).

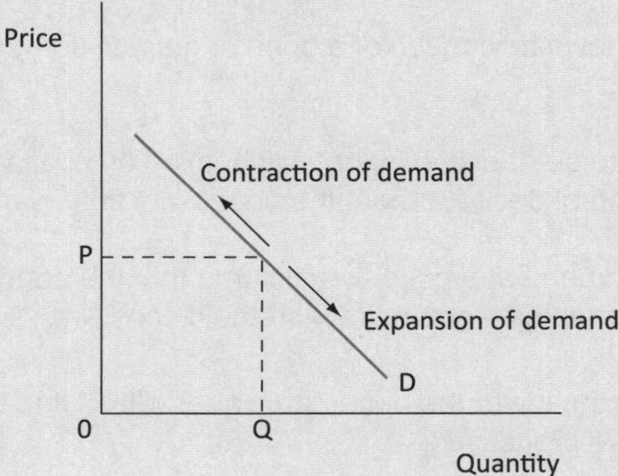

2.2 Market demand

Market demand shows the total amount of effective demand from all the consumers in a market. It is an *aggregate*, like the supply curve for an industry. *Market demand* is usually shortened to demand and represented by a straight-line curve on a graph. The demand curve for most normal goods is negatively inclined sloping downwards from right to left for reasons explained in the previous section.

2.3 Conditions of demand

Individual and market demand consider exclusively the influence of price on the quantity demanded, assuming other factors to be constant. These factors, termed the conditions of demand, will now be considered, with price held constant.

Any change in one or more of the conditions of demand will create shifts in the demand curve itself.

- If the shift in the demand curve is outward, to the right, such a shift is called an *increase* in demand.
- If the shift in the demand curve is inward, to the left, such a shift is called a *decrease* in demand.

It is important to distinguish such increases and decreases in demand that result from a shift in the demand curve as a whole from *expansions* and *contractions* in demand that result from price changes leading to movements along the demand curve itself.

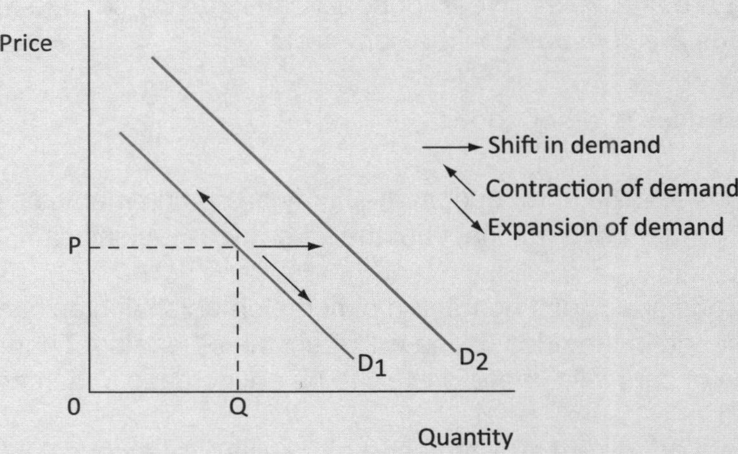

The main conditions of demand are as follows:

- Income

  Changes in income often affect demand.

  For example, lower direct taxes would raise disposable incomes and, other things being equal, make consumers better off and so they spend more on holidays. For *normal* goods an increase in income leads to an increase in demand. Other examples could include cars, jewellery, fashion clothing and CDs.

  For *inferior* goods, however, a rise in income leads to a **lower** demand for the product as consumers, now being richer, substitute better quality and preferred goods and services for the original ('inferior') good or service. An example of this is public transport. Here, as incomes rise, the demand for public transport falls as consumers substitute private transport such as cars.

- Tastes

  Tastes, in particular fashions, change frequently and it may make the demand for certain goods volatile.

  For instance, in the UK the only type of beer that saw an increase in sales in 2009 was "real ale", primarily because many women had started drinking it.

Tastes, of course, can be manipulated by advertising and producers to try to 'create' markets, particularly for ostentatious goods, for example, air conditioners which our ancestors survived perfectly well without. Some goods are in seasonal demand (e.g. cooked meat) even though they are available all year round, because tastes change (i.e. more salads are consumed in the summer).

- The prices of other goods

  Goods may be unrelated, or they may be complements or substitutes. The former have no effect but the latter two are significant.

  If goods are in joint demand (i.e. complements such as cars and tyres) a change in the price of one will affect the other also. Therefore, if the price of cars falls, there is likely to be an increase in demand for tyres.

  Where goods are substitutes (e.g. Quality Street chocolates and Roses chocolates), a rise in the price of one will cause an increase in demand for the other (and thus the demand curve will shift to the right).

  Sometimes, technological breakthroughs mean that new products come into the market. For instance, the advent of ink cartridge pens reduced the demand for fountain pens, because the former became a cheaper (and less messy) substitute.

- Population

  An *increase* in population creates a larger market for most goods, thereby shifting demand outwards. For instance, an influx of immigrant workers will raise the demand for most essential goods. Changes in population distribution will also affect demand patterns. If the proportion of old people relative to young people increases, then the demand for products such as false teeth, wheelchairs and old people's homes will increase to the detriment of gripe water, nappies and cots.

In the analysis of how the demand and supply model works, the distinctions between *increase/decrease* in demand and *expansion/contraction* in demand are very important. Remember:

- If a *price change* occurs, there will be a *movement along the demand curve* and the result will be either an *expansion* or a *contraction* in demand;
- If the *conditions of demand* change, there will be a *shift in the demand curve* and the result will be either an *increase* or a *decrease* in demand.

Test Your Understanding 1

A demand curve is drawn assuming all but one of the following remains unchanged. Which item can vary?

A The price of competitors' products

B The cost of labour to make the product

C The price of the product

D The level of growth in the economy.

Test Your Understanding 2

Which one of the following would lead to the demand curve for health supplements shifting to the right?

A Adverse publicity that suggests such supplements may be harmfull.

B A fall in the disposable income of consumers

C A fall in the price of the supplements

D An increase in the size of the population due to people living longer

Test Your Understanding 3

Which one of the following would not lead to a shift in the demand curve for overseas holidays?

A An advertising campaign by holiday-tour operators

B A fall in the disposable income of consumers

C A rise in the price of domestic holidays

D A rise in the exchange rate for the domestic currency

3 Elasticity of demand

Elasticity, generally, refers to the relationship between two variables and measures the responsiveness of one (dependent) variable to a change in another (independent) variable: There are several types which are useful to economists.

3.1 Price elasticity of demand (PED)

This concept explains the relationship between changes in quantity demand and changes in price.

- Price elasticity of demand explains the responsiveness of demand to changes in price.
- The co-efficient of price elasticity of demand (PED) is calculated by:

$$\frac{\text{Percentage change in quantity demanded}}{\text{Percentage change in price}}$$

The formula can be applied either at one point (point elasticity) or over the whole curve (arc elasticity). It is critical that percentage or proportional changes are used rather than absolute ones.

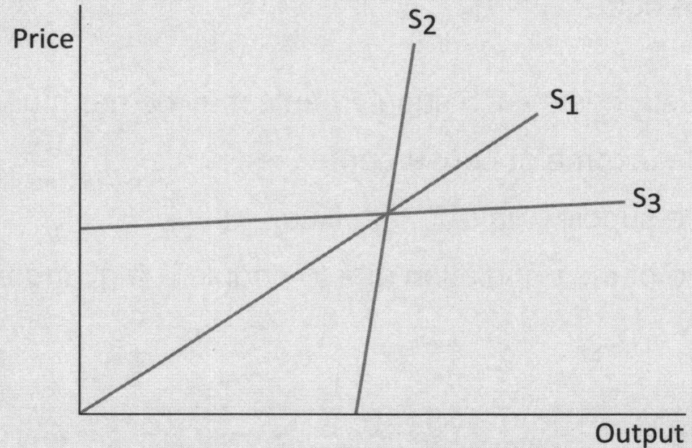

D_1 shows unit elasticity.
D_2 shows inelastic demand.
D_3 shows elastic demand.

A normal demand curve will always slope downwards from left to right indicating that a price rise will lead to a *contraction* in demand and a price fall will lead to an *expansion* in demand.

Illustration 1 – PED

Suppose we are currently selling a product at a price of $20 with a resulting demand of 500,000 units per annum. A marketing manager has suggested dropping the price to $19 and claims that demand will rise to 550,000 units.

Calculate the PED.

Solution

- Percentage change in price = –5%
- Percentage change in demand = +10%
- PED = (+10)/(–5) = –2

In CBA questions expect PED to be negative because price and quantity demanded are inversely related. A summary of price elasticity is given below:

Description of curve's elasticity	Coefficient value	Actual examples
Relatively inelastic	Between 0 and –1	Tea, salt
Unit elasticity	–1	–
Relatively elastic	Between –1 and -∞	Cameras, air travel

Note: if demand is completely insensitive to price, then the PED will be 0 and demand would be described as "perfectly inelastic". An example of this would be a vertical demand curve. Similarly a horizontal demand curve would have PED = -∞, "perfectly elastic".

Generally, if the demand curve is fairly steep, a large change in price will cause only a relatively small change in demand, indicating an *inelastic* demand curve.

Test Your Understanding 4

A business currently sells 100,000 units of a product per month at a price of $5. The sales manager has suggested dropping the price to $4.90 with the argument that the quantity demanded will rise to 105,000 units.

Calculate the PED

A – 50,000

B – 4

C – 2.5

D – 0.25

Test Your Understanding 5

A business, currently selling 10,000 units of its product per month, plans to reduce the retail price from $1 to $0.90. It knows from previous experience that the price elasticity of demand for this product is –1.5. Assuming no other changes, the sales the business can now expect each month will be:

A 8,500

B 10,500

C 11,000

D 11,500

Supplementary reading – PED and gradient

While we might expect a steeper demand curve to be less elastic, elasticity and gradient are not the same thing. It is often wrongly assumed that two demand curves with the same shape will have the same elasticity coefficient. Even for a straight line demand curve (i.e. constant gradient) the PED will vary depending where exactly you are on the curve.

Consider the following demand curves:

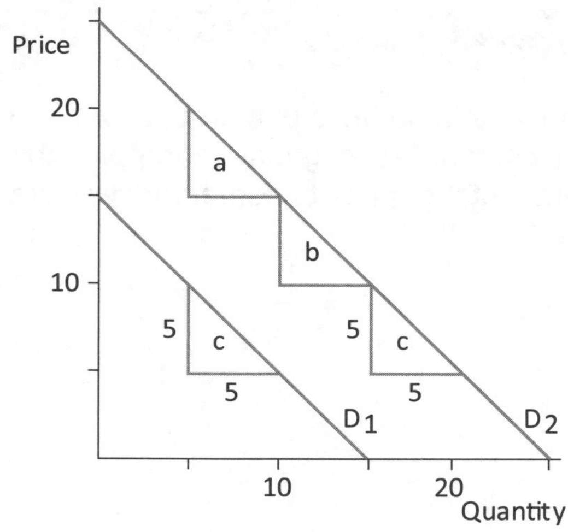

Price	Demand D1	Demand D2
5	10	20
10	5	15
15		10
20		5

The PED coefficients for the same range of D1 and D2 are calculated for a price fall (triangle *c*).

For D_1 (triangle *c*) the quantity demanded increases from 5 to 10 (i.e. = +5/5) as the price falls from 10 to 5 (i.e. –½). Elasticity is therefore calculated as (5/5) ÷ (– ½) = –2.

In contrast, D_2 (triangle c) shows that quantity demanded increased from 15 to 20 (i.e. + 1/3) when the price fell from 10 to 5 (i.e. – 1/2) Elasticity is therefore calculated as

1/3 ÷ (–1/2) = 2/3.

This demonstrates the importance of the position of the demand curve. Generally, a curve further from the origin will tend to be less elastic, as shown above.

The numerical value of the elasticity coefficient also varies according to:

- whether a price fall or price rise is calculated.

  For example, D_2 elasticity = –2/3 when price fell from 10p to 5p. However, a price rise of 5p to 10p gives –1/4 (i.e. –1/4 ÷ 1). This occurs because elasticity shows relative percentage changes and the base from which the calculations are made differs.

- which part of the demand curve is selected. Elasticity varies from point to point on a straight-line demand curve (but not on a rectangular hyperbola). As calculation moves down a linear curve from top left to bottom right the elasticity value falls, that is, the curve becomes relatively more inelastic.

  For example, the price elasticity of demand for a price fall of 5p on D_2 at

  – *a* = –4 (i.e. 1 ÷ (/1/4)), whereas at
  – *b* = –3/2 (i.e. 1/2 ÷ (–1/3)) and at
  – *c* = –2/3 (i.e. –1/3 ÷ (1/2)).

Supplementary reading – The point method for calculating PED

So far we have calculated PED by considering a movement along a demand curve – i.e. we started at one point and then changed both price and quantity. This is known as the arc method.

With a straight line demand curve the PED calculated will only depend on where we started (as this determines how we calculate the percentages) but not on how far along the demand curve we move.

Unfortunately if the demand curve is a curve then the PED will depend on both the starting point AND on how far we move. We thus cannot really talk of the elasticity at a point because it depends on our calculation. This is clearly absurd and so we need a more precise method of calculating PED. The solution is the point method and requires a knowledge of the equation of the demand curve and of differential calculus. While both are off-syllabus it is worth being aware that using the point method means that the PED only depends on the point chosen again.

3.2 Factors that influence PED

There are several factors which determine the price elasticity of demand:

- Proportion of income spent on the good

  Where a good constitutes a small proportion of consumers' income spent, then a small price change will be unlikely to have much impact. Therefore, the demand for unimportant items such as shoe polish, matches and pencils is likely to be very inelastic. Conversely, the demand for quality clothing will probably be elastic.

- Substitutes

  If there are close and available substitutes for a product, then an increase in its price is likely to cause a much greater fall in the quantity demanded as consumers buy suitable alternatives. Thus, the demand for a specific variety box of chocolates may be fairly elastic because there are many competing brands in the market. In contrast, the demand for a unique product such as the Timeform Racehorses Annual for racing enthusiasts will tend to be inelastic.

- Necessities

  The demand for vital goods such as sugar, milk and bread tends to be stable and inelastic; conversely luxury items such as foreign skiing holidays are likely to be fairly elastic in demand. It is interesting to note that improvements in living standards push certain commodities such as televisions from the luxury to the necessity category. However, with luxuries the income elasticity of demand (see below) is more significant than the price elasticity of demand.

- Habit

  When goods are purchased automatically, without customers perhaps being fully aware of their price, for example, newspapers, the demand is inelastic. This also applies to addictive products such as cigarettes, cocaine and heroin.

- Time

  In the short run, consumers may be ignorant of possible alternative goods in many markets, so they may continue to buy certain goods when their prices rise. Such inelasticity may be lessened in the long run as consumers acquire greater knowledge of markets.

- Definition of market

  If a market is defined widely (e.g. food), there are likely to be fewer alternatives and so demand will tend to be inelastic. In contrast, if a market is specified narrowly (e.g. orange drinks) there will probably be many brands available, thereby creating elasticity in the demand for these brands.

Test Your Understanding 6

Using the factors above discuss whether you consider the demand for petrol to be price elastic or inelastic.

3.3 The link between PED and total revenue

The PED can also be calculated by examining *total revenue*. This method is most useful to business people.

- If total revenue increases following a price cut, then demand is price elastic.
- If total revenue increases following a price rise, then demand is price inelastic.

Conversely, if total revenue falls after a price cut, then the demand is inelastic; and after a price rise it is elastic. If total revenue remains unchanged, then the demand is of unitary elasticity.

Illustration 2 – PED and revenue

Suppose a product is currently priced at $20 with associated demand of 50,000 units per annum. The directors would like to boost revenue and are considering a price cut to $19. Research suggests that the PED is –0.8.

Determine the expected change in demand and total revenue.

Solution

- Suggested % change in price = –5%
- Given a PED of –0.8, the expected % change in demand will be –5% × –0.8 = +4%
- Thus demand will rise to 52,000 units
- Currently revenue = 20 × 50,000 = $1,000,000
- Predicted revenue with price cut = 19 × 52,000 = $988,000

Revenue has fallen. Given inelastic demand this was expected. A price increase would boost revenue here rather than a price cut.

Note: This illustrates how useful knowledge of elasticity is to managers when making pricing decisions.

Test Your Understanding 7

If the demand for a good is price elastic, a fall in its price will lead to:

(i) a rise in unit sales.
(ii) a fall in unit sales.
(iii) a rise in total sales revenue.
(iv) a fall in total sales revenue.

A (i) and (iii) only
B (i) and (iv) only
C (ii) and (iii) only
D (ii) and (iv) only

Test Your Understanding 8

Answer the following questions based on the preceding information. You can check your answers below.

(1) Describe the shape of a typical demand curve.

(2) What are 'inferior' goods?

(3) What is the price elasticity of demand?

(4) The price of a good falls by 10 per cent but the quantity demanded increases from 100 to 120 units. Calculate the price elasticity of demand.

(5) List four factors that influence price elasticity of demand.

(6) What is the difference between a shift in demand and an expansion of demand?

4 Supply

4.1 The supply curve of a firm

A supply curve shows how much producers would be willing to offer for sale, at different prices, over a given period of time.

The supply curve of a firm is underpinned by the desire to make profit. It demonstrates what a firm will provide to the market at certain prices. Given that cost is one of the main determinants of supply an increase in price will usually result in greater supply. Thus supply curves are usually upward sloping.

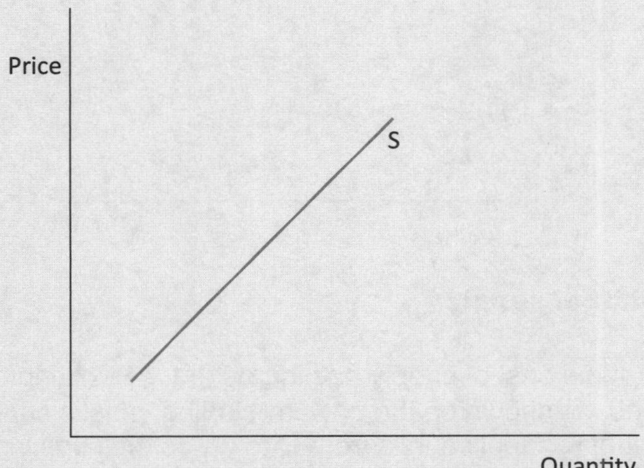

4.2 The supply curve of an industry

Assuming that all the firms in an industry are identical, a market supply curve is composed of all the supply curves of the individual producers in the industry added together. The industry supply curve is an aggregate, which shows what producers are willing to offer for sale at any given price. For example

	Quantity supplied			
Price	Firm A	Firm B	Firm C	Industry
0	0	0	0	0
1	30	15	20	45
2	20	30	25	75
3	30	45	30	105
4	40	60	35	135
5	50	75	40	165

Thus, the supply curve of an industry is similar to that of its individual component firms but at a higher level.

As with the demand curve, changes in price cause movement up and down the supply curve but the supply curve itself is not moving. This is referred to as either a change in the quantity supplied or an *expansion/contraction* of supply.

4.3 Conditions of supply

A change in factors other than the price will move the supply curve itself.

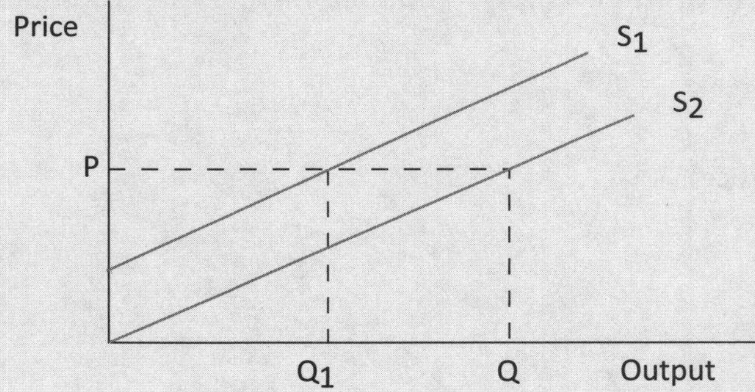

An upward shift of supply

This means that the cost of supply has increased. At existing prices less will now be supplied, as shown on the upward-sloping, elastic supply curve. At price P, the quantity supplied falls from Q to Q_1 as the supply curve shifts from S_2 to S_1.

This results from:

- *Higher production costs*. The costs of production may increase because the factors of production become expensive. Thus conditions such as higher wage costs per unit, higher input prices and increased interest rates will lead to reductions in supply.
- *Indirect taxes*. The imposition of an indirect tax makes supply at existing prices less profitable. With an indirect tax the costs of production are raised directly because the tax must be paid on each good sold irrespective of how much of the tax can be recouped via a higher price. The profit margin is reduced (by some varying amount) as an indirect effect.

A downward shift of supply

For example, a shift in the supply curve from S_1 to S_2 illustrates an increase in supply with more being supplied at each price, showing that the cost of production has fallen or lower profits are being taken.

Lower unit costs may arise from:

- *technological innovations*, for example, the advance of microchip technology lowered the cost of computers and led to large increases in supply;
- more *efficient use of existing factors* of production, for example, introduction of a shift system of working might mean fuller use of productive capacity, leading to lower unit costs. Improvements in productivity may be secured by maintaining output but with fewer workers;
- *lower input prices*, such as, cheaper raw material imports and lower-priced components could bring down production costs.
- a reduction or abolition of an *indirect tax* or the application or increase in subsidies.

4.4 Elasticity of supply

The elasticity of supply is calculated by the formula:

$$\frac{\text{Percentage change in quantity supplied}}{\text{Percentage change in price}}$$

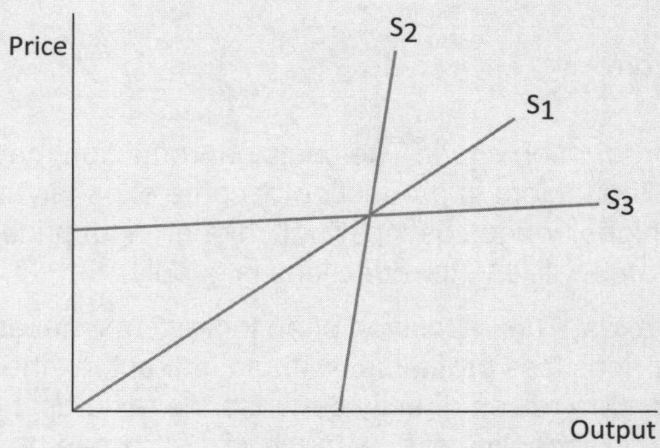

S_1 intersects the origin and shows unit elasticity.
S_2 intersects the output axis and shows inelastic supply.
S_3 intersects the price axis shows elastic supply.

A normal supply curve will always slope upwards from left to right indicating that suppliers are willing to supply more the higher is the price. Thus a price rise will lead to an *expansion* in supply and a price fall will lead to a *contraction* in supply.

Therefore, the value of the price elasticity of supply (PES) is always positive.

- If a change in price induces a *larger proportionate* change in the quantity supplied, the price elasticity of supply will have a value of more than 1 and supply is said to be *price elastic.*
- If a change in price induces a *smaller proportionate* change in the quantity supplied, the price elasticity of supply will have a value of less than 1 and supply is said to be *price inelastic.* The extreme case would be perfectly inelastic where supply is completely unaffected by price.
- If a change in price induces an *equally proportionate* change in the quantity supplied, the price elasticity of supply will have a value of 1 and supply is said to have *unit elasticity*.

4.5 Factors that influence elasticity of supply

There are several factors which affect the elasticity of supply:

- *Time.* Supply tends to be more elastic in the long run. Production plans can be varied and firms can react to price changes. In some industries, notably agriculture, supply is fixed in the short run and thus perfectly inelastic. However, in manufacturing, supply is more adaptable.
- *Factors of production.* Supply can be quickly changed (elastic) if there are available factors, such as trained labour, unused productive capacity and plentiful raw materials, with which output can be raised. Although one firm may be able to expand production in the short run, a whole industry may not, so there could be a divergence between a firm's elasticity and that of the industry as a whole.
- *Stock levels.* If there are extensive stocks of finished products warehoused, then these can be released onto the market, making supply relatively elastic. Stock levels tend to be higher when business people are optimistic and interest rates are low.
- *Number of firms in the industry.* Supply will tend to be more elastic if there are many firms in the industry, because there is a greater chance of some having the available factors and high stock. Also, it is possible that industries with no entry barriers or import restrictions could expand supply quickly as new firms enter the industry in response to higher prices.

Test Your Understanding 9

Using the above factors comment on whether the supply of fresh milk is price elastic or inelastic.

Test Your Understanding 10

Answer the following questions based on the preceding information.

(1) Which factors affect the elasticity of supply?

(2) What effect will higher wages have on the supply curve?

5 The price mechanism

5.1 Equilibrium

Now we have looked at demand and supply in detail, let us consider how the price mechanism sets a price.

The way to see how market forces achieve equilibrium is to consider what happens if the price is too high or too low:

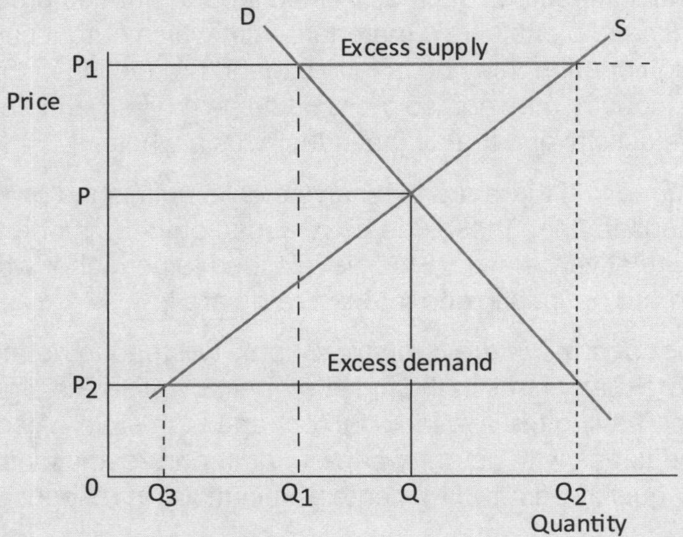

The graph shows the *intended demand* and *planned supply* at a set of prices. It is only at price *P* where demand and supply are the same. If the demand of consumers and the supply plans of sellers correspond, then the market is deemed to be in *equilibrium*. Only at output *Q* and price *P* are the plans of both sellers and buyers realised. Thus *Q* is the *equilibrium quantity* and *P* is the *equilibrium price* in this market.

There is only one equilibrium position in a market. At this point, there is no tendency for change in the market, because the plans of both buyers and sellers are satisfied. At prices and outputs other than the equilibrium (*P*, Q) either demand or supply aspirations could be fulfilled but not both simultaneously.

- For instance at price P_1, consumers only want Q_1 output but producers are making Q_2 output available. There is a **surplus**, the excess supply being Q_1Q_2 output.

  Assuming the conditions of demand and supply remain unchanged, it is likely that the buyers and sellers will reassess their intentions.

This will be reflected in the short term by retailers having unwanted goods, returns made to manufacturers, reduced orders and some products being thrown away and so suppliers may be prepared to accept lower prices than P_1 for their goods.

This reduction in price will lead to a *contraction* in supply and an *expansion* in demand until equilibrium is reached at price *P*.

- Conversely, at a price of P_2, the quantity demanded, Q_2, will exceed the quantity supplied, Q_3. There will be a **shortage** ($Q_2 - Q_3$), demonstrating the *excess demand*.

  This will be reflected in the short term by retailers having empty shelves, queues and increased orders. Furthermore there may be high second-hand values, for example on ebay. The supplier will respond by increasing prices to reduce the shortage.

  This excess demand will thus lead to a rise in the market price, and demand will *contract* and supply will *expand* until equilibrium is reached at price *P*.

A supply and demand analysis can be applied to many different markets:

- Supply of and demand for money gives an equilibrium price that can be interpreted as the level of interest rates in an economy – covered in Chapter 5.
- Supply of and demand for a particular currency gives an equilibrium price in the form of an exchange rate – covered in Chapter 8.

Test Your Understanding 11

When the price of a good is held above the equilibrium price, the result will be:

A excess demand

B a shortage of the good

C a surplus of the good

D an increase in demand

Test Your Understanding 12

When the price of a good is reduced and held below the equilibrium price, the result will be all except one of the following:

A excess demand

B a shortage of the good

C a surplus of the good

D an expansion in demand

5.2 Shifts in supply and or demand

As well as signalling information in a market, price acts as a *stimulant*. The price information may provide incentives for buyers and sellers. For instance, a price rise may encourage firms to shift resources into one industry in order to obtain a better reward for their use.

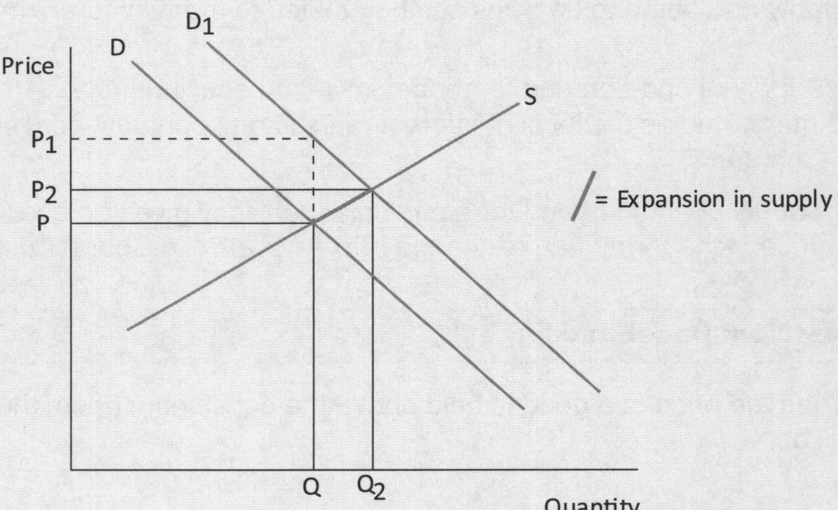

- For example, suppose the equilibrium is disturbed when the conditions of demand change. Consumers' tastes have moved positively in favour of the good and a new curve D_1 shows customers' intentions.
- Supply is initially Q, at the equilibrium, and it is momentarily fixed, so the market price is bid up to P_1.
- However, producers will respond to this stimulus by expanding the quantity supplied, perhaps by running down their stocks.
- This expansion in supply to Q_2 reduces some of the shortage, bringing price down to P_2, a new equilibrium position, which is above the old equilibrium P.

Note that if we had drawn the diagram with steeper supply (and demand curves), then the price fluctuations would have been greater. Thus the more inelastic the demand and supply of a good are, the greater will be price volatility when either demand or supply shifts.

The longer-term effects of these changes in the market depend upon the reactions of the consumers and producers. The consumers may adjust their preferences and producers may reconsider their production plans. The impact of the latter on supply depends upon the length of the production period. Generally the longer the production period, and the more inelastic the supply is, the more unstable price will tend to be.

- Price acts as a signal to sellers on what to produce.
- Price rises, with all other market conditions unchanged, will act as a stimulus to extra supply.
- Equilibrium price is where the plans of both buyers and sellers are satisfied.

Test Your Understanding 13

Much of the world's coffee is grown in South America. By use of supply and demand curves explain what would happen to the price of coffee if bad storms in South America damaged much of the coffee crop.

5.3 Factor markets

Supply and demand analysis can also be applied to factor markets.

Land

The supply of land is affected by factors such as:

- price
- legislation (e.g. in the UK some land cannot be built upon as it is classified as "greenbelt")
- the availability of planning permission
- government policy on house building and development.
- the policies of some firms to buy up land to hold extensive land banks

The demand for land is dependent on:

- price
- the price of property – as house prices increase, so builders will be willing to pay more for land upon which to build

- the trade cycle – for example in a high growth period the demand for new properties (and hence the land to build them on) increases greatly
- demographic changes such as birth rates, death rates, divorce rates and immigration – for example, in many countries people are living longer thus increasing the demand for property

Labour

The supply of labour is affected by factors such as:

- wage levels
- benefit levels – how comfortable is someone who does not work
- legislation regarding discrimination
- education and skills – are people sufficiently qualified to apply for the jobs that exist?
- labour mobility
- demographic changes such as birth rates, death rates, emigration and immigration – for example, in some countries emigration has resulted in skills shortages and hence higher wage levels

The demand for labour is dependent on:

- wage levels
- the prices of and demand for the goods or services that the workers would produce – for example there is always high demand for teachers and doctors
- the trade cycle – for example in a high growth period the demand for many products (and hence the labour to make them) increases greatly

Test Your Understanding 14

A government has decided to lower the qualifications required for workers to be employed as teachers. What will be the impact on the number of teachers employed and on the average wage of teachers?

A Average wage will rise and employment will fall

B Average wage will rise and employment will rise

C Average wage will fall and employment will fall

D Average wage will fall and employment will rise

6 Interference with market prices

There may be occasions when the equilibrium price established by the market forces of demand and supply may not be the most desirable price. With such cases the government might wish to set prices above or below the market equilibrium price.

6.1 Minimum price

In certain markets government may seek to ensure a minimum price for different goods and services. It can do this in a number of ways such as providing subsidies direct to producers (e.g. the Common Agricultural Policy). Alternatively, it can set a legal minimum price (e.g. a statutory minimum wage). To be effective legal minimum prices must be above the current market price.

If the government sets a minimum price above the equilibrium price (often called a price floor), there will be a surplus of supply created.

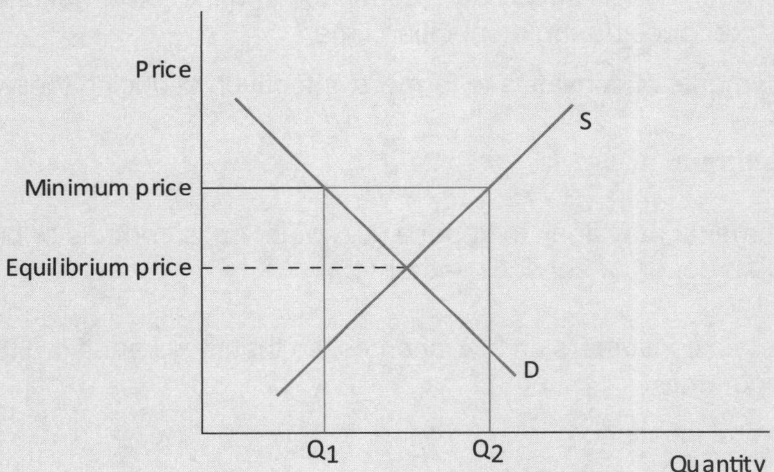

In the diagram this surplus is Q_1Q_2.

If this minimum price was applied in the labour market it would be known as a minimum wage and the surplus would be the equivalent of unemployment, which would be a waste of a factor of production.

If applied to physical goods, then price floors cause surpluses of products which have to be stored or destroyed. With the EU Common Agricultural Policy (CAP) this has, over the years, resulted in the EU storing large quantities of food ("butter mountains"), selling the surplus to countries outside the EU (such as Russia) and even paying farmers not to grow the product in the first place but to remove land from agricultural use (so called "set aside" conditions).

Another way of looking at the same problem is to state that it leads to a misallocation of resources both in the product and/or the factor market which causes lower economic growth. There also may be the temptation for firms to attempt to ignore the price floor, for example, by informal arrangements with workers, which would lead to a further waste of resources in implementing such arrangements as well as raising issues of fair treatment for the workers involved.

In summary government-imposed minimum prices cause:

- Excess supply
- Misallocation of resources
- Waste of resources.

Note: Alternative approaches to protect farmers include

- the use of deficiency payments, where farmers are paid the difference between a legislatively set target price and the lower national average market price during a specified time
- payments of subsidies to farmers, effectively reducing their costs

6.2 Maximum price

Governments may seek to impose maximum price controls or price ceilings on certain goods or services, either to:

- benefit consumers on low incomes, so that they can afford the particular good, or to
- control inflation.

To be effective, a legal maximum price must be set below the equilibrium price. The effect will be to create a shortage of supply.

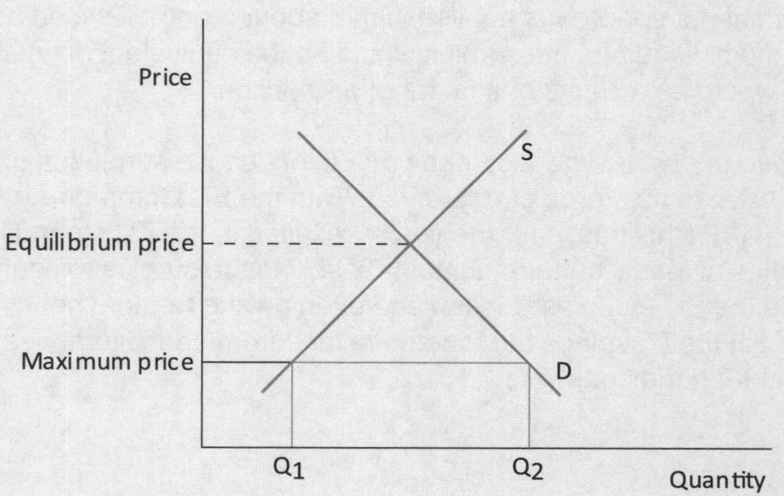

This shortage is $Q_1 Q_2$. If the shortages of supply persist then problems can arise. The limited supply has to be allocated by some means other than by price.

This can be done by queuing, by rationing or by some form of favouritism, for example, by giving preference to regular customers. The difficulty with any of these alternative mechanisms is that they can be considered arbitrary and unfair by those who fail to secure the product. A consequence of the shortage can be the emergence of black markets. This is where buyers and sellers agree upon an illegal price which is higher than that which has been officially sanctioned at the maximum price.

Maximum prices can also lead to a misallocation of resources. Producers will reduce output of those products subject to price controls as these products are now relatively less profitable than those products where no price controls exist. In the housing market this may lead to fewer apartments for rent as landowners develop office blocks rather than residential houses. Alternatively the quality of the product may be allowed to drop as a way of reducing costs when profits are constrained by price controls. This failure to maintain property can mean that apartments fall into disrepair.

In summary, government-imposed maximum prices cause:

- Shortages of supply
- Arbitrary ways of allocating a product
- Misallocation of resources.

Test Your Understanding 15

A government introduces a minimum price below free market price. Which one of the following describes the consequences of this?

A There will be no effect on market price or producer incomes

B Suppliers will withdraw from the market due to falling incomes

C Unsold surpluses of the product will build up

D Demand for the product will contract

Supplementary reading – The CAP

The Common Agricultural Policy

As members of the European Union, Britain participates in the Common Agricultural Policy (CAP). This is a buffer stock system combined with an external tariff. This tariff protects European suppliers from foreign competition. The European Union sets target prices for foodstuffs and buys stocks at intervention prices if target prices are not achieved.

The intervention price (P_I) is usually above the (world) market price (P_M) with the result that excess quantities are supplied (Q_1Q_3). These are the famous butter mountains and wine lakes. Thus a stable and high price is sustained to the benefit of European farmers. A tariff, equivalent to P_MP_T, is placed on imports to further protect domestic suppliers.

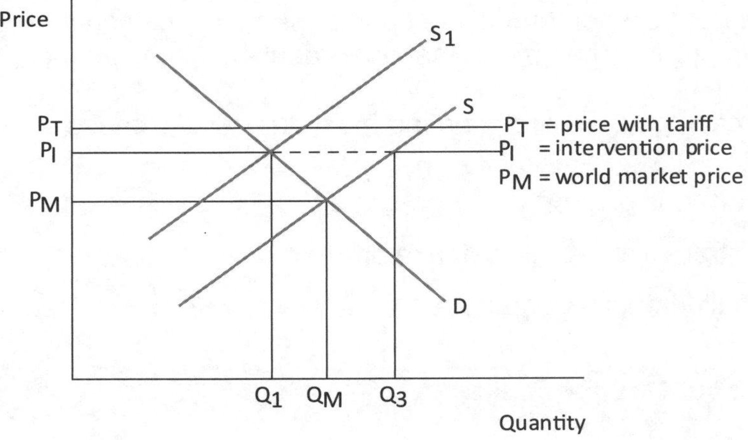

However, consumers pay a price (P_I) above the market price (P_M). This entails a loss of consumer welfare. The EU stores the surplus quantity of food. Even if a bad harvest shifts supply to S_1, then the same price is received by farmers (although their income falls as quantity is lowered); but the Community does not have the costs of storage.

The increase in farm efficiency and high intervention prices led to growing stocks in the 1980s. Thus, in the case of butter, milk quotas were introduced in an attempt to limit the excess supply and reduce the costs and waste of intervention.

It went further in the 1990s by bringing in *set-aside* conditions, although it was agreed in 2008 to abolish these.

7 Agricultural prices and the cobweb theorem

7.1 Agricultural prices

Agricultural markets are sometimes regulated because of the inherent instability in prices. This is mainly due to supply issues, although demand factors can also play a part.

Supply

- Significant changes in supply can occur due to natural events such as harvest failure.
- Furthermore, in the short run supply is often inelastic - for example, if a farmer wishes to increase wheat output, then more seed must be planted but this will not have an impact until it has grown and then been harvested.

Demand

- Price fluctuations may also be caused by demand factors. For instance, industrial demand for raw materials varies erratically, depending on consumer demand for the final product, stock levels and the interest and exchange rate cost of holding materials ready for use. It is usually in the primary goods sector, particularly agriculture and raw materials, where price is most unstable.
- For example, the downturn in 2013 in the UK for ready meals containing beef (due to the horse meat scandal) resulted in a drop in demand for minced beef, affecting retailers, distributors and, ultimately, farmers.

Rapid changes in demand for primary products when matched by inelastic supply causes erratic movements in prices and in the incomes of producers.

While price changes generally may have beneficial dynamic effects, frequent and large price variations can be harmful. They can create uncertainty, which is bad for trade, and convey misleading information, which might cause market failures. Thus, governments may intervene in the market and adjust prices in certain circumstances.

7.2 Cobweb theorem

The cobweb theory shows the instability to which agricultural prices are subject. This involves large fluctuations in the prices of foodstuffs and in the incomes of farmers, both of which governments believe to be economically and politically undesirable.

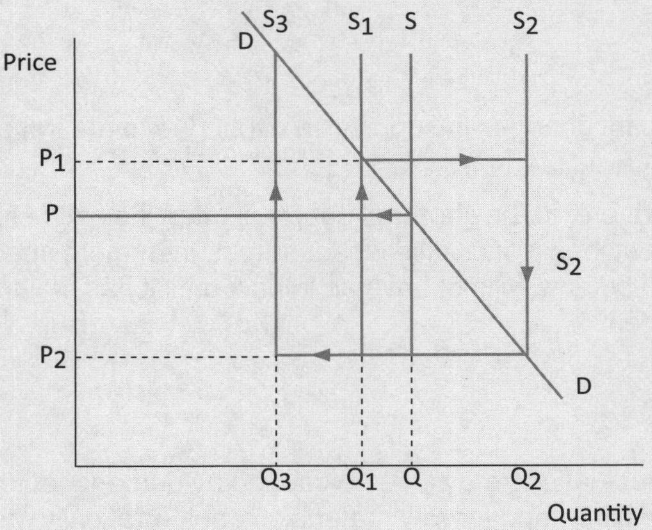

This theory was originally used to explain the fluctuations in pig prices in the United States:

- At the initial equilibrium (*P*, *Q*) pig farmers felt that the market price was too low, so they transferred resources to other activities.
- This action lowered the following year's supply to S_1; but the ensuing shortage raised prices to P_1.
- This price rise acted as a stimulant and so in the following year more pigs were raised (S_2).
- However, this increase in supply glutted the market, leading to a dramatic price fall to P_2.
- Thus, a high price was followed by a high supply and therefore a low price (and then a low supply).

To prevent such price fluctuation for primary products, such as cocoa, tin, etc., *buffer stock systems* have been developed by the world's main suppliers. They form cartels to regulate prices, which fluctuate within fairly narrow ranges. The bigger stockholders buy surpluses if a large supply threatens to push prices through the floor. Alternatively, they sell stocks if shortages threaten to force prices above the ceiling. Apart from providing fairly constant prices for buyers, the policy also maintains fairly stable incomes for producers.

Test Your Understanding 16

Which of the following statements are true or false.

A Government setting an effective minimum price that is higher than the equilibrium price that would otherwise result always leads to over-production. TRUE/FALSE

B Minimum wages will always lead to unemployment. TRUE/FALSE

C Cobweb theory can apply in all markets to explain price instability. TRUE/FALSE

D Maximum price controls force markets to act efficiently. TRUE/FALSE

Test Your Understanding 17

Answer the following questions based on the preceding information. You can check your answers below.

(1) When does excess supply occur?

(2) What mainly causes the price instability of agricultural goods?

(3) How can producers attempt to overcome the problems that the cobweb theory illustrates?

(4) What does the operation of the CAP and similar schemes tend to cause?

8 Market failure

8.1 Introduction

In theory market forces should result in allocation of resources in a way that maximises the utility (benefits) for consumers. However, in some circumstances, markets can lead to sub-optimal allocation of resources, leading to under- or over-production of certain goods and services.

This inability of a market to allocate resources in a way that maximises utility is called market failure.

Government can then have a role to intervene to ensure that a market functions efficiently.

8.2 Public goods

Without government intervention some goods would not be provided at all by a market economy. These are often referred to as *public goods*.

Public goods have the following properties:

- **non-excludability** – a person can benefit from the good without having to pay for it (the "free rider" concept). Provision of the good for one member of society automatically allows the rest of society also to benefit.
- **non-rivalry** – consumption of the good by one person does not reduce the amount available for consumption by others.

As a result a market for this type of goods does not exist and so must be provided by the state.

Illustration 3 – Public goods

Imagine you needed a street light outside your home. You might ask your neighbours to share the cost as they too will benefit from its installation. If they refuse and you go ahead, paying for it all yourself, you cannot stop them from benefiting from its presence.

Under such circumstances, in which you have to bear all the costs but benefit no more than any other resident in the street, would you go ahead and buy the light?

In these circumstances consumers are very unwilling to purchase goods and services and there is a role for government to provide them centrally, funded out of general taxation.

Other public goods include defence, a police force and lighthouses.

Test Your Understanding 18

Pure public goods are goods:

A which are produced by the government

B whose production involves no externalities

C whose consumption by one person implies less consumption by others

D where individuals cannot be excluded from consuming them

As the government is providing public goods on a nationwide basis, it can benefit from *economies of scale.* This could lower costs and the industry would strive for technical efficiency. There is no *allocative efficiency* because consumers do not have a choice – the services, such as police, prisons, fire, are provided whether they like it or not. However, a consumer who seeks more protection could buy additions in the marketplace, like burglar alarms, underground concrete bunkers, security men, etc.

8.3 Externalities

Externalities are social costs or benefits that are not automatically included in the supply and demand curves for a product or service.

Social costs arising from production and consumption of a good or service are described as negative externalities and social benefits as positive externalities.

Supply and demand curves only take into account private costs and benefits, i.e. the costs that accrue directly to the supplier or the benefits that accrue directly to the consumer.

Illustration 4 – Externalities

If you smoke, drive a car or drink alcohol, who actually pays the cost of the product? In part you do in the form of the price you pay for each packet of cigarettes, litre of fuel or bottle of wine. These are the private costs.

However, there are other costs. They are social costs that are met by society as a whole – the cost of healthcare for smokers, the environmental damage of burning fossil fuels and the cost of Accident and Emergency treatment for drunk drivers. These could all be described as "negative externalities".

Some would argue that one of the roles of government is to ensure that such externalities get incorporated into decision making, for example by fining polluters ("polluter pays policies") or higher taxes on alcohol.

Illustration 5 – Using taxes to control externalities

One way of reducing negative externalities such as pollution would be to tax the supplier concerned, thus adding to their costs.

This would shift the supply curve to the left (S_1 to S_2), resulting in an equilibrium with higher prices (P to P_2) and lower quantity (Q to Q_2):

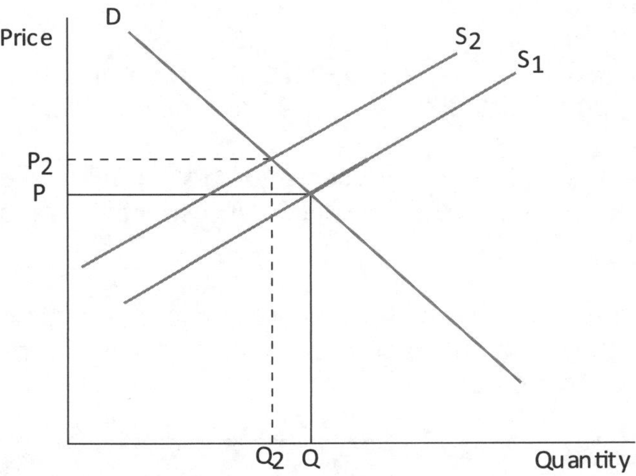

The more significant the tax, then the greater the impact.

Supplementary reading – Externalities

An externality occurs when the costs or benefits of an economic action are not borne or received by the instigator. Externalities are, therefore, the spill-over effects of production and consumption which affect society as a whole rather than just the individual producers or consumers.

- Externalities created by nationalised industries can be good and bad. For example, the railways may be beneficial by relieving roads of congestion and maintaining communications for isolated communities, but may be detrimental in terms of noise and air pollution.
- The pricing policies considered so far have been based purely on private costs. If any pricing policy was to maximise net social benefit (or minimise net social cost) then costs would need to include such externalities.

- Calculate *social costs*. These would indicate the true cost to society of production to incorporate into decision making. However externalities are very difficult to calculate as they are not always attributable, for example noise, and their impact is not universally identical.
- Use *indirect taxes and subsidies*. Where private costs of production or consumption are below social costs, an indirect tax could be imposed so that price is raised to reflect the true social costs of production. Taxes on alcohol and tobacco can be justified on these grounds. Subsidies to home owners to install roof insulation will reduce energy consumption and help conserve a scarce resource for wider social benefit.
- Extend *private property rights* so that those suffering negative externalities can charge the polluters for the harm they are causing. If the right level of charges are made then this should result in a socially efficient level of production being achieved. Emission charges on firms discharging waste are an example of this approach.
- *Regulations*. A government can set maximum permitted levels of emission or minimum levels of environmental quality. The European Union has over 200 pieces of legislation covering environmental controls. Fines can be imposed on firms contravening these limits.
- *Tradable permits*. A maximum permitted level of emission is set for a given pollutant, for example carbon emissions, and a firm or a country is given a permit to emit up to this amount. If it emits less than this amount, it is given a credit for the difference, which it can sell to enable the buyer to go above its permitted level. Thus the overall level of emissions is set by a government or regulatory body, whereas their distribution is determined by the market.

Despite the many measures to deal with externalities, the issue of achieving the socially optimal level of production remains unresolved. Problems of calculating externalities and the correct level of taxation; issues of avoidance and enforcement; administrative costs can all mean that market failure and how to deal with it has yet to find an optimum solution.

Test Your Understanding 19

Which of the following statements are true or false?

A The cost of packaging for cigarettes is a negative externality. TRUE/FALSE

B The benefits to society from education are a positive externality. TRUE/FALSE

C The fine incurred for polluting a watercourse is a negative externality. TRUE/FALSE

D Damage to pine forests from pollution is a negative externality. TRUE/FALSE

8.4 Merit goods

One way of looking at merit goods is in terms of externalities. Merit goods are characterised by external social benefits (i.e. positive externalities) in consumption or by lack of knowledge of the private benefits in consumption. This would lead to under consumption of such services and health and education.

Moreover, merit goods are also ones that it is generally agreed should be available to all, irrespective of the ability to pay. Thus governments often provide health and education services even though, unlike public goods, these can be provided by the market.

Thus merit goods may be underprovided by the market because of

- ignorance of consumers of the private benefits
- failure of the market to reflect the social benefits
- excessive prices limiting access to these services

Note: some consumers possess the means and the willingness to buy merit goods, such as education and healthcare.

Furthermore, the private sector often provides alternatives, although these are often seen as 'different', or even superior goods/services, for example, private school education, private health schemes. In the case of state-provided merit goods, economies of scale can often be achieved, so the cost of education per student is about three times cheaper in the state sector than in the private sector, for example.

8.5 Demerit goods

A demerit good is a good or service which is considered unhealthy, degrading, or otherwise socially undesirable due to the perceived negative effects on the consumers themselves. The concern is that a free market results in excessive consumption of the goods.

Examples include smoking (tobacco), excessive consumption of alcohol, recreational drugs, gambling and junk food.

While some would argue that the consumption of reasonable amounts of alcohol is acceptable and should not be legislated against by a "nanny state", they would also agree that excessive binge drinking causes significant problems both for the user and others. (Note: with demerit goods we are particularly looking at the effect on the user in contrast with negative externalities where we considered the impact on society as a whole).

Government responses usually involve regulating or banning consumption, banning advertising of these goods and the use of higher taxes (sometimes known as "sin taxes").

Test Your Understanding 20

Which of the following are examples of merit goods?

A street lighting TRUE/FALSE

B education TRUE/FALSE

C healthcare TRUE/FALSE

D defence TRUE/FALSE

8.6 Competition policy and fair trading regulations

The final market failure to be addressed is the problem posed by large businesses. The argument is that unchecked, market forces may result in powerful companies who can abuse their market power and charge excessively high prices to consumers. Government intervention is thus needed to ensure that consumers are protected from such abuses.

The subject of competition and its regulation forms the basis of the next chapter.

Test Your Understanding 21

Which one of the following is not a valid economic reason for producing a good or service in the public sector?

A The good is a basic commodity consumed by everyone

B It is a public good

C There is a natural monopoly in the production of the good

D It is a merit good

Test Your Understanding 22

The following passage is based on a newspaper article:

British cod – the staple of fish and chips – is on the verge of becoming an endangered species, according to the Worldwide Fund for Nature (WWF), the conservation group. It stressed that the crisis in the fishing industry was due to poor management and to over-fishing. The total weight of cod caught in the North Sea had halved since the 1960s. Similar falls in catches had occurred for other types of fish.

The WWF proposes the establishment of fishing free zones to protect areas where young fish grow and develop. The WWF said that such a strategy would lead to increased fish stocks and a larger fishing catch for fisherman within five years. However, the problem may become less urgent as consumer demand for this type of fish may decline in the long run. Higher prices themselves may discourage consumers and some observers believe that for many consumers fish and chips may be an inferior good and, in many cases, faces a growing number of alternatives.

Required:

Using *both* your knowledge of economic theory and material contained in the above passage:

(a) State whether each of the following would lead to a shift in the demand curve for fish or a movement along the demand curve for fish.

(i) An increase in the number of substitutes for fish.

(ii) A rise in the price of fish.

(iii) An outward shift in the supply curve of fish.

(iv) A rise in income of fish consumers. **(4 marks)**

(b) State whether each of the following is true or false.

(i) If the demand for fish is very price elastic a fall in supply will raise prices a great deal. **(1 mark)**

(ii) If the supply of fish is price inelastic, a reduction in supply will have a smaller effect on price than if the supply were price elastic. **(1 mark)**

(iii) Price changes affect demand by leading to a shift in the demand curve for the product. **(1 mark)**

(iv) Effective advertising might raise sales by shifting the demand curve to the right. **(1 mark)**

(v) If the demand for fish was perfectly price inelastic, a change in income would have no effect on demand. **(1 mark)**

(vi) The longer the time period considered, the greater becomes the price elasticity of demand for goods. **(1 mark)**

(Total marks: 10)

Test your understanding answers

Test Your Understanding 1

C

When drawing a demand curve only the price is allowed to vary but all conditions of demand are kept constant.

Test Your Understanding 2

D

A larger population would presumably want more supplements, especially if they are older and more health conscious.

A and B would shift the curve to the left. C would result in movement along the curve but not a shift in the curve itself.

Test Your Understanding 3

D

Correct answer is D since a change in exchange rates effectively changes the price of foreign holidays and leads to a movement along the demand curve not a shift in the curve itself

Test Your Understanding 4

C

- % change in price = –2%
- % change in demand = +5%
- PED = (+5)/(–2) = –2.5

Test Your Understanding 5

D

- % change in price = –10%
- PED = –1.5
- % change in demand = –10% × –1.5 = +15%
- The price cut will thus raise demand and sales by 15%, that is, from $10,000 per month to $11,500 per month.

Test Your Understanding 6

The six factors given can be applied as follows:

(1) *Proportion of income spent* – high petrol prices mean that petrol expenditure is a high proportion of most people's disposable income, which would suggest demand should be price **elastic**.

(2) *Substitutues* – drivers cannot substitute a different fuel for use in their cars and so would not consider petrol to have any close substitutes. This would indicate that demand should be **inelastic**. (Note: you may have considered substitutes to driving here, such as using public transport. How close a substitute you consider this to be will depend on your location and the availability of public transport in your area. Most people would probably conclude that it is not a close substitute).

(3) *Necessity* – many drivers consider using a car to be a necessity, suggesting demand will be **inelastic**.

(4) *Habit* – many drivers get used to using their cars and would not switch to public transport, even if a good local service was available. This would again indicate **inelastic** demand.

(5) *Time* – if a driver wanted to switch from a petrol powered vehicle to electricity or diesel, then they would need to sell their vehicle and buy another. This is unlikely to happen quickly suggesting **inelastic** demand.

(6) *Definition of market* – If the demand is defined as petrol in general then the above arguments would indicate that demand would be **inelastic**. However, if we specify a particular brand of petrol, then there will be very close substitutes offered by other suppliers resulting in highly **elastic** demand.

Test Your Understanding 7

A

If the demand for a good is price elastic, the demand for it will change more than proportionately to the change in price. Thus a price fall will raise unit sales and will increase total sales revenue.

Test Your Understanding 8

(1) Downward sloping from top left to bottom right is the shape of a typical demand curve.

(2) Inferior goods are goods for which the demand decreases as income rises. Thus a rise in income would lead the demand curve to shift to the left as opposed to the right for normal goods.

(3) Price elasticity of demand shows the responsiveness of demand to a change in price.

(4) The price elasticity of demand is –2 (i.e. + 20%/–10%). The demand for the good is therefore price elastic.

(5) Income, substitutes, necessities, time, definition of the market.

(6) A shift in demand occurs when the conditions of demand change, whereas an expansion of demand is the result of a fall in price.

Test Your Understanding 9

We can assess the elasticity of supply for milk as follows:

(1) *Time* – in the short run the number of dairy cows available and their milk output is difficult to increase, indicating **inelastic** supply.

(2) *Factors of production* – even though more workers could be employed to milk the cows and more land acquired for them to graze on, the main problem would be the fact that all of the milk of existing cows will be being sold already, so farmers will have to buy new cows from a different market. This would suggest supply was **inelastic**.

(3) *Stock levels* – fresh milk cannot be stored for long so there will not be stocks that could be utilised, indicating **inelastic** supply.

(4) *Number of firms in the industry* – this will depend on the country concerned and whether or not a system of quotas operates. In some markets new firms may be able to set up quickly but the barriers in others may be significant.

In summary one would expect supply to be inelastic, at least in the short run.

Test Your Understanding 10

(1) The elasticity of supply is determined by time, the factors of production, stock levels and the number of firms in the industry.

(2) Higher wages will cause the supply curve to shift upwards and parallel to the original supply.

Test Your Understanding 11

C

When the price of a good is held above the equilibrium price suppliers will be willing to supply more at this higher price. However, consumers will demand less. The combined effect of this is to create a surplus of the goods.

Test Your Understanding 12

C

When the price of a good is held below the equilibrium price suppliers will be willing to supply less at this lower price. However, consumers will demand more. The combined effect of this is to create an expansion in demand, a shortage of the goods and excess demand.

Test Your Understanding 13

In the short term the price would rise:

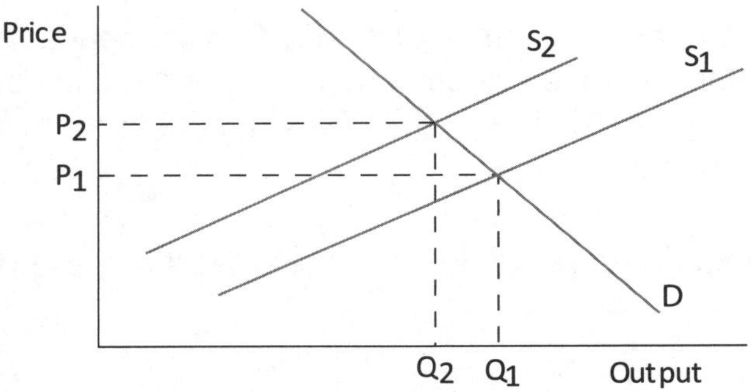

The poor harvest with shift the supply curve to the left but the demand curve is unlikely to move.

The equilibrium will move from P_1, Q_1 to P_2,$Q_{2,}$ giving a price rise.

In the longer term the price will fall as supply moves back to the right, either because it is the next harvest or because new suppliers are attracted to the industry by high prices (note this would involve repurposing land to grow coffee that was previously used for something else).

Test Your Understanding 14

D

A reduction in entry qualifications to a profession should lead to an increase in the supply of workers to that profession and the supply curve will shift to the right (S2). The result will be greater employment (Q2) and a lower price or wage rate (P2).

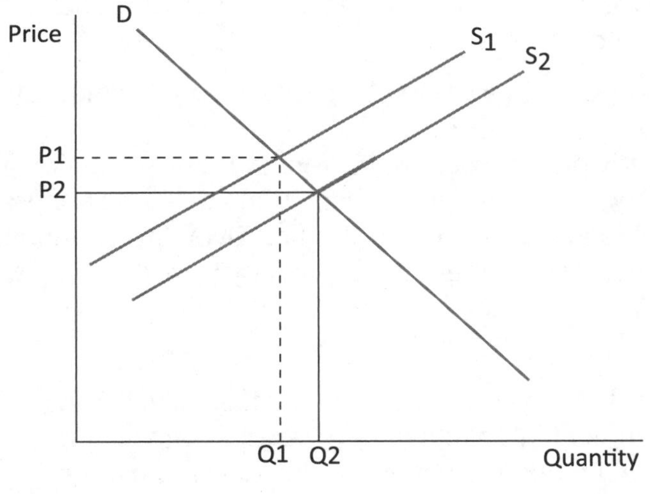

Test Your Understanding 15

A

The free market price will not change. B confused a maximum price with a minimum price, and C and D refer to a minimum price set above free market price.

Test Your Understanding 16

A Government setting an effective minimum price always leads to over-production. TRUE
Setting a price higher than the market equilibrium will stimulate supply. As long as the government does not also rig supply through, for example, quotas, then this will result in over-production.

B Minimum wages will always lead to unemployment. FALSE
A minimum wage will only cause unemployment if it is set above the equilibrium wage rate

C Cobweb theory can apply in all markets to explain price instability. FALSE
Cobweb theory really only applies well where there is a long time lag between price changes and suppliers responding to such change. It is this time lag that leads to the disequilibrium. Given the 12 month time lag between harvests farmers are always trying to catch up with market conditions.

D Maximum price controls force markets to act efficiently. FALSE
Whilst some government intervention (e.g. taxation of polluting products) can force a market to act efficiently, maximum price controls have the opposite effect. Before price controls supply and demand can find equilibrium lower prices resulting from controls result in an imbalance between demand and supply. There is an extension in demand due to the lower prices but a contraction in supply leading to scarcity.

Test Your Understanding 17

(1) Excess supply occurs when the amount supplied is greater than the amount demanded at a given price, that is when the price is above the equilibrium level.

(2) The price instability of agricultural goods is caused by wide variations in the supply, which is naturally inelastic in the short run.

(3) Producers can overcome the fluctuations in agricultural goods prices by price-fixing within a narrow range. This requires them to co-operate through a cartel and storing surplus stocks, which are then released on to the market if there is insufficiency.

(4) The operation of the CAP causes higher prices, excess supplies and storage costs, but it does stabilise farm prices.

Test Your Understanding 18

D

D is the right answer since pure public goods are those which must be provided communally, e.g. defence or public transport.

A is imprecise as the government provides more than just public goods.

B is incorrect as public goods are likely to involve externalities.

C is incorrect since the consumption of a public good by one person must not, by definition, reduce the amount available for another person.

Test Your Understanding 19

A FALSE – The cost of packaging is paid for by the supplier and is therefore included in the supply curve.

B TRUE – Not only does the individual benefit from education but so does society as a whole through a more productive workforce.

C FALSE – The cost of the fine is met by the company and not by society as a whole. For something to be an externality it has to be shared by society.

D TRUE – Society as a whole bears the cost of the pollution, in terms of replanting forests, the lost utility of their enjoyment and the negative impact it has on the environment.

Test Your Understanding 20

A Street lighting FALSE

B Education TRUE

C Healthcare TRUE

D Defence FALSE

Education and healthcare result in positive externalities but can be provided by the private sector are often purchased by individuals – they are merit goods.

Street lighting and defence would not be provided effectively by the private sector due to the problems of charging for them; non-rivalry, non-exclusivity, free rider problem – they would be classified as public goods rather than merit goods.

Test Your Understanding 21

A

Because a commodity is consumed by everyone (e.g. food), it does not follow that it has any special features such that it cannot be produced efficiently in a competitive market in the private sector. All other responses are valid reasons why a good or service should be produced wholly, or partly, in the public sector.

Test Your Understanding 22

(a)

- (i) a shift of the demand curve.
- (ii) a movement along the demand curve.
- (iii) a movement along the demand curve.
- (iv) a shift of the demand curve.

(b)

- (i) *False*; price will rise much more if demand is price inelastic.
- (ii) *True*; because supply is inelastic, the reduction in supply is mitigated as is the effect on price.
- (iii) *False*; price changes lead to movements along the demand curve.
- (iv) *True*; advertising may get consumers to buy more at every price.
- (v) *False*; a change in income would lead to a shift in the demand curve.
- (vi) *True*; the longer the time period, the easier it is to find substitutes.

chapter

4

The Competitive Process

Chapter learning objectives

On completion of their studies students should be able to:

- explain market concentration and the factors giving rise to differing levels of concentration between markets, including acquisitions and combinations
- identify the impacts of the different forms of competition on prices, output and profitability
- explain the main policies to prevent abuses of monopoly power by firms.

1 Introduction

Competition is an extremely important topic in your CIMA studies for two reasons:

(1) Competitive rivalry

All firms face competition but some markets are more competitive than others. To be profitable firms need to understand the degree and nature of competition and formulate a suitable competitive strategy in response.

There are many factors affecting the level of rivalry, for example

- The extent to which competitors are in balance – roughly equal sized firms in terms of market share or finances often leads to highly competitive marketplaces;
- The stage of the industry or product life cycle – during market growth stages all companies can grow naturally whilst in mature markets growth can only be obtained at the expense of someone else;
- Difficulties in differentiating your product emphasises price as a key aspect.

Within economics we are particularly interested in looking at the number of firms in a market and what that means in terms of competition, prices and profitability.

(2) Market failure and government regulation

In the last chapter we considered market failure and the need for government intervention. The final market failure to be addressed is the problem posed by large businesses. The argument is that unchecked, market forces may result in powerful companies who can abuse their market power and charge excessively high prices to consumers.

Government intervention is thus needed to ensure that consumers are protected from such abuses.

2 Market structures

2.1 Markets

The word 'market' is used in many contexts. In economic theory a market is where *goods and services are bought and sold*, although it may not be an actual place.

For instance, foreign currencies are bought and sold through international telephone deals and telex transfers between bank accounts. The buyers and sellers must be in *contact* and in modern societies the exchange is via the medium of *money*. The traders involved are willingly participating in the exchange and usually require information on the *prices* of the goods/services involved.

Most markets in practice are unorganised and decentralised. Governments may influence markets generally through legal constraints but they do not decide how much is traded. This is usually determined by price, which acts as a signal and as an incentive.

2.2 Forms of market structure

The purpose of this section is briefly to describe the main characteristics and assumptions which define each form of market. The detailed operation of each form is considered in the next section.

There are two extreme and largely theoretical forms of market: *perfect competition* and *monopoly*, which are polar opposites. In between, under the broad heading of imperfect competition, there are three other structures which have more grounding in reality. These are *monopolistic competition*, *oligopoly* and *duopoly*. All of these market structures are defined largely in terms of the number of suppliers in the market:

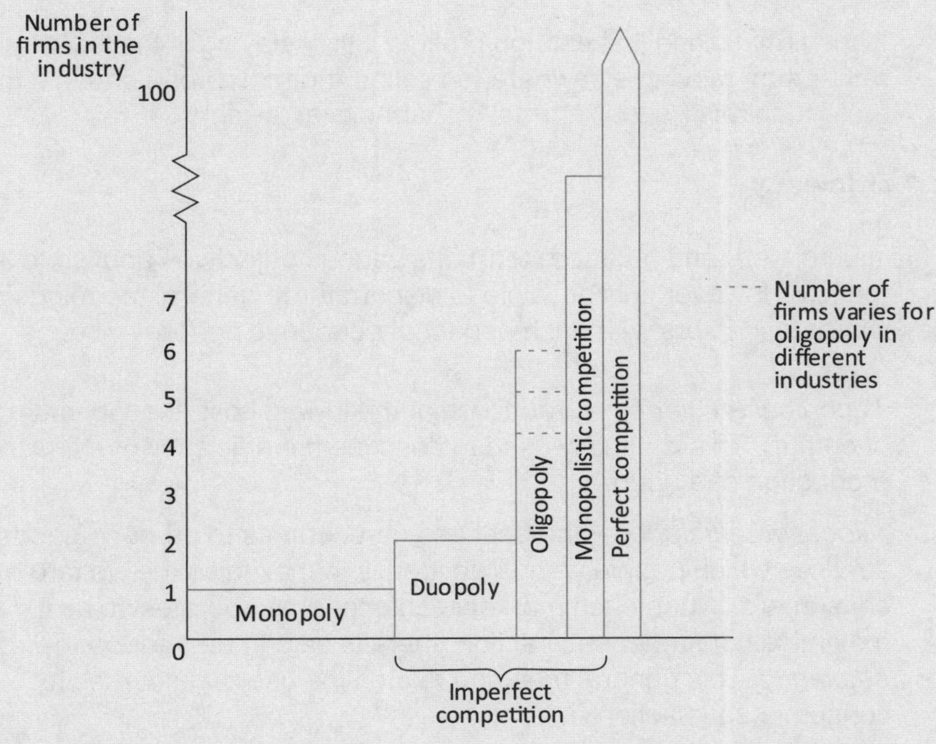

2.3 Discussing market structures

These will be discussed in more detail below using the following approach:

- Structure

  This is defined in terms of seller concentration, the number of firms, type of product and the existence or otherwise of barriers to entry.

- Conduct: pricing behaviour

  How much freedom does the firm have to set any price it wants – is the firm a price taker or maker?

  How is price related to the firm's average total cost at the chosen level of output?

- Efficiency

  See below

- Profit

  Is the firm making just enough profit to justify staying in the industry rather than moving elsewhere (so called "normal" profit) or can it make more than this ("super-normal" or "abnormal" profit)

2.4 Efficiency

This much-used (and -abused) term has various adjectives applied to it in economics. However, it is possible to discern three general meanings and associate descriptors with each aspect of economic performance.

- *Technical efficiency* – production at the lowest cost (the 'optimum' level of output). This is usually used to describe the efficiency of a firm in the production of a good.
- *Allocative efficiency* – the best use of resources to produce goods and services which people want. The idea is to maximise the welfare of consumers. When each market in an economy operates so as to maximise consumer satisfaction, there is said to be *economic efficiency*. This general meaning relates the use of resources to consumer satisfaction.
- *X-inefficiency* – this considers the gap between the theoretical best practice ATC curve and the typical firm's actual ATC curve. If the market has barriers to entry, then the firm is likely to be X-inefficient and if no barriers are present it is likely to be x-efficient.

The issue is further complicated by *time*. The most efficient firm at one point in time may not be so at a later date. For example the relative technical efficiency of one firm may change over time as a result of investment. Similarly, people's preferences for goods may change and so utilities alter, thereby affecting allocative efficiency.

The result of such changes is that identification of productive and economic efficiency for the whole economy at a macro level is impossible. Thus, it makes more sense to concentrate on considering technical and allocative efficiency in markets in a micro analysis.

Test Your Understanding 1

A lack of barriers to entry in an industry is likely to result in firms being X-efficient.

True/False

Supplementary reading – Types of markets

There are many markets in all types of modern economy, ranging from large-scale and official, for example, the Stock Exchange, to small and illegal, like a drug addict buying heroin from a street pusher. Some markets are very specialised, for example, the copper exchange on the London Metal Exchange. Markets tend to be dynamic, expanding and becoming more sophisticated to meet particular needs. Thus, not only can major commodities be bought and sold at prevailing prices (spot market), they can also be purchased now for an agreed price to be supplied at a future date. Such a *futures* market meets industry's need to plan future production.

Markets are also *segmented*. They can be divided by:

- *Geography*. The market for primary products may be international, national, regional or local depending on the suppliers and customers involved.
- *Time*. Demand and supply conditions can change, particularly when services are sold. For instance, travel on the railways may be cheaper from Monday to Thursday (than on Friday) for the same service. Such price discrimination between off-peak and peak times makes the market less homogeneous.
- *Customer type*. Suppliers may discriminate between their customers. For instance, large regular customers may get preferential quantity discounts off the listed prices, which other consumers pay.

Economic analysis needs to simplify the understanding of all these diverse markets. Thus we shall consider the product or goods markets. These markets refer to newly produced goods and services, and avoid the pricing of second hand goods.

Supplementary reading – Measuring market concentration

Market concentration

The growth of firms has increasingly led to greater domination of individual markets by few firms. This is referred to as *market concentration* and describes the extent to which the largest firms in an industry control their output, sales and employment. Concentration ratios can take two forms.

- Market and seller concentration

  This measures the share of production, sales or employment of the largest few firms in an industry or market. Often a five-firm concentration ratio is used. Traditionally, manufacturing industries are the most concentrated. In 2004 the United Kingdom had five-firm concentration ratios of over 85 per cent in car, cement, steel and tobacco production. There is also increasing concentration in service industries such as accountancy, advertising, banking and food retailing. The growth in five-firm concentration ratios is driven by the desire to exploit economies of scale.

  High concentration ratios are associated with a high degree of market or monopoly power by the largest firms in an industry or market sector. Sometimes concentration ratios overstate the extent of market power in an industry held by the leading five firms. This occurs when there is a significant amount of competition from imports. However, concentration ratios may also understate the true level of market power held by the leading five firms where local or regional monopolies exist, as in the case of supermarkets.

- Aggregate concentration ratio

  This measures the share of total production or employment contributed by the largest firms in the whole economy. The oldest concentration ratio used in the United Kingdom is the 100-firm ratio used in manufacturing. This measures the share of the largest 100 private firms in total manufacturing net output. This ratio rose from 14.8 per cent in 1900 to 41.7 per cent in 1975 but fell back to 32 per cent in 2001.

Increases in firm size implicit in the rise in concentration ratios have occurred more by takeovers and mergers than by internal growth of the leading firms. We will examine the effect on market competition and structures later.

3 The growth of firms

Firms grow through internal expansion and integration. A firm may expand by producing and selling more of its existing products or by extending its range of products.

Integration occurs when firms join together, by either merger or takeover. A *merger* is an amalgamation of at least two firms into one orgainisation. It is usual for shareholders in the old firm to exchange their old shares for shares in the new firm in agreed proportions.

A *takeover* differs from a merger in that the initiative for acquisition comes from the offering company and the board of the target company is opposed to, or not fully in favour of, the bid.

There are three main types of integration: horizontal, vertical and diversification.

Horizontal integration

Firms in the *same industry* and at the *same stage* of production join together. The reasons for such integration include:

- *To obtain the benefits of economies of scale.* A big retailer will have much more buying power than two smaller retailers and so will be able to lower their input costs. The increased financial muscle enables the large retailer to negotiate better terms with their suppliers. In manufacturing industry, horizontal integration was justified in the 1960s as a 'synergy' between companies on the basis of '2 + 2 = 5'.
- *To reduce competitive rivalry.* By taking over rivals a firm can reduce competition, possibly allowing it to increase prices and margins. An extreme case of this would be a duopoly where one firm acquires the other, thus becoming a monopoly.
- *To increase market share*. If a takeover reduces competition, the acquiring company can probably raise its market share. In retailing, mergers usually mean more outlets through which to sell the products of the two companies. Outside retailing, horizontal mergers have declined since the 1970s, partly because of the legislation on monopolies.

- *To fight off imports*. This defensive motive was behind the proposed GEC–Plessey merger (which the Department of Trade supported but the Ministry of Defence opposed in evidence to the Monopolies Commission), as they competed in an electronics industry which the Americans and Japanese were infiltrating from their dominant international positions.
- *To pool technology*. The wasteful duplication of research facilities can be avoided and the beneficial sharing of technical 'know-how' can be developed when manufacturers integrate, for example, Renault–Nissan.

Vertical integration

Vertical growth occurs when one firm moves into another stage of production, which might otherwise be independent, in the same industry. This integration may be *backwards* towards the source of supply, for example, Ross Foods, which sells frozen food, purchasing its own fleet of trawlers; or *forwards* when the producer buys out stages nearer the market, for example, Ross Foods purchasing a retail outlet. The reasons for vertical integration include:

- *The elimination of transaction costs*. This will increase cost efficiency between the various stages of production, by reducing delivery costs and eliminating the profits of middlemen.
- *Increasing entry barriers*. By gaining more control over supplies and/or sales, it will become more difficult for new competitors to enter the market.
- *Securing supplies*. By controlling its own sources of supply as a result of backward integration, a firm can achieve more flexible production. For instance a brewer experiencing increased demand could readily use his own lorry fleet to collect hops from stock and thereby temporarily raise production levels.
- *Improving the distribution network* with better market access. Forward integration into marketing enables a firm to control the conditions under which its goods are sold. For instance, a brewer can dictate pricing, advertising and display of his beer to a 'tied' public house.
- *Gaining economies of scale*; these benefits are common
- *Making better use of existing technology*

Diversification

This occurs when one firm expands into an industry with which it was previously unconnected, for example, Virgin records into travel. Some mergers are classed as *lateral* where the goods being newly produced by the expanding firm have a close link with their main products, for example, cars and lorries.

However, increasingly integration creates *conglomerates*, that is, groups of companies pursuing different activities in different industries. These organisations sell off the inadequate parts of underperforming companies and develop those with potential. The conglomerates thus behave like investment bankers.

The reasons, other than short-term profit motives, for diversifications are:

- *To minimise risks*. If its main line is subject to trade fluctuations or going out of fashion, a firm may diversify into an expanding area to protect itself, for example, British American Tobacco purchasing Eagle Star. Such takeovers seek financial security, and higher corporate growth;
- *To make full use of expertise*. Dynamic management can use the expertise residing in a company in seemingly unconnected areas. Thus Centrica, initially a company selling gas, took over the AA, a motoring organisation, so as to fully utilise its large customer data base and sell a greater range of products.
- *To achieve economies of scale*. Particularly in *administration*. Thus a merger might lead to the fuller utilisation of, and greater return from, departments such as data processing, accounts and exports.

However, mergers are not always successful. Sometimes diseconomies of scale occur when merged managements experience personality clashes and become divided. Rationalisation does not always lead to lower cost production and may alienate customers and workers. The same is true of takeovers which lead to asset stripping and to less production and redundancies.

In 1995, the phrase *'vertical disintegration'* entered the dictionary. This explains the hiving off by a company of many of its service sectors or product centres, often to management buyouts, in order to reduce costs and concentrate on its core business. Such a policy is not quite the same as a *demerger*, where a firm sells off a brand (or brands) to an existing large company. The latter is often a rival and thus augments its market share.

Test Your Understanding 2

The most likely reason for a government to discourage a horizontal merger between two car manufacturers is:

A such mergers do not allow the firms to benefit from any economies of scale

B by increasing their control over the sources of supply (the supply chain), the merged firm will have an unfair advantage over its rivals

C consumers might lose out if the merged firms acquire market dominance

D By controlling the distribution network, the merged firm could prevent potential new manufacturers joining the market

Test Your Understanding 3

Z is a food producer which specialises in making high quality cakes and desserts for social events. Z has recently acquired the dairy company from which it previously bought the milk and cream it used in its products. What method of growth has Z used to expand?

A Backward vertical integration

B Organic growth

C Forward vertical integration

D Horizontal integration.

4 Perfect competition

Definition

Perfect competition is an idealised model of a competitive market and has the following characteristics:

- *Many buyers and sellers*, so no one individual, can influence price by their actions.
- Buyers and sellers are *rational* economic beings. This translates into firms being profit maximisers.
- Buyers and sellers have *perfect information* about the product.
- The product is *homogeneous*. Hence there is no brand differentiation.

- There are *no entry barriers*. Buyers and sellers are free to enter and leave the market and there is no government interference in the market.
- *Perfect mobility* exists in the market both for products and factors of production.
- *Normal profits* are earned in the long run as any abnormal profits/losses are removed by competitive forces.

Example

In reality, perfect markets rarely exist. An approximation is the Stock Exchange or local farmers' markets.

Implications

- There is one market price that all suppliers sell at. These suppliers can sell their entire output at this price so they have no incentive to cut prices. However, any attempts to increase prices are doomed as customers will switch to one of their many competitors who sell identical products. All firms are thus "price takers".

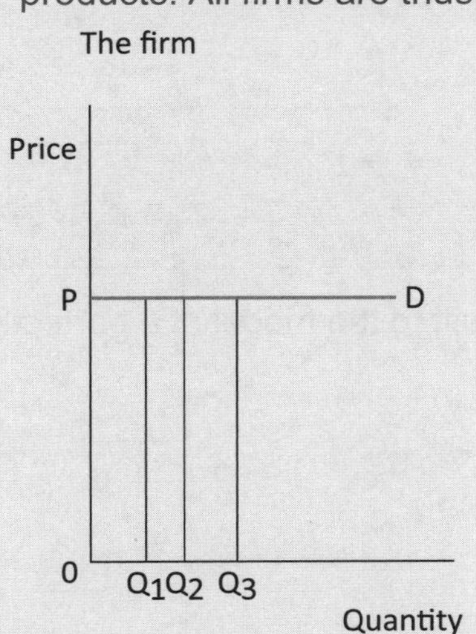

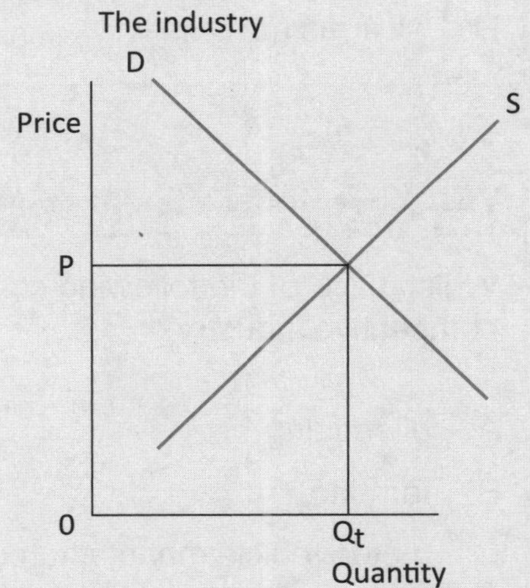

The degree of competition forces firms to operate at their minimum cost, implying technical efficiency.

- Furthermore the level of rivalry has resulted in the lowest prices possible, implying allocative efficiency. This also means that firms are only just making the minimum profit they need for it to be worth staying in the industry ("normal profits")

Even though we are dealing with a theoretical extreme, this model does suggest that high levels of competition are "good" for consumers (minimum prices) and good for the economy (firms operating at minimum cost).

However there are some potential issues here

- a lack of choice for consumers
- if firms are only making normal profits, then they may not be able to afford to spend additional sums on "discretionary" expenditure such a staff welfare, product innovation or protecting the environment. (note: a firm facing perfect competition has a high incentive to develop new and different products, precisely to get away from the current market)

Test Your Understanding 4

In a perfectly competitive market, all producers charge the same price because:

A They are all profit maximisers

B They have the same costs

C The product is homogeneous

D All firms are small

Test Your Understanding 5

Which ONE of the following comes closest to the model of a perfectly competitive industry?

A oil refining

B farming

C motor vehicle manufacture

D banking

5 Monopoly

Definition

A monopoly is when a market has a single producer of a good with no close substitutes.

This is usually due to barriers preventing other firms from entering the market. Barriers to entry can take a number of forms, including:

- Legal barriers, e.g. patents or the award of a state monopoly to a utility company
- Natural barriers reflecting the cost structure of an industry, e.g. high start-up costs
- Integration in which monopolists control production, distribution and retail aspects of the industry making it very hard for a new entrant to become established.

Note: As we shall see later, in *practice* British legislation identifies a firm in the private sector as holding a monopoly if its market share exceeds 25%.

Example

In 1989 the water industry in England and Wales was reprivatised in the form of 10 regional monopolies.

Implications

In a pure monopoly the firm is the industry, and thereby controls market supply. Rather than market forces setting an equilibrium price where supply equals demand, the monopolist can choose where they want to be on the demand curve:

- either they fix the price and let demand determine the amount supplied, or
- fix supply and let demand determine the market price.

This effectively means that the monopolist has a vertical supply curve

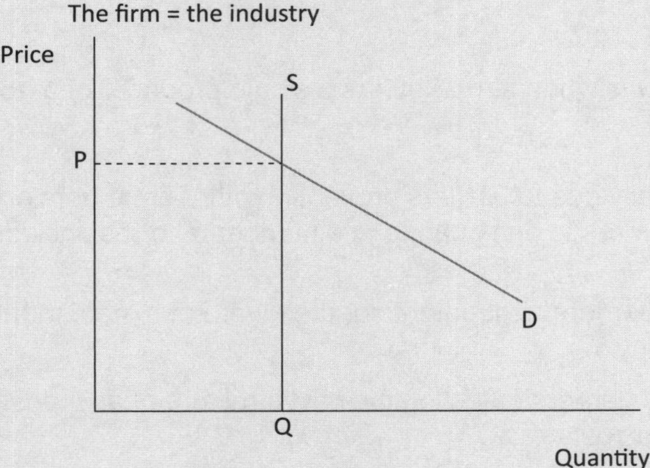

The monopolist will choose a position that maximises their profit, which usually means the following:

- the firm makes '*supernormal'* profits – i.e. higher than the minimum needed to stay in the industry. The ability to secure such profits is the result of restricting output so that prices are raised.
- the price is likely to be higher and the quantity supplied lower than would be seen under perfect competition
- the firm may not be operating at minimum cost
- These mean that we have neither technical nor allocative efficiency.

Taken together, this would suggest that monopolies are bad for both customers and the economy and so represent a market failure requiring state intervention.

However, the situation is not so clear cut:

- Since the monopoly is making supernormal profits, then they can afford to spend additional sums on "discretionary" expenditure such a staff welfare, product innovation or protecting the environment.
- However, you could argue that the monopolist has little incentive to develop new products as they already have a captive market. If anything, it may restrict choice by eliminating uneconomic brands.
- Furthermore, monopolists can keep out potential competitors by setting very low prices if necessary ("limit pricing"). Some firms try to set prices so low to kill off existing rivals in order to become a monopoly ("predatory pricing").

- A monopolist may be able to achieve significant economies of scale that mean that its cost of production is lower than that under perfect competition, even if the monopolist is not forced to operate at their minimum cost.
- Continuing this argument, the resulting price may be lower than that under perfect competition, even though the monopolist has higher margins.

On balance however, most governments feel they need to act to prevent abuses of market power by large organisations.

Test Your Understanding 6

Which one of the following would not discourage entry of new firms into an industry?

A perfect consumer knowledge

B economies of scale

C high fixed costs of production

D brand loyalty

Test Your Understanding 7

Which of the following is a natural barrier to firms entering an industry?

A large initial capital costs

B the issuing of patents

C a government awarded franchise

D the licensing of professions

Supplementary reading – Further comments on monopolies

In a capitalist economy, a monopolist would be a profit maximiser. However, in a planned economy it is unlikely that state monopolies would have such a goal. In the United Kingdom mixed economy the previously nationalised industries operated like monopolies and sought large profits, for example, gas and electricity. Although facing competition from one another in the market for energy, each had a monopoly in its own fuel since there were entry barriers which limited the ability of new firms to enter the market. However, the law creating the sole supplier rights of such public monopolies is not sacrosanct. The government sets price controls on their operation and opened them up to competition and eventual full privatisation.

Supplementary reading – Price discrimination

A monopolist may be able to subdivide one market into two or more sectors, and then set different prices (price discriminate) between different customers, although selling the same product. There are several ways to discriminate:

- by **time** – a golf club will charge non-members a higher green fee to play at weekends than during the week;
- by **customer** – a golf club will charge non-members playing with a member less than non-members would otherwise pay;
- by **income** – a hairdresser may charge a pensioner less than a breadwinner because the former has a lower income;
- by **place** – a hairdresser may charge extra for providing the service at the customer's home, as opposed to what would be charged at the salon.

These pricing strategies are likely to be successful if several conditions are fulfilled:

- at least *two distinct markets* with no *seepage* between them so that a higher price can be charged in one of the markets. If there was seepage then enterprising consumers could buy the good in the lower-priced market and then resell it in the other market, perhaps undercutting the discriminating monopolist;
- a *market imperfection*, such as transport costs, which gives the supplier a monopoly and thus keeps out competitors who might undercut him in his high-price market;
- *differing demand elasticities* so that the monopolist can gain extra profit from his price discrimination. A higher price would be set in the more inelastic market.

6 Imperfect Competition

Between perfect competition and monopoly, several forms of market exist, exhibiting some of the characteristics of the two extreme structures.

5.1 Monopolistic competition

Monopolistic competition is characterised by:

- Large number of producers who supply similar but not homogeneous products.
- Products are differentiated in style, image and price.
- There is not one prevailing market price. Firms may compete on price to try and gain market share at the expense of rivals.
- Consumers lack perfect knowledge but have a choice of products. This choice may be extended if new firms enter the industry perhaps attracted by the prospect of abnormal profits.
- There are no entry barriers; new firms can enter the industry and existing firms can leave at little cost. The lack of barriers to entry would suggest that in the long run only normal profits can be made.
- Prices are likely to be higher than under perfect competition but the customer now benefits from more choice.
- For example, the market for greetings cards

5.2 Oligopoly

An oligopoly is characterised by:

- A few large firms with a high concentration ratio.
- The behaviour of firms is often dependent on their rivals' actions and hence the market has a degree of uncertainty about it. A firm is not certain how rivals will respond to action initiated by itself. Consequently, there is *interdependence* in decision making.
- Consumers in oligopolistic markets lack detailed market information and are susceptible to the market strategies of the suppliers.
- New firms are unlikely to enter an oligopoly. The entrenched dominance often involving economies of scale enable them to fight off new competition. However, advances in technology and the financial power of transnational corporations mean that existing oligopolies can be challenged today.

There are a number of strategies which an oligopolist firm might adopt:

- co-operate with the other large firms.

  In such a *collusive oligopoly*, a common policy is agreed on pricing and market sharing and joint profit maximisation is the objective. The market structure then resembles the *monopoly* model. However, this may not be possible in practice because of restrictive practices legislation. This is considered under competition policy later in this chapter.

- make their own decisions and ignore their rivals.

  A firm could estimate its demand curve and set a price. The effect of this depends upon other prevailing prices for what are broadly similar goods/services, and how the rivals react.

  A higher price may lower sales and lead to a fall in market share if rivals do nothing. A lower price may increase sales but only if rivals do nothing. If rivals also lower prices, demand for the firm's product will be inelastic and lower profits will be the result.

  If rivals follow suit when the firm initiates a price rise, it becomes the *market leader*. This position is akin to that of a monopolist, who can make price changes with impunity. If rivals copy a price cut, there may *be price warfare*. Each firm is seeking to maintain its market share and protect its profits. The price cuts will benefit the consumer, as may some of the non-price competition.

- become a price follower by awaiting the action of the price leader.

  This strategy makes the firm a price taker.

- avoid price based competition.

  A firm may feel that any change in its price would be disadvantageous because of the reasons outlined above. Price stability is often associated with oligopolistic behaviour as firms choose not to raise or lower prices as they cannot be sure how rival firms will react to any such price changes.

  This is why there is often substantial non-price competition with oligopolies, for example, by advertising. Firms often produce several branded goods in the same market. Hence products are not homogeneous.

As long as collusion and price fixing do not occur, it could be argued that consumers may benefit from an oligopoly through a wide range of branded goods, price stability and after-sales servicing. In addition if price stability facilitates accurate forward planning by producers, then consumers might gain from better products and lower costs of production in the long run.

Note: A duopoly is just one example of an oligopoly and hence all of the comments above hold.

Test Your Understanding 8

Under monopolistic competition, excess profits are eliminated in the long run because of:

A the lack of barriers to entry

B the effects of product differentiation

C the existence of excess capacity

D the downward sloping demand curve for the product

Test Your Understanding 9

Company G operates in an industry with the following characteristics:

- four large firms who control 80% of the market, along with many smaller firms
- significant barriers to entry
- similar but not homogenous products
- long run price stability

Which of the following market structures best describe the above scenario?

A Monopoly

B Oligopoly

C Monopolistic competition

D Perfect competition

Test Your Understanding 10

Answer the following questions based on the preceding information. You can check your answers below.

(1) What is a market?

(2) What are the main assumptions of perfect competition?

(3) In a monopoly, if a firm fixes the price, what determines the amount supplied?

(4) Imperfect competition can be divided into three submarkets. What are they?

(5) What is allocative efficiency?

7 Regulation

6.1 Competition policy

As markets have become more heavily concentrated among fewer firms and competition has become more imperfect, so more controls have been applied to restrictive trade practices and pricing. The economic justifications for such a policy are fairly clear.

- Collusion by suppliers and the operation of cartels usually lead to higher prices and/or monopoly profits and possibly lower output.
- These in turn reduce consumer welfare
- Furthermore, they are a diminution in allocative efficiency. However, it must be remembered that extra profits may lead to investment in research, which could eventually benefit consumers via new products.

6.2 Scope of regulation

There are three aspects to this which involve government regulation:

- **Mergers and acquisitions**

  Many countries have bodies that monitor and assess mergers and acquisitions to see if the resulting organisation has excessive market power that is deemed to be against the public interest.

  In the UK this role is taken by the Competition and Markets Authority (formerly the Competition Commission) and a 25% market share or above is seen as a possible indicator of a "substantial lessening of competition" that may warrant further investigation.

- **Restrictive trade practices**

  Activities such as collusion over price fixing reduce competition within a market and undermine consumer sovereignty.

  In the UK, the Office of Fair Trading (OFT) investigates anti-competitive behaviour in markets.

- **State created regional monopolies**

  Many countries have gone through a process of privatisation thus converting state owned organisations into private companies. In many cases these result in regional monopolies, for example with water and other utilities.

  To control such monopolies government set up industry regulators, such as OFWAT, which regulates water and sewerage providers in England and Wales.

  Regulators will negotiate with firms over key issues of pricing and required investment to leave an appropriate level of return for shareholders, for example, a maximum ROCE.

Supplementary reading – Regulation in the UK

As examples of how governments regulate markets, we will look at the role of various bodies in the UK

The Competition and Markets Authority – mergers and acquisitions

The Competition and Markets Authority (CMA), formerly the Competition Commission, is an independent public body which conducts in-depth inquiries into mergers, markets and the regulation of the major regulated industries, ensuring healthy competition between companies in the UK for the benefit of companies, customers and the economy.

Mergers may be investigated to see whether there is a realistic prospect that they will lead to a substantial lessening of competition (SLC), unless it obtains undertakings from the merging parties to address its concerns or the market is of insufficient importance. In the UK one factor that is considered is whether the combined businesses supply (or acquire) at least 25 per cent of a particular product or service in the UK (or in a substantial part of the UK), and the merger results in an increase in the share of supply or consumption.

The CMA has wide-ranging powers to remedy any competition concerns, including preventing a merger from going ahead. It can also require a company to sell off part of its business or take other steps to improve competition.

For example, in August 2008, they provisionally found that there were competition problems arising from BAA's dominant position as owner of seven UK airports with adverse consequences for passengers and airlines. The proposed remedy in respect of BAA was to order it to sell two of its London airports and either Glasgow or Edinburgh airport in Scotland.

The Office of FairTrading – restrictive practices

The Office of Fair Trading (OFT) regularly discovers anti-competitive behaviour, particularly when frustrated retailers are threatened by manufacturers that their supplies of products will be curtailed if they continue to sell them at cut prices or as loss leaders (against the maker's wishes). This suggests that competitive policy in the area of restrictive trade practices needed to be strengthened.

In 2003 Argos and Littlewoods were fined £22 million by the OFT for fixing the price of toys and games together with Hasbro.

Similarly ten businesses including Manchester United, were fined a total of £18.6 million in October 2003 for fixing the price of Umbro replica football kits.

Specific industry regulators

As privatisation of large nationalised industries usually transformed public monopolies into private monopolies, the government accepted the need to create *regulatory watchdogs*. These bodies, such as the Office of Telecommunications (OFTEL) to supervise British Telecom, were performing a role which government departments did formerly.

On 28 December 2003 the Office of Communications (OFCOM) was established. It is now the regulator for the media and telecommunications industries and replaces five other regularity bodies including OFTEL. OFCOM will regulate standards of taste and decency on all TV and radio channels. It will licence commercial TV and radio. It will also oversee the telecommunications industry, where OFTEL was seen to have performed poorly particularly in relation to the regulation of BT and the deregulation of directory inquiries.

The role of specific industry regulators (SIRs) is essentially two-fold.

- First, when large state monopolies were privatised, they lacked effective competition. SIRs can introduce an element of competition by setting price caps and performance standards. In this way consumers can share in the benefits of competitive behaviour even if competition does not actually exist in the market.
- Second, SIRs can speed up the introduction of competition in such markets by reducing barriers to entry for new firms.

Supplementary reading – Regulation in the EU

The European Commission

The Commission of the European Union can use its powers, directly derived from the Treaty of Rome, to control the behaviour of monopolists and to increase the degree of competition across the European Union. It has long had powers, similar to those now adopted by the United Kingdom in the 1998 Competition Act, to prohibit price fixing, market sharing and production limitations. In this context they do not allow 'dual pricing'.

This is a system whereby exports to other EU countries are not allowed to be charged at different prices. For instance, Distillers sold whisky at higher prices in France and tried to restrict British buyers from purchasing the whisky more cheaply in England for resale at lower prices in France. The European Court adjudged that Distillers was distorting competition by trying to prevent its dual pricing being undermined.

Test Your Understanding 11

Company L is a large manufacturer of very high quality hi-fi equipment. In a recent newspaper article it was accused of putting pressure on small retailers to stock its full range of products (or it wouldn't be allowed to stock any), to charge the full recommended price with no discounts and even insisting that rival products were not stocked.

Which aspect of government regulation would seek to investigate and address this behaviour?

A Takeovers and mergers regulation

B Restrictive trade practices regulation

C Predatory pricing monitoring

D Regulation of state monopolies through industry-specific regulators

8 Public verses private provision of goods and services

7.1 The public sector

The public sector contains a range of businesses *sponsored* by the government, and often run by officials who are *accountable* (often very indirectly) to elected politicians.

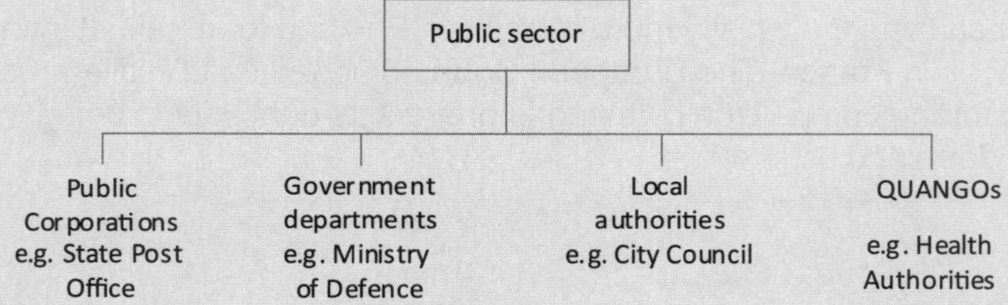

The blend of public and private provision varies from one country to another and the experience in the UK is useful to illustrate some of the issues involved.

During the 1980s, the UK public sector shrank as a result of privatisation, both through the sale of state assets and the hiving-off of public services to other agencies. Local authorities were forced to offer some services for tender (e.g. school meals) while others were taken away (e.g. transport). Government departments became subject to market criteria in their operations, while new QUANGOs (Quasi Autonomous Non Governmental Organisations) with commercial ethics and private sector business personnel were encouraged, for example, London Docklands Development Corporation.

7.2 Public corporations/nationalised industries

These are state-owned organisations (public corporations and nationalised industries are virtually synonymous except in legal terms) created by Acts of Parliament and given specific responsibilities.

In the UK many were created by the Labour government of 1945–51. For example, the National Coal Board was set up in 1947 when the UK coal industry was nationalised. This involved around 200 companies being bought up at a total cost of £338 million.

Their assets are publicly owned but they are not usually required to make a profit. A minister exercises general control and is responsible to Parliament. However, the day-to-day management is by a *board* appointed by the minister.

Arguments for nationalisation

- Low costs

  Cost advantages may be obtained through economies of scale, and the avoidance of waste and duplication. These points are particularly true of 'natural' monopolies such as gas, water and other public utilities.

- Capital

  Sufficient capital should be available for investment, because of government support.

- Provides uneconomic services for consumers.

  This argument places social benefit above private profit and is the justification for keeping small railway stations open, for example.

- Allows strategic control over key resources.

  This was an important factor for many countries after the second world war but is less so today, as privatisations of steel and electricity indicate.

- Protects employment and minimises social costs.

  For example in the UK, the keeping open of 'uneconomic pits' could be justified on this argument, because of the opportunity cost to the local communities based on coal mines (and steel plant) closures. Not only did closure mean lost output, it also meant extra public spending on unemployment benefit and the intangible social costs of 'loss of community', increased marital stress, higher crime, etc.

- Gives a fairer distribution of wealth

  Public sector surpluses could be used for the benefit of society rather than profits being expropriated by capitalist owners. This argument also justified high wages and job security for public employees, as well as more sympathetic management.

7.3 Privatisation

Privatisation involves transferring ownership of a business, enterprise, agency, public service or property from the public sector to the private sector, either to businesses or to private non-profit organizations.

The term is also used to mean government out-sourcing of services to private firms, such as refuse and waste collection.

Typically there are two main strands to privatisation:

Sale of state assets

This could involve the sale of

- whole industries (e.g. the Indian Government is currently investigating privatising its national railways),
- firms (e.g. the West German government sold its majority stake in Volkswagen to small investors in a public share offering in 1961) or
- parts of local authorities (e.g. in the UK approximately 2 million council houses were sold into private hands during the 1980s and 90s).

Introduction of competition into areas previously monopolised by state suppliers

This can involve

- deregulation of various industries (e.g. bus travel) and
- compulsory competitive tendering (e.g. local authority refuse collection services).

A major ongoing privatisation is that of Japan Post and involves both the Japanese post service and one of the largest banks in the world. This process was started in 2007 following generations of debate and is expected to last around ten years to complete.

Arguments for privatisation

- Improved 'efficiency' in sleepy state monopolies.

  The experience of many countries is that overmanning and wasteful investment occurred in state monopolies because of demoralised management (and frequently changed government objectives) and immunity to takeover.

  Thus it was claimed that the fear of takeover in the private sector and competition would lead to *innovation* in the search for profit, for example, use of minibuses after the deregulation of bus services. These pressures would also give managers an incentive to minimise costs and shake out unproductive labour.

  For example, in the UK the privatisation of British Telecom resulted in 15,000 jobs being cut in 1993.

- Wider share ownership.

  It is argued that if employees become shareholders they work harder and strike less, thereby engendering economic gains to firms. Furthermore, the increase in the number of adults with shares will create empathy with the private profit motive and better understanding of business problems.

- Improved quality

  The argument is that quality will have to improve because privatised concerns will have to compete to survive and be responsive to consumer complaints. For example, in many countries the deregulation of long-distance bus travel has seen significant price cutting and better quality coaches.

- Greater economic freedom

  Privatised companies will not be subject to the 'dead hand' of state control. For example, nationalised industry chairmen were sometimes pressured by government ministers to make decisions for political reasons, for example, hold prices steady during a period of incomes policy. Market forces should have more influence.

- Will provide funds for the Treasury.

  Selling off state assets will allow a reduction in the public sector borrowing requirement and tax cutting.

For example, in March 2012, Greece invited bids for state-owned gas company DEPA, as it moved ahead with a privatisation programme meant to raise €19bn by 2015.

Note: the current crisis in the Eurozone has resulted in a number of governments looking at privatisation as a way of raising funds to reduce debt levels. Such moves have met with heated resistance in some countries. For example, in January 2012 The Spanish government suspended plans to privatise its two main airports, a plan they had hoped would raise €5bn.

Criticisms of privatisation

- Fewer services and higher prices

  For example, experiences in bringing competition into rural transport is that unprofitable routes are closed.

- Private monopolies are created.

  For instance, in the UK BT had 70 per cent of the domestic market in the 1990s and faced only limited competition. Thus there were few pressures to reduce costs and it was able to raise prices and make over £1 billion profits annually.

- Quality of service has diminished,

  Particularly where local authority functions have been contracted out, for instance, costs have been saved by reducing staff, paying lower wages and reducing what was provided, like schools cleaned less frequently.

  Any gains in technical efficiency as cost per unit has fallen is thus an illusion as quality of service has simultaneously declined.

  For example, the performance of the private security firm G4S at the London Olympics 2012 was considered so poor that the British armed forces were called in to rectify the situation.

- Asset sales were underpriced

  Sales of state assets have often been criticised for setting prices too low to attract buyers and this created big capital gains for private investors.

  For example in the UK one estimate of the sale of Railtrack shares was that they were underpriced by £2 billion.

- Only the profitable parts of the public sector are sold off

  Private enterprise will only be interested in the more profitable parts of the public sector. Unless the privatisation process is managed to avoid, the end result will be that there is less public income in the future to contribute to government spending.

  Furthermore the previous tendency of state enterprises to cross-subsidise disappears and less profitable aspects eventually get closed down.

- Impact on balance of payments

  The sale of shares to overseas buyers means that *other governments can influence the decisions of domestic firms* and dividend payments go abroad, thereby weakening the balance of payments.

- Top executives of privatised companies have paid themselves *large salaries and generous share options*, while simultaneously preaching wage restraint to their trade unionists.

  This seems most unfair and hardly likely to induce high productivity and employee commitment.

- Competition has not been enhanced.

  Often privatisation has resulted in local monopolies that subsequently need the intervention of specific industry regulators to control investment and pricing decisions.

- The poor often suffer.

  The UN Development Program notes that water privatisation has hurt many in the developing world, where poor people pay some of the highest prices for water. For example, the poorest 20% of households in El Salvador, Jamaica, and Nicaragua spend up to 10% of their income on water.

Pricing

As many privatised companies are now private monopolies, they would be expected to conform to profit maximisation principles. Indeed, in most cases they have.

However, this does not create technical or allocative efficiency. As the model for such efficiency is perfect competition, the government has tried to create competition.

For example in the UK, when electricity was privatised, the power generation was split between National Power and Powergen. However, this was rather artificial and still only gave a duopoly.

A major problem for the government of creating competition has been that it makes the nationalised industry to be sold less likely to be profitable and thereby depresses the share price, and so raises less money than required.

A different approach has been to impose *price limits* on privatised monopolies. For example, in the UK electricity had a *price formula*:

$$RPI - X + Y$$

where RPI is the change in retail prices index; X is a percentage deduction (designed to squeeze costs); and Y is a percentage addition (for costs which cannot be passed on).

7.4 Public–private partnerships

Public-private partnerships (PPP), of which the best known example is the private finance initiative (PFI), describes any private sector involvement in public services including the transfer of council homes to housing associations using private loans, and contracting out services like rubbish collection to private companies. The PFI refers to a strictly defined legal contract for private consortiums, usually involving large construction firms, to design, build, finance and manage a new public project, typically a school or hospital, over a 30-year period. The building is not publicly owned but leased by a public authority.

The perceived advantages of the PFI are:

- Finances public projects without the need for government to borrow funds or raise taxes.
- Risk is transferred to the private provider. If the private consortium misses performance targets, it will be paid less.
- Introduces private sector qualities such as efficiency and innovation into the public sector, thereby, raising the quality of provision

Critics of PFI, however, point out:

- The methods of financing used to make public projects more expensive. The Edinburgh Royal Infirmary cost £180 million to build but will cost £900 million over its 30-year contract. This includes the operating costs but, as government has access to cheap funds, it would still have been cheaper to build and manage using traditional public sector funding.
- There is also a question mark over how much risk is genuinely transferred to the private sector given the government's record of bailing out private companies managing troubled public services.

- Efficiency savings have been made at the expense of quality deterioration in the service, for example hospital cleaning.

However it will take a much longer period of time, when the first PFI contracts have been completed, before the real costs and benefits of this form of PPP can be judged.

Test Your Understanding 12

Answer the following questions based on the preceding information. You can check your answers below.

(1) Give three arguments for nationalisation.

(2) What were three reasons for privatisation?

(3) How do merit goods differ from public goods?

Test Your Understanding 13

Which one of the following is not a valid economic reason for producing a good or service in the public sector?

A The good is a basic commodity consumed by everyone

B It is a public good

C There is a natural monopoly in the production of the good

D It is a merit good

Test Your Understanding 14

Which of the following statements about a policy of privatising a public sector industry are true?

(i) It will permit economies of scale.

(ii) It is a means of widening share ownership.

(iii) The industry would become more responsive to the profit motive.

(iv) It is a source of funds for the government.

A (i) and (ii) only

B (i), (ii) and (iii) only

C (i) and (iii) only

D (ii), (iii) and (iv) only

Supplementary reading – Public and merit goods revisited

Public and merit goods were discussed in chapter 3. These are provided by the government because the free market under produces them. *Public goods* are products such as *defence* where one person's consumption does not diminish someone else's (*non-rivalry*) and that person cannot stop someone else benefiting from it (*non-exclusivity).* This enables free-riders to take advantage and so the person would not be prepared to pay for the service. Hence the government provides defence at *zero price* but taxpayers fund the service.

As the government is providing public goods on a nationwide basis, it can benefit from *economies of scale.* This could lower costs and the industry would strive for technical efficiency. There is no *allocative efficiency* because consumers do not have a choice – the services, such as police, prisons, fire, are provided whether they like it or not. However, a consumer who seeks more protection could buy additions in the marketplace, like burglar alarms, underground concrete bunkers, security men, etc.

With *merit goods*, government provision is made in the interests of the general well-being of the nation. However, the private sector provides alternatives, although these are often seen as 'different', or even superior goods/services, for example, private school education, private health schemes.

In the case of state-provided merit goods, economies of scale could be achieved and technical efficiency sought. The cost of education per student is about three times cheaper in the state sector than in the private sector. However, it is rather difficult to maximise technical efficiency as shown by the failure to close small local hospitals and village schools. Ironically, the support for these threatened organisations comes from local users, thereby indicating that consumer needs are being met. Also, they are making a rational choice because a local service is better than a more distant (alternative) one in terms of time and travel cost. Free marketeers would thus point to the folly of zero pricing, which negates allocative efficiency.

Test your understanding answers

Test Your Understanding 1

True

The lack of barriers to entry will mean that new firms can easily enter the market (if they wish), increasing the level of competition. While some firms will survive by finding a niche or through being differentiators, many will be under pressure to find cost efficiencies or exit the market. In the long run such firms will have to become X-efficient to survive.

Test Your Understanding 2

C

Horizontal mergers occur when two firms in the same business merge, and there is a danger that such a merger could create a monoploy (which is an extreme form of market dominance). Options B and D both relate to vertical integration: B illustrates the potential issue with backward vertical integration and D a potential issue with forward vertical integration. The economies of scale available from larger production quantities are one of the main benefits of horizontal mergers (so option A is incorrect).

Test Your Understanding 3

A

Z has acquired one of its suppliers, which is backward vertical integration.

Test Your Understanding 4

C

You may feel that all four answers have some merit. However, the key reason is the fact that all suppliers have exactly the same product and so cannot avoid the competition or carve out a niche for themselves. In perfect competition if a product is homogeneous, all suppliers will sell it at the same price. There is no benefit to be gained from cutting price, as demand is infinite at the current market price. Raising price will lead to total loss of demand due to perfect consumer knowledge and a lack of economic friction.

Test Your Understanding 5

B

A perfectly competitive industry must have many producers none of which can have any dominance in the market. They are all price-takers. You might feel that applying these concepts is tricky because the **extent** of the industry is not clearly defined – are we discussing a particular country or considering a global market or a typical one? However, if we look closely at the specific industries given we can see that A, C and D are typically characterised by a small number of major companies, leaving answer B.

Test Your Understanding 6

A

Economies of scale and brand loyalty will both deter new firms from entering an industry as they would be competing against firms who are already operating with these benefits.

High fixed costs of production will also make it difficult for new firms to break into the market as they will have to raise substantial amounts of finance against a nil track record.

Test Your Understanding 7

A

Only A is a 'natural' barrier to entry, not legally created.

Test Your Understanding 8

A

New firms are attracted into the market by the existence of supernormal profits, and are able to enter because of the lack of barriers to entry.

Test Your Understanding 9

B

An oligopoly is mainly characterised by a small number of firms controlling most of the market. The long run price stability would indicate that firms are choosing non-price competition (e.g. through advertising) to avoid the problems of interdependence and uncertainty.

Test Your Understanding 10

(1) A market is where goods and services are bought and sold.

(2) The assumptions of perfect competition are:
many buyers and sellers;
homogeneous product;
perfect information;
freedom of entry and exit.

(3) Demand for the product.

(4) Imperfect competition can be subdivided into monopolistic competition, oligopoly and duopoly.

(5) Allocative efficiency refers to the best use of resources producing goods and services which people want.

Test Your Understanding 11

B

This is an example of restrictive trade practices as L is accused of restricting the trade of other firms, here its retailers.

Test Your Understanding 12

(1) Nationalisation can be justified because it provides low costs of production, uneconomic services which otherwise might not exist and strategic control over key resources.

(2) Three reasons for privatisation are funds for the Treasury, greater economic freedom for producers and improved efficiency within the organisation.

(3) Public goods are freely provided by the government as there is non-rivalry and non-exclusivity in their use. Merit goods are provided by the government as it is believed they should be made available to all irrespective of the ability to pay.

Test Your Understanding 13

A

Because a commodity is consumed by everyone (e.g. food), it does not follow that it has any special features such that it cannot be produced efficiently in a competitive market in the private sector. All other responses are valid reasons why a good or service should be produced wholly, or partly, in the public sector.

Test Your Understanding 14

D

Privatisation does not produce larger firms and often leads to smaller firms when public sector monopolies are broken up into smaller companies (e.g. railways) on privatisation. Thus the privatisation process cannot increase the scope for economies of scale. All the other responses are valid reasons for privatisation.

chapter

5

The Financial System I

Chapter learning objectives

After completing this chapter you should be able to:

- identify the factors leading to liquidity surpluses and deficits in the short, medium and long run in households, firms and governments
- explain the role of various financial assets, markets and institutions in assisting organisations to manage their liquidity position and to provide an economic return to holders of liquidity
- explain the financial and economic functions of financial intermediaries
- explain the role of commercial banks in the process of credit creation and in determining the structure of interest rates;
- explain the role of the 'central bank' in ensuring liquidity and in prudential regulation
- explain the origins of the 2008 banking crisis and credit crunch;

1 Introduction – The financial system

1.1 The financial system

'The financial system' is an umbrella term covering the following:

- Financial markets – e.g. stock exchanges, money markets.
- Financial institutions – e.g. banks, building societies, insurance companies and pension funds.
- Financial assets and liabilities – e.g. mortgages, bonds, bills and equity shares.

1.2 Financial markets

The financial markets can be divided into different types, depending on the products being issued/bought/sold:

- Capital markets which consist of stock-markets for shares and bond markets.
- Money markets, which provide short-term (< 1 year) debt financing and investment.
- Commodity markets, which facilitate the trading of commodities (e.g. oil, metals and agricultural produce).
- Derivatives markets, which provide instruments for the management of financial risk, such as options and futures contracts.
- Insurance markets, which facilitate the redistribution of various risks.
- Foreign exchange markets, which facilitate the trading of foreign exchange.

1.3 Financial intermediaries

Within each sector of the economy (households, firms and governmental organisations) there are times when there are cash surpluses and times when there are deficits.

- In the case of surpluses the party concerned will seek to invest/deposit/lend funds to earn an economic return.
- In the case of deficits the party will seek to borrow funds to manage their liquidity position.

Faced with a desire to lend or borrow, there are three choices open to the end-users of the financial system:

(a) Lenders and borrowers contact each other directly

This is rare due to the high costs involved, the risks of default and the inherent inefficiencies of this approach.

(b) Lenders and borrowers use an organised financial market

For example, an individual may purchase corporate bonds from a recognised bond market. If this is a new issue of bonds by a company looking to raise funds, then the individual has effectively lent money to the company.

If the individual wishes to recover their funds before the redemption date on the bond, then they can sell the bond to another investor.

(c) Lenders and borrowers use intermediaries

In this case the lender obtains an asset which cannot usually be traded but only returned to the intermediary. Such assets could include a bank deposit account, pension fund rights, etc.

The borrower will typically have a loan provided by an intermediary.

Financial intermediaries have a number of important roles.

- Risk reduction

  By lending to a wide variety of individuals and businesses, financial intermediaries reduce the risk of a single default resulting in total loss of assets.

- Aggregation

  By pooling many small deposits, financial intermediaries are able to make much larger advances than would be possible for most individuals.

- Maturity transformation

  Most borrowers wish to borrow in the long-term whilst most savers are unwilling to lock up their money for the long-term. Financial intermediaries, by developing a floating pool of deposits, are able to satisfy both the needs of lenders and borrowers.

- Financial intermediation

  Financial intermediaries bring together lenders and borrowers through a process known as financial intermediation.

Supplementary reading – Functions and qualities of money

Functions of money

The different forms of money include gold, notes, coin and bank account. As long as something is acceptable and enables the performance of certain functions, it can be regarded as money.

There are four main functions of money.

(1) A medium of exchange. The existence of money means that buyers and sellers can meet and trade, without the problems associated with barter.

   – Without money, trade was limited because some goods were indivisible, a rate of exchange might be disputed and the wants and needs of the buyer needed to match identically with the needs and wants of the seller.

   – With money, small quantities can be purchased, prices are largely fixed at the point of sale, and buyers and sellers do not need to reciprocate.

(2) A store of value. When people receive money they may not spend it all on consumption.

   – Thus money needs to be capable of storage until required for consumption while simultaneously maintaining its value during the saving period.

   – If there is inflation, the value of savings held in money form or denominated in money terms will lose value; money will not be performing this function very well and the desire to save may be reduced.

(3) A unit of account. In this role, money allows goods to be compared in a common denomination which people understand – namely money.

   – The prices of goods and services reflect their scarcity values and costs of production and enable consumers to make rational judgements.

   – Thus money enables people to establish relative values.

(4) A standard of deferred payment. This means the ability to determine the value of future payments in contracts specifying prices and payments measured in money terms.

The issue of 'what is money?' has led to much discussion among economists and to various definitions and measures of money in the economy. If something performs the above functions and is acceptable to people it will be used as 'money'.

In order to fulfil the functions of money, an asset must have certain characteristics.

Qualities of money

In order to fulfil all of the functions of money, a financial asset should have the following characteristics:

- *Acceptability*. All participants in a transaction must be willing to accept money in exchange for real goods and services in order to fulfil the function of acting as a medium of exchange.
- *Durability*. It is important, especially with cash, that money does not physically deteriorate, especially if the money is used as means of storing value over time.
- *Stable value*. The purchasing power of money must be stable otherwise money cannot act as a store of value or a standard of deferred payment.
- *Portable and divisible*. Money needs to be convenient for small transactions and easily transported.

The overall quality which money derives from these features is *liquidity*: the ability to turn a financial asset into a form – effectively cash, that can be used as a medium of exchange – the primary function of money.

This raises the question of what should, and what should not, be classified as money.

- Cash clearly meets all of the above requirements.
- Both bank and building society accounts which give customers (fairly) immediate access to their money also meet these requirements and are included in most measures of the total of money in the economy. These accounts give their holders liquidity, the vital characteristic of money. They also perform the storage function.
- However, credit cards which are treated as 'money' by their users and enable customers to buy goods are really only money substitutes. This is because they do not perform the storage function.

Test Your Understanding 1

Most lenders wish to offer their funds for the short term whereas most borrowers want to borrow over the longer term. Resolving this mismatch is known as:

A risk reduction

B aggregation

C maturity transformation

D pooling

Test Your Understanding 2

The linking of net savers with net borrowers is known as:

A the savings function

B financial intermediation

C financial regulation

D a store of value

2 Liquidity surpluses and deficits

The lack of synchronisation between payments and receipts, has a variety of origins and affects individuals, businesses and governments.

2.1 Individuals

The lack of synchronisation in payments and receipts for individuals can occur in the short, medium and long term.

Receipts

Household income comes in a variety of forms. The main ones being:

- wages and salaries
- income from investments, property and savings
- social security and pension payments.

The common feature of these is that the flow of such income tends to be regular, but not continuous. Typically wages and salaries are paid monthly (and bonuses annually) as are social security and pension payments. Income from investments may be monthly, but are more commonly bi-annually or annually.

Payments

	Payments	Dealing with a lack of synchronisation
Short term	Consumption expenditure is typically more or less continuous and irregular. Most households spend some money every day but rarely exactly the same amount. Some payments may match receipts, for example monthly direct debits and monthly salaries but this relates only to certain types of expenditure.	Households can: • retain a *stock of cash* to meet day-to-day expenditure • use *credit* such as credit cards and overdrafts facilities • *save* in periods when receipts exceed payments to finance periods when the reverse happens. In all of these cases, households use the services of financial intermediaries: bank accounts, credit cards and overdrafts. **Note:** there will also be times when individuals have a surplus of funds and would thus look for opportunities to invest and earn a return. There are a wide range of deposit accounts available with different yields, time periods and conditions over withdrawal (e.g. notice periods).

Medium term	The infrequent purchase of expensive items such as • consumer durables, including cars • holidays and • medical bills. Again these expenditure flows are unrelated to the flow of income.	The solutions for households are broadly twofold: • to *save* over a period of time prior to the purchase • to *borrow* and repay over a period of time. Again both of these require appropriate financial instruments; in the first case efficient means of saving such as deposit accounts, and in the second case, cost effective means of borrowing, including bank loans and consumer credit.
Long term	Even in the long term there may be a mismatch between payments and receipts. This arises from the very long-term nature of some income and spending decisions. Examples of this include: • housing property • savings for pensions.	A range of specialist mortgage products have been developed to enable people to buy property. A range of specialist pension products have been developed to help people to generate income for when they retire and no longer receive a salary.

2.2 Business

As with individuals, businesses will find that flows of payments and flows of receipts rarely match. This is often referred to as the cash flow problem and can occur in the short, medium and long run.

Receipts

Receipts for the business come mainly from sales revenue. The pattern of receipts will depend on the nature of the business (e.g. whether there a seasonal aspect to trade), the system of invoicing (e.g. monthly), credit terms and whether customers stick to the payment terms.

Payments

	Payments	Dealing with a lack of synchronisation
Short term	All business have day-to-day costs to meet: • wages and salaries • regular flow of physical inputs such as energy, raw materials and components In effect, businesses need working capital.	For businesses the solutions to this cash flow problem are: • retaining a large stock of cash to meet periods of low or delayed income • access to credit, for example trade credit of various kinds to pay for physical inputs • access to overdraft facilities with their banks. Of course when receipts are lower than payments businesses need access to credit and overdraft facilities, but when the reverse happens secure, and preferably profitable, savings instruments are required.
Medium term	Cash flow issues might arise in the medium term for businesses. Examples where this may arise include: • sales revenue is received long after the first costs are incurred such as in building and construction activity, shipbuilding and aerospace • where contracts specify part payments long before delivery • reorganisation costs are incurred before benefits from lower costs or increased revenues are achieved.	Businesses thus require medium-term finance, typically 2–3 years, to meet these medium-term financial problems.

<table>
<tr>
<td>Long term</td>
<td>Most long-term financing problems in business arise out of their investment activities. This may take a variety of forms:

• investment in physical capital
• investment in long-term Research and Development programmes (R&D)
• take-overs and mergers of existing businesses</td>
<td>These activities may involve very large capital outlays with the prospect of increased incomes delayed well into the future. Businesses thus need long-term finance and have three main options:

• the use of internally generated funds
• equity capital through the issue of shares
• debt capital including mortgages, bank borrowing and bonds.

In the latter two cases, businesses need access to the capital market as sources of funds for long-term investment.</td>
</tr>
</table>

2.3 Government

Receipts

The government may have some income from profitable state industries or charges made to consumers for state-provided services, but the vast bulk of its income comes from taxation. The main sources of taxation revenue are:

- a range of *indirect taxes* (sales taxes) such as value added tax and excise duties on alcohol, petrol and tobacco products;
- *direct taxes* on individuals most importantly income tax and social security taxes
- *direct taxes* on business organisations such as corporation tax.

Some of these flows of taxation revenue are quite regular, such as income tax paid through the pay-as-you-earn system in the United Kingdom, but many are not. The flow of receipts from corporation tax, for example, can be very uneven with significant payments towards the end of the tax year. This, as with households, implies a problem of synchronisation of payments and receipts.

Payments

	Payments	Dealing with a lack of synchronisation
Short term	In the short term, governments must finance their day-to-day activities such as: • payments of wages and salaries to government employees • payment of social security and state pensions to the unemployed and the retired • payments to providers of goods and services to enable the day-to-day running of the government activities.	Most of these payments are spread over the financial year and are relatively stable from one month to another. It is therefore difficult to match tax revenue to the payments made for these items. Thus the government, like households, needs short-term financial facilities so that it can meet its day-to-day running expenses. The credit and savings needs of government in this respect are often met by the central bank, one of whose functions is to act as banker to the government and to manage the government's finances.

	Payments	Dealing with a lack of synchronisation
Medium term	Governments also have medium-term financial commitments that largely arise from investment activities in the public sector. Governments engage in investment when they finance such as: • school and hospital building • construction projects for the economic infrastructure, for example motorway and railway construction • loans to private sector activities to help finance investment by those organisations; this typically occurs in high technology and risky activities such as aerospace.	These expenditures are not likely to be evenly spread over the years. Indeed, governments may deliberately concentrate such expenditures in some years rather than other as part of a fiscal policy designed to manage the trade cycle. In this case, government will raise such expenditure in recessions exactly when receipts from taxation are likely to be low as consumer incomes and spending fall. Thus governments may run *budget deficits* which have to be financed by borrowing from the private sector.

Long term	Governments often take responsibility for financing very long-term investment projects in the development of the infrastructure of the economy, for example nuclear power and telecommunications.	Since it is possible for governments to be net savers or net borrowers over very long periods of time, they may need the services of financial intermediaries over that period. It is more likely that governments will be net long-term borrowers: • given that the projects such as nuclear power are investments, not current consumption, borrowing is an acceptable means of finance for these projects • governments can continue to borrow in the very long run as long as there is sufficient taxation income to finance the subsequent debt. Even if governments do not engage in additional long-term borrowing, all have debts accumulated from the past – the national debt. This must be managed as there is no real possibility of repaying it. Thus governments need the services of financial intermediaries to manage and renew this debt.

2.4 Linkages

The above inflows and outflows are obviously linked. For example,

- In January 2011, the UK government increased the rate of VAT from 17.5% to 20% to increase its revenues.
- However, this also meant that households would need to find more cash to buy the same things they had bought previously. This sum was estimated at around £400 per family and resulted in cutbacks in expenditure and increased levels of debt.
- This also had a knock-on effect on businesses who saw a decline in their sales and cash receipts.

Supplementary reading – Further detail on finance for business

Finance for business

There are financial problems for businesses when there is a lack of synchronisation in the flows of payments and receipts. The financial needs of business vary and take a variety of forms. In general their needs can be classified as:

- funds to finance day-to-day business including payments for wages and salaries, raw materials and components – *working capital*;
- funds to finance the purchase of new capital equipment or to finance acquisitions and mergers – *investment capital*;
- suitable instruments for investing any surplus funds as part of the *asset management function*.

In acquiring funds to finance their activities, businesses have a large range of different types of financial instruments from which to choose. But in making the choice, businesses will follow a general rule that the instrument should be appropriate to the use to which the funds are to be put. Thus:

- short-term instruments should be chosen to finance the short-term needs of *working capital*;
- long-term instruments should be chosen to finance the long-term needs of *investment*.

With the investment of surplus funds a similar rule is generally adopted and the instrument chosen will be balanced between profitability and the needs to match the term of the instrument to the period during which the funds will not be needed.

In most economies and for most businesses, the bulk of the financial needs of those businesses are met by internally generated funds. For the rest of their financial needs, businesses can employ a range of financial instruments. The most important of these are:

Short-and medium-term instruments

These are typically acquired from the money markets. The most important are:

- short-term bank loans and overdrafts, the latter are expensive and avoided if possible;
- bills of exchange, these are typically of 3–6 months duration are sold with a promise to repay at that date;

- commercial paper which are debt securities issued by the largest companies;
- trade credit which allows business to delay payment for raw materials, components, business services, etc.
- leasing and hire purchase.

Financial intermediaries have thus built up a wide range of instruments to meet the short- and medium-term financial needs of business. However, there has been a persistent complaint in many countries over recent years that the system has been poor at meeting the financial needs of small and newly established businesses. This explains the growth various government measures designed specifically to help the small business sector.

Long-term instruments

In meeting their long-term financial needs, businesses have a broad choice between two forms of long-term finance:

- *equity* finance
- *debt* finance.

Equity finance is available to limited liability companies through the issue of shares. For publicly quoted companies, additional shares ('rights issues') can be issued via the Stock Market. This is discussed in the next section.

The alternative is long-term borrowing. This might be done by long-term commercial paper for the largest firms. Funds may also be raised by forms of Preference Shares on which fixed rates of interest are paid and mortgaged.

Although there is a wide choice of instruments for larger firms, especially those quoted on the stock market, there have been problems in many economies for small and new businesses. A persistent complaint has been the difficulty that small firms face in acquiring the finance they need from the financial system. In response many governments have created a series of initiative designed to meet the specific financing needs of small firms.

Mezzanine finance, in effect, combines aspects of both debt and equity finance. Although the finance is initially given as a loan (debt capital), the lender has the rights to convert to an equity interest in the company if the loan is not paid back in time and in full.

Test Your Understanding 3

Peter is looking to finance the purchase of a new car. Which of the following in the most likely form of finance he would use?

A Mortgage

B Credit card

C Overdraft

D Personal loan

Test Your Understanding 4

ABC Chocolate manufactures a range of different chocolate novelties for sale in major supermarkets. It has seasonal trade and finds the period before Christmas difficult from a cash management point of view as it has to pay out wages and for ingredients before the holiday period but often has to wait until the New Year before receiving payment from major customers.

Which of the following would be a suitable way of managing this cash flow problem?

A Issue new equity shares

B Overdraft

C Leasing arrangement

D Mortgage

Test Your Understanding 5

What is meant by the term 'Mezzanine finance'?

A Short-term loans to help a firm through a cash flow crisis

B Foreign currency loans

C Loans by non-financial institutions

D Finance that is neither pure debt not pure equity

3 Financial products

3.1 Main considerations

There are a wide range of contracts and financial instruments issued by financial institutions for lending /borrowing. (Note that the term 'financial claims' can be used to refer to both).

Whether borrowing or lending the main considerations when choosing which product to use are as follows:

- Yield/cost

  For example, investing in certificates of deposit typically gives a lower return than investing in equities. (However, see the comments on risk below.)

- Risk

  The main determinant of cost (yield) is risk. For example, if a company wishes to raise funds by an issue of bonds, then the yield it must offer to investors (or the cost to the company) must be sufficient to compensate them for the perceived risks of the bond.

- The amounts involved/divisibility

  For example, the minimum amount for a certificate of deposit is £50,000.

- The time period the funds are required/available for

  For example, treasury bills usually have an initial maturity of 91 days.

- Liquidity

  This looks at how easy it is to sell the asset to release funds early if required. For example, shares in an unquoted company are much harder to sell to release funds than Treasury bills which have a recognised market.

- Transaction costs

  For example, the arrangement fees for mortgages.

3.2 Capital and money markets

The time to maturity has traditionally been used to make a distinction between 'capital' markets and 'money' markets:

- Capital markets – maturities > 1 year – examples include equities, bonds and mortgages
- Money markets – maturities < 1 year – examples include certificates of deposit and bills of exchange

3.3 Ordinary shares ('equity')

Ownership of companies is conveyed via ordinary shares. Ordinary shareholders also have voting rights. Shares have a nominal or par value (e.g. '£1 ords'), which is usually different from the market value if quoted. Companies often raise funds through the issue of shares.

Characteristics	
Return	• Potentially very high returns if the company is profitable. • Returns will be in the form of dividends and/or increases in share prices.
Risk	• Shares carry high risk. • If company profits fall, then there is a danger of zero or low dividends, combined with a fall in share value. Furthermore, if, in a worst case scenario, the company gets liquidated, then the shareholders only get paid if there is any money left after settling all other claims. In such situations the shareholder usually get nothing.
Timescales	• The company usually has no intention of buying back the shares, so equity is considered long-term.
Liquidity	• for unquoted companies it is very difficult to sell the shares but for quoted companies the shares are highly liquid, so investors can "cash in" at any point.

3.4 Bonds

Just as the total equity of a company is split into shares, loans may be broken down into smaller units (e.g. one bond may have a nominal or par value of £100). Different varieties include debentures and loan stock and may be issued by companies, local authorities and governmental organisations.

Bonds will normally have a nominal value (e.g. £1,000), a coupon rate (e.g. 5%) and redemption terms (e.g. redeem at par in 2015). The annual interest is the product of the nominal value and the coupon rate (e.g. £1,000 × 5% = £50 per annum).

Characteristics	
Return	• Typically bonds have low returns because they are a lower risk investment. • Returns will be in the form of interest and (possibly) gain on redemption.
Risk	• Bonds are usually lower risk than equity. • For example the bonds may be secured and the interest rate fixed. • Note: you can get high-risk, unsecured ("junk") bonds as well.
Timescales	• The maturity is defined on the bond and varies from very short term (e.g. Treasury Bills) to long term (e.g. 25-year corporate bonds). • Some bonds are redeemable but others irredeemable.
Liquidity	• If the bonds are unquoted then the investor has no choice except to wait for redemption. • However, if quoted, then they will be easier to liquidate by selling on bond markets. • For example government bonds are usually very liquid. • Note: high risk bonds will be sold at a large discount on face value.

3.5 Certificates of deposit ('CD')

A CD states that a deposit has been made with a bank for a fixed period of time, at the end of which it will be repaid with interest. The minimum amount invested is £50,000.

Characteristics	
Return	• Very low returns due to low risk
Risk	• Very safe.
Timescales	• 3 and 6 month maturities are the most common.
Liquidity	• Can be readily sold on money markets

3.6 Credit agreements

A credit agreement is an arrangement where one party borrows or takes possession of something in return for future payment. For example – credit cards and store hire purchase contracts.

Characteristics	
Return	• Usually high interest rates. • For example, store cards typically cost around 25 – 30% per annum.
Risk	• The credit card company faces the risk of default – that the card holder will not repay the amount borrowed – as such cards are usually unsecured.
Timescales	• Usually intended to be short term, although some individuals can get into financial difficulties by running up large debts on credit cards that they cannot repay.
Liquidity	• The debt cannot be resold by the lender but the borrower may be able to repay early if funds permit.

3.7 Mortgages

A mortgage is a loan to finance the purchase of property, usually with specified payment periods and interest rates.

Characteristics	
Return	• The interest cost is usually relatively low as the mortgage will be secured on the property bought.
Risk	• As stated above, usually considered low risk. • However, a fall in house prices would reduce the value of security offered. (e.g. in the 1990s this gave rise to 'negative equity' in the UK).
Timescales	• Long term – e.g. between 10 and 35 years.
Liquidity	• The traditional position was that the mortgage could not be resold by the lender to recover their funds but the borrower could repay the loan early, albeit with possible penalties. • However, one contributory factor in the banking crisis of 2008 was the way lenders effectively sold their mortgage books to other institutions via the use of 'Collateralised debt obligations' or CDOs. These are discussed further below.

3.8 Bills of exchange

A bill of exchange is usually issued by companies to finance trade and promises to pay a certain sum at a fixed future date to the other party. In many respects it is very similar to a post-dated cheque.

- When a financial intermediary accepts a bill of exchange it is effectively loaning money to a private trader upon promise of a refund by another trader.
- The bill is a contract between the two traders, with the buyer promising to pay a sum of money in return for goods on a certain date to the seller.
- The seller may sell the bill or cash to a financial intermediary who will discount it. A bank will discount the bill by paying less than the face value, knowing that it will receive the full value at a later date. The difference between the two sums of money is the interest.

Characteristics	
Return	• As stated above there is usually no interest paid but the return is the difference between the discounted amount for which it is sold/bought and the full face value on redemption. • For example, a bill bought for £4,900 is redeemed for £5,000 after three months. Thus £100 profit is made on an outlay of £4,900 over three months, giving a return of approximately 8.2 per cent per annum.
Risk	• The level of risk varies – some bills may be guaranteed by banks
Timescales	• Short term – 3 and 6 month maturities are the most common.
Liquidity	• Can be resold on money markets.

3.9 Inter-relationships

All the markets in a money market closely inter-mesh with each other and in that way the market may be regarded as an entity. The players are the same and they pass the ball between each other.

However, since the global "credit crunch" of 2008, the liquidity in the money markets has reduced as the different players have begun to view each other with suspicion. The credit crunch is covered in more detail later in this chapter.

Illustration 1 – Inter-relationships within money markets

- A large company might deposit $500,000 with Bull's Bank, which issues it with a CD.
- Bull's Bank then looks at the local authority market, decides that rates there are rather low, and instead lends the money for a week on the inter-bank market to another bank that is short of funds.
- A week later local authority rates have improved and Bull's Bank lends the $500,000 to a big city council.
- Meanwhile, the large company has decided to bring forward an investment project and wants its $500,000 quickly to help pay for some sophisticated new electronic equipment. It sells the CD to a bank, which might either carry it to maturity or sell it to any of the banks – except Bull's Bank.

All these transactions, with the possible exception of the CD deals, will have taken place through a broker who sits at the end of a telephone switching the funds from one market to another as rates move and potential borrowers and lenders acquaint the broker with information about their requirements.

Test Your Understanding 6

Ian has surplus funds that he wishes to invest. Which of the following would be the least risky investment?

A Certificates of deposit from a global bank.

B Equity shares in a new growing company.

C Unsecured loan stock

D National lottery tickets

Test Your Understanding 7

Which of the following is not a characteristic of bills of exchange?

A Interest is paid monthly

B Can be resold on money markets

C Maturities typically between 3 and 6 months

D May be guaranteed by banks

4 Calculating yields on financial products

4.1 Equity

The total return to shareholders will incorporate both dividends and growth in the share price.

Dividend yield is measured as:

$$\text{Dividend Yield} = \frac{\text{dividend per ordinary share}}{\text{market price of the share}} \times 100\%$$

Thus if a company is paying 30 cents per ordinary share and each share has market price of $7.50 then the dividend yield would be:

$$\frac{30 \text{ cents}}{750 \text{ cents}} \times 100\% = 4\%$$

This figure looks only at the current dividend so does not incorporate future growth expectations.

4.2 Bonds

There are a number of different ways of calculating the yield on bonds:

(a) the bill rate

(b) the running rate or interest yield

(c) the gross redemption yield

Illustration 2 – Yields on bonds

Consider a bond with characteristics as follows:

- Nominal value $100
- Coupon rate 8%
- Redemption terms – to be redeemed at par in 5 years time
- Current market value – $108.40

Calculate the following yields:

(a) Bill rate

(b) Running yield

(c) Gross redemption yield

Solution

(a) The bill rate – this is just another name for the coupon rate, here 8%.

This rate does not consider the market value of the bond or the capital gain/loss on redemption.

(b) The running yield, also known as the "interest yield", given by

Running yield = (annual interest/market value) × 100% = (8/108.40) × 100% = 7.38%

If you bought the bond for $108.40, then annual interest of $8 gives a return of 7.38% on your investment each year. Note that this approach takes into account the market value of the bond but ignores the impact of a capital gain or loss on redemption

(c) The gross redemption yield

The gross redemption yield gives the annualised overall return to the investor and incorporates both interest and capital gains and losses. For the above bond the gross redemption yield is 6%. Note this is lower than the running yield because it incorporates the loss you would make on redemption – you bought the bond for $108.40 but it gets redeemed at $100.

Calculation of gross redemption yield is outside the syllabus but the principles are still useful to see:

The redemption yield is the required return of investors, which is determined primarily by their perceived risks but also by interest rates.

This then determines the market price as follows:

Market price = Present value of future receipts (interest and redemption proceeds), discounted at the investors' required return

To calculate the redemption yield involves doing this process in reverse – given the market value, what discount rate satisfies MV = PV of future receipts?

4.3 The role of risk

As stated above, the main determinant of the overall yield to an investor is their perceived risk.

This in turn determines the market price for the bond or share.

Suppose a company is currently paying a dividend of 20 cents per share and is expected to do so in the future. If the share price is $1, then the net dividend yield will be 20%. Suppose that adverse environmental factors then cause investors to consider the shares more risky so that they now want a return of 25%. If the company still pays 20 cents per share, then the only way the yield can rise to 25% is if the share price falls:

Net dividend yield = (annual dividend/market value) × 100%

0.25 = (0.20/market value) × 100%

This would give a revised market value of 80 cents.

The order is very important here:

Risk determines required return, which determines the market value.

4.4 The term structure of interest rates and yield curves

Most people believe that the annual interest rate on a loan remains the same regardless of period of the loan. So, if the interest rate charged on a two-year loan was 5% then it would be 5% on a six-year loan of the same risk class.

However, lenders in the financial markets normally demand higher interest rates on loans as the term (i.e. length of time) to maturity increases – that is there is a 'term structure' of the interest rate. The yield curve shows this relationship.

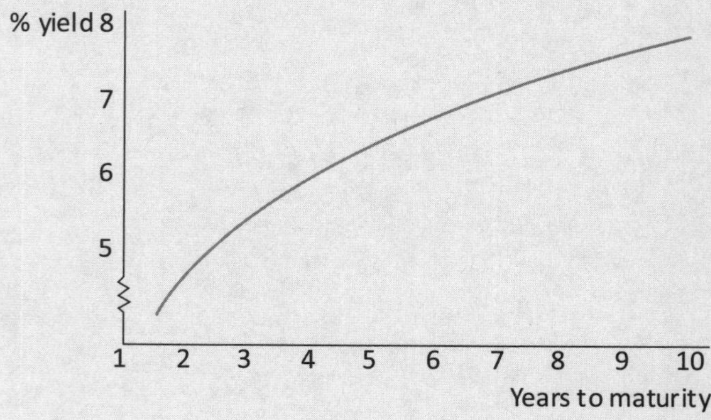

The longer the term of a security, the higher will be its gross redemption yield – the return to the investor.

Analysis of term structure is normally carried out by examining risk-free securities such as UK government stocks, also called gilts. Newspapers such as the Financial Times show the gross redemption yield (i.e. interest yield plus capital gain/loss to maturity) and time to maturity of each gilt on a daily basis.

The normal shape of the yield curve would suggest that it is cheaper to borrow in the shorter term. For example, if a firm wishes to borrow for ten years, then it would be cheaper to take out a five-year loan and then replace it with another five year loan (in five years, time) than to take out a single ten-year loan.

The main reasons why some firms do not do this are:

- Risk – the ten-year loan could be arranged with a fixed rate for the whole term. If two five-year loans are used, then the rate for the second loan would depend on prevailing rates in five years' time, which could be higher than current rates.
- Arrangement fees.

One way of linking risk and yield structures for bonds is through credit rating agencies.

Supplementary reading – Credit rating agencies

The role of credit rating agencies

If a company wants to assess whether a firm that owes them money is likely to default on the debt, a key source of information is a credit rating agency.

They provide vital information on creditworthiness to:

- potential investors
- regulators of investing bodies
- the firm itself.

The assessment of creditworthiness

A large number of agencies can provide information on smaller firms, but for larger firms credit assessments are usually carried out by one of the international credit rating agencies. The three largest international agencies are Standard and Poor's, Moodys and Fitch.

Certain factors have been shown to have a particular correlation with the likelihood that a company will default on its obligations:

- The magnitude and strength of the company's cash flows.
- The size of the debt relative to the asset value of the firm.
- The volatility of the firm's asset value.
- The length of time the debt has to run.

Using this and other data, firms are scored and rated on a scale, where AAA is the least risky (investment grade) and C would be much more risky ("junk" bonds)

Credit spreads

There is no way to tell in advance which firms will default on their obligations and which won't. As a result, to compensate lenders for this uncertainty, firms generally pay a "spread" or premium over the risk-free rate of interest.

The yield on a corporate bond is therefore given by:

> Required yield on corporate bond = Yield on equivalent treasury bond + credit spread

Credit rating agencies publish tables of credit spreads detailing the premium for bonds of differing risks and maturities.

For example, suppose a company wants to issue some 5 year bonds with a credit rating of BB. The required yield would be made up of two elements

- The expected yield on the yield curve for 5 years – suppose this is 4%
- A premium (the credit spread) to reflect the maturity of 5 years and the credit rating of BB – suppose this is 2.5%
- The required yield on the new bonds would thus be 4% + 2.5% = 6.5%

Test Your Understanding 8

A $100 stock with market price of $80 and a dividend of $5 will generate a yield of:

A 5%

B 8%

C 6.25%

D 12.5%

Test Your Understanding 9

Which of the following yields does not need knowledge of a bond's market value to calculate it?

A Running yield

B Gross redemption yield

C Bill rate

D Interest yield

5 Understanding interest rates

5.1 A central rate of interest

It is clear that there is no such thing as *the* rate of interest because there are many rates of interest, which reflect varying risk. However, there has always been a central rate around which the others vary and to which governments have paid great attention. This has usually been the rate at which the central bank would lend to the money market, based on the treasury bill rates (see below for further detail on how central banks set interest rates).

In 2010/11 in the UK the "base rate" was 0.5%. However, the rate that banks would lend to businesses was much higher with the end result that firms still struggled to borrow money at low rates.

5.2 Real and nominal interest rates

The real interest rate puts interest rates in the context of inflation. It shows the interest rate, allowing for inflation.

For example, suppose inflation is 3% and you deposit $100 in a deposit account paying 4% per annum

- The "nominal" or "money" rate of interest is 4% so you will end up with $104 in the account
- However, you are not 4% better off. 3% of the increase merely covers inflation so you will feel that your wealth has only increased by around 1%. This is the "real" rate of interest received.

Note: You will not be expected to do calculations on real and money rates. However, the correct way of determining the real rate in the above example would be

$1 + r = (1 + m)/(1 + i)$, where r = real rate, m = money rate and i = level of inflation

$1 + r = 1.04/1.03 = 1.0097$, giving $r = 0.0097$ or 0.97%

When the nominal rate of interest is higher than the rate of inflation there is a positive real rate. This means that borrowers are losing in real terms but savers are gaining.

Conversely, when the rate of inflation exceeds the nominal rate of interest there is a negative real rate of interest. In such a case, borrowers gain and savers lose.

For decision-making by individuals and businesses, it is the real rate of interest which is the important variable.

5.3 Determining interest rates

The interest rate can be viewed as the "price" of money determined by market forces of supply and demand.

Demand

The demand for money is the preference for holding one's financial assets in the fully liquid form of cash rather than in some relatively illiquid form such as bonds and shares. This is due to 3 motives:

- The transactions motive – people need to buy goods and services
- The precautionary motive – kept to meet unforeseen personal and financial contingencies

- The speculative motive – some people wish to hold money in order to speculate with it

Changes in the demand for money are unlikely to be very large in the short run although there may be significant seasonal variations in the demand for money.

Supply

The supply of money is different however since the supply of money is partly determined by the credit creation activities of the banks and a change in their policy and behaviour could affect the supply of money and hence the rate of interest.

Moreover, since the ability of banks to create credit is constrained by the supply of cash and very liquid assets in the financial system, central banks may be able to influence the supply of money and interest rates by effecting changes in the amount of liquid asset in the financial system.

Supplementary reading – Motives for holding cash

Transactions Motive

As money is a medium of exchange giving liquidity, and people need to buy goods and services, clearly they require money for this purpose. Such money is usually held in cash and current accounts.

The demand for money for transactions purposes will be largely affected by the following:

- *The level of real income.* As living standards rise, expenditure rises and hence the demand for money to finance those transactions will increase. Thus the supply of money needs to be increased over time to match this rise in expenditure.
- *The rate of inflation.* In periods of inflation the demand for money for transactions purposes will increase, not because there is an increase in the real volume of expenditure, but because the total monetary value of those transactions has risen due to the rise in prices.
- *The frequency of wage and salary payments.* People paid monthly will probably have a higher average current account balance than those paid weekly.

Precautionary Motive

As money acts as a store of value, people wish to keep it in order to meet unforeseen personal and financial contingencies.

- Such money tends to be held by individuals in bank and building society deposit accounts which are fairly accessible in an emergency.
- However, the expansion of private insurance, the wider provision of state benefits and the ease of transfer between deposit and current accounts have meant that people commit less income to saving for this purpose.
- It is unlikely that small increases in income affect the level of precautionary demand for money, although generally those on higher incomes tend to have higher savings balances.
- However, there is a clear link between precautionary savings and inflation. At times of rapid inflation, people tend to save more so as to maintain the real value of their money balances in case of emergency.

Speculative Motive

As money gives immediate liquidity, some people wish to hold money in order to speculate with it.

- An individual may hold cash ready to undertake potentially profitable risks, varying from betting to the purchase of assets. The amount of money held for speculation is largely dependent on individual income levels.
- However, the main money speculators are financial institutions, rather than individuals.
- Potential speculators are interested in the real rate of interest from asset buying. Thus their calculations take into account inflation. As a simple general rule, it is probably reasonable to say that the speculative demand for money is lowest at times of highest inflation, other things being equal. This is because money held ready for a suitable speculation is losing its value even more quickly at times of rapid inflation, and potential speculators recognise this real cost.
- Since there is an inverse relationship between interest rates and bond / share prices, the demand for money for speculative purposes is related to expectations about future movements in interest rates. If interest rates are expected to rise (fall) in the immediate future, investors will expect a fall (rise) in bond and share prices. In these circumstances they will wish to hold large (small) amounts of cash and relatively smaller (larger) amounts of bonds and shares.

Test Your Understanding 10

Daniella has received a salary increase from €30,000 to €36,000 per annum. Given inflation for the next year is expected to be 5%, what percentage increase in salary has Daniella received in ***real*** terms?

Answer____________% (give your answer as a percentage to one decimal place)

Test Your Understanding 11

Which of the following are the likely consequences of a fall in interest rates?

(i) A rise in the demand for consumer goods.
(ii) A fall in investment.
(iii) A fall in government spending.
(iv) A rise in the demand for housing.

A (i) and (ii) only
B (i), (ii) and (iii) only
C (i), (iii) and (iv) only
D (ii), (iii) and (iv) only

Test Your Understanding 12

The following financial data refer to an economy for the period 2001–2006.

	2001	*2002*	*2003*	*2004*	*2005*	*2006*
Interest rates						
Bank base rate (%)	8.5	7.0	5.5	6.8	5.8	6.0
Instant-access account deposit rate (%)	6.3	4.9	3.8	4.2	2.8	2.3
90-day-access account deposit rate (%)	8.8	6.2	4.5	4.9	3.9	3.9
Mortgage rate	11.0	9.4	7.7	8.4	7.0	7.4
Share prices						
Stock market index	2521	2900	2919	2314	3711	4710
Inflation						
Percentage rise in consumer prices	4.0	1.6	2.3	3.5	2.7	2.7

Required:

Using *both* your knowledge of economic theory and material contained in the table:

(a) With respect to the data given:
- (i) using the bank base rate calculate the real rate of interest for 2003;
- (ii) calculate the real mortgage rate of interest for 2004;
- (iii) state whether real share prices rose or fell between 2002 and 2003.

(3 marks)

(b) State whether each of the following are true or false.
- (i) Rising real interest rates will encourage savings and investment.
- (ii) Interest rates will only affect business investment if that investment is financed by borrowing.
- (iii) Rising interest rates in a country tend to raise the exchange rate for that country's currency.
- (iv) Producers of consumer durable goods are more sensitive to changes in interest rates than supermarkets.
- (v) Central banks cannot increase the money supply and raise interest rates at the same time.

(5 marks)

(c) State whether the effect of a rise in interest rates will be to
  (i) increase or decrease government spending;
  (ii) reflate or deflate the economy.

(2 marks)
(Total marks = 10)

6 Financial intermediaries

6.1 Introduction

It is common to split financial intermediaries into two types:

(1) Deposit-taking institutions (DTIs), such as banks and building societies

(2) Non-deposit-taking institutions (NDTIs), such as insurance companies, pension funds, unit trust and investment trusts.

This distinction is made for three reasons:

- The deposit liabilities of DTIs form the bulk of a country's money supply (see below) so DTIs are more important to government economic policy and, hence, Central bank attention.
- DTIs are subject to more regulation.
- The level customers deposit is more discretionary than other products (e.g. once an insurance contract is entered into, the customer is committed to making monthly payments).

6.2 Banks

The main business of banks includes offering financial services, taking deposits and extending credit. In the UK their activities are regulated by the Financial Services Authority (FSA).

Banking activities are traditionally split between the following:

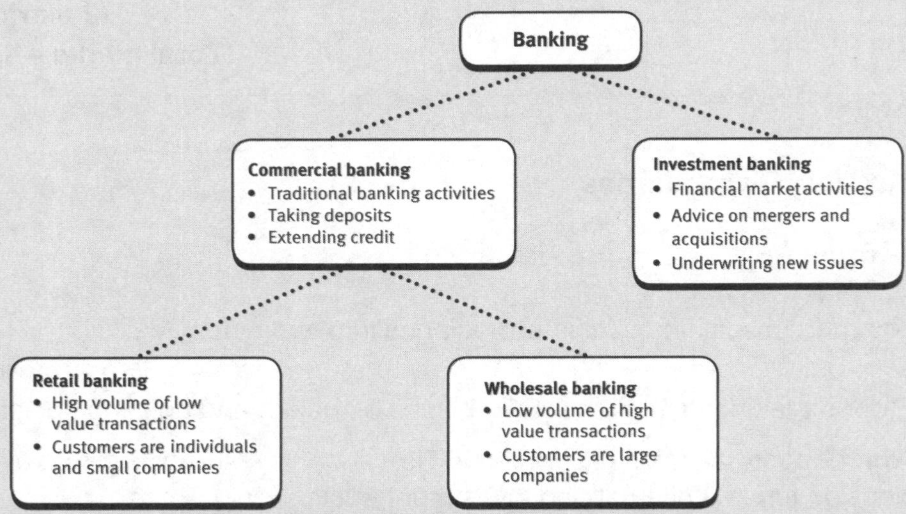

Supplementary reading – Financial organisations

Retail banks

The retail or commercial banks' main activities are as follows.

Safeguarding money

Customers' deposits are kept in deposit and current accounts.

- *Deposit (time)* accounts are operated for savers who receive interest for storing their money at the bank. The rate of interest received varies with movements in the bank's base rate. If interest rates in the money market rise, then bank base rate is increased so depositors receive more interest on their deposits.
- *Current (sight)* accounts do not usually gain significant amounts of interest, although they do provide the holder with a chequebook facility. Customers can settle debts by writing cheques or by using debit cards, and also withdraw cash on demand (i.e. no charges) in current accounts while the customer stays in credit.
- The distinction between deposit and current accounts is becoming less clear cut, as banks devise new financial instruments. For example, high interest cheque accounts continue the traditional features of deposit and current accounts and were invented to attract specific customers.

Transferring money

Banks move cash between their branches when required. In operating the cheque clearing system they transfer money between accounts within a branch, between different branches and between different banks.

- Each clearing bank has an account at the central bank. In effect, every time one of a bank's customers writes a cheque, which is presented at another bank, the payer's bank has its account at the central bank debited. Conversely, the recipient's bank has its account credited. In practice, at daily clearing, each bank totals up its accounts with every other bank and the net amount owed (or gained) is deducted from (or credited to) its account.
- This is a money transmission service. It is also undertaken by the use of direct debits, standing orders and credit transfers.

Lending money

When goldsmiths realised that only a small proportion of their gold deposits was required daily, they decided to put the gold to work by lending and charging interest. The banks perform a similar profit-earning function by providing loans and overdrafts to customers. Generally the rates of interest charged to businesses are less than those levied on personal borrowing. Such loans generally take two forms:

- When a customer has a current account, he or she might seek an *overdraft*. Usually, *overdrafts* are for short periods of time, allowing customers to write cheques to a value greater than the funds in the current account. Interest is charged on a daily basis on the actual amount by which the customer is overdrawn. This tends to be a cheaper form of borrowing, if prior authority is given by the bank. Overdrafts are more informal and more flexible than loans, although penalty rates of interest may be charged for unauthorised borrowing.
- *Loans.* These tend to be for larger amounts and over longer periods of time. They are often tied to particular purchases and are repaid over longer periods of time.

Facilitating trade

Modern banks provide numerous services which facilitate easier trading. The accepting of commercial bills and the provision of foreign exchange make international trade smoother in operation. Similarly the development of advisory services for small firms, the participation in loan guarantee schemes and the giving of financial advice and market information encourage domestic trade.

Wholesale banks

In addition to retail banks there are also wholesale banks. These are also known as investment or secondary banks. The most common of these banks are:

- merchant banks such as Morgan Grenfell
- overseas banks operating in countries other than their home country.

Merchant banks are banking brokers who bring together the lenders and borrowers of large sums of money, for example business companies. Merchant banks:

- Operate in a high-risk area and deal in very large deposits and loans primarily from industry and commerce. They often borrow from each other on what is known as the *inter-bank market*.
- Advise companies on money management.
- Negotiate bills of exchange. A bill of exchange is a trading contract, usually for three months, upon which a trader can usually get credit.
- Underwrite the launching of new shares, for example Lazard Bros. organised the privatisation of Britoil in 1985.
- Supervise company takeovers on the stock market.
- As accepting houses, they guarantee commercial bills for companies.

They are thus wholesalers of money in the system.

Also, overseas banks now operate in most financial centres and their banking activity is mainly related to:

- financing international trade
- international capital movements
- international currency transactions.

In practice the distinction between retail and wholesale banks has become less clear in recent years. Many banks which previously operated only as retail banks have taken on many of the functions of wholesale banks, especially in relational to international transactions. They have often achieved this by setting up or acquiring specialist subsidiary companies.

Discount houses are another type of unofficial bank, which are unique to Britain. These nine institutions operate in the money market by borrowing from the commercial banks for a short period (which may be as little as overnight) and lending for up to three months. They make a profit on the difference between the interest rate paid and charged.

Non-bank financial intermediaries

These institutions are not officially authorised by the Bank of England, although they are informally watched. However, they often perform banking tasks and since financial deregulation in the 1980s they have competed with banks for business. The best-known type of non-bank in the United Kingdom is the building society. Some are owned by their members ('mutual' building societies), others by shareholders. They tend to 'borrow short' and 'lend long' (via mortgages), profiting from interest-rate differentials and fulfilling the function of *maturity transformation*.

Since the 1980s, building societies have become more independent and competitive. No longer are society interest rates kept in harmony by the Building Societies Association, so there is more competition between them. In addition, competition with banks and other authorised institutions has increased, particularly in home loans and high-interest, instant-access accounts. However, building societies are still constrained by the requirement that they can lend only a maximum of 5 per cent of their assets for personal finance. Many building societies have become banks in recent years.

Another trend has been the growth of financial conglomerates. Formerly financial institutions tended to specialise, for example building societies and mortgages. Now they are branching out into non-traditional lines of business and offering mortgages. The diversification has also brought estate agents, unit trusts and big High Street retailers into financial intermediaries. In the mid-1990s, several building societies decided to 'go public' and become banks. The process takes a while, such that it was not until 1997 that the Halifax, Woolwich and Alliance & Leicester emerged on to the stock market. Thus the distinction between banks and building societies is now blurred and institutions providing the entire range of financial services are dominating the financial system.

Many other financial institutions exist, mostly providing specialist financial services. The most important of these are:

- *Investment and unit trusts* which accept savings by selling shares and invest these savings, mainly in company shares;
- *Pension funds* which accept savings from their customers, both individuals and companies, normally on an ongoing basis, to invest and to provide retirement pensions for their customers
- *Insurance companies* which invest their premium income in a range of assets but mainly long term such as shares and property.

- *Finance companies* which provide medium-term credit for business and individual customers. Others act as leasing companies (leasing out capital equipment to businesses) and factoring companies (providing funds for businesses using their creditors as collateral).

6.3 Credit creation

The credit multiplier

Banks create credit as a way of making profit. They are able to do this because not all of the cash that is deposited at a bank will be regularly withdrawn. Furthermore, when a bank lends money to a borrower, some of that money may be deposited back in the bank by another customer who deals with the borrower. This provides more cash reserves. In practice, the banks have discovered that at most 10 per cent of the deposited cash will be withdrawn, thereby leaving the remainder for loans and/or investment. This percentage is known as the cash ratio.

Illustration 3 – Credit creation

The use of the cash ratio makes possible the multiple creation of credit by banks. Suppose the following sequence occurs.

- A bank opens with a deposit by 'customer A' of $1,000 on day 1.
- On day 2 the bank manager decides, on the basis of the 10 per cent cash ratio, to make a loan to business woman 'B' of $900.
- In the course of their business dealing, 'B' pays $400 to 'C', who banks at the same bank.
- When 'C' pays in $400 on day 3, this raises the cash at the bank to $500 and total liabilities (deposit accounts) to $1,400.
- These liabilities only necessitate $140 in cash (i.e. 10 per cent ratio) which means that the bank can put the 'excess' cash of $360 to work. This is done on day 4 when investments to that account are made. This broadens the bank's asset structure.
- Alternatively, the bank could have lent the $360 to another customer seeking a loan.

This sequence can be shown as follows:

	Liabilities		Assets	
Day one	Deposit	A – 1,000	Cash	1,000
Day Two	Deposit	A – 1,000	Cash B-loan	100 900
Day Three	Deposit	A – 1,000 C – 400	Cash B-loan	500 900
Day Four	Deposit	A – 1,000 C – 400	Cash B-loan Investment	140 900 360

The process of credit creation can continue as long as the ratio of cash/liquid assets to total deposits is maintained. The term 'deposit multiplier' (or credit multiplier) denotes the amount by which total deposits can increase as a result of the bank acquiring additional cash. This amount equals the reciprocal of the cash ratio:

$$\text{Change in total deposits} = \frac{1}{\text{cash ratio}} \times \text{the initial cash deposit}$$

Hence a cash ratio of 10% gives a balance sheet multiplier of 10: the total increase in the money supply is ten times the initial cash deposit. The credit multiplier (the amount by which credit expands in the economy) is, strictly speaking, the balance sheet multiplier –1, since 10% of the rise in the balance sheet consists of the initial cash deposit rather than created credit.

Thus the amount of credit that banks can create depends on two factors:

- the cash and near cash liquid assets they hold.
- the size of the credit multiplier

6.4 Central banks

All countries have a central bank: in the United Kingdom, the Bank of England; in the USA, the Federal Reserve Board; in the eurozone, the European Central Bank and in Japan, the Bank of Japan. These are normally government-owned organisations. Although the functions of central banks vary a little from country to country, there are some common functions of these organisations.

The main functions of central banks are as follows.

Banker to the banks

All commercial banks keep accounts at the central bank. These accounts:

- act as a liquid reserve for the commercial banks; thus acting as lender of the last resort
- facilitate transfers from one bank to another arising out of the cheque clearing system.

In most countries these accounts are compulsory and must be equal to a minimum percentage of the commercial banks liabilities.

Banker to the government

The central bank provides a range of banking services for the government and for government departments:

- accounts of government departments are held at the central bank and used in the same way as bank accounts in commercial banks; thus taxation revenue is paid into, and government expenditure paid out of these accounts;
- debt management which involves organising the raising of new borrowing for government when they run budget deficits, redeeming old debts when they run budget surpluses and managing the national debt.
- the central bank operates monetary policy on behalf of the government and is largely concerned with managing the supply of money in the economy, rates of interest and the rate of exchange for the currency.
- it manages the country's reserves of foreign currency; in the United Kingdom this is done through the Exchange and Equalization account which may be used to buy and sell sterling on the foreign exchange market in order to smooth out excessive fluctuations in the value of sterling.

Supervision of the banking system

The central bank normally has the duty of supervising the financial system and ensuring that the banks in the system meet the requirements laid down for them. These normally concern:

- *Capital adequacy*. To ensure that banks have sufficient capital to meet problems arising from business losses or loss of value in their assets, for example losses arising from bad debts.
- *Liquidity*. To ensure banks can meet the normal day-to-day requirements of their customers for cash.

In order to support the banking system should a problem of liquidity arise, the central bank also acts as *lender of the last resort*. In this role the central bank will be willing to rediscount bills or buy bank government stock ('repos') thus providing cash for the banking system.

The Bank of England and Northern Rock

In the autumn of 2007 the UK based building society Northern Rock faced major problems in raising the funds it needed to continue its business. This was the result of a shortage of credit in the inter-bank market where financial institutions lend to each other. The result was a growing fear that Northern Rock would collapse because of a shortage of liquidity. This fear led to customers withdrawing deposits and a classic 'run on the bank' ensued. In these circumstances the Bank of England stepped in and loaned up to £25 billion to Northern Rock albeit a rate of interest higher than prevailing market levels. In effect the Bank of England had acted as 'lender of the last resort'.

Note issue

The central bank has the sole right of note issue in an economy. These notes are liabilities on the central banks balance sheet and the matching assets are largely government securities. Paper currency is no longer backed by gold.

Supplementary reading – Central banks and monetary policy

The central bank can alter interest rates by selling or buying bank ('redeeming') government stock. The central bank buys and sells treasury and commercial bills, and government bonds in the money market. This activity is known as 'open market operations'.

- If it seeks a multiple contraction of credit it will sell bills. The cheques paying for them will be drawn on the banks, whose deposits will fall and whose balances at the Bank of England will be lowered. Their cash base will be lowered and their potential to create credit will be limited.
- If it seeks a multiple expansion of credit it will buy bills. The result will be an increase in the commercial banks deposits at the central bank and thus their cash base will be increased and their ability to create credit will be raised.

When selling bills in an attempt to restrict credit, the central bank may find that, in practice the commercial banks can restore their cash base by reclaiming money at call from the discount houses (in the United Kingdom) and other financial organisations.

- The discount houses when they find themselves short of cash always sell bills to the Bank of England. Since 1981, the arrangement has been that they offer the bills to the bank at the prevailing market rate, which the bank can accept or reject.
- Thus, if the Bank of England wishes to see interest rates rise, it rejects the market rate offered by the discount houses and offers to buy at a new higher interest rate, thus penalising the discount houses.
- As the discount houses do not wish to make losses on their own loans they raise interest rates and the increase is thus transmitted through the money market.

Thus the central bank can either restrict the credit creating ability of banks by reducing the amount of cash in the financial system or it can force a rise in interest rates through the system. A similar outcome can be achieved by central bank operations in the market for government longer-term securities (in the United Kingdom, 'gilt-edged' securities). If the central bank:

- increases its sales of government bonds, the price will fall and the effective interest rate (the yield) will rise;
- decreases its sales of government bonds, the price will rise and the effective interest rate (the yield) will fall.

In addition, the government and central bank might operate rather more directly on the ability of commercial banks to create credit through bank *assets ratios*. Banks are required to a proportion of their total assets in certain specified assets. The basic idea behind these ratios was to ensure *prudential standards of liquidity* but by varying these required ratios, the central banks could, in principle, affect the credit multiplier. In practice little sue is now made of this and most reliance is placed on open market operations and on interest rate policy.

Monetary policy in the UK

During the first half of 2008 the main concern of the Bank of England was the threat of rising inflation. The large rise in food and energy prices, especially the price of oil which rose to over $150 a barrel, was the main reason for a rise in rate of inflation which peaked at 5.2% in September. As a result the Bank kept interest rates at relatively high levels. Some members of the monetary policy committee voted for increases in rates despite the fears of one member, David Blanchflower, that the real threat was a collapse in house prices & a severe recession. By the autumn the threat of inflation had faded as food & energy prices fell, the price of oil to $40 a barrel in December, & the crisis in the banking system & the onset of a severe recession became the primary problems. The result was a rapid reversal of monetary policy. The Bank cut its interest rate by 0.5% in October, by 1.5% in November & by 1% in December. The result was the lowest Bank of England rate of interest for a generation ending up at 0.5%.

Less than a year later, prices were rising again and by late 2011 the rate of inflation was above 5%, reaching the highest annual rate since June 1991.Since then, inflation has falled back again, with inflation in 2015 now well below the Bank of England's 2% target rate for the first time since November 2009.

Test Your Understanding 13

Which *one* of the following is not a function of a central bank?

A Management of the National Debt

B Holder of the foreign exchange reserves

C The conduct of fiscal policy

D Lender of the last resort

(2 marks)

Test Your Understanding 14

(1) What is a cash ratio?

(2) What is the relationship between liquidity and profitability of banks assets?

(3) How could a central bank reduce the supply of credit in the financial system?

(4) How could a central bank reduce the demand for credit in the financial system?

(5) What are capital adequacy rules?

7 Financial markets

Financial markets

Financial institutions operate in a range of financial markets. The most important of these are:

- money markets
- capital markets
- international markets.

Money markets

In most economies, the financial markets are dominated by the *money market*. It is here that banks, companies, local authorities and the government operate via the discount houses in buying and selling short-term debt. The discount houses are described as market makers in bills. This is because they will buy (or sell) treasury and commercial bills to enable holders to transform their assets into liquidity (or their cash into paper financial assets).

One important element of this function is the obligation of the discount houses to purchase each week the full issue of treasury bills. These are issued in order to make up the difference between government expenditure and reserves. Other buyers may purchase most of the treasury bills but the discount houses guarantee to make good any shortfall in demand.

- The price which the discount house pays reflects the market rate of interest.
- A high bid price makes a low rate of interest, because the difference between the price paid and the maturity value (usually three months later) is effectively the interest paid on the loan.

- For example, a bill bought for £4,900 is redeemed for £5,000 after three months. Thus £100 profit is made on an outlay of £4,900 over three months, approximately 8.2 per cent per annum.

The main commercial bill is a bill of exchange (discussed earlier). These treasury and commercial bills are also often resold before maturity, again facilitating liquidity for the seller. The discount houses, in turn, raise their funds by borrowing 'money at call' from the banks, at very low rates of interest. They make a profit by charging slightly higher rates of interest when buying bills.

The 1970s and 1980s saw enormous financial innovation and the creation of new markets. These are known as *parallel money markets*. A key characteristic is that transactions are mainly between financial intermediaries, firms and local authorities but not the government. Secondary markets were developed in:

- bank liabilities, such as *certificates of deposit*
- and in bank assets, such as *resaleable bank loans*.

Such markets as the inter-bank market evolved to enable banks to accommodate fluctuations in customers' transactions by making loans to one another. With the increase in financial deregulation since the mid-1980s, new parallel markets in local authority debt, inter-company deposits and finance house borrowing have also sprung up.

The stock market

In the United Kingdom this encompasses several markets:

- the "full" equities/securities market where ordinary shares, preference shares and debentures are traded;
- the Alternative Investment Market (AIM) where smaller companies gain access to capital, under less stringent and less costly entry procedures;
- government bonds/gilts market where government sells short (up to 5 years) medium (5–15 years), long (over 15 years) and undated stock.

The phrase 'capital instruments' refers to the means (e.g. shares, bonds, etc.) by which organisations raise finance.

In October 1986 the 'Big Bang' occurred and the United Kingdom Stock Exchange radically changed. Its central function as a market for the purchase and sale of secondhand securities remained but its operations and procedures were reformed.

- Previously, an individual bought shares through a stockbroker.

- The broker acted as an adviser and an agent for his client (who was charged a commission) and bought shares from a stockjobber.
- The jobber was a dealer in securities who was willing to buy and sell at a price and hold on to unrequired shares. He did not deal with the general public.
- This system of single capacity was ended in October 1986 and the broker and jobbing functions were merged. The new dealer, of which there are about 200, has become known as a market-maker.

Equity market

Transactions in company securities are the most numerous but average only £15,000 per transaction. These can be subdivided into equities (ordinary shares) and loan capital securities.

- Equities bestow full voting rights on the shareholder and an entitlement to dividends, once the preference shareholders and the holders of loan capital have been paid out.
- Preference shareholders receive a fixed dividend and get their capital repaid before ordin-ary shareholders if a company is wound up.
- Company bond sand debentures do not confer ownership rights but their holders receive a fixed rate of interest over a set period of time. In 1978 'traded options' were introduced, whereby an option holder can buy/sell a quantity of a company's shares at a fixed price on a specified date.

In 1985, convertible securities became prominent. They combine both debt and equity. The holder of the debt has the option of converting to equity, if desired. The securities market performs two main functions:

- It is a primary market for newly issued shares. Typically, a company's new shares are issued by an issuing house with the help and advice of a stockbroker. There are several possible methods of issuing new shares – by an offer for sale, by placing, by tender and by public issue: issuing a prospectus.
- In addition, existing companies wishing to raise capital may introduce a rights issue. This gives existing shareholders the right to subscribe cash for more shares in proportion to their existing shareholdings. The stockbroker's involvement is to obtain stock exchange approval for the issue, which a merchant bank usually undertakes.
- A secondary market exists for the buying and selling of existing shares. Although this does not contribute to economic production, it has some value. It raises the liquidity of company shares because buyers of new issues know that they can sell in the future. In addition, the worth of a company can be calculated from its share price.

- Furthermore, a company can raise further capital by an issue of extra shares more easily and cheaply if it has a high market share price. This was very clear in the stock market boom of 1986–87.

The stock market is usually given as an example of a perfectly competitive market because there are many buyers and sellers with excellent knowledge and rapid reactions to price changes. Share prices are published daily and they reflect demand changes. For instance market-makers will 'mark down' the prices of shares for which they have a plentiful supply.

Alternative investment market (AIM)

In the United Kingdom there exists a market for shares in smaller companies. This was originally the Unlisted Securities Market (USM) set up in 1980. The purpose was to enable smaller companies raise sums up to £250,000 through share issues. The AIM which replaced the USM caters for smaller companies with none of the formal requirements regarding the age of the company and its market capitalisation for the main stock market.

Government bond market

Government stocks, such as Gilt-edged stocks in the United Kingdom, are fewer in number than shares but marketed in greater volume, averaging £250,000 per transaction on long dated stock.

- The method of sale since 1979 has been by tender rather than at a fixed price (tap).
- However, the Bank of England usually sets the minimum tender price and when there is an excess demand all allotments are made at the lowest accepted price. These bonds are sold in £100 units, usually at a fixed interest rate.

There is a wide choice of interest payments and redemption dates to make bonds attract-ive to buyers. The main buyers are pension funds and life assurance companies who are attracted by a fixed certain income.

- As explained elsewhere the market price varies with the interest payment (called the 'coupon').
- For example, if interest rates are around 5 per cent then a bond with a £10 coupon will trade at around £200 (10/200 = 5 per cent). If interest rates then rise to 6 per cent, the bond price will move to £166 (10/166 = 6 per cent).

The supply of bonds is determined by the stock of bonds, which basically constitute the national debt. Public sector borrowing, which necessitates debt sales, will increase the supply of bonds.

Test Your Understanding 15

Which of the following would be expected to lead to a rise in share prices on a stock market?

A A fall in interest rates

B A rise in the rate of inflation

C A fall in share prices in other stock markets

D An expected fall in company profits

Test Your Understanding 16

A 30 year Treasury bond that was issued last year is sold in a:

(i) money market
(ii) capital market
(iii) primary market
(iv) secondary market

A Both (i) and (iii)
B Both (i) and (iv)
C Both (ii) and (iii)
D Both (ii) and (iv)

8. Understanding the 2008 banking crisis and credit crunch

In 2008 there was global banking crisis which then led into a credit crunch and, for some countries, recession. This section looks at the causes of the banking crisis and the knock-on effects mentioned.

8.1 Contributory factors

Contributory factor 1: US sub-prime mortgage lending

In 2001 the US faced recession, due partly to the events of 9/11 and the Dot com bubble burst, so the US government was keen to stimulate growth. As part of this in 2003 the Federal Reserve responded by cutting interest rates to 1% – their lowest level for a long time.

Low Interest rates encouraged people to buy a house, resulting in house price rises. As house prices began to rise, mortgage companies relaxed their lending criteria and tried to capitalise on the booming property market. This boom in credit was also fuelled by US government pressure on lenders to grant mortgages to people who, under normal banking criteria, presented a very high risk of default. These were the so called 'sub-prime mortgages', with, many borrowers taking out adjustable rate mortgages that were affordable for the first two years.

This 'sub-prime market' expanded very quickly and by 2005, one in five mortgages in the US were sub-prime. Banks felt protected because house prices were continuing to rise so if someone defaulted the bank would recover its loan.

In 2006 inflationary pressures in the US caused interest rates to rise to 4%. Normally 4% interest rates are not particularly high but, because many had taken out large mortgage payments, this increase made the mortgage payments unaffordable. Also many homeowners were coming to the end of their 'introductory offers' and faced much higher payments. This led to an increase in mortgage defaults.

As mortgage defaults increased the boom in house prices came to an end and house prices started falling. In some areas the problem was even worse as there had been a boom in building of new homes which occurred right up until 2007. It meant that demand fell as supply was increasing causing prices to collapse, meaning that banks were no longer able to recover loans when borrowers defaulted. In many cases they were only ending up with a fraction of the house value.

Contributory factor 2: 'Collateralised debt obligations' or CDOs.

Normally if a borrower defaults it is the lending bank or building society that suffers the loss. As a result they are very diligent to verify the credit worthiness of potential borrowers and whether they have the income and security to repay loans. However, in the US mortgage lenders were able effectively to sell on mortgage debt in the form of CDOs to other banks and financial institutions. This was a kind of insurance for the mortgage companies. It means that other banks and financial institutions shared the risk of these sub-prime mortgages.

Using the income from their mortgage book as security, banks sold CDO bonds with a three-tier structure:

(1) Tier 1 was "senior" or "investment grade" and supposed to be very low risk but with a low return.

(2) Tier 2 was the "mezzanine tranche" and had medium risk and return

(3) Tier 3 was the "equity tranche" and had highest risk and return.

As money was received on mortgages, it was used to pay the Tier 1 bond holders their interest first, then Tier 2 and finally Tier 3, so if borrowers defaulted, then Tier 3 holders would suffer first and so on, like a waterfall effect.

Unfortunately losses were so great that Tier 3 and Tier 2 and in some cases Tier 1 investors were affected. At the very least, the value of Tier 1 bonds fell due to the perceived risks.

Contributory factor 3: Debt rating organisations

The CDO bonds were credit-rated for risk, just like any other bond issues. Maybe because these sub-prime mortgage debts were bought by 'responsible' banks like Morgan Stanley and Lehman Brothers, or maybe because they didn't fully understand the CDO structures, risk agencies gave risky Tier 1 debt bundles AAA safety ratings. Normally AAA would denote extremely low risk investments.

This encouraged many banks and financial institutions to buy them, not realising how risky their financial position was. The trillions of dollars of sub-prime mortgages issued in the US had thus become distributed across the global markets ending up as CDOs on the balance sheets of many banks around the world.

Many commentators have seen this factor as an example of a regulatory failure within the financial system.

Contributory factor 4: Banks' financial structure

Unlike most other commercial enterprises, banks are very highly geared with typically less than 10% of their asset value covered by equity. A drastic loss of asset value can soon wipe out a bank's equity account and it was this risk which led some banks to start selling their asset-backed securities on to the market.

However, the sellers in this restricted market could not find buyers; as a result, the values at which these "toxic assets" could be sold plummeted and many banks around the world found themselves in a position with negative equity.

Contributory factor 5: Credit default swaps

As an alternative (or addition) to using CDOs, the mortgage lenders could buy insurance on sub-prime debt through credit default swaps or CDSs.

For example, AIG wrote $440bn and Lehman Brothers more than $700bn-worth of CDSs. These were the first institutions to suffer when the level of defaults started to increase.

Warren Buffett called them "financial weapons of mass destruction"

8.2 Implications and consequences

Implication 1: The collapse of major financial institutions

Some very large financial institutions went bust and others got into serious trouble and needed to be rescued. For example,

- In September 2008 Lehman Brothers went bust. This was the biggest bankruptcy in corporate history. It was 10 times the size of Enron and the tipping point into the global crash, provoking panic in an already battered financial system, freezing short-term lending, and marking the start of the liquidity crisis.
- Also in September 2008 the US government put together a bail out package for AIG. The initial loan was for $85bn but the total value of this package has been estimated at between 150 and 182 billion dollars.
- In the UK the Bank of England lent Northern Rock £27 billion after its collapse in 2007.

Implication 2: The credit crunch

Banks usually rely on lending to each other to conduct every-day business. But, after the first wave of credit losses, banks could no longer raise sufficient finance.

For example, in the UK, the Northern Rock was particularly exposed to money markets. It had relied on borrowing money on the money markets to fund its daily business. In 2007, it simply couldn't raise enough money on the financial markets and eventually had to be nationalised by the UK government.

In addition to bad debts, the other problem was one of confidence. Because many banks had lost money and had a deterioration in their balance sheets, they couldn't afford to lend to other banks. Even banks that had stayed free of the problem began to suspect the credit worthiness of other banks and, as a result, became reluctant to lend on the inter-bank market.

The knock on effect was that banks became reluctant to lend to anyone, causing a shortage of liquidity in money markets. This made it difficult for firms to borrow to finance expansion plans as well as hitting the housing market.

Many companies use short-term finance rather than long-term. For example, rather than borrowing for, say 10 years, a company might take out a two-year loan, with a view to taking out another two-year loan to replace the first, and so on. The main reason for using this system of "revolving credit" is that it should be cheaper – shorter-term interest rates are generally lower than longer-term. The credit crunch meant that these firms could not refinance their loans causing major problems.

Implication 3: Government intervention

Many governments felt compelled to intervene, not just to prop up major institutions (e.g. Northern Rock and AIG mentioned above) but also to inject funds into the money markets to boost and stimulate liquidity.

Efforts to save major institutions involved a mixture of loans, guarantees and the purchase of equity. For example, in 2008/9 the UK government invested £45.5bn in the Royal Bank of Scotland, ending up with an 82% stake.

Usually, central banks try to raise the amount of lending and activity in the economy indirectly, by cutting interest rates. Lower interest rates encourage people to spend, not save. But when interest rates can go no lower, a central bank's only option is to pump money into the economy directly. That is quantitative easing (QE). The way the central bank does this is by buying assets – usually financial assets such as government and corporate bonds – using money it has simply created out of thin air. The institutions selling those assets (either commercial banks or other financial businesses such as insurance companies) will then have "new" money in their accounts, which then boosts the money supply.

By March 2012 the UK Government had injected £325bn into the financial system through quantitative easing.

The end result was that many governments found themselves with huge levels of debt with the corresponding need to repay high levels of interest as well as repay the debt.

Implication 4: Recession and "austerity measures"

The events described above resulted in a recession in many countries. Despite the falling tax revenues that accompany this, some governments would normally try to increase government spending as one measure to boost aggregate demand to stimulate the economy.

However, the high levels of national debt have resulted in governments doing the opposite and making major cuts in public spending. This is partly to be able to reduce the level of debt but also because of fears over credit ratings. If the rating agencies fear that a country will default on its debt, then its credit rating will be downgraded resulting in higher costs for future debt.

Implication 5: Problems refinancing government debt

In 2010/2011 some countries tried to refinance national debt by issuing bonds:

- A problem facing the Spanish government at the end of 2010/2011 was the need to raise new borrowing as other government debt reached maturity. Spain successfully sold new bonds totalling nearly €3bn on 12/1/11 in what was seen as a major test of Europe's chances of containing the debt crisis gripping parts of the region. This was in addition to the Spanish government cutting spending by tens of billions of euros, including cuts in public sector salaries, public investment and social spending, along with tax hikes and a pension freeze.
- The problem of refinancing is more severe for countries whose national debt has a short average redemption period (Greece is about 4yrs) but much less of a problem where the debt is long dated (e.g. the UK where the average maturity is about 14 years).

For others they needed help from other countries and the IMF.

- Greece received a €110bn rescue package in May 2010
- At the end of 2010 Ireland received a bailout from the EU, the UK and the IMF. The total cost is still being debated but could be as high as €85bn.
- In May 2011 Portugal received a bailout of €78bn.

For many, this was compounded by seeing their national debt downgraded by credit rating agencies:

- For example, on 20 September 2011, Italy had its debt rating cut by Standard & Poor's, to A from A+.

Implication 6: The Eurozone crisis and fears over "contagion"

The above issues of governments trying to boost their economies while reducing national debt have been particularly visible within the Eurozone. This is due to a number of factors:

- As well as trying to manage their own economies, governments of countries within the Eurozone are committed (at least in theory) to staying within the rules of the Eurozone - for example, that debt should not exceed 60% of GDP.

- Concerns over the possibility of Greece defaulting on its loans have resulted in Eurozone ministers insisting on even greater austerity measures before they will release further funds. At one point commentators wondered whether Greece would vote to stop being part of the Eurozone. The cost of Greece dropping out of the Eurozone was estimated at over one trillion euros.
- Credit rating agencies have been concerned about "contagion" - i.e. the possibility of problems in countries such as Greece spreading throughout the Eurozone, possibly resulting in the collapse of the Euro as a major currency. For example, on 13 January 2012, credit rating agency Standard & Poor's downgraded France and eight other Eurozone countries, blaming the failure of Eurozone leaders to deal with the debt crisis.
- By February 2013 ongoing fears over a continuing recession led to the credit rating agency Moody's downgrading the UK's rating from AAA to AA+.

Supplementary reading – UK National Debt

History of UK national debt

After a period of financial restraint, national debt fell to 29% of GDP in 2002. Despite a long period of economic expansion, this then increased to 37% in 2007. This was primarily due to the government's decision to increase spending on health and education. There had also been a marked rise in social security spending.

In 2011, national debt increased sharply to 64% of GDP because of:

- Recession (lower tax receipts, higher spending on unemployment benefits)
- Financial bailout of Northern Rock, RBS and other banks.

In December 2014, national debt reached 90% of GDP.

However, the debt situation can be improved through:

- Economic growth which improves tax revenues and reduces spending on benefits
- Improved performance of banks increases prospect of regaining financial sector intervention
- Government spending cuts and tax rises (e.g. VAT) which improve public finances.(However, there is also a danger spending cuts could reduce economic growth and therefore hamper attempts to improve tax revenues.)

Note that other countries have a much bigger problem.

- Japan – 227%,
- Italy - 132%
- US – 102%.

Also the UK has had much higher national debt. e.g. after the second world war it was over 180% of GDP.

Cost of National Debt

The cost of National debt is the interest the government has to pay on the bonds and gilts it sells. In 2015, the debt interest payments show an annual cost of around £57bn (3.2% of GDP).

Test Your Understanding 17

One contributory factor to the financial crisis that started in 2008/9 was the way lenders were able to repackage mortgages as three tier bonds with different risk profiles. These bonds were known as what?

A CDFs

B CDAs

C CDOs

D CDs

Test Your Understanding 18

What is the main reason why governments would not normally consider using quantitative easing to boost economic growth?

A It would result in the government having to increase taxes to pay for it.

B It would generate high inflationary pressure.

C It would result in excessive savings, thus creating a leakage in the economy.

D It would crowd out private investment

Test your understanding answers

Test Your Understanding 1

C

The time period money is lent/borrowed is called the maturity.

Test Your Understanding 2

B

By definition

Test Your Understanding 3

D

The easiest way to see this is to consider the timescales involved. The car is a medium term asset and so should be financed using medium term finance.

A mortgage (A) is long term and more suitable for buying a house.

(B) and (C) are short term methods of finance more used to manage short term discrenecies between receipts and payments.

Test Your Understanding 4

B

The easiest way to see this is to consider the timescales involved. The shortfall is short term and relates to the lack of synchronisation between receipts and payments.

Both share issues (A) and mortgages (D) are long term and more suitable for buying new premises or buying a competitor.

(C) is a medium term method of finance more used to acquire plant and machinery or motor vehicles.

Test Your Understanding 5

D

Mezzanine finance is a type of 'middle ground' finance which has characteristics of both debt and equity.

Test Your Understanding 6

A

Risk looks at the degree of uncertainty of future cash flows. The CD will be the least risky out of the options given.

(B) – equity is normally considered high risk but may give high returns

(C) – the loan stock is unsecured making it more risky

(D) – Lottery tickets are highly risky and will most likely result in Ian having much less money at the end than he started with.

Test Your Understanding 7

A

Interest is not normally paid but the "return" comes from the difference between the discounted value when buying and the full redemption value.

Test Your Understanding 8

C

The yield of an asset is the relationship between the income derived from it and the price that has to be paid to acquire it. In this case the market price is $80 and the income gained is $5. The yield in percentage terms is $5 divided by $80 3 100. This is 6.25%

Test Your Understanding 9

C

The bill rate is the same as the coupon rate

(A) and (D) are the same as can be calculated as (annual interest / market value) × 100%

(B) involves determing the discount rate at which the market value = present value of future receipts (interest and redemption).

Test Your Understanding 10

Answer = 14.3%

- Increase in money terms = "m" = 20%
- Inflation = "i" = 5 %
- 1 + r = (1 + m)/(1 + i) = 1.20/1.05 = 1.143, giving r = 14.3%

Test Your Understanding 11

C

A fall in interest rates will encourage investment, not a fall. Lower interest rates reduce government expenditure on servicing the national debt, and will encourage consumers to take on more credit, including borrowing for house purchase. Thus C is the correct solution.

Test Your Understanding 12

(a)

- (i) 3.1%
- (ii) 4.9%
- (iii) fell

(b)

- (i) *False*. High interest rates encourage savings but discourage business investment.
- (ii) *False*. A rise in interest rates raises the opportunity cost of using internal funds to finance investment.
- (iii) *True*. Higher interest rates encourage capital inflows which increase the demand for the currency.
- (iv) *True*. Consumer durables are often bought on credit.
- (v) *True*. If the supply of money increases, its price, the rate of interest, will go down.

(c) A rise in interest rate would:
raise government spending as the cost of financing government debt would increase.
deflate the economy since it would discourage expenditure.

Test Your Understanding 13

C

Fiscal policy is concerned with the government budget and the balance of taxation and public expenditure. This is the responsibility of the government, not the central bank.

Test Your Understanding 14

(1) The amount of cash kept by banks in readiness to pay withdrawals as a proportion of their total assets.

(2) The most liquid assets, for example cash, are the least profitable; and the least liquid assets, for example advances and loans to customers, are the most profitable.

(3) The central bank would need to reduce the liquidity of the financial system as this is the basis upon which credit is created. It can do this by selling government stocks to financial institutions.

(4) The central bank could raise interest rates as interest is the price of credit and a higher price will reduce demand.

(5) Capital adequacy rules attempt to ensure that banks have sufficient capital to cover potential bad debts on risk assets.

Test Your Understanding 15

A

A fall in company profits would clearly discourage the purchase of shares and so share prices would fall. Since stock markets are linked, a fall in one market tends to lead to a fall in share prices in other markets. A rise in inflation would lead to some business pessimism and might be expected to lead to a rise in interest rates. However, since share prices and interest rates move in opposite directions, A is the correct solution.

Test Your Understanding 16

D

The bond can be sold in a capital market and a secondary market.

Test Your Understanding 17

C

CDO = Collateralised debt obligations

Test Your Understanding 18

B

Quantitative easing is not "normally" considered as it would rapidly increase the money supply, resulting in high inflation.

Instead other measures, such as reducing interest rates could be considered. However, during the ongoing financial crisis many countries already have very low interest rates and the threat of high inflation is not considered significant compared to the need to boost liquidity in the banking system and hence the economy.

chapter

6

The Macroeconomic Context of Business I: The Domestic Economy

Chapter learning objectives

After completing this chapter you should be able to:

- explain determination of macroeconomic phenomena, including equilibrium national income, growth in national income price inflation, unemployment, and trade deficits and surpluses
- explain the stages of the trade cycle, its causes and consequences for the policy choices of government
- explain the consequences of the trade cycle for organisations
- explain the main principles of public finance (i.e. deficit financing, forms of taxation) and macroeconomic policy
- describe the impacts on organisations of potential policy responses of government, to each stage of the trade cycle.

Overview

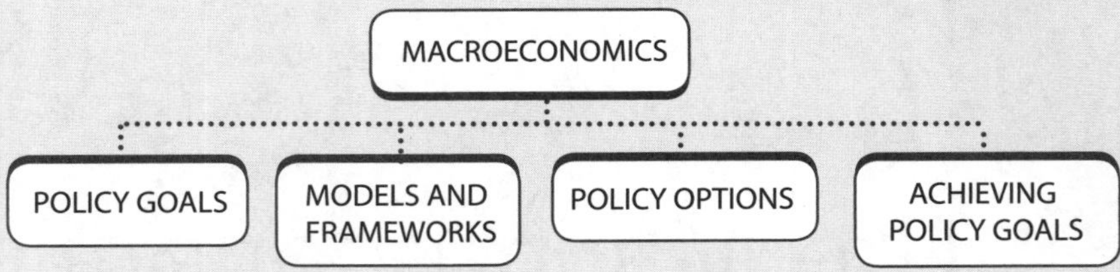

In this chapter we will look at macro-economics and the domestic economy by focussing on the following:

- *Policy goals* – after explaining what is meant by "macro-economics" we will look at the different policy goals that face all governments:
  - growing the economy,
  - reducing inflation,
  - creating jobs and
  - managing trade with other countries.
- *Models and frameworks* – to understand how to achieve these goals there are a number of economic models and frameworks you need to understand first. These include:
  - how to measure the size of the economy,
  - the circular flow of funds model and its components,
  - how to apply supply and demand arguments to the whole economy and
  - different economic schools of thought, including Classical, Keynesian and Monetarist viewpoints
- *Policy options* – next we look at the range of policy options available to governments, including:
  - fiscal and
  - monetary policies.
- *Achieving policy goals* – finally we consider the range of policies that could be implemented to try to achieve the policy goals we started with and their likely implications.

1 Macroeconomics and government policy goals

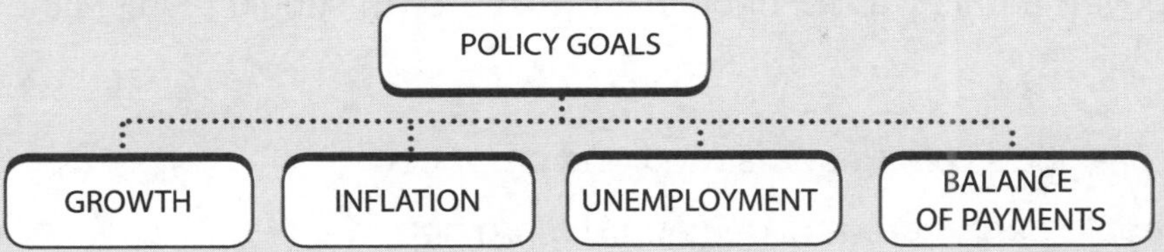

1.1 Macroeconomics

In Chapter 3 we looked at the interaction of supply and demand in individual markets. Macroeconomics focuses on the workings of the economy as a whole, including:

- the overall ('aggregate') demand for goods and services
- the output of goods and services ('national output' or 'national product')
- the supply of factors of production
- total incomes earned by providers of factors of production ('national income')
- money spent in purchasing the national product ('national expenditure')
- government policy.

These will be discussed in more detail throughout this chapter.

1.2 Government macroeconomic policy

Typically, governments will have four macroeconomic policy objectives:

- Economic growth – how can productive capacity be increased?
- Inflation – how can we ensure that general price levels do not increase?
- Unemployment – how can we ensure that everyone who wants a job has one?
- Balance of payments – how should we manage our financial relationships and trade with other countries?

1.3 Stagnation and economic growth

Most governments want economic growth. Growth should result in the following:

- more goods being demanded and produced
- people earn more and can afford more goods
- more people should have jobs.

On the face of it, therefore, growth should result in an improved standard of living in a country and higher profitability for businesses.

However, growth is not without its problems.

- Is economic growth fast enough to keep up with population growth?
- Growth rates have to exceed inflation rates for benefits to arise (i.e. "real" growth has to occur).
- Growth may be in 'demerit' goods, such as illegal drugs.
- Growth may be at the expense of the environment or through exploitation of the poor.
- The gap between rich and poor may grow, as the benefits from growth are not evenly distributed.
- Rapid growth means rising incomes and this often 'sucks in' imports, worsening the balance of trade, rather than benefiting domestic producers.

1.4 Inflation

Most governments want stable prices and low inflation. The main reasons given include the following:

- Inflation causes uncertainty and stifles business investment.
- Not all incomes rise in line with inflation – the poor and those on fixed incomes suffer the most.
- In extreme cases of inflation, the function of money may break down, resulting in civil unrest.
- Inflation distorts the working of the price mechanism and is thus a market imperfection.

Note that high inflation can affect savings in different ways:

- inflation erodes the future purchasing power of funds so people may decide to save less but spend more now.
- an alternative argument is that higher prices reduce individuals' real wealth and so they spend less. This could result in higher savings (the "real balance" effect).

1.5 Unemployment

Even in a healthy economy some unemployment will arise as people change jobs. However, mass unemployment is a problem due to the following:

- The government has to pay out benefits to the unemployed at a time when its tax receipts are low. This can result in the government having to raise taxes, borrow money and cut back on services.
- Unemployment has been linked to a rise in crime, poor health and a breakdown in family relationships.
- Unemployment is a waste of human resources and can restrict economic growth.

High unemployment could give firms higher bargaining power allowing them to pay lower wages to prospective employees.

1.6 Balance of payments

In the long-term government seeks to establish a broad balance between the value of imports into, and exports from, the country.

To run a persistent surplus or deficit can have negative macroeconomic effects.

- A long-term trade deficit has to be financed. The financing costs act as a major drain on the productive capacity of the economy.
- A long-term trade surplus can cause significant inflationary pressures, leading ultimately to a loss in international confidence in the economy and a lack of international competitiveness.

1.7 Trade cycles

Many economies exhibit fluctuations in economic activity over time with an underlying trend of output growth.

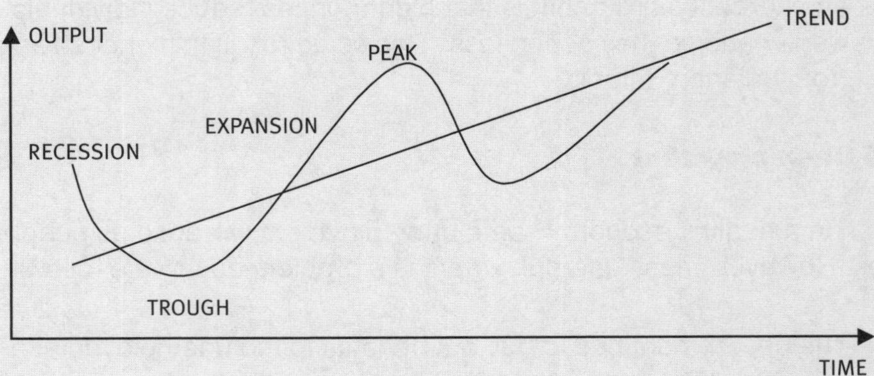

Some economists argue that one role of governments is to smooth out this pattern to avoid 'boom and bust' years.

Illustration 1 – The Great Depression

The Great Depression

The Great Depression was a worldwide economic downturn that lasted through most of the 1930s. It was focused on North America and Europe, but had knock-on effects around the world.

- Construction virtually stopped in many countries as demand fell sharply.
- Unemployment and homelessness soared.
- Cities based on heavy industry suffered particularly badly.
- Rural areas and farmers suffered as prices for crops fell by 40-60%.
- Mining and logging areas were also hit hard as there was little alternative economic activity.

Supplementary reading – The economic diamond

Objectives of economic policy

A useful illustration of the economy's performance and the success of economic policy is the 'economic diamond' showing the main economic objectives of governments. Although the priority among the objectives varies with the government's values and political motives the following four objectives are typical of most governments:

- *Price stability*. A low annual rate of inflation.
- *Full employment.*
- *External balance* implying no long-term tendency for balance of payments current account deficits.
- *Economic growth* as measured by the annual rise in GDP.

In effect, the bigger the diamond is, the better the performance of the economy and the more successful economic policy might be judged. Of course the conduct of economic policy by any government in a market economy is constrained by many factors, most of which are outside of the control of governments.

The most important of these constraints are:

- *previous policies* which cannot be abandoned or altered by new governments since there has to be a degree of continuity in policy to ensure a reasonably stable economic environment in which individuals and businesses can work.
- *information* which is always limited and imperfect and limits the value of economic predictions upon which economic policy making must be based.
- *time lags* between the design and implementation of economic policy and the point at which they start to have an effect on the economy.
- *political limitations* which constrain what is possible and acceptable to the electorate and may condition what governments are prepared to do.

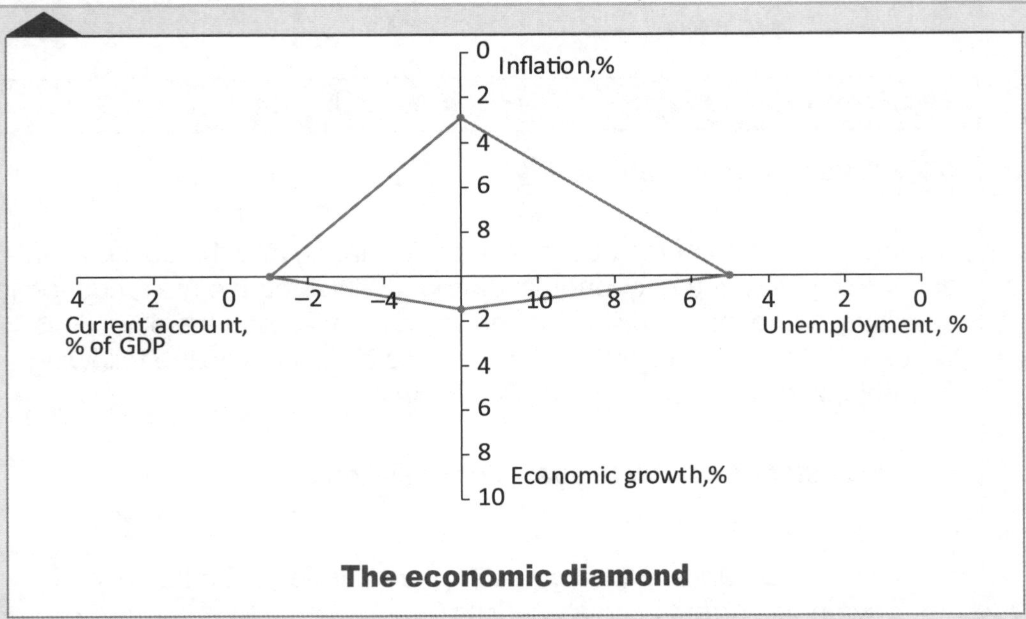

The economic diamond

Test Your Understanding 1

Which of the following is NOT an objective of macroeconomic policy?

A Economic growth

B Control of Inflation

C Lower levels of taxation

D A balanced balance of payments

Test Your Understanding 2

Which of the following statements is true?

A Economic growth always brings benefits to all members of a society. TRUE/FALSE

B Economic growth can lead to an increase in imports. TRUE/FALSE

C Inflation does not affect those on fixed incomes as much as those in employment. TRUE/FALSE

D Inflation encourages investment in a national economy. TRUE/FALSE

Test Your Understanding 3

Why is a 'boom and bust' economy a problem?

2 Measuring the size of the economy

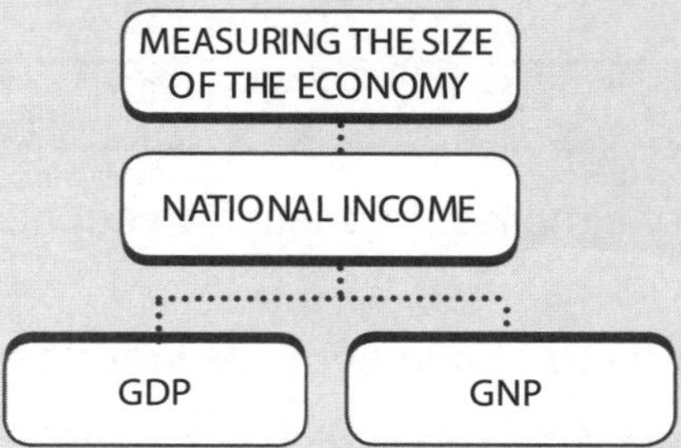

In order to address these policy goals we first need to understand the following:

- How large is the economy?
- How fast is the economy growing?
- Why do inflation and unemployment occur?
- How may we assess the ability of the economy to generate economic welfare for its citizens?

2.1 National Income

The starting point is to measure the size of the economy by using the concept of national income.

The definition of national income is:

the total value of the goods and services produced by a country's resources over a year.

Given the scale of economic activity in a modern economy, the accounting needed to measure national income is very complex. Measurement is done in three ways:

- by national **output** = value of finished goods and services produced
- by national **income** = total incomes earned by providers of factors of production
- by national **expenditure** = money spent in purchasing the national product

Each of these methods should give the same answer.

When goods and services are produced, people receive incomes, and thus in theory the addition of the prices of all the goods and services should equal the sum of all the income of the population. Similarly, those figures should equate with the total amount of spending by the population on goods and services. However, numerous adjustments have to be made when calculating by each method.

Illustration 2 – National Income calculation

Let us consider a very simplistic model of an economy.

- Company A has a forest and supplies wood to Company B
- Company B makes furniture, which it then sells to the general public.

Let us suppose that the results for the period are:

	Company A	**Company B**
Sales to public	–	200
Sales from A to B	100	(100)
Wages	(10)	(30)
Rent	(12)	(10)
Interest	(5)	(10)
Profit	73	50

We can estimate national income in each of the three methods given above:

- National product = value of finished goods = value of furniture only = 200
- National expenditure = money spent buying the furniture = 200
- National income = wages + rent + interest + profits
  = 40 + 22 + 15 + 123 = 200

National income can be used for a variety of purposes. In particular, when we wish to measure

- the *productivity* of an economy the appropriate measure of national income is gross domestic product (GDP) – this measures the value of all output within the country and excludes any income generated by assets held overseas by the country's residents;

- the *standard of living* in an economy the appropriate measure is gross national product (GNP) – this refers to the value of the output produced (and incomes earned) by all of a country's residents in a year

However, measurement of growth is difficult given the black market and goods that are excluded from national income calculations.

In a closed economy with no economic relations with the rest of the world, the measures of GDP and GNP would be identical; in an open economy with international flows of payments for factor services, they may differ.

Supplementary reading – GDP and GNP

Gross domestic product (GDP)

This measures the value of all output within the country and excludes any income generated by assets held overseas by the country's residents.

This term is often referred to by economists because it shows the value of the output produced in an economy during one year. If it increases in real terms, then there has been economic growth.

Gross national product (GNP)

This term refers to the value of the output produced (and incomes earned) by all of a country's residents in a year. To calculate this, the following must be added/deducted to the figure for GDP for a country.

- Add – income (profits, rents, interest) earned by domestic companies and individuals abroad and remitted back to the home country.
- Deduct – income (profits, rents, interest) earned by overseas companies and individuals operating in the home country and remitted back to their countries of origin reduces GNP.

Note: The above statistics are "gross" because no deduction has been made to reflect depreciation (also known as "capital consumption").

Supplementary reading – National Income calculations

Two of the three methods used to calculate national income are illustrated below (note National Income calculations are **not** on the syllabus)

UK GDP by expenditure method 2013

	Percentage
Total actual individual consumption	77.5
Government expenditure	7.6
Total gross capital formation (note)	17.0
Exports	29.8
Imports	–31.7
Statistical discrepancy	–0.2
GDP at market prices	**100**

Source: ONS

(**Note:** capital expenditure on tangible and intangible fixed assets, changes in inventories and acquisitions less disposals of valuables)

UK GDP by income method 2013

	Percentage
Compensation of employees (e.g. wages)	51.2
Total gross operating surplus (from corporations and government)	30.6
Mixed income	5.8
Taxes less subsidies	12.3
Statistical adjustment	0.1
GDP at market prices	**100**

Source: ONS

2.2 Business use of national income data

National income data is of particular use to governments in formulating economic policy and to business when making strategic business choices. For businesses, especially large businesses operating in more than one country, national income data is helpful in making several types of strategic decision.

- *Sales and production strategy*. If a business knows that prospective rate of growth of income in its markets and the income elasticity of demand (see Chapter 2), it can predict its potential sales growth in those markets.

- *New markets*. Data on growth of income in different countries helps businesses to identify potential new markets. Many international businesses clearly see that rapid economic growth in China will make it a major future market for a wide range of both consumers and capital goods.
- *Location decisions*. National income data may also help businesses to choose appropriate locations for production facilities. Businesses prefer to locate in prosperous and dynamic countries. However other data indicating the *competitiveness* of particular locations including costs, taxation levels, the exchange rate, may be more significant in these decisions.

For governments, national income data is particularly important since sound policy making requires plentiful and accurate information about what is happening in the economy. Thus detailed national income data is essential. However effective economic policy making requires not only the national income data itself, but also an understanding of the factors and processes which determine the level and growth of national income. These are analysed using the framework of the circular flow of income.

Test Your Understanding 4

GDP is better than GNP when discussing the standard of living in an economy.

True/False

Test Your Understanding 5

GNP (gross national product) may be best defined as:

A the total of goods and services produced within an economy over a given period of time

B the total expenditure of consumers on domestically produced goods and services

C all income received by residents in a country in return for factor services provided domestically and abroad

D the value of total output produced domestically plus net property income from abroad, minus capital consumption

3 Understanding national income: the circular flow model

Note: In the circular flow model there is extensive use of symbols to represent variables in the model. The most important of these are as follows:

Y national income
C consumption
S savings
I investment
T taxation
G government expenditure
X exports
M imports

Also note that the terms *companies* and *firms* are used interchangeably.

3.1 The circular flow model

Imagine a simple economy in which there are only producers (firms) and consumers (households). This economy does not have a government and it does not trade with the rest of the world, nor does any private sector investment take place.

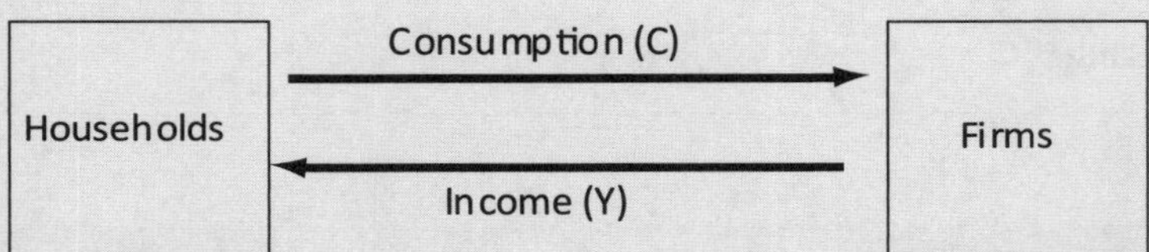

In this scenario there is a simple circular flow of funds. Households earn factor incomes (Y) by selling their labour to firms. In return the households buy and consume (C) the goods and services produced by the firms. At this point it is assumed that households spend all that they earn, i.e. income is equal to expenditure (also referred to as demand or aggregate demand) in the home economy.

Note: In all of these models real things (goods, services and work) go in one direction, payment for these (consumption expenditure, wages) go in the opposite direction.

In this simple economy equilibrium (when the circular flow is neither increasing nor decreasing) will exist when income equals consumption or aggregate demand and is possible to write:

Consumption = Income

Furthermore, in this simple case total expenditure (E) is made up of consumption only, so we can state that in equilibrium

Expenditure = Income

E = Y

3.2 Injections and withdrawals

The initial model of the circular flow was rather unrealistic as it ignored the possibility of overseas trade, the influence of government, and the fact that households might save some of their income.

A more realistic model would recognise that the circular flow can experience:

- Injections are additions to expenditure from outside of the circular flow itself;

  Injections boost the circular flow and include exports (X), government investment (G) and private sector investment (I).

- Withdrawals are some element of income in the circular flow that is not passed on as expenditure.

  Withdrawals (also known as leakages) reduce the circular flow and include imports (M), taxation (T) and savings (S).

Remember that with exports goods flow out of the country but money flows into the country; with imports, goods flow into the country and money flows out of the country.

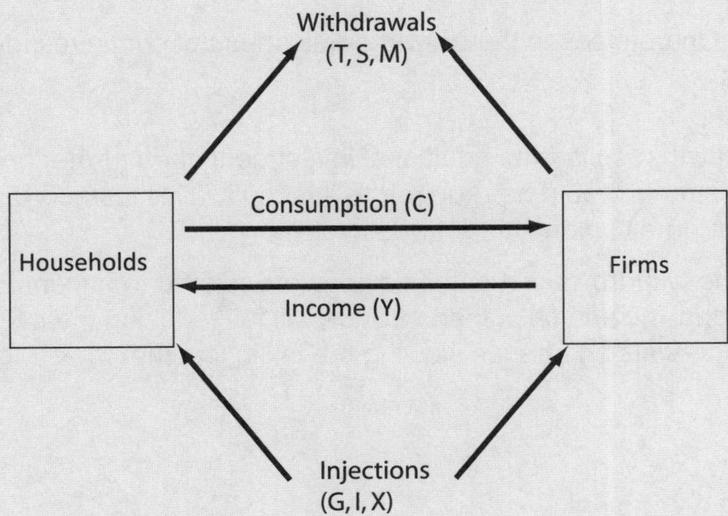

3.3 Equilibrium

An economy making full use of its resources will be moving towards a state of rest, or equilibrium. For equilibrium to be established in the circular flow, planned injections must equal planned withdrawals.

Equilibrium in national income is where

J (injections) = W (withdrawals or leakages)

$$I + G + X = S + T + M$$

Where I = investment
G = government expenditure } *injections*
X = exports

And S = savings
T = taxations withdrawals } *withdrawals*
M = imports

It is not necessary that pairs of injections and withdrawals (such as imports and exports or taxation and government expenditure) are equal. Equilibrium only requires that the sum of injections is equal to the sum of withdrawals.

But if:

- J > W, additions to the circular flow exceed withdrawals and so the level of national income will rise;
- J < W, additions to the circular flow are less than withdrawals so the level of national income will fall.

Note that in both cases the growth or fall does not continue indefinitely. For example

- If growth results from additional investment, then further ongoing investment would be required to sustain it. This issue is discussed in more detail below under trade cycles.
- Some withdrawals such as savings are related to national income. If national income falls, then savings will fall reducing the overall level of withdrawals and hence slowing the fall in income.

Supplementary reading – More complex circular flow of funds

Clearly more complex models can be devised (see diagram below).

- Households may save via financial institutions which may channel these savings to firms to finance investment.
- Governments tax incomes and may use these revenues either to purchase goods and services from the firms sector or to provide support incomes for certain households.
- International trade occurs. Exports will represent additional spending on the firm sector but imports will represent a diversion of spending away from the firm sector towards firms in other countries.

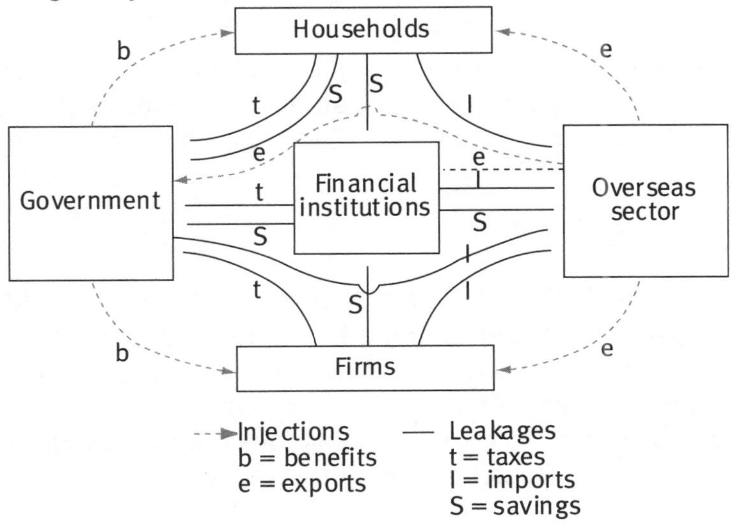

4 Understanding the components of the circular flow of funds

4.1 Consumption (C)

The spending by people, or households on the circular flow model is termed *consumption*. The single most important determinant of the level of consumption is the level of income. This is true for both individuals and the economy as a whole.

The extent to which consumption changes with income is termed the *marginal propensity to consume (MPC)*.

The marginal propensity to consume is calculated by the formula:

$$\text{MPC} = \frac{\text{Change in consumption, } \Delta C}{\text{Change in income, } \Delta Y}$$

Thus, if a person's disposable income increases from $100 to $120 per week and her consumption increases from $90 to $105 per week, her MPC would be 0.75 (i.e. 15:20).

The MPC varies considerably between economies, with some (e.g. Japan), having relatively low MPCs and some (e.g. the USA), having relatively high MPCs. Generally, it is assumed that the MPC is positive but likely to fall as income rises.

Supplementary reading – Factors affecting consumption

Factors influencing the level of household consumption are:

- Income

  Consumption is normally based on current income. Another possibility is that people's consumption is determined by their previous income or their expected future income.

- Wealth

  At an individual level, an increase in wealth may raise MPC because less saving is needed. In the economy as a whole, a more equal wealth distribution is likely to raise consumption. The nature of wealth may also be significant; liquid wealth, such as savings under the bed, is likely to raise consumption, whereas illiquid wealth will probably have little effect on consumption.

- Government policy

  By taxation and public spending, the government can influence the level (and pattern) of consumption. An increase in direct taxation lowers disposable incomes and thereby reduces the capacity for consumption. Alternatively, higher government spending, particularly on state benefits, raises incomes and stimulates consumption.

- The cost and availability of credit

  The cheaper the cost (the rate of interest) and the greater the availability of credit, the more likely it is that consumption will occur. Credit is particularly influential when consumer durables are purchased. The United Kingdom has high levels of consumption financed by credit partly because of the wide range and sophistication of the credit instruments available.

- Price expectations

  In certain circumstances, when price rises are anticipated, consumption might be brought forward. This temporarily raises MPC.

These factors can be described as 'objective' influences. In contrast, there are 'subjective' influences which determine individual behaviour, irrespective of the other factors. For instance, some cultures encourage high levels of savings (e.g. Japan). It is also usually argued that consumption by individuals in urban areas is higher than in rural areas.

Test Your Understanding 6

Which of the following is **least** likely to result in a fall in consumption spending in an economy?

A An increase in the rate of income tax

B An increase in interest rates

C An increase in the rate of inflation

D A reduction in the availability of credit

4.2 Savings (S)

Saving is defined as the amount of income not spent. It is therefore sometimes regarded as a residual; the amount of income left after consumption has been determined. Thus the factors determining saving are mainly the mirror image of the factors determining consumption.

Supplementary reading – Factors affecting savings

The factors influencing saving are as follows.

- Income

  Both for the individual and the economy, the level of saving is determined mainly by income.

- Interest rates

  In theory, an increase in the rate of interest will mean that people need to save less in order to achieve a given target of income earned in interest. However, this income effect can be offset by the substitution effect. With higher interest rates, people might save more and spend less, as saving is now more attractive.

- Inflation

  However, to rational consumers the money rate of interest is less important than the real interest rate (i.e. allowing for inflation). Even if the nominal rate of interest is high, a low real rate of interest might discourage savings. However, consumers might suffer from the *money illusion* and save more when nominal interest rates are high even if inflation reduces the real rate of interest.

- Credit

  When credit is easily available consumers might acquire as much credit as they are saving; in effect there is no net saving. In some countries, notably the USA and the United Kingdom, the expansion of credit in recent years has meant that net household savings rates have fallen to historic lows.

- Contractual savings

  Most household saving is contractual and regular such as payments into pension schemes. As the need to finance pensions increases, especially in developed economies with ageing economies, this form of saving is expected to increase.

Most saving is undertaken by households and the company sector. Governments save when they run budget surpluses and dis-save when they run budget deficits. The savings deficits of any one sector of the economy have to be financed by the saving of other sectors. Thus if the company sector plans to invest more than it is saving, it will have to borrow from other sectors which are net savers. This raises the question of what determines the level of investment in the economy.

4.3 Investment (I)

Expenditure on investment covers:

- fixed capital formation (e.g. plant, machinery, roads, houses);
- the value of the physical increase in stocks of raw materials, work in progress and finished goods.

Investment is undertaken by the public sector and the private sector (the latter featuring firms and households) and it enhances the capacity of the economy.

- The capital stock of the economy is increased by the amount of net investment undertaken each year.
- Net investment is the difference between gross (total) investment and replacement investment (capital consumption), which accounts for the deterioration of the existing capital equipment stock.

Note: do not confuse investment (I) and savings (S).

If we revisit the idea of assessing investments using discounted cash flows, then we can say that the main determinants of the level of investment are:

- Expectations about future cash flows

  These expectations will be influenced by the anticipated revenue from the output of the investment compared with the anticipated costs of the investment.

- The business's cost of capital

  This will be affected by the availability and cost of finance, inflation and also the perceived risks of the cash flows.

Supplementary reading – Additional factors affecting investment

Other factors that influence investment include the following:

- The state of business confidence

  If businesses are optimistic, they are likely to expect greater returns than if they are pessimistic. (Note this will affect estimated cash flows and perceived risk in the NPV approach)

- Technological innovation

  If capital becomes more productive this is likely to raise the level of investment at any given rate of interest. Note: economists talk about the "marginal efficiency of capital" as a way of calculating the return on invested funds. For an investment to be worthwhile the MEC must exceed the interest rate.

- Government policy

  Inconsistent and varying economic policies might increase business uncertainty and thereby deter investment. In contrast, reductions in corporation tax and improved tax allowances will increase the expected income stream and encourage investment. Also changes in interest rates will have direct effects on the profitability of investment.

Test Your Understanding 7

Brenda has decided to spend less but instead invest $100 more in a bank deposit account.This will increase the level of investment in the economy by $100.

True/False

4.4 The government and external sectors

The factors determining the level of government expenditure and taxation and the main influences on the balance of imports and exports will be discussed in later sections.

4.5 Linkages between different elements of the circular flow

There are two key linkages that you need to be aware of:

The accelerator

For growth to occur the economy has to be able to increase output of goods and services. Unless spare capacity exists this will require additional investment in capital goods.

(**Note:** Failure to increase output at a time of rising demand would simply result in inflation - more money chasing the same amount of goods).

The accelerator principle views investment as a function of changes in national income i.e. as national income rises and desired consumption increases, firms will respond, investing in new capital goods to meet this extra demand. This in turn increases aggregate demand further within the economy, increasing pressure for more investment.

Thus when an economy starts to grow, this in itself can fuel further growth. Unfortunately the reverse is also true as a reduction in the size of an economy will result in a cut in investment accelerating the decline further.

The multiplier

This idea shows the change in national income resulting from a change in planned investment (in the simple model) or a change in government spending or a change in the overseas trade sector). It looks at the effect of injections (less withdrawals) into the circular flow of income.

Changes in injections, government expenditure, investment and exports may cause a more than proportional increase in national income. This is termed the *multiplier effect*.

Multiplier effects can occur in many ways. When any planned injection into the circular flow increases and other injections and withdrawals remain unchanged, then national income will lead to the use of more factors of production whose earnings will be spent, thereby adding to the income of others who may then spend more, and so on. . . . Thus an initial injection of additional expenditure in the circular flow will lead to a series of additional rounds of expenditure.

Determinants of the multiplier

A simple economy

The increase in national income caused by successive rounds of spending will not go on forever since with each round some extra income will be lost to the circular flow through the operation of *withdrawals.* Thus each succeeding round of spending becomes smaller and smaller. If withdrawals were 20 per cent of income (e.g. a marginal propensity to save of 0.2) the increases in income in each round from an initial increase in spending of $100 would be:

Round 1	$100	
Round 2	$80	($100 minus $20 which is saved)
Round 3	$64	($80 minus $16 which is saved)
Round 4	$51.2	($64 minus $12.8 which is saved)

In a simple economy the obvious withdrawal is saving. In this simple economy, with no government and no external sector, the value of the multiplier (K) is shown in the following equation.

$$K = \frac{1}{1 - MPC} = \frac{1}{MPS}$$

Where MPC marginal propensity to consume
MPS marginal propensity to save

If one assumed an MPC of 0.8 the multiplier would have a value of 5 and an increased injection of $10 m would increase total national income by $50 m. This is important for government policy making.

Illustration 3 – Explaining trade cycles

Although there a number of explanations for trade cycles, attempts have been made to combine the accelerator and multiplier effects to explain the behaviour:

- Something happens to boost Investment - for example, innovation or war.
- The increase in investment triggers the multiplier effect leading to rising incomes.
- Rising incomes increase consumption and therefore demand.
- Higher expected demand triggers the accelerator effect as firms invest further to meet demand.
- The extra investment then triggers the multiplier again leading to rising incomes and so on.

This means that once the economy starts growing, then it will continue to grow giving a strong upward swing in the trade cycle.

However, this process cannot continue indefinitely as the economy will eventually reach full capacity i.e. all factors are employed. As this point is reached investment tails off and incomes start to fall triggering a reverse multiplier. As incomes fall so does consumption and demand. This is in turn reduces investment and so on, resulting in the downward part of the trade cycle.

Supplementary reading – Policy making and the multiplier

It is clear that if a government wishes to engage in some form of *demand management* policy, that is using its levels of taxation and expenditure to influence the level of aggregate demand and hence the level of national income, it will need to have some knowledge of the working of the multiplier and its value in their economy.

- The government will also need to be aware that the value of the multiplier can vary not only over time as savings rates and the propensity to import changes, but also between government policy instruments.
- Expenditure tends to have a higher multiplier value than tax cuts since in the first round all public expenditure is 'spent' but some of the tax cuts may be saved.
- Some expenditure has immediate spending effects (e.g. increased pensions) whereas some (e.g. long-term investment projects) may only have their full effect over a period of years.
- Some economists (including monetarist and new classical economists) argue that the multiplier value of government expenditure is zero since an increase has to be financed via government borrowing from the private sector which 'crowds out' an equivalent amount of private expenditure.

Test Your Understanding 8

Which of the following is **least** likely to result in a fall in investment spending in an economy?

A An increase in government expenditure'

B An increase in interest rates

C An increase in the rate of inflation

D A reduction in the availability of credit

Test Your Understanding 9

Answer the following questions based on the preceding information. You can check your answers below.

(1) Name two withdrawals from the circular flow.

(2) What is an injection into the circular flow?

(3) When, in theory, is an economy in equilibrium?

(4) What does the consumption function show?

(5) Apart from households and firms, what else is a major consumer of goods and services?

(6) Define net investment.

(7) What does the accelerator theory show?

(8) What does the multiplier show?

(9) What is the formula for calculating the multiplier, K?

5 Aggregate supply and demand

The common economic issues facing all economies include the twin problems of inflation and unemployment. Much government economic policy effort is devoted to attempts to prevent either of these undesirable outcomes. In order to understand these economic policies it is first necessary to see how unemployment and inflation might arise in a market economy. The starting point for this understanding is the aggregate demand and aggregate supply model.

5.1 The aggregate demand and aggregate supply model

The circular flow model discussed in Section 4 showed how the total demand for goods and services in the economy was made up of several elements: consumption, investment, government expenditure and net exports (i.e. exports minus imports). Together these made up aggregate monetary demand or simply just aggregate demand (AD).

$$AD = C + I + G + (X - M)$$

However, an understanding of how the economy functions and why problems may occur cannot be explained solely in terms of the demand for goods and services; we also need to know about the ability of the economy to produce goods and services. This is known as aggregate supply (AS).

5.2 Aggregate demand (AD)

In the circular flow model, AD was related to the level of national income and the level of expenditure; in the aggregate demand and supply model, it is related to national income and to the price level. This makes possible a discussion of the origin of both unemployment and inflation.

It is assumed that aggregate demand

- is made up of all components of expenditure in the economy, consumption, investment, government expenditure and net exports;
- is inversely related to prices since a price fall would raise everyone's real (purchasing power) wealth and thus tend to raise spending;
- may shift if any one component (e.g. investment or exports) changes through the multiplier effect.

Thus the AD curve slopes down from left to right but may shift.

5.3 Aggregate supply (AS)

The aggregate supply in an economy refers to the willingness and ability of producers in an economy, largely the business sector, to produce and offer for sale, goods and services. It is assumed that aggregate supply

- is the collective result of decisions made by millions of business producers, large and small to produce and sell goods and services;
- is positively related to the price level since, other things being equal, a rise in the price level will make sales more profitable and thus encourage businesses to expand output;
- is limited by the availability of resources (labour, capital, etc.) so that at full employment, output cannot be increased any further;
- can only shift in the long run as the result of a change in the costs of production or in the availability of factors of production.

Thus the AS curve slopes upward from left to right and does not shift in the short run.

5.4 Equilibrium

National equilibrium will be where the aggregate demand (AD) curve intersects with the aggregate supply (AS) curve; here the total demand for goods and services in the economy is equal to the total supply of goods and services in the economy.

The particular value of this model is that it demonstrates the effect of changes in either aggregate demand or aggregate supply on both the level of national income and on the price level. Given the reasonable assumption that the level of employment in an economy in the short to medium run is a function of the level of national income, the model can show how inflation and unemployment might arise in an economy and how governments might respond to these problems.

Changes in aggregate demand

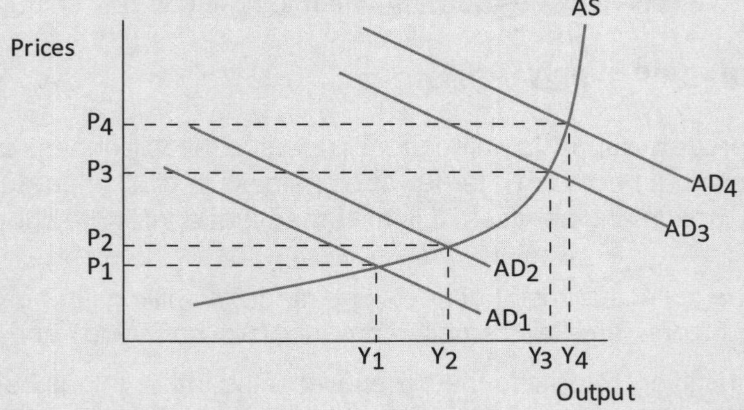

Example 1

Suppose that the economy is initially in equilibrium at a level of national income and employment denoted by Y_1. If there was an increase in aggregate demand from AD_1 to AD_2

- the new equilibrium would be at national income level Y_2;
- national income would have risen from Y_1 to Y_2 and unemployment would have fallen;
- the price level would have risen from P_1 to P_2.

In this case most of the effect of an increase in AD is felt in the form of rising income and employment and there is only a small inflationary impact. Thus in this case, if the government wished to reduce unemployment an expansion of AD by reducing taxes or by raising government expenditure would be an appropriate and effective policy.

Example 2

Suppose that the economy is initially in equilibrium at a level of national income and employment denoted by Y_3 . If there was an increase in aggregate demand from AD_3 to AD_4

- the new equilibrium would be at national income level Y_4;
- national income would have risen from Y_3 to Y_4 and unemployment would have fallen;
- the price level would have risen from P_3 to P_4.

In this case most of the effect of an increase in AD is felt in the form of a rise in the price level and there is only a small effect in raising national income and reducing unemployment. Thus in this case if the government attempted to further reduce unemployment by expanding AD the effect would be very small and the price would be a significant increase in inflationary pressure. Indeed, at this point the AS curve becomes very steep because the economy is approaching full employment; a more appropriate policy for government here might be to restrain AD by raising taxes and reducing government expenditure thus shifting aggregate demand from AD_4 to AD_3 .

Of course, shifts in the AD curve may occur for reasons other than government policy. A recession, characterized by falling output and employment and reduced inflationary pressure will result from a leftward movement in the AD curve caused by, among other things,

- a fall in investment if business confidence is damaged;
- a fall in consumer expenditure if consumers lose confidence or if they reach the limits of their ability to finance extra credit;
- a fall in exports if there is a major loss of competitiveness or there is a recession in the country's major trading partners.

Since 2009 this has been the experience of many developed economies, as declining consumer and business confidence led to falling aggregate demand and contracting national income. The result was a serious recession affecting much of the world economy.

By 2013, however, some countries were seeing renewed growth. The US economy grew at an annual rate of 2.5% in the first three months of the year, helped by the strongest consumer spending figures in two years.

Likewise, the economy may expand and experience a period of business boom characterised by rising output and employment and increasing inflationary pressures conditions if there is a rightward movement in the AD caused by, among other things,

- an investment boom if business is confident and profitable;
- a rapid rise in consumer expenditure if consumers are confident and have access to affordable credit;
- a rapid rise in exports if there is a major gain in competitiveness (e.g. from a depreciation of the currency) or there is a boom in the country's major trading partners.

Changes in aggregate supply

It is also possible that, in the long run, the aggregate supply in the economy might change. This is shown as shifts in the aggregate supply curve.

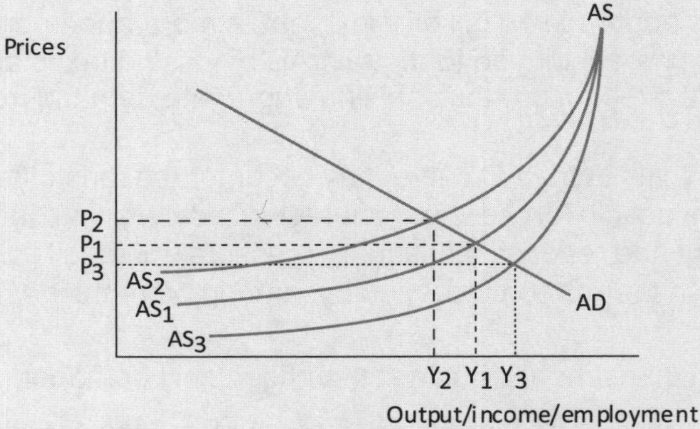

Example 1

The economy might suffer from *supply-side shocks* which reduce the ability or willingness of productive businesses in the economy to produce and sell goods and services. If this occurred the AS would shift to the left, for example, from AS_1 to AS_2. The result would be a rise in the price level from P_1 to P_2 and a fall in output from Y_1 to Y_2. This combination of falling output and rising inflation is sometimes referred to as *stagflation*. Such supply-side shocks might arise from:

- a major rise in energy and/or raw material prices such as the oil price rises in the 1970s and early 1980s;
- a major rise in labour costs; the problems of many of the European Union larger economies in past years may be partly the result of social and labour legislation significantly raising the cost of labour for businesses;

- a significant fall in productivity in businesses due to major technological problems; some fear that attempting to deal with global warming by emissions controls may have something of this effect on economies.

Example 2

The economy might also experience a rightward shift in the AS curve such as from AS_1 to AS_3. This would produce a highly beneficial result that national income and employment would expand from Y_1 to Y_3 and the price level would fall from P_1 to P_3. This might be seen as the opposite of stagflation. Such shifts to the right in the aggregate supply curve might arise from:

- favourable developments in the economy reducing costs such as falling energy and raw material prices or big productivity improvements from technological change;
- deliberate government *supply-side policies* designed to shift the AS curve to the right such as privatisation, business tax reductions or labour market reforms.

5.5 Demand and supply side policies

Managing a national economy that interacts fully with the global economy is complex and full of uncertainty. Different theories exist regarding how to manage the economy. Three of the most important are outlined below.

The classical view (do nothing)

- Classical economic theory involved doing nothing – a 'leave it alone' approach.
- It was thought that the economy would automatically move to equilibrium with full employment.
- In the event of a depression, for instance, the price of factors of production would fall. This would increase demand for them, leading to their utilisation and the re-establishment of economic growth.
- This theory was severely challenged by the Great Depression in the 1920s and 30s when, despite wages falling significantly, the economy did not respond by growing. During the Great Depression the economy seemed unable to stimulate itself to grow. Out of this failure grew the more interventionist approach advocated by John Maynard Keynes.

The Keynesian view (demand side)

- Keynes believed that an economy could become stuck at many different equilibrium points, ones that did not necessarily involve full employment. He cited the Great Depression as evidence for this, where the global economy got stuck in low gear and was unable to grow.
- He argued that it was government's role to move the economy to a better equilibrium, i.e. one closer to full employment.
- Simply put, this involved government borrowing money and injecting it into the economy to stimulate economic growth. Increased future tax revenues would then allow the government to repay this money.
- Conversely, if an economy was growing too fast and experiencing inflation, government could slow the economy down by increasing levels of taxation, reducing the amount of money in the economy.
- Effectively, Keynes argued for manipulation and management of aggregate demand in the economy (demand side economics).

The monetarist view (supply side)

- Monetarists revived the earlier classical view and believe that there is only one true equilibrium point in the national economy. Equilibrium will only occur when supply is equal to demand in all markets in an economy.
- Monetarists believe that the economy will automatically gravitate towards this 'natural' equilibrium unless hindered by market imperfections.
- Thus it is the role of government to 'free up' the economy by removing these imperfections. Once this is done the role of government should be minimal.
- Market imperfections include the following:
  - inflation
  - government spending and taxation
  - price fixing
  - minimum wage agreements
  - regulation of markets
  - abuses of monopoly power.
- Monetarist solutions to economic problems are often described as supply side economics as they focus on improving the supply of factors of production in an economy.

Supplementary reading – Further details on supply side policies

Monetary and fiscal policy are primarily concerned with influencing the level of aggregate monetary demand in the economy. In terms of the aggregate demand and supply model these policies are aimed to shift the AD curve to the right when the problem is unemployment and to the left when the problem is inflation. However, concern over the effectiveness of such policies, has led to a shift of emphasis towards *supply side policies*.

The object of supply side policy is to shift the aggregate supply curve to the right. In terms of the aggregate demand and supply model, this would have effect of raising national income and lowering unemployment at the same time as reducing inflationary pressures in the economy.

Supply side policy typically consists of a wide range of measures the most important of which are:

- shifting taxation away from direct to indirect taxation and reducing marginal rates of taxation to encourage work and enterprise;
- reducing social security payments and tailoring them to encourage the unemployed to seek employment;
- an emphasis on vocational education and training to improve work skills in the labour force;
- reducing the power of trade unions and employee organisations to limit entry into occupations and to raise wages above equilibrium levels;
- deregulation and privatisation to encourage enterprise and risk-taking.

In the longer run such policies appear to have been successful. In the USA and the UK where such policies have been most widely adopted, both unemployment and inflationary pressures fell significantly in the 1990s and into the current decade.

However, supply side policies have had other, less desirable consequences. The most significant of these have been:

- making the taxation system much more regressive: in the UK the proportion of income paid in tax by the poorest 20% of the population is higher than that paid by the richest 20%;
- a more unequal distribution of income;
- a greater degree of uncertainty for workers in the labour market and with less employment protection;
- a fall in the relative (and sometimes absolute) standard of living of many who are dependent on social security payments.

Test Your Understanding 10

In an aggregate demand and supply diagram, if the aggregate supply curve shifted to the left, the consequences would be:

A national income and the price level would both fall

B national income and the price level would both rise

C national income would fall and the price level would rise

D national income would rise and the price level would fall

Test Your Understanding 11

Which one of the following would cause a fall in the level of aggregate demand in an economy?

A A decrease in government expenditure

B A fall in the propensity to save

C A fall in the level of imports

D A decrease in the level of income tax

Test Your Understanding 12

Which one of the following would cause the aggregate supply curve of an economy to shift to the right?

A A decrease in government expenditure

B Increased investment in new technologies in industry

C A fall in interest rates

D Lower unemployment

Test Your Understanding 13

State whether each of the following would affect the AD curve or AS curve and state whether the curve would move to the right or to the left.

Factor	AD	AS	Right	Left
A fall in business confidence due to political scandals				
An increase in tariffs on imported goods				
A major increase in world oil prices				
An increase in trade union power and militancy				
An increase in interest rates				
New training initiatives for the unemployed				

6 Trade cycles

The trade cycle and government policy

Aggregate demand and supply analysis has shown how the trade cycle of recessions, recoveries and booms followed by further recession might occur and how government policy might be used to deal with these problems.

Stage of trade cycle	Features	Causes	Policy response
Recession	• falling output/income, • high and rising unemployment, • reduced inflationary pressure, • improving trade balance as imports fall • public finance will be adversely affected due to reduced tax income and increased benefits payments	• falling domestic AD from lower levels of: consumer spending, investment, exports, government expenditure • world recession	•raise AD by reducing taxation, raising public expenditure, lowering interest rates •Note: this will further increase the need for government borrowing
Stagflation: special type of recession	• falling output, income and employment, • rising inflationary pressure	• supply-side shocks reducing aggregate supply • could have a recession due to low AD combined with imported cost-push inflation	• supply-side policy to raise aggregate supply • prices and incomes policy
Recovery	• output and income begin to rise, • unemployment begins to fall, • only moderate inflationary pressure • improving public finances	• returning confidence in business and consumer sectors, • effect of government expansionary policy undertaken in recession	•reduction in expansionary policy to prevent too strong a boom

Boom	• high output and employment, • rising inflationary pressure, • deteriorating trade balance as imports rise • Higher net income for government allows repayment of debt	• high and rising AD from higher levels of: consumer spending, investment, exports, government expenditure	•reduce AD by raising taxation, reducing public expenditure, higher interest rates

Of course there might be a period of economic growth with all the features of a boom but without undue inflationary pressure, if the aggregate supply of the economy continually increases. The ability of some economies such as the United Kingdom and the USA to maintain steady growth with high levels of employment but without serious inflationary pressures in recent years may have been, at least partly, the result of supply-side reforms in these countries since the 1980s.

Implications for businesses

The main implication of trade cycles will be the impact on likely demand for the firm's products

- A firm selling staple goods such as milk and bread will be less affected than one selling new cars for example.
- Manufacturers of capital goods such as machinery will see a major downturn in demand in recessions but a large up swing in a growth phase.
- A firm that supplies to the public sector will be particularly concerned with government spending plans. For example, if a government wishes to try to spend their way out of a recession by building new roads and schools, then clearly this would present major opportunities for building contractors.
- A firm may need to consider its portfolio of products to reduce the risk associated with trade cycles, perhaps by diversifying geographically.

Other implications include

- In times of economic downturn unemployment will be higher, so the firm will have more bargaining power over employees so may be able to pay lower wages than in boom times.

- Success may also be influenced by being able to determine when best to act – for example, increasing production in response to an anticipated upturn in economic activity.
- If the government adjusts interest rates as part of its policies, then this will affect the firm's cost of borrowing.

Supplementary reading – Trade cycles

- A recession starts when demand begins to fall. Firms respond to the fall in demand by reducing their output, causing a decline in purchases of raw materials and an increase in unemployment, as workers are laid off.
- The reduction in demand will feed through into households' incomes, causing these to fall too, resulting in a further reduction in demand.
- The economy will quickly move into a slump, with low business confidence, depressed 'animal spirits' and little incentive to carry out investment.
- Once in the slump, it can take a long time before the economy begins to recover. One of the most difficult things to restore is business and consumer confidence.
- Eventually, though, economic activity begins to pick up. It may be a new invention that tempts entrepreneurs to invest, it may be that replacement investment can be put off no longer or a war may force the government to inject expenditure into the economy.
- The extra investment will push up incomes, which will persuade consumers to spend and this will induce yet more investment, reducing unemployment.
- The economy will expand, pushing upwards into a boom. After some time, however, full capacity will be reached and demand will become stable. The reduction in investment starts off the downward spiral once again.

7 Fiscal and monetary policy options

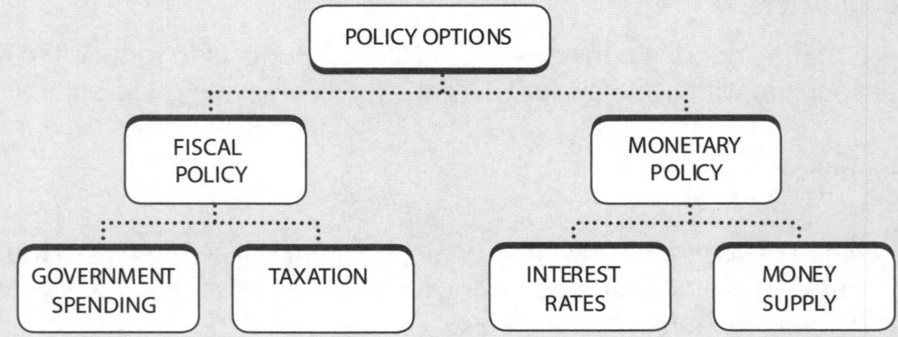

In the previous sections we looked at policy options for managing trade cycles and the different schools of thought relating to whether governments should focus on demand management or supply side policies. Here we look at fiscal and monetary policy.

7.1 Fiscal policy options

- Fiscal policy refers to a government's taxation and spending plans and is usually understood within the context of demand side policies (see section 5.5 above).

Government budget

- In the medium- to long-term it is suggested that a government should aim to achieve a balanced budget, i.e. one in which government expenditure is matched by government income.
- For a number of macroeconomic reasons that are explored in this chapter, governments may decide to run either a budget deficit or a budget surplus.

Government income < expenditure = budget deficit

Government income > expenditure = budget surplus

Government income = expenditure = a balanced budget.

Note: Don't confuse a balanced budget with the balance of payments. The former refers to the relationship between government income (from taxation) and spending, while the latter refers to the flow of funds into and out of a country.

Running a budget deficit

- If a government intends to run a budget deficit, then this has to be financed through borrowing – this borrowing is referred to as the Public Sector Net Borrowing (PSNB).
- Running a budget deficit has frequently been used to promote economic growth and reduce unemployment by closing a 'deflationary gap'.
- A deflationary gap exists if the level of aggregate demand in the economy is less than that required to ensure full employment. The resulting level of national income is too low to provide employment opportunities for all those seeking work.
- By running a budget deficit, the government is injecting more into the economy than it is taking out and can boost aggregate demand and reduce unemployment. This is known as an 'expansionary' policy.

- One criticism of increasing government spending to influence the economy is that higher public spending will "crowd out" private expenditure. For example, higher public borrowing may increase interest rates and make private sector borrowing more expensive.

Running a budget surplus

- If aggregate demand lies above the level necessary to generate full employment, this can lead to inflation (too much money chasing too few goods). In this situation an 'inflationary gap' is said to exist.
- Fiscal policy can also be used to control inflation. If an inflationary gap exists, government can seek to reduce aggregate demand by running a budget surplus, effectively taking money out of the economy. This is known as a 'contractionary policy'.

7.2 Monetary policy options

- Monetary policy refers to the management of the money supply in the economy and is usually understood within the context of monetarism (see section 5.5 above).
- Monetary policy can involve changing interest rates, either directly or indirectly through open market operations and setting reserve requirements for banks.
- Like fiscal policy, monetary policy can be described as expansionary or contractionary. An expansionary policy increases the total supply of money in the economy, and a contractionary policy decreases the total money supply. Expansionary policy is traditionally used to combat unemployment in a recession by lowering interest rates, while contractionary policy has the goal of raising interest rates to combat inflation.

Money supply

- The term "money supply" refers to the total amount of money in the economy. There are many measures of the money supply, including the following:

  M0 Notes and coins in circulation and balances at the country's Central Bank.

  M4 Notes and coins and all private sector sterling bank/building society deposits (96% of which are deposits).

Reserve requirements

- Typically banks operate a fractional reserve system, i.e. only a part of their deposits are kept in cash on the assumption that not all customers will want their money back at the same time. The proportion of deposits retained in cash is known as the reserve asset ratio or liquidity ratio.

Open market operations

- By buying and selling its own bonds the government is able to exert some control over the money supply.
- For instance, by buying back its own bonds it will release more cash into circulation. Conversely, when it sells bonds it receives cash in return, reducing the amount of money in circulation thus restricting the ability of banks to lend.

Interest rates

- High interest rates suppress demand for money due to the increased cost of borrowing. Over a period of time the money supply will then react to this reduced demand for money by contracting. Monetarists view interest rate manipulation as a key control over inflation.
- In some countries, such as the UK, the setting of interest rates is the responsibility of the Central Bank. In others it may be a government minister.
- Interest rates are discussed in more detail in section 8 below.

Supplementary reading – The problem of government borrowing

When governments run budget deficits and borrow to finance those deficits a distinction can be made between two elements in those deficits:

- a *cyclical* element in which the deficit arises as a result of the downswing phase of the trade cycle and will decrease or even turn into a surplus in the upswing phase of the trade cycle;
- a *structural* element in which the deficit is the result of a permanent imbalance between expenditure and taxation and will not be affected by the trade cycle.

A cyclical deficit is much less concern since over the whole trade cycle, budget deficits would be broadly balanced by budget surpluses. However, a structural deficit implies continuous borrowing by governments and an increasing total debt ('national debt') owed by the government. There are some reasons to believe that many countries are facing pressures are tending to increase public expenditure on a long-term basis and hence threatened the emergence of structural budget deficits.

These pressures include:

- *an ageing population* which increases public expenditure on health care for the elderly and on state pensions;
- *inflation* in the prices of public sector goods and services which are mainly labour intensive and thus tend to show the fastest rate of inflation;
- *spending commitments* for public and merit goods especially social welfare, education and health, which are difficult to decrease in the face of voter opposition;
- *tax changes* as it is always politically much easier to reduce taxes than to raise them thus making raising more tax revenue problematic.

Thus many governments are faced with the problem of financing budget deficits. The ways in which this might be done can be distinguished by:

- *from whom* the government borrows; this might be the non-bank private sector such as pension funds or individual households;
- *the type of liability* the government issues where the main distinction is between different degrees of liquidity of those liabilities. Long term government securities (in the United Kingdom, 'gilts') are the principal liabilities of governments.

For most governments the PSNB arising from the budget deficit is mainly financed by the sale of long-term government debt to the private (non-bank) sector of the economy. This is likely to have some effects on the economy but the nature of those effects is subject to some debate among economists.

- Some, mainly Keynesians, believe that the effects are real in that a budget deficit financed in this way will tend to affect the real variables in the economy, raising output and employment via the effect of the deficit on aggregate demand.
- Others, including monetarists and new classical economists, believe that the effects are *monetary* in that government borrowing injects liquid assets into the economy thus boosting the money supply and casing inflation. Moreover, government borrowing may push up interest rates thus reducing private spending. This reduction in private spending will offset the government expenditure financed by borrowing – a process known as 'crowding out'.

The problems of financing budget deficits and the potential problems arising from the need to service (pay interest on) the national debt have led governments across the world to adopt policies designed to control the level of government borrowing.

In the European Union, a condition of joining the single currency (euro) was a maximum size of national debt and of current government borrowing in relation to the national income of the country concerned. Once a country has joined the single currency and adopted the euro, it is obliged to keep control of its government borrowing via the 'stability pact' which specifies maximum amounts that governments can borrow. The crisis in the Eurozone has shown that these rules were clearly not working in many countries, especially Greece, Spain and Italy, and new rules, with real sanctions, are being introduced

In the United Kingdom since 1997 the government has tried to adopt the "golden rule" for government finances. This states that over the economic cycle, the Government will borrow only to invest and not to fund current spending.

This rule states that

- over the whole trade cycle, government current expenditure on goods, services and transfer payments should not exceed its taxation income;
- only government investment expenditure may be financed by government borrowing;
- the overall burden of public debt should not go above sustainable levels, generally taken to mean equal to 40 per cent of GDP.

However, the effect of the recession in the UK from 2008 onwards forced the government to effectively abandon this golden rule.

Budgetary rules under pressure?

The serious recession in the UK which developed from 2008 onwards had a two-fold effect on the government budget. In the autumn of 2008 the government predicted that the effect of the recession would be to greatly increase the size of its budget deficit. This was inevitable as the recession would reduce tax revenues as output and incomes fell, and would raise expenditure on unemployment payments. The effect would be a budget deficit in 2009/2010 and subsequent years so large that it would effectively break all three fiscal rules.

However, the problem did not stop there. The government felt that in order to limit the severity of the recession, it would need to inject extra spending into the economy in order to raise aggregate demand. The government therefore proposed to accelerate some public investment programmes and reduce some tax rates in the following year. The biggest of these tax cuts was a temporary reduction in VAT from 17.5% to 15%. This would make the budget deficit even bigger.

The overall result was that the government predicted that its borrowing would peak at £118bn in 2009/2010 (equivalent to 8% of GDP). The government was thus forced to adopt much looser 'temporary operating rules' for its budgetary policy.

The coalition government is still trying to close the UK's gaping budget deficit. The government hoped, in 2010, that five years of tax increases and spending cuts would repair the public finances, but progress has been much slower than planned and the deficit is about 5% of GDP in 2015.

Test Your Understanding 14

The PSNB (public sector net borrowing) is:

A the accumulated debts of the government

B the total amount borrowed by all members of the public

C the amount borrowed by the government and public authorities in a given period

D the amount borrowed to finance a balance of payments deficit

Test Your Understanding 15

According to the advocates of supply-side economics, which one of the following measures is most likely to reduce unemployment in an economy?

A Increasing labour retraining schemes

B Increasing public sector investment

C Increasing unemployment benefits

D Decreasing the money supply

Test Your Understanding 16

The crowding-out effect refers to:

A low wages leading workers to leave an industry

B firms wishing to locate production away from congested areas

C public expenditure displacing private expenditure

D increased rates of taxation leading to lower total tax revenue

8 Interest rate management

Monetary policy is concerned with managing the monetary environment in order to influence the decisions of economic agents including consumers, investors and businesses. It can do this by affecting either the *availability* of credit or the *price* of credit. The main feature of monetary policy is the policy of changing interest rates since they are the price of credit.

8.1 The effects of interest rate changes

Changes in interest rates affect the economy in many ways. The following consequences are the main effects of an increase in interest rates:

- Spending falls.

  Expenditure by consumers will be reduced. This occurs because the higher interest rates raise the cost of credit and deter spending.

  If we take incomes as fairly stable in the short term, higher interest payments on credit cards/mortgages, etc. leave less income for spending on consumer goods and services.

- Investment falls.

  A rise in interest rates will reduce the net return to investment and thus discourage businesses from undertaking new investment projects.

- Asset values fall.

  The market value of financial assets, such as bonds, will drop, because of the inverse relationship between bond prices and the rate of interest. This, in turn, will reduce many people's wealth.

  It is likely that they will react to maintain the value of their total wealth and so may save, thereby further reducing expenditure in the economy.

The total effect of these consequences of a rise in interest rates is to shift the aggregate demand curve to the left. This will lower inflationary pressures but at the cost of reducing the level of economic activity and raising unemployment.

In addition to these domestic effects there may be some external effects of a rise in interest rates.

- Foreign funds are attracted into the country.

  A rise in interest rates will encourage overseas financial businesses to deposit money in domestic banking institutions because the rate of return has increased, relative to that in other countries.

- The exchange rate rises, at least in the short term.

  The inflow of foreign funds raises demand for the currency and so pushes up the exchange rate.

  In the longer term, high interest rates can stifle economic growth, potentially making domestic firms less competitive in global markets. This can reduce export demand, resulting in a fall in exchange rates.

The overall effect – and in most cases its intended effect – of a rise in interest rates is to reduce the inflationary pressures in the economy.

8.2 The impact on businesses

Clearly businesses will be affected both directly and indirectly by changes in interest rates. These effects fall into three categories.

- Costs

  Some of the costs of a business, such as the cost of credit and the cost of stockholding, are directly determined by the rate of interest the business has to pay.

- Investment decisions

  The rate of interest is the cost of acquiring external investment funds, or the opportunity cost of using internal funds; a change in interest rates will therefore affect the profitability of investment projects.

- Sales revenue

  The volume of sales will decrease if interest rates rise: this is partly because this will generate deflationary pressure in the economy and partly because some sales, for example consumer durable goods, are often based on credit.

Of course, the reverse would happen if interest rates were to be *reduced*. This would be a reflationary policy and appropriate when inflationary pressures are weak and the economy is experiencing low levels of output and high unemployment. In this case lower interest rates would reduce business costs, raise the profitability of investment projects and thus encourage investment, and raise sales revenue as consumes have access to cheaper credit. Thus the thrust of monetary policy affects the economy as a whole and impacts in many ways on the businesses that make up the economy.

Supplementary reading – UK interest rate policy

In the case of the United Kingdom, the government in 1997 established a Monetary Policy Committee at the Bank of England. It gave the seven members, including five external experts, the power to decide the central rate of interest in the United Kingdom.

- The committee has a target rate of inflation of 2.0 per cent.
- Should the rate of inflation vary from this target by 1 per cent or more, the Bank of England is required to provide a written explanation to the Chancellor of the Exchequer.

- It is generally assumed that this would be most likely to occur if the rate of inflation exceeded the 2.0 per cent target. However, by 2001 it was clear that inflation was undershooting the target and it was just as likely that the Bank of England would have to explain why the rate of inflation had fallen by 1 per cent below the target.
- Despite inflation being above 2% in 2011 and 2012, the MPC has kept interest rates at 0.5% to counter the global recession and to boost lending and liquidity in financial markets.

In the EU, the European Central Bank manages monetary policy for the eurozone and a similar process operates with the central bank being given an inflation target. Even in those countries where a formal target does not exist, central banks are required to regard the rate of inflation as the main policy target for monetary policy and to conduct interest rate policy accordingly.

Test Your Understanding 17

Which of the following would not be due to an interest rate cut?

A Increase in consumer spending

B Increase in private sector investment

C Decrease in the value of corporate bonds

D Short term drop in the exchange rate

Test Your Understanding 18

An increase in the money supply will cause

A Interest rates to rise, investment spending to rise, and aggregate demand to rise

B Interest rates to rise, investment spending to fall, and aggregate demand to fall

C Interest rates to fall, investment spending to fall, and aggregate demand to fall

D Interest rates to fall, investment spending to rise, and aggregate demand to rise

9 Taxation

There are many aims to taxation and their priority varies with the political complexion of the government. However, all governments are agreed on the need to raise revenue.

Taxation can also be used to:

- Change markets.

  Certain potentially harmful goods, such as cigarettes and alcohol, may be heavily taxed, thereby lowering the quantity demanded and reducing consumption levels. Over 75 per cent of the price of cigarettes goes in tax; and at times higher taxes on petrol have been used to deter consumption and induce energy conservation also.

- Influence the level of aggregate monetary demand.

  AD can be reduced by raising taxation and can be raised by reducing taxation.

- Finance the provision of public and merit goods.

  The collective provision of certain public goods, such as defence, paid for from taxation revenue, enables it to be given free to everyone. Similarly, the zero price provision of a merit good such as education provides access to everyone, when market-priced supply might lead to under-consumption by many, which society might consider to be undesirable.

- Change the distribution of income and wealth.

  Direct taxes and especially progressive direct taxes fall most heavily on upper groups while indirect taxes and regressive taxes in general fall most heavily on lower income groups. Changing the balance between different taxes can thus alter income distribution.

Supplementary reading – Types of taxation

Taxes can be classified in several ways:

- What is taxed?

  The three main categories are:

Income	*Expenditure*	*Capital*
Income tax	VAT	Inheritance tax
Corporation tax	Excise duties	Capital gains tax
National insurance	Customs duties	

  However, there are also taxes on property ownership (e.g. council tax in the United Kingdom), car use (motor vehicle licence duty), television use (licence fee), a firm's payroll (employers' social security taxes), and oil royalties (petroleum revenue tax).

- Who is levying the tax?

  Most taxes are imposed by central government but some local government authorities are given the power to raise taxes.

- Who is paying the tax?

  Usually a distinction is made between direct and indirect taxes. With a direct tax the person receiving the income pays the tax to the authorities, for example income tax. In contrast, most taxes on expenditure are termed indirect, because the purchaser who benefits from the consumption is charged, usually in the purchase price, but the actual tax revenue is remitted, for convenience, by the seller to the authorities. Although the seller pays in the nominal sense he/she may be able to pass on the burden of the tax to the purchaser through a higher price.

- What percentage of income is paid in tax?

  The main categories here are:

  – *progressive*. A larger percentage of income is paid in tax as income rises, e.g. income tax (above a certain minimum).

  – *regressive*. A smaller percentage of income is paid in tax as income rises, e.g. VAT (on most goods and services).

  – *proportional*. The same percentage of income is paid in tax at all income levels.

Thus, with a progressive tax the average rate of taxation rises with income, whereas with a regressive tax the average rate falls. The average rate of tax is constant with a proportional tax. The marginal rate of taxation (percentage of extra $1 income paid in tax) also varies between these different types of tax. The marginal rate is higher than the average rate with a progressive tax but lower with a regressive tax as income rises. The two rates are equal for a proportional tax.

Supplementary reading – Principles of taxation

Adam Smith outlined four principles of taxation.

(1) *Certainty*. If people know what is expected of them in terms of what, when, how and where to pay, then the system operates efficiently and evasion is minimised.

(2) *Convenience*. The PAYE system in the United Kingdom operates on this basis and the payment of local authority tax by monthly instalments has developed for this reason.

(3) *Equitable*. They should be fairly based on an individual's ability to pay. Equality of sacrifice is often subject to conflicting interpretations, but it is usually agreed that a progressive element to income tax is fair in that the better off can bear a higher tax burden more easily than those on low incomes.

(4) *Economy*. Taxes should be cheap to collect.

Since Smith's day, other principles have been added. These include:

- *Efficiency*. A tax needs to achieve its objective efficiently and not undermine other aims and taxes. For instance, if the basic rate of tax is reduced to encourage effort but taxpayers substitute more leisure, then it is not operating efficiently.
- *Flexibility of a tax*. A tax needs to be capable of variation in order to fit with changes in economic management.

Supplementary reading – The tax yield

Direct taxes

The government is particularly concerned with the yield from taxation, both in total and per individual tax. It is probably easier to calculate the yield from changes in direct taxes, particularly those on income, than from changes in indirect taxes. However, higher income tax rates may lead to evasion and tax avoidance schemes. It has been argued that the growing black economy has resulted from higher taxes, and such activities obviously mean a loss of government revenue. Also, citizens may substitute leisure for work because they dislike the marginal tax rate on their earnings and this may slightly lower the tax yield. In recent years it has been argued that lower rates of taxation, especially of income tax, may actually raise the total tax yield. This is based on Laffer curve analysis which suggests that there is an optimum rate of tax for maximising total revenue. If taxes go above this level, tax revenues will fall. This suggests a strong case for reducing tax rates.

Five main arguments have been used to justify the reduced payment of income tax:

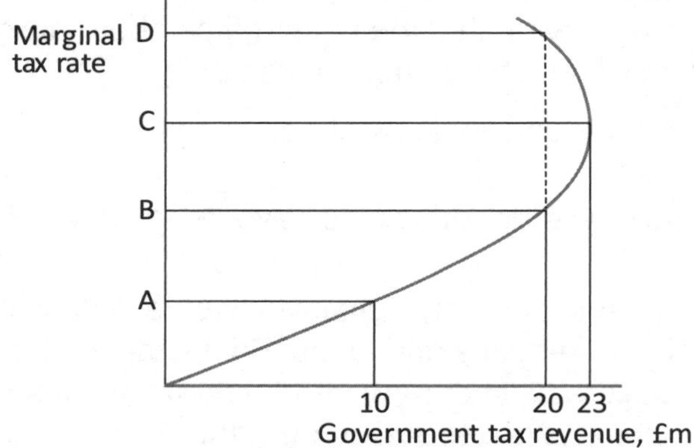

- High levels of income tax are a disincentive to work. For instance, in the United Kingdom in 1986 the marginal rate of tax and national insurance combined was 39 per cent on most incomes between £95 and £300 per week, and this deterred people from overtime working. It also acted as a disincentive to the self-employed and small companies, who faced higher marginal tax rates. In the diagram above, when the tax rate exceeds *C* total government revenue falls because workers substitute leisure. Thus it could be argued that the tax is no longer efficient. So a tax cut from *D* to *C* would actually increase tax yield by £3 m (23–20). Similarly, taxes could be reduced from *D* to *B* without any negative impact on tax revenues. Furthermore, it was claimed that in America in 1981–83 such a policy had raised extra revenue. However, critics have argued that it is virtually impossible to separate out the effects of a cut in tax rates from other economic things that are going on at the same time. Furthermore, the 'disincentive to work' argument takes a narrow view of worker motivation. Also, there is really no satisfactory way of measuring work effort, because the number of working hours fails to capture variables such as dedication, loyalty, drive, pride and long-term career choice.
- In the 1970s Britain experienced a 'brain drain' when well-qualified and well-paid (by British standards) professionals, such as doctors, golfers, etc., emigrated, particularly to the USA. One explanation given was the high rates of income tax, with a top marginal rate of 83 per cent. This exodus meant that British investment in human resources had been wasted.
- High tax rates mean that fewer funds are available for investment. It was claimed that people on high incomes invested their savings.
- Reductions in tax liability may lead to lower wage claims, and thus dampen inflation. This may occur because the tax reductions raise the workers' net disposable income and so they do not seek such high future wage claims, in their attempt to keep better off.
- Lower direct taxes would reduce the poverty trap, encouraging unemployed workers to accept low paid employment as the post tax income would now be higher.

However, the evidence to support these claims is rather mixed and the long term consequences of reduced direct taxation are not entirely clear.

Indirect taxes

The effect on yield of taxation on goods and services depends on consumer preferences, demand elasticities and time. When a good has price inelastic demand, then sales will not fall by much and tax will be collected. However, if the good has high price elasticity of demand then demand will fall steeply when the price rises as result of the imposition of a tax. This effect would become stronger in the long run and the total revenue gained would be greatly reduced. For this reason the heaviest indirect taxes are typically levied on those goods with very low price elasticities of demand. These goods include tobacco and cigarettes, alcohol and petrol.

Test Your Understanding 19

A progressive tax is one where the tax payment:

A rises as income increases

B falls as income increases

C is a constant proportion of income

D rises at a faster rate than income increases

Test Your Understanding 20

The following data refer to the principal sources of taxation revenue for the government of a developed economy

Government tax revenue: main tax sources as a percentage of total tax revenue

	200X	200Y
	%	%
1. Income taxes	34.1	30.0
2. Social security taxes	19.2	20.0
3. Corporation tax	6.8	7.9
4. Value added tax	14.7	22.9
5. Excise duties	15.9	14.3
6. Other expenditure taxes*	7.7	3.7
7. Capital gains tax	0.9	0.6
8. Inheritance tax	0.7	0.6

*includes stamp duty and motor vehicle duties

Required:

Using *both* your knowledge of economic theory *and* material contained in the table:

(a) State whether each of the following is a direct tax or an indirect tax:

(i) income tax;

(ii) corporation tax;

(iii) value added tax;

(iv) excise duties;

(v) social security taxes. **(5 marks)**

(b) State whether each of the following statements is true or false.

(i) Between 200X and 200Y the burden of taxation this economy shifted from indirect towards direct taxation.

(ii) Retailers cannot pass all of an indirect tax onto the customer.

(iii) Most tax revenue is gained when indirect taxes are levied on goods with high price elasticity of demand.

(iv) Taxes will have act as a disincentive if the income effect outweighs the substitution effect.

(v) Indirect taxes are likely to more regressive than direct taxes **(5 marks)**

(Total marks = 10)

10 Achieving policy objectives

The above (and other) policy options discussed can be blended to achieve economic objectives as follows.

10.1 Engineering a recovery from a recession

Policies to promote growth in order to get out of a recession include the following:

Cutting interest rates

- This can be interpreted either as part of Keynesian demand management (cutting interest rates should boost aggregate demand) or monetarism (to boost the money supply).

Running a budget deficit

- The classic Keynesian response to a recession.
- Monetarists would argue that the way the government finances the increase will have a negative effect elsewhere (e.g. higher taxation), thus reducing its effectiveness.

10.2 Enabling long term growth

Supply-side policies

Supply side policies attempt to increase the total quantity of factors of production especially capital as well as raise levels of productivity. Such policies should increase the economic capacity of the economy and include:

- Increasing the availability and quantity of skilled labour:
  - Training schemes to increase skills
  - Childcare vouchers to encourage single parents to enter the labour market
  - Using the income tax and benefits systems to encourage workers to work harder and longer hours
- Encouraging research and development, for example by government sponsorship of university research in cutting edge technologies
- Modernisation of the transport system, such as the motorway network, to enhance the distribution networks of firms.
- Provides smaller firms with assistance in the form of market information, advice on exporting, management training, technical assistance as well as tax concessions.
- Deregulation of markets.

Other

- Regional development grants and tax incentives to boost investment.
- Protectionist measures to reduce imports (e.g. quotas).
- Creating a stable economy to boost confidence (e.g. by achieving low inflation).

Supplementary reading – Further details on economic growth

Factors influencing economic growth

The growth potential of an economy is dependent upon two things:

- The amount of economic resources. The more factors of production there are, in the form of land, labour, enterprise and capital, the greater the potential for economic growth.
- The productivity of these factors of production.

Improvements in productivity are important for economic growth as it will not only increase output from a given stock of factors of production but it will also improve the competitiveness of an economy. *Productivity* is the amount of output produced per unit of input. As a result higher rates of productivity would lower unit costs of production for a firm, leading to greater competitiveness. The firm could, therefore, expect to gain sales in domestic and international markets. Lower costs could enable a firm to lower its prices, thereby expanding the market, and encourage it to raise its levels of investment. This in turn would expand productive potential and lead to still higher productivity which in turn can produce a virtuous circle of economic growth. Productivity growth is, therefore, clearly an important ingredient in achieving a higher rate of economic growth in an economy.

Capital can play a major part in economic growth.

- The greater the capital/output ratio, the higher the productivity of labour. The greater the levels of investment, the faster will be the growth in the capital stock.
- The higher the quality of capital, the more advanced will be the technology progress. This will occur when machinery is updated and when investment in research and development is high.

Labour also influences economic growth via its quantity and quality.

- Demographic factors such as the size and gender/age composition of the population determine the size of the work force. *The participation* rate measures the proportion of any age group which makes itself available for work. The greater this is, the greater the size of the working population.
- Education and training are likely to make a work force more adaptable and enterprising. This in turn will improve mobility of labour and raise its productivity

Policies to promote economic growth

Due to the importance of economic growth in raising standards of living, governments have always taken an interest in policies to promote it. A necessary condition is that levels of *aggregate monetary demand* are kept sufficiently high to see that existing productive capacity is fully used and that firms are encouraged to expand potential production by further investment.

- Governments can use fiscal and monetary policy to keep aggregate monetary demand close to its full employment level.
- Tax rates can be cut and interest rates lowered to encourage consumer and investment spending.

Doubts exist regarding the success of such policies. The preferred route in the United Kingdom is to use fiscal and monetary policy so as to control inflation and reduce uncertainty in government economic policy rather than as a way of stimulating aggregate monetary demand. Government policy tries to create favourable economic conditions for firms to thrive, thereby raising economic growth.

However government policies will also seek to encourage *aggregate supply* in order to expand production in the economy. In the United Kingdom this has been linked to a recognition that productivity in the United Kingdom is lower than in other developed economies.

Supply-side policies attempt to increase the total quantity of factors of production especially capital as well as raise levels of productivity. Such policies can be market driven or interventionist in nature. *Market driven* policies seek to create as free a market as possible within which private enterprise and entrepreneurial activity can thrive. Such policies aim to reduce the role of government in the economy and place a greater emphasis on the role of the individual in driving economic activity.

- Thus privatisation of government industries, e.g. electricity, gas and water in the United Kingdom, and deregulation, as with the London Stock Exchange in 1986, have been introduced.
- Similarly an internal market was introduced in several public services notably the National Health Service. The intention was to generate competition in sectors previously devoid of it and hence raise efficiency.
- The dependency culture was also attacked by reducing welfare payments for the unemployed and making it more difficult to qualify for such benefits. This should expand the numbers seeking work as people cannot so readily rely on State benefits for support, thus raising the supply of labour, one of the factors of production.

Supply-side policies also seek to offer greater incentives in the economy. Marginal rates of taxation can be cut for workers and firms.

- This should encourage workers to work harder and longer hours as they will retain a greater amount of their earnings.
- It might also encourage previously non-active persons, such as housewives, to enter the labour market as the opportunity costs of not doing so has now risen.
- Consequently the amount of labour as well as its productivity could rise as income tax rates are reduced, thus raising economic growth.
- Cuts in business tax would raise the level of retained profits, providing more funds for firms to reinvest in the business and thus raising the capital stock in the economy.

Finally, market driven policies will seek to reduce the amount of controls in the economy. This could involve regulations which include unnecessary restrictions on business activity, for example, licensing laws, or the amount of bureaucratic form-filling required from small firms.

- In the United Kingdom retail restrictions have been lifted so that shops can open seven days a week and the licensing laws on the sale of alcohol liberalised.
- The VAT threshold on small firms has been raised while all foreign exchange controls were removed in 1979, thereby permitting the free inflow and outflow of capital.
- The powers of trade unions have also been reduced in the United Kingdom. These include enforced secret ballots before a union can call a strike, restrictions on secondary picketing and the outlawing of union closed shops.

The overall impact of these measures has been the liberalisation of labour and capital markets in the United Kingdom.

However not all firms and entrepreneurs automatically thrive in a free market. Consequently supply-side policies are often *interventionist* in order to promote further economic growth in an economy. In most developed economies governments support the infrastructure to give firms a stronger foundation from which to conduct their businesses.

- This can take the form of modernisation of the transport system, such as the motorway network, which will enhance the distribution networks of firms.
- Education and training may be upgraded which will provide firms with potentially a more adaptable and productive supply of labour.

- The government may sponsor research and development in universities in order to provide an economy with an advantage in respect of leading edge technologies.
- In the United Kingdom the government recognises the importance of small and medium size firms to the economy. It provides them with assistance in the form of market information, advice on exporting, management training, technical assistance as well as tax concessions. Thus there are many ways in which inventionist policies of government can strengthen the position of firms in a market economy and enhance economic growth.

10.3 Unemployment

Reducing unemployment is not straightforward. At any moment in time unemployment may have a variety of causes, each of which may require a different and incompatible solution.

Cyclical unemployment

- This is sometimes referred to as demand-deficient, persistent or Keynesian unemployment.
- In this case unemployment is caused by the fact that aggregate demand in the economy is too small to create employment opportunities for all those willing, and able, to work.
- Keynesian economists refer to this as a deflationary gap and would seek to remove it by boosting aggregate demand.
- Monetarists would seek to reduce cyclical unemployment by appropriate supply-side measures as they would argue that cyclical unemployment does not really exist.

Frictional unemployment

- This refers to those people who are short-term unemployed as they move from one job to another.
- While not seen as a problem, it can be reduced by the provision of better information through job centres and other supply-side policies.

Structural and technological unemployment

- This is caused by structural change in the economy, leading often to both a change in the skills required and the location where economic activity takes place.

- Boosting aggregate demand (a demand-side policy) is likely to have little impact on structural unemployment. Supply-side policies are likely to be more effective, including:
  - government funded retraining schemes
  - tax breaks for redevelopment of old industrial sites
  - grant aid to encourage relocation of industry
  - business start-up advice and soft loans
  - help with worker relocation costs
  - improved information on available employment opportunities.

Seasonal unemployment

- Demand for some goods and services is highly seasonal, e.g. demand for fruit pickers. This in turn creates highly seasonal demand for workers. This can create regional economic problems in areas where a significant proportion of the workforce is employed in these seasonal industries.

Real wage unemployment

- This type of unemployment can occur in industries that are highly unionised. By keeping wages artificially high by the threat of strike action and closed shops, the number of people employed in the industry is reduced.
- Monetarists would see this as a prime example of a market imperfection and would address it by reducing union powers and abolishing minimum wage agreements.

Illustration 4 – Unemployment

In the 1980s the UK experienced a huge decline in its traditional heavy industries in the north. At the same time new high technology industries were established in the south.

Workers in the former heavy industries were at a double disadvantage. Not only were they in the wrong location but they also had the wrong skills required by the new industries.

Test Your Understanding 21

Structural unemployment is best defined as that caused by:

A the long-term decline of particular industries

B the trade cycle

C an insufficient level of aggregate demand

D seasonal variations in demand for particular goods and services

Test Your Understanding 22

Match each of the scenarios given below with one of the following types of unemployment.

Types

- Cyclical
- Structural
- Seasonal
- Frictional
- Real Wage

Scenarios

A A worker loses their job because of the introduction of new technology.

B After the Wall Street Crash of 1929, millions of Americans were unable to find work.

C Jobs in the car industry have been reduced due to a strong union and high wages.

D A management accountant has just been made redundant but is due to start a new job in three weeks' time.

E Bar staff are out of work in November in a European holiday resort.

Test Your Understanding 23

In recent years, a number of skilled workers have left Country A to work in neighbouring countries, because the tax rates in the neighbouring countries are lower than Country A's tax rates. The resulting decrease in the supply of skilled labour in Country A is likely to lead to:

A A lower equilibrium wage and a lower quantity of labour employed.

B Structural unemployment.

C A higher equilibrium wage and a lower quantity of labour employed.

D Frictional unemployment.

Supplementary reading – Further details on unemployment

Keynesian v Monetarist views

Keynesians view unemployment as being largely demand deficient, i.e. the equilibrium national income is too small to generate employment opportunities for all those wishing to work. The solution to this is for government to boost aggregate demand. In response to this, the economy will move to a new equilibrium closer to full employment.

For example, in response to falling aggregate demand during a recession Keynesian economists would advocate an increase in government spending to boost aggregate demand. This should then feed through into increased employment opportunities as firms respond by increasing the supply of goods.

Monetarists would react differently. They would advocate cuts in interest rates to encourage business investment. Further, they would seek to improve the operation of markets by removing government subsidies, freeing up labour markets by reducing the power of unions, and encouraging people into work by keeping unemployment benefits low.

Fundamentally, Keynesian economics does not allow for the co-existence of inflation and unemployment. Keynesian economists would argue that if unemployment exists there is insufficient demand in an economy whereas inflation indicates excessive demand.

In the mid-1970s many countries experienced high and growing levels of unemployment, together with record levels of inflation. This combination of economic variables was called stagflation and presented Keynesian economics with a real challenge.

Monetarists recognise a concept called the natural rate of unemployment. Even if an economy is at capacity, significant unemployment can still exist due to imperfections in the labour market, including:

- workers having the wrong skills relative to those demanded by the economy
- workers being located in the wrong place relative to economic activity
- workers having inadequate information about job opportunities
- occupational immobility due to trade unions and other restrictive working practices.

The natural rate of unemployment essentially has a structural cause. Boosting aggregate demand will do nothing to remove this problem. Inappropriate boosting of demand when the economy cannot respond for structural reasons will lead to inflation and will not decrease unemployment, i.e. stagflation.

Monetarists view the role of government as one of reducing or removing these labour market imperfections, i.e. reduction in the natural rate of unemployment.

Whilst monetarists recognise that demand-deficient unemployment can occur they would not seek to manipulate aggregate demand directly.

Typical monetarist policies aimed at removing demand deficient unemployment would involve:

- cutting interest rates to encourage business investment
- providing business start-up advice and support
- providing low-cost finance for business start up
- offering tax incentives for research and development
- offering incentives to encourage inward investment in the national economy.

10.4 Inflation

Inflation has a number of causes and solutions.

Demand-pull inflation

- If demand for goods and services in the economy is growing faster than the ability of the economy to supply these goods and services, prices will increase – the classic case of too much money chasing too few goods.
- Demand-side policies would focus on reducing aggregate demand through tax rises, cuts in government spending and higher interest rates.
- One type of demand-pull inflation is that due to excessive growth in the money supply
- Monetarists argue that inflation can result from an over expansion of the money supply. In effect increasing the money supply increases purchasing power in the economy, boosting demand for goods and services. If this expansion occurs faster than expansion in the supply of goods and services inflation can arise.
- The main monetarist tool for controlling such inflation is to reduce the growth in the money supply through higher interest rates.

Cost-push inflation

- If the underlying cost of factors of production increases, this is likely to be reflected in an increase in output prices as firms seek to maintain their profit margins irrespective of the level of aggregate demand.
- Reasons for cost increases include rising factor prices, rising import prices and increases in indirect taxes.
- For example, in an economy in which imports are significant, a weakening of the national currency will increase the cost of imports and could lead to domestic inflation. This can be reduced by policies to strengthen the national currency (see later).

Expectations effect

- If anticipated levels of inflation are built into wage negotiations and pricing decisions then it is likely that the expected rate of inflation will arise. Whilst the expectations effect is not the root cause of inflation it can contribute significantly to an inflationary spiral, particularly when underlying levels of inflation are high and rising.
- This spiral can be managed by a 'prices and incomes' policy where manufacturers agree to limit price rises in response to union agreements to limit wage claims.

- In the 1970s the UK government sought to control the inflationary effect of rising oil prices by setting ceiling prices for basic goods and services and, through the extensive nationalised industries of the day, wage increases. Ministers specified what the price of bread and milk would be and by how much the wages of workers in specific sectors would be allowed to rise.

Illustration 5 – Inflation

In 1975 the UK had inflation of nearly 25%. This reflected a number of factors:

- Poor macroeconomic management by government. In seeking to reduce unemployment the government had injected significant sums into the UK economy. However, due to growing structural problems the economy was unable to grow and the net result of this increased demand was to trigger an inflationary spiral.
- The effects of the quadrupling of the oil price in 1973/74 were still being felt in the UK economy.
- Strong unions and weak management led to poor control over wage demands.

In summary the high inflation was a mix of both cost push and demand pull.

As mentioned above, the UK government at the time tried to implement a prices and incomes policy.

Illustration 6 – Inflation

After the collapse of communism in the former Soviet Union, inflation in Russia during the early 1990s reached 5,000%, according to some estimates. This was due to the government policy of financing redevelopment through a rapid growth in the money supply.

Supplementary reading – The Quantity Theory of Money

Demand pull and cost push were essentially Keynesian explanations of inflation. However, monetarists reject the idea of cost-push inflation, believing that inflation is caused by increases in the *money supply* leading to excess demand for goods and services. In their view, changes in the money supply affect prices but not output and employment, except in the short run.

Monetarism is based on the *quantity theory of money*.

MV = PT

M = money supply
V = velocity of circulation (frequency with which money is spent)
P = average price of a transaction
T = volume of transactions

Monetarists believe the different factors vary as follows:

- In a given period monetarists believe that V is constant.
- T is limited by the supply of goods and services in the economy and hence linked to the level of national income/output in the economy. As the economy grows, then so does T
- Therefore if the money supply M grows more quickly than the economy (i.e. the growth in T), for the equation to remain in balance P has to increase, i.e. inflation occurs as the average price of a transaction increases.

Supplementary reading – The Phillips curve

The Phillips curve

It is generally believed that unemployment and inflation are linked. Phillips correlated changes in United Kingdom money wages and the level of unemployment. The relationships suggested that when unemployment was 2.5 per cent, the rate of change in money wages would be non-inflationary. As wages accounted for 70 per cent of production costs and it was assumed that cost-plus pricing was adopted, it was concluded that prices and unemployment were also correlated. If an economy was run at a 2.5 per cent level of unemployment, it was suggested that the general price level would be stabilised. Thus the Phillips curve is normally shown as a relationship between the level of unemployment and the rate of inflation

Thus the Phillips curve seemed to show a stable relationship between inflation and unemployment.

This means that

- the lower the rate of unemployment, the higher the rate of inflation;
- the higher the rate of unemployment, the lower the rate of inflation;
- there was a trade off between employment and price stability;
- governments could not simultaneously achieve price stability and full employment.

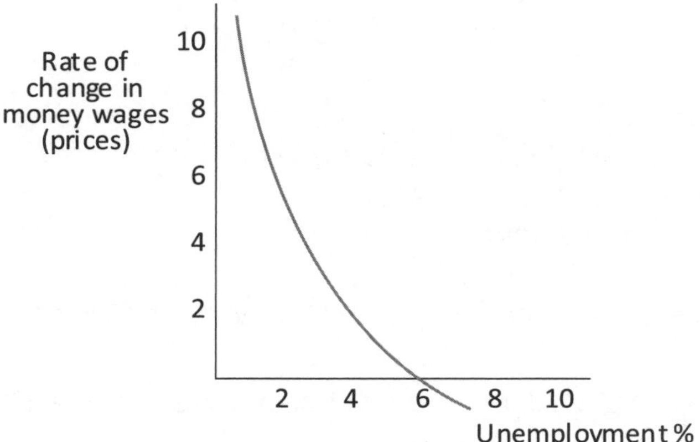

The Phillips curve

The Phillips curve was neutral between the cost-push and demand-pull theories of inflation and between the Keynesian and monetarist schools of thought. It only showed a link between wage inflation and unemployment levels and did not necessarily specify causation.

- The demand-pull theorists interpreted low unemployment as an indication of excess demand which served to 'pull' up wages in the labour market.
- The proponents of cost-push inflation saw a low level of unemployment as a measure of trade union strength, enabling them to 'push' up wages when employers were vulnerable because wage costs could be passed on as higher prices in the buoyant economy.

For a government, the Phillips curve seems to offer the option of lower unemployment and higher inflation or higher unemployment and lower inflation. This gave policy makers a choice, but still meant that one major economic objective could not be fulfilled. Price stability and full employment appeared to be mutually exclusive.

Development of the Phillips curve

By the time the Phillips curve had become established, 1970, the inverse relationship between unemployment and inflation began to break down. Monetarists were not surprised, as they had argued that the trade-off was at best temporary. As unemployment grew at higher rates of inflation (stagflation), Keynesian demand management was discredited. However, in the 1980s, the trade-off reappeared but at a higher absolute level. In effect, the Phillips curve appeared to have shifted to the right.

Several explanations have been put forward to explain this.

- *Structural unemployment.* The growth of structural and voluntary unemployment meant that there could be high pressure of demand for labour even if the unemployment figures suggested otherwise. This would mean a higher level of unemployment for each level of inflation.
- *Increased trade union power.* This would suggest that trade unions were able to secure higher wage increases at any given level of unemployment, thus generating higher inflation.
- *Cost pressures.* External cost rises such as that resulting from the oil price rises in the early and late 1970s would cause a higher rate of inflation at every level of unemployment. Administered prices in uncompetitive markets would contribute to this process.

Both of these arguments would suggest that the Phillips curve had moved outwards to the right as shown below. Thus the employment/inflation trade-off still existed but that the inflation price of full employment had greatly risen. Cost-push pressures shift PC to PC_1.

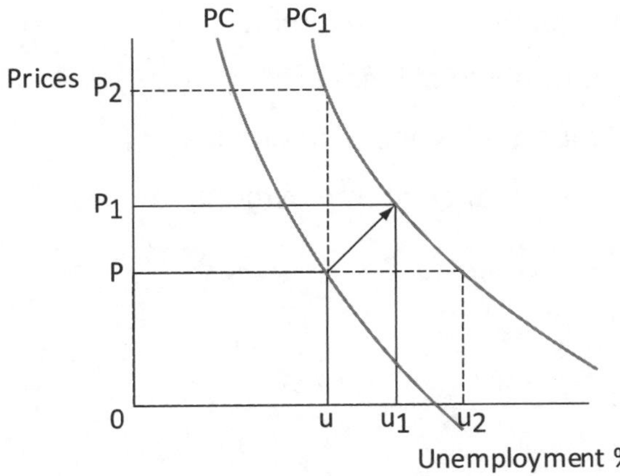

A shift in the Phillips curve

- At an unemployment level of U_1 the rate of inflation will now be P_1.
- If the government expanded aggregate demand to reduce unemployment to U, the resulting rate of inflation would rise to P_2 – higher than the P rate of inflation when the economy was on the original Phillips curve, PC.

This appears to be the experience of many economies during 1970 and 1980s. Between 1995 and 2008, some economies (e.g. the USA and the UK) managed to combine low inflation with falling unemployment. This suggests that the Phillips curve may have moved back to the left. This may be the result of:

- the effects of the *supply side policies* adopted in many countries from mid 1980s onwards;
- declining trade union power and militancy;
- a reduction in structural unemployment as structural change slows down;
- a temporary fall in real energy prices down to 2005.

Test Your Understanding 24

Answer the following questions based on the preceding information. You can check your answers below.

(1) What could be the underlying causes of demand-pull inflation?

(2) In cost-push inflation, cost rises are 'exogenous'. What does that mean?

(3) What is the quantity theory of money?

(4) Suggest four effects of inflation.

(5) List three important types of unemployment.

(6) Specify three costs of unemployment.

Test Your Understanding 25

The following data refer to an economy over a period of 13 years. Consider the data and answer the following questions:

Year	Rate of growth of GDP1 %	Govt. borrowing[2] $bn	Balance of payments[3] $bn
1994	–2.0	+11.8	+2.6
1995	–1.1	+10.5	+6.7
1996	+1.7	+4.8	+4.6
1997	+3.7	+11.5	+3.5
1998	+2.0	+10.3	+1.4
1999	+4.0	+7.4	+2.2
2000	+4.0	+2.5	–0.9
2001	+4.6	–1.4	–5.0
2002	+4.9	–11.9	–16.5
2003	+2.2	–9.3	–22.5
2004	+0.6	–2.1	–18.2
2005	–2.3	+7.7	–7.6
2006	–0.5	+28.9	–8.5

(1) Annual rate of growth of gross domestic product (GDP)

(2) Government borrowing (PSNB) '+' denotes net borrowing, '–' denotes repayment of previous debt.

(3) Balance of payments, current account: '+' denotes surplus, '–' denotes deficit.

Required:

Using *both* your knowledge of economic theory and the data contained in the table:

(a) With respect to the data in the above table, identify 2 years of economic recession in this economy and state whether in a recession: **(2 marks)**

(i) government borrowing increases or decreases;

(ii) the current account of the balance of payments moves towards deficit or surplus. **(2 marks)**

(b) State whether, other things being equal, the following would increase or decrease the level of government borrowing (the PSNB) or have no effect:

(i) a rise in exports;

(ii) a fall in unemployment. **(2 marks)**

(c) State whether each of the following is *true* or *false*.

(i) A current account deficit must be financed by a surplus on the capital and financial accounts.

(ii) If the government has a budget deficit it must borrow from abroad to finance it.

(iii) The national debt is the amount of money owed by the government to other countries.

(iv) The government budget acts as an automatic stabiliser in the trade cycle. **(4 marks)**

(Total marks = 10)

Test your understanding answers

Test Your Understanding 1

C

Lower taxation is not a policy objective. Rather it is a policy instrument that could be used to encourage economic growth.

Test Your Understanding 2

A Economic growth always brings benefits to all members of a society. **FALSE**

The benefits of economic growth are often very unevenly spread across a population. Those missing out on growth can experience a relative decline in their standard of living.

B Economic growth can lead to an increase in imports. **TRUE**

Rising incomes that accompany economic growth can lead to an increase in imports as consumers choose to spend their income on foreign rather than domestically produced goods.

C Inflation does not affect those on fixed incomes as much as those in employment. **FALSE**

Fixed incomes do not increase in line with inflation, e.g. 10% on $10,000 savings will not increase if a country is experiencing inflation. Those in employment would expect to receive pay rises broadly in line with inflation ensuring that the spending power of their income is not eroded.

D Inflation encourages investment in a national economy. **FALSE**

Inflation tends to discourage investment in a national economy in a number of ways. This includes a loss in confidence by both domestic and international investors.

Test Your Understanding 3

The main implications of 'boom and bust' are:

	Boom	**Bust**
Individuals and households	On the whole a boom time will be good for households: • low unemployment • rising house prices • high levels of confidence • increasing consumer spending. But: • People may be tempted to over-stretch borrowings. • Possible inflation, the main problem with 'boom and bust'.	The main problem with 'boom and bust' is the 'bust': • job losses • people losing their homes when unable to pay mortgages • fall in labour mobility due to negative equity • bankruptcy • low confidence.
Firms	• growth in profitability • extra competition as new firms are established. • May be tempted to over-stretch themselves through growing too quickly (which can give cash flow problems) and / or excessive borrowing.	• corporate failures • fall in profits • excess capacity.

Most people and firms would prefer steady growth without the high risks associated with the extremes of 'boom and bust'.

Test Your Understanding 4

False

GNP is better because it focuses on the incomes received by residents rather than only on those activities within the economy.

Test Your Understanding 5

C

GNP is a measure of all incomes received by residents. (A) is incorrect since it refers to domestic output and incomes, (B) is incorrect since it ignores incomes spent on imports and (D) is incorrect since it considers depreciation (capital consumption) and is a measure of net, not gross, national product.

Test Your Understanding 6

C

In some circumstances higher inflation can result in an increase in consumption spending as people prefer to spend now while their money has greater purchasing power.

Test Your Understanding 7

False

Do not confuse investment and savings. What Brenda has done is save more, so the level of savings will increase by $100 not the level of investment.

You could argue that the bank, having additional funds, would increase its lending to businesses who could then use it for investment (e.g. building new factories) but it is highly unlikely that investment will rise by exactly $100. The counter argument is that the reduction in consumption demand may result in a fall in investment levels.

Test Your Understanding 8

A

Excluding any (largely spurious) crowding out effects there is no reason to expect an increase in government expenditure to lead to a fall in investment. Given the impact on GDP, the opposite might be expected..

- B – an increase in interest rates will make fewer projects worth undertaking (higher cost of capital means lower NPVs)
- C – higher inflation creates uncertainty and thus stifles investment
- D – less credit means firms will struggle to raise funds for investment

Test Your Understanding 9

(1) Withdrawals from the circular flow are savings, taxes and imports.

(2) An injection into the circular flow is any additional expenditure that does not arise from the circular flow of income itself.

(3) At equilibrium, injections and withdrawals are equal.

(4) The consumption function shows how the level of consumption changes as the level of income changes.

(5) There are two other major consumers of goods and services: the government and overseas consumers (via exports).

(6) Net investment is the volume of investment in capital goods over and above that required to replace worn-out capital, that is depreciation.

(7) The accelerator theory shows that changes in consumption expenditure may induce much larger proportional changes in investment expenditure and thereby contribute to the trade cycle.

(8) The multiplier shows that an increase in expenditure (e.g. investment, government expenditure or exports) will produce a much larger increase in total income and expenditure through successive rounds of spending.

(9) The multiplier can be calculated as $K = 1/(1 - \text{MPC})$ where MPC is the marginal propensity to consume.

Test Your Understanding 10

C

On the aggregate supply and aggregate demand diagram AS/AD the horizontal axis is national income and the vertical axis is the price level. If the AS curves shifts to the left then, national income must fall. Since the AD curve is normally sloped down left to right the new AS curve will intersect is a higher point. Thus the price level will rise.

Test Your Understanding 11

A

(D) would increase consumer incomes and therefore demand. (B) would mean consumers spending a higher proportion of their income. (C) would imply an increase in demand for home-produced goods. A is correct because government expenditure is one component of aggregate demand.

Test Your Understanding 12

B

(A) and (C) will impact aggregate demand not supply and (D) is a consequence of the supply curve moving to the right not a cause.

Test Your Understanding 13

Factor	AD	AS	Right	Left
A fall in business confidence due to political scandals	X			X
An increase in tariffs on imported goods	X		X	
A major increase in world oil prices		X		X
An increase in trade union power and militancy		X		X
An increase in interest rates	X			X
New training initiatives for the unemployed		X	X	

Test Your Understanding 14

C

The PSNB refers to borrowing by the governments and other public sector authorities when their expenditure exceeds their income. (B) and (D) are incorrect since the first refers to private borrowing and the second to the balance of payments, not the government budget. (A) is incorrect: this is the accumulation of previous borrowing, not the current level of borrowing.

Test Your Understanding 15

A

Supply-side theorists believe unemployment is the result of problems with the supply of labour. (B) and (D) are concerned with aggregate demand and the demand for labour, and are therefore incorrect. (C) is incorrect since supply-side theorists believe that generous unemployment benefits encourage unemployment.

Test Your Understanding 16

C

The crowding-out effects refers to the process by which an increase in public expenditure may be offset by a fall in private expenditure. If the public expenditure is financed by taxation, private expenditure will fall. If it is financed by borrowing, interest rates are likely to increase, thus discouraging private expenditure.

Test Your Understanding 17

C

The value of bonds is inversely proportional to interest rates. As rates fall, the value will increase.

(A) and (B) could be due to a cut in interest rates as finance will become cheaper for both individuals and businesses.

(D) is correct as, in the short run, a cut in interest rates will result in funds leaving the country to find higher interest rates elsewhere. This will increase supply of the currency and hence a drop in its value.

Test Your Understanding 18

D

If the supply of money is increased, then the price of money - in effect, interest rates - will be reduced. Lower interest rates mean the cost of capital used in investment decisions will also be reduced, meaning that the net present valu of investment projects will increase. This will lead to an increase in government spending. Investments represent an injection into the economy, so a growth in investments will lead to an increase in aggregate demand.

Test Your Understanding 19

D

B refers to a regressive tax and (C) refers to a proportional tax. (A) is insufficient since the tax payment could rise with regressive and proportional taxes. (D) is correct since it identifies a progressive tax as one where the proportion of income taken in tax rises.

Test Your Understanding 20

(a)

(i) direct tax

(ii) direct tax

(iii) indirect tax

(iv) indirect tax

(v) direct tax

(b)

(i) *False*. The burden of taxation shifted towards indirect taxation.

(ii) *True*. A retailer can only pass on all of a tax onto customers if the demand for the good is perfectly price inelastic.

(iii) False. Most revenue is gained from taxing goods with very low price elasticity since consumers continue to buy even when the price has risen such as in the case of tobacco, petrol and alcohol.

(iv) *False*. A rise in taxation makes people take more leisure because of the substitution effect but to take less because of the income effect. Only if the substitution effect is strongest is there a net disincentive effect.

(v) *True*. Indirect taxes are unrelated to income and therefore tend to be strongly regressive.

Test Your Understanding 21

A

(D) is incorrect since it clearly refers to seasonal unemployment. (B) and (C) refer to unemployment caused by a lack of aggregate demand; this would cause unemployment in the economy as a whole. Structural unemployment is that which occurs irrespective of the overall level of demand and affects only certain industries.

Test Your Understanding 22

A Structural

B Cyclical

C Real wage

D Frictional

E Seasonal

Test Your Understanding 23

C

Workers leaving Country A to work in foreign countries means the labour supply curve in Country A will shift to the left (inwards). This resulting equilibrium between supply and demand now occurs at a higher wage rate but a lower quantity than before.

Test Your Understanding 24

(1) The principal cause is aggregate monetary demand exceeding the supply of goods and services at current prices. This could result from increases in injections into the circular flow when the economy is at or near full employment.

(2) Exogenous cost rises are those that occur from outside of the economic system and are not the result of excessive aggregate demand. These could include increases in import prices or wage increases due to trade union pressure rather than the demand for labour.

(3) The quantity theory of money claims that there is a stable link between the stock of money in the economy and the level of prices; if the money stock (supply) increases, this will raise the price level at some future date.

(4) Inflation may: reduce the international competitiveness of the trade sector of an economy; shift wealth from the holders of financial assets to the holders of debts; discourage savings as the value of savings decreases; distort consumer expenditure as consumers attempt to anticipate price changes.

(5) The main types of unemployment are: structural, frictional, cyclical, seasonal and voluntary.

(6) The costs of unemployment include the loss of output, the loss of tax income to the government, the loss of income to the unemployed and damage to the unemployeds' skills and health.

Test Your Understanding 25

(a) The years of recession are 1994, 1995, 2005 and 2006 and in a recession
(i) government borrowing would *increase*.
(ii) the balance of payments current account would move towards a *surplus*.

(b) (i) A rise in exports would have *no direct effect* on the government budget and therefore on government borrowing.

(ii) A fall in unemployment would lead to *lower* government borrowing as expenditure on unemployment pay fell and tax receipts rose.

(c) (i) *True*. The balance of payments always balances so a deficit (surplus) on one account is always matched by a surplus (deficit) on the other.

(ii) *False*. If the government has a budget deficit is must borrow but it can do this domestically as well as internationally.

(iii) *False*. Most government borrowing is done domestically so the bulk of the national debt is debt owed by the government to individuals and organisations in its own country.

(iv) *True*. In a recession taxes fall and expenditure rises thus limiting the recession; the reverse occurs in a boom period.

chapter

7

The Macroeconomic Context of Business II: The International Economy

Chapter learning objectives

After completing this chapter you should be able to:

- explain the concept of the balance of payments and its implications for government policy
- identify the main elements of national policy with respect to trade
- explain the impacts of exchange rate policies on business
- explain the concept of globalisation and the consequences for businesses and national economies
- explain the role of major institutions promoting global trade and development.

1 Introduction

In the previous chapter we looked at the main policy objectives of governments

- Economic growth – how can productive capacity be increased?
- Inflation – how can we ensure that general price levels do not increase?
- Unemployment – how can we ensure that everyone who wants a job has one?
- Balance of payments – how should we manage our relationship and trade with other countries?

In this chapter we look in detail at the last of these.

2 International trade

2.1 The benefits of international trade

Ignoring political reasons for trading, it is possible to identify a number of significant advantages relating to international trade:

- World trade allows *specialisation* enabling different nations with differing skills and resources to gain the rewards from the division of labour. In theory, nations specialise in the production of goods for which they have a natural advantage.

  For instance, Saudi Arabia extracts oil, Argentina rears beef and Britain provides financial services.

  Specialisation usually enables an industry to benefit from large-scale production and make the maximum use of resources.

- The *economies of scale* which can be obtained are determined by the size of the market.

  As international trade opens up new markets, it facilitates economies of scale. Such efficiency has benefits for the trading economies because it should produce lower prices and better products, leading to improvements in general living standards.

- *Competition* should be fostered by world trade, particularly free trade.

  A domestic market which is controlled by a monopolist might be subject to a foreign competitor. Alternatively, the market of a few complacent home suppliers might be revitalised by the entry of foreign firms (e.g. Japanese and American companies in British consumer goods industries).

- *Lower prices and greater choice* should be available to consumers.

  The increased choice which results from international trade is particularly evident in the food industry. Many consumers are now used to being able to eat fruits and vegetables from all over the world and all year round.

Supplementary reading – Comparative advantage

Specialisation is based on the concept of comparative advantage. While you do not need to know the details of this theory the basic idea will help you understand international trade.

The law of comparative advantage states that two countries can gain from trade when each specialises in the industries in which each has the lowest opportunity cost.

Comparative advantage between countries – illustration

Imagine a global economy with two countries and two products. Each country needs both products and at present all needs are met by domestic production. Each country has the same resources available to it and they are split equally between the two products.

Suppose the current situation with regard to production is as follows:

	Units of X per day	**Units of Y per day**
Country A	1,200	720
Country B	960	240
Total daily production	2,160	960

As the situation currently stands, country A has an absolute advantage in production of both X and Y.

Given this what are the benefits of A trading with B?

To answer this question we need to consider the opportunity costs incurred by producing X and Y.

- If country A were to focus on making X only, it would give up 720 units of Y to produce an extra 1,200 units of X, i.e. the opportunity cost of 1 unit of X is 720/1,200 = 0.6 units of Y.
- If country B were to focus on making X only, it would give up 240 units of Y to produce an extra 960 units of X, i.e. the opportunity cost of 1 unit of X is 240/960 = 0.25 units of Y.
- The opportunity cost of producing X is lower for country B than it is for country A. It follows that B has a comparative advantage in production of X and should specialise in this product.

If country B is to make product X, it follows that country A should make product Y. An analysis of opportunity costs supports this conclusion.

- If country A were to focus on making Y only, it would give up 1,200 units of X to make 720 units of Y, i.e. the opportunity cost of 1 unit of Y is 1,200/720 = 1.67 units of X.
- If country B were to focus on making Y only, it would give up 960 units of X to make 240 units of Y, i.e. the opportunity cost of 1 unit of Y is 960/240 = 4 units of X.
- Since country A has the lowest opportunity cost for production of Y, it should specialise in production of this product.

The impact of this decision by each country to specialise in production of the good for which they have the lowest opportunity cost on world output is shown below:

Specialisation based on lowest opportunity cost

	Units of X per day	**Units of Y per day**
Country A	0	1,440
Country B	1,920	0
Total daily production	1,920	1,440

Summary

- The important thing is comparative cost which is based on opportunity cost
- Because of this every country has a comparative/competitive advantage in some goods or services
- This will reflect their natural endowment of factors of production
- Trade enables countries to specialise where they have a comparative advantage and this raises world output and all countries gain from the process.

Supplementary reading – Practical limitations on specialisation

The advantages which can be gained from specialisation and international trade may be limited in practice by many of the following:

- Factor immobility

  I n the real world, factors tend to be fairly immobile in the short run, and over longer periods in some industries, for instance, coal. However, improved technology has lowered factor costs and thereby facilitated more international trading.

- Transport costs

  Although the production of certain bulky intermediate goods, such as cement, may be cheaper abroad, the distribution costs are so great that domestic suppliers still have a stranglehold over the market. However, generally transport costs in world trade are falling, thereby stimulating trade.

- The size of the market

  Specialisation and the resultant possible economies of scale are only justified if the production can be sold. No longer can any individual European country support a commercial or military aircraft building industry from the size of its own domestic market. Consequently pan European production facilities were established to produce the A380 airbus and the Euro fighter.

As the standard of living improves around the world so the sizes of markets grow. Generally, the development of new products, particularly in fields such as microelectronics, encourages world trade, as it creates new markets.

- Government policies

  Governments may install barriers to trade for political, economic and social reasons. For example the United Kingdom prohibits trade with Zimbabwe and restricts arm sales to certain countries.

Test Your Understanding 1

The existence of international trade is best explained by the fact that:

A countries use different currencies

B countries have different economic systems

C opportunity costs vary from one country to another

D specialisation enables a country to export certain goods and services

Test Your Understanding 2

Which of the following is not a benefit of free trade for a country?

A Greater competition

B Greater choice for consumers

C Greater opportunities for specialisation

D More jobs created in that country

2.2 Protectionism

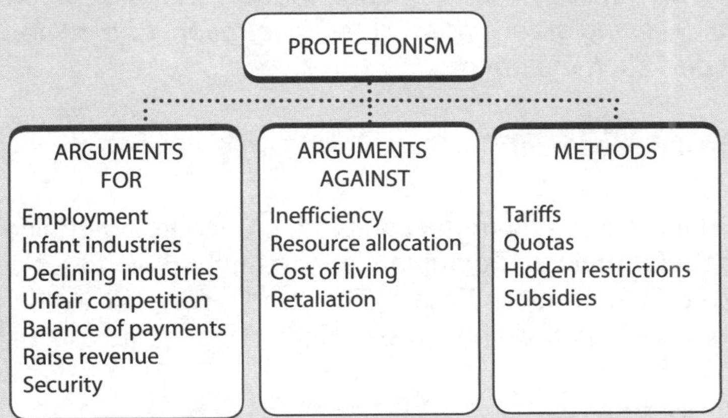

Many countries do not engage in free trade but seek, through a variety of mechanisms, to restrict the flow of imports into the domestic economy.

The main reason is simply that domestic producers want protection from imports in order to make higher profits at the expense of consumers. However, national governments provide a number of 'justifications' for protectionism:

- To protect employment

  For example, if a nation with an advantage successfully exports a good (e.g. Chinese textiles), then this may result in redundancies in a recipient nation (e.g. Britain).

- To help an infant (sunrise) industry

  The classic argument for protection is that new industries require help during their infancy because of the high initial costs and lack of economies of scale. If this help was not provided and they had to face competition from fully developed similar industries, it is claimed that these industries might not survive. Import controls might enable a new industry to build a solid domestic base and benefit from economies of scale before embarking upon international competition.

  For example, India uses a range of tariffs and controls to enable its domestic firms to become firmly established in its rapidly developing economy.

- To protect declining industries to buy time for structural readjustment

  For example, the US government has made various attempts to protect its declining steel industry (see illustration 1 below for further details of one such instance)

- To prevent unfair competition

  A government may justify protection by reference to the trading policies of its competitor nations. For instance, certain third-world producers try to sell fake British goods in Britain. These imitations break the copyright and patent laws in purporting to be of British origin, and are justifiably banned.

  Another unfair practice, which is not illegal, is dumping. This involves selling exports at artificially low prices, in order to gain a start in foreign markets. For instance, Japanese excavators were sold for export at 45% of the production cost. The losses abroad were subsidised by profits at home. Furthermore, the larger output, because of increasing exports, enabled economies of scale to be attained and unit costs lowered.

  (**Note:** The WTO agreement does not pass judgement on the rights or wrongs of dumping. Its focus is on how governments can or cannot react to dumping – it disciplines anti-dumping actions, and it is often called the "Anti-dumping Agreement".)

  Unfair trading can be more subtle than either of the above two varieties. Governments often subsidise their industries to enable them to compete in world markets, and the EU is not without its critics for giving such help to farmers. Clearly, it is very difficult to decide objectively what constitutes 'fair trading'.

- To protect the balance of payments

  One remedy suggested for persistent balance of payments deficit is the use of import controls.

  Many Western countries have a high marginal propensity to import, which means imports grow more than proportionately as the domestic economy expands. The result is that frequent payments deficits have caused deflationary domestic policies, which inhibited domestic investment and weakened doemstic industry. In addition, the rise in imports will reduce the market share of domestic firms, thereby making them less viable and less optimistic.

- To raise revenue

  Protective tariffs will raise revenue for the government if such duties are levied on goods with inelastic demand.

- To maintain security

  Essential products may be produced at home even when foreign goods may be more efficient, for example, defence equipment.

Arguments against protectionism

- Inefficiency is encouraged

  If domestic firms are protected from international competition, then they may settle for their existing market share and profits. Such complacency will discourage innovation and risk-taking. New technology may not be introduced and overmanning may persist. The protected industry (e.g. the textiles industry) may lobby to make temporary help permanent.

- Resources are misallocated

  By maintaining existing patterns of trade, resources do not move from declining industries, which are protected, to expanding industries. In addition, protection for one industry (e.g. steel) may adversely affect another (e.g. buyers of steel) because unit costs are raised.

- The cost of living is raised

  Protection will probably raise prices and so domestic consumers have to pay higher prices for (the taxed) imported goods or for (the protected) home-produced goods.

- Retaliation may occur

  Protection by one nation may provoke its trading partners to take similar action, and this will reduce the volume of world trade with the attendant consequences outlined above. This may weaken confidence, as the internationally accepted rules for trading are weakened when governments take unilateral action.

The methods of protection

Trade barriers fall into two groups – tariffs and non-tariff barriers (NTBs), which include everything else detailed below.

- Tariffs

  The most common import control is the tariff. This tax may be ad valorem – a given percentage of the import price – or specific (a set amount per item). It is sensible to levy tariffs on imports with an elastic demand if the objective is to reduce the volume of imports. However, if a tariff is imposed in order to raise revenue, then goods with inelastic demand should be chosen. Tariffs, therefore, act on the price of goods/services.

- Quotas

  In contrast, quotas are restrictions on the quantity of imports. The WTO has tried to stop quotas, although it does permit exceptions for nations with severe balance of payments difficulties.

  A more acceptable and modern type of protection which aims to limit the amount of a certain good being imported is the Voluntary Export Restraint Agreement (VERA). In 1991 the EC applied a VERA to the Japanese car industry, which was supposed to have halted its exports to Europe when sales of Japanese cars exceeded 16% of the market.

- Hidden restrictions

  Also, there are hidden import restrictions and procedures which can be utilised to subtly undermine foreign competition.

  Administrative devices include complicated forms, special testing regulation and safety certification, unusual product specification and the specialisation of customs posts.

  For instance, the colour of yellow Trebor Refreshers had to be modified for sale in Japan because they were considered an optical health danger. Such devices may frustrate exporters and thereby protect domestic producers from imports.

  In addition, the British government like others has used official persuasion to exclude imports; for example Ford Motor Company reduced the imports out of its European factories from 50 to 30% of its United Kingdom sales because of government pleas.

Public procurement can also be used to assist domestic firms. Government departments may deliberately buy goods from domestic firms even though they may not be the 'best on the market' (e.g. computer software for the Inland Revenue in 1993).

- *Subsidies*

As well as restricting imports, governments often *encourage exports* by various means. The systematic use of *export credits* and official support for export deals by departments is increasingly becoming part of Britain's trading strategy. Such measures make exporting cheaper and easier; a theme which is furthered by the government-sponsored international promotions and exhibitions.

However, the most blatant help given to exporters is the direct subsidy, for example, the subsidies given by both national governments and the European Commission to European steel firms. This is outlawed by the WTO and so done in more subtle ways nowadays. For instance, VAT on exports is refunded by the British Government to the producers. Similarly, some European governments subsidise domestic producers. For example, Germany gives subsidies on electricity which indirectly helps German manufacturers' costs of production.

International friction has increased because of the expansion of protectionism. There is friction between governments (e.g. between countries of the EU over beef and livestock movements), and between governments and trading blocs. The EU is often in dispute with the United States over steel and agriculture exports and with Japan over many manufactured goods.

Illustration 1 – Retaliation

In March 2002 the USA and Europe were on the brink of war (a trade war) over steel.

The US government imposed a 30% tariff on imports of steel in order to protect its struggling steel industry. President Bush blamed cheap imports for the closure of 32 steel firms in the USA. In 2003 the World Trade Organisation ruled these tariffs to be illegal and the EU planned to retaliate with sanctions worth $2.2 billion.

Shortly after the USA appeal against the WTO ruling was rejected the US President withdrew the tariff and the threat of a trade war subsided.

Test Your Understanding 3

Which of the following is not an example of protectionism?

A Subsidy to exporters

B Fixed exchange rate

C VERA

D Import tariff

Test Your Understanding 4

Which of the following is not an argument in favour of protectionism?

A To protect domestic jobs

B To reduce inflationary pressure

C To raise revenue via tariffs

D To protect declining domestic industries while they restructure

3 Trade agreements

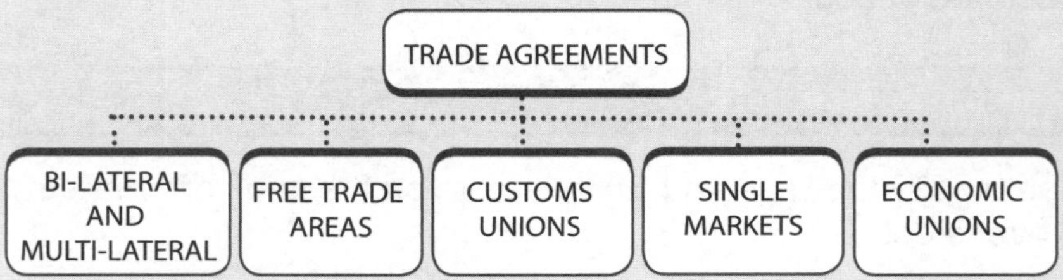

In many parts of the world, governments have created trade agreements and common markets to encourage free trade. However, the World Trade Organisation (WTO) is opposed to these trading blocs and customs unions (e.g. the European Union) because they encourage trade between members but often have high trade barriers for non-members.

From a business perspective such agreements give major opportunities to firms within the area specified but create barriers to entry for those outside. This is the reason why Japanese car manufacturers have built factories within the EU, so they can avoid quotas.

The different types of agreement are as follows:

3.1 Bi-lateral and multi-lateral trade agreements

These are agreements between two or more countries to eliminate quotas and tariffs on the trade of most (if not all) goods between them. example include

- The Closer Economic Relations (CER) agreement between Australia and New Zealand.

3.2 Free trade areas

If the members of a multi-lateral free trade agreement are all in the same geographical area then it is sometimes described as a free trade area. Examples include

- The North American Free Trade Agreement (NAFTA) between Canada, the United States, and Mexico.
- The ASEAN Free Trade Area (AFTA) is an agreement by the Association of Southeast Asian Nations (Brunei, Indonesia, Malaysia, Philippines, Singapore, Thailand, Vietnam, Laos, Myanmar and Cambodia).
- South Korea is currently negotiating a free trade agreement with the EU. Trade between South Korea and the EU totalled $92.2 billion in 2010.

3.3 Customs unions

A customs union is a free trade area with a common external tariff. The participant countries set up common external trade policy, but in some cases they use different import quotas. examples include

- Mercosur is a customs union between Brazil, Argentina, Uruguay, Paraguay and Venezuela in South America.

Countries may chose to move from a FTA to a customs union to eliminate some of the trade distortions of FTAs where different member countries have different export rules to the same target country. To avoid local regulations producers may sell to a partner in another member country with less stringent regulations who then sells to the target customer. This results in the need for rules to determine the origin of goods.

3.4 Single markets (economic communities)

A single market is a customs union with common policies on product regulation and free movement of goods and services to which has been added free movement of factors of production, notably capital and labour.

Advocates argue that this gives a more "level playing field" for producers in different countries as they all have to meet the same standards.

Examples include

- The Economic Community of West African States (ECOWAS).

3.5 Economic unions

An economic and monetary union is a single market with a common currency.

The largest economic and monetary union at present is the Eurozone. The Eurozone consists of the European Union member states that have adopted the Euro.

Arguments abound regarding the effects of regional trading blocs.

- Their supporters say that they encourage *trade creation by harmonizing economic policies* and standards within member countries and reducing prices as trade restrictions are removed.
- Opponents state that they lead to *trade diversion*. Member countries buy within the regional trading bloc when cheaper sources are available outside.
- Common external tariffs can encourage a regional fortress mentality which can lead to conflicts between different regional trading blocs. For example, NAFTA has complained over the EU's agricultural imports while the EU has complained over NAFTA's restrictions on steel imports.
- The fear is that regional trading blocs could lead to the development of protectionism worldwide at a time when the WTO is seeking to create free trade.

Test Your Understanding 5

Which of the following are necessary characteristics of a single market?

(i) a multi-lateral trade agreement between nearby countries

(ii) a common external tariff

(iii) free movement of factors of production

(iv) a single currency.

A (i) only

B (i) and (ii)

C (i), (ii) and (iii)

D (i), (ii), (iii) and (iv)

4 The balance of payments

4.1 Balance of payments

The balance of payments is an account showing the financial transactions of one nation with the rest of the world over a period of time.

The balance of payments is split into three parts:

- current account (goods and services)
- capital account (e.g. buildings) and
- financial account (e.g. cash flows)

The nature of the accounting system for the balance of payments (similar to double entry book keeping) ensures that the accounts, as a whole, will always balance to zero. However there may be deficits or surpluses on each of the three accounts that together make up the balance of payments.

When discussing debits and credits we conventionally look at the current account, where exports are a credit entry and imports a debit.

4.2 The current account

This is composed of two parts.

(a) *Visible trade*. This is trade in goods.

Exports by Britain are shown as credits (e.g. machinery sold to Saudi Arabia); while imports are debits (e.g. French perfume sold in Britain). The difference between the totals is known as the balance of trade.

	Visible balance £m
1996	–13,086
1999	–27,372
2003	–47,290
2006	–83,631
2009	–81,790
2012	-107,900

Source: ONS

(b) *Invisible trade*. Invisible trade includes trade in services, investment income and transfers of money between individuals and national bodies.

The income earned from the sale of British services abroad is known as an invisible export (e.g. consultancy fees paid to a British firm for advice on a Saudi Arabian building project). In contrast, invisible imports arise when British citizens spend money on foreign services (e.g. a British tourist to Texas pays for accommodation).

The invisible account can be considered in three sectors:

- *Interest, profits and dividends* (IPD).
- *Services*.
- *Transfers*. e.g. government transfers to embassies, military bases and contributions to international organisations, including the EU.

	Invisible balance £m
1996	+6,703
1999	+5,655
2003	+32,369
2006	+35,850
2009	+63,355
2012	+74,000

Source: ONS

Current account balance

This combines the visible and invisible trade. Generally a surplus balance is a good sign, and can indicate a prosperous and expanding economy. Britain's current account was in surplus in the early 1980s but has been in deficit ever since.

A deficit (surplus) on the current account will be balanced by a surplus (deficit), that is a net inflow (outflow) on the combined capital and financial accounts. However, as changes in the current account affect national income, a deficit means a decrease in spending power (and a net withdrawal from the circular flow), which is *deflationary*.

	Visibles £m	Invisibles £m	Current account balance £m	%GDP
1996	–13,086	+6,703	–6,717	–0.9
1999	–27,372	+5,655	–21,717	–2.4
2003	–47,290	+32,369	–14,921	–1.3
2006	–83,361	+35,850	–47,781	–3.6
2009	-81,790	+63,355	-18,345	-1.3
2012	–107,900	+74,000	–33,900	–3.3

Note: These accounts do not exactly balance because of the exclusion of some minor items and different basis for calculation of some items.

Source: ONS

4.3 The capital and financial accounts

These accounts show transactions in Britain's external assets and liabilities. It records *capital and financial movements* by firms, individuals and governments. It also includes the balancing item. A positive *balancing item* indicates unrecorded net exports, while a negative total shows unrecorded net imports. Since 1988 Britain had some unusually high balancing items. The figure arises because of the errors and omissions which occur in the collection of such detailed and numerous statistics based on enormous numbers of international transactions.

Types of flow include:

- Real foreign direct investment, such as a UK firm establishing a manufacturing facility in China. Direct investmnet refers to investment in an enterprise where the owners or shareholders have some element of control over the business.
- Portfolio investment, such as a UK investor buying shres in an existing business abroad. With portfolio investment, the investor has no control over the enterprise.
- Financial derivatives are any financial instrument whose underlying value is based on another asset, such as foreign currency, interest rates, commodities or indices.
- Reserve assets are foreign financial assets that are controlled by monetary authorities - namely the Bank of England. These assets are used to finance deficits and deal with imbalances. Reserve assets include gold and foreign exchange held by the Bank of England.

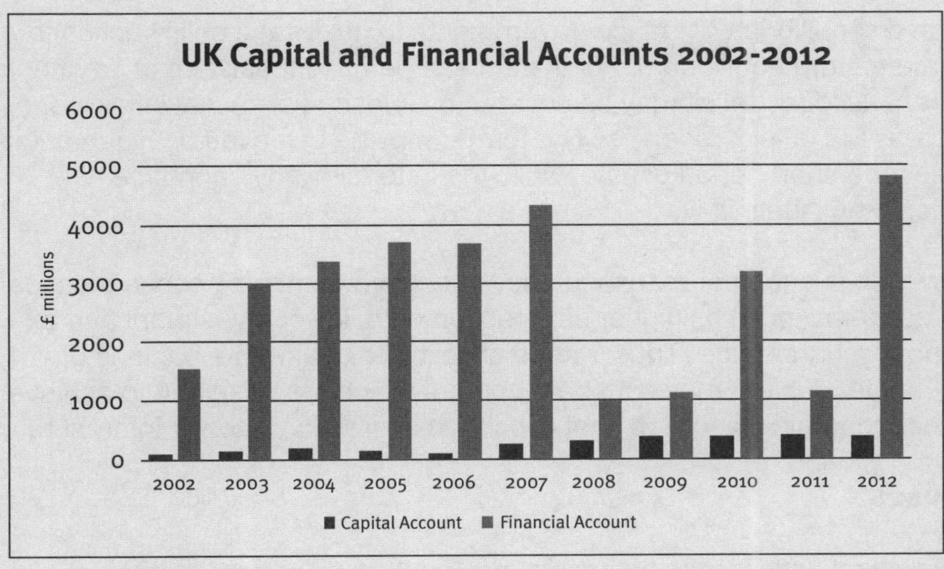

Test Your Understanding 6

The current account of the balance of payments includes all of the following items except which one?

A The inflow of capital investment by multinational companies

B Exports of manufactured goods

C Interest payments on overseas debts

D Expenditure in a country by overseas visitors

4.4 Equilibrium and disequilibrium

The balance of payments accounts always balance for technical reasons:

Current account + capital account + financial account + balancing items = 0

However, economists are concerned with the component parts of the structure. Persistent imbalances in certain sections, such as the visible trade and the current account, indicate *fundamental disequilibrium.*

For example:

- Countries with persistant deficits on their current accounts include the USA, the UK, Spain, Italy and France.
- Countries with persistant surpluses on their current accounts include China, Japan and Germany.

Such disequilibria will induce governments to undertake policy action to create/restore equilibrium. For instance, a persistent balance of payments current account deficit may be covered by substantial capital inflows or by a decrease in official reserves. The former may be achieved by higher interest rates for a short period of time, while the latter similarly cannot be undertaken indefinitely.

However, this temporary expediency may have damaging consequences for the economy, such as higher debt repayments, lower investment and a higher exchange rate. Thus, remedial action to deal with a balance of payments problem may constrain policies which are designed to achieve other economic objectives, that is economic growth via lower interest rates.

Causes

A structural deficit in the balance of payments current account is usually due to a high demand for imports alongside a weak export performance in manufacturing products.

(a) *Import penetration*. This can arise from imports taking larger shares of static markets or from imports maintaining their shares of expanding markets. Import penetration has increased for many reasons.

- Growth in consumer spending is often largely supported by imports.
- Imports may have become more competitive than domestic substitutes.
- Domestic currencies may be overvalued
- Foreign currencies may be undervalued (a criticism often made of the Chinese Yuan)
- Domestic producers have lacked competitiveness in non-price factors such as design, reliability, delivery and pre and after sales service.

(b) *Export performance.* The factors determining exports are similar to those affecting the demand for imports.

- First, the willingness and ability of domestic producers to supply abroad. For instance, a growing home market and a lack of surplus capacity will inhibit exporting and lead to concentration on home sales.
- Second, the price competitiveness of exports.
- Third, firms in some countries tend to have more surplus capacity which can be quickly utilised to raise output for domestic consumption when incomes rise.

4.5 Policies

Many policies have been advocated to restore a balance of payments account to equilibrium, usually when deficits have been a regular feature and there is evidence of fundamental disequilibrium.

Do nothing

The primary advantage of a floating exchange rate is that it is claimed to lead to automatic correction of a balance of payments disequilibrium. For example,

- If imports exceed exports, then a balance of payments deficit exists.
- In sterling terms, this means that more sterling is being sold to buy imports than is being bought to purchase UK exports.
- This excess of supply of sterling over demand for sterling will lead to a weakening of sterling against other currencies.
- This makes imports into the UK more expensive and exports from the UK cheaper.
- As a result, export volumes should start to rise and import volumes fall, gradually removing the balance of payment deficit.

Deliberate depreciation of the exchange rate

The objective behind depreciation and devaluation has been to induce *expenditure-switching* by consumers. This occurs in two ways:

- dearer imports hopefully lead domestic consumers to buy domestic goods instead,
- while cheaper exports cause foreign consumers to purchase exports rather than foreign products.

With a "dirty floating" exchange rate system, intervention to change the exchange rate will be through the central bank buying or selling currency onto markets.

However, a depreciation/devaluation will not immediately benefit a balance of payments in practice.

- There is an initial worsening of the current account because volumes are fixed and prices adjust automatically. However, eventually demand and supply become more elastic and so consumption and production patterns change, creating an improvement in the accounts.

- Furthermore, there is some evidence that, following a depreciation, exporters maintain their foreign exchange price (i.e. raise their prices measured in the domestic currency) rather than lowering them; this raises their short-run profits at the expense of long-run sales growth.

Deflation

An effective, but generally undesirable, policy used to return a balance of payments deficit to equilibrium has been domestic deflation to induce *expenditure-reduction* by consumers.

- The government, through either tight fiscal or restrictive monetary policy, curbs demand at home.
- The balance of payments is improved because the growth of import demand is weakened and domestic suppliers, facing a static home market, might switch resources towards export markets in order to fully utilise capacity.
- Additional gains from government deflationary policies can be to weaken trade union bargaining power through the fear of unemployment and by restraining production costs help to reduce inflation.

Although deflation improves the current account of the balance of payments, it has unfortunate costs for the economy.

- The tightening of fiscal policy, by either tax increases or expenditure cuts, and the restrictions on money supply, both reduce the demand for goods.
- Less demand means less supply and so unemployment rises.
- The general effect is to constrain the rate of economic growth, by depressing business optimism, lowering investment and under-utilizing resources.

Deflation is often used in conjunction with depreciation (devaluation) of the currency to improve the current account of the balance of payments.

Import controls

These have the effect of causing expenditure switching rather than expenditure reduction. *Quotas* prevent the purchase of imports, while *tariffs* raise import prices and possibly lower outgoings (assuming elastic demand for imports). The advantage gained from implementation will probably only be temporary because the basic weakness of price uncompetitiveness has not been changed. The likelihood would be that a fundamental disequilibrium would return once the import controls were lifted.

In Britain's case, wide-ranging import controls are not a realistic option. As a member of the WTO Britain has disavowed such a policy, while membership of the EU obviates such a unilateral action. There is also the danger of retaliation by our trading partners, with the consequent diminution in world trade.

Supply-side policies

These were policies which attempt to improve the efficiency of the supply base of the economy. By freeing up markets, increasing incentives, deregulating and removing the dead hand of the state from economic activity, it is claimed that the economy can be revitalised and achieve non-inflationary economic growth. The intention is to transform attitudes and behaviour so that British competitiveness re-emerges. Although the renaissance of any economy cannot happen overnight, the British economy has managed a period of sustained economic growth for a period 1995–2007. However there is little evidence that this has brought about any permanent improvement in the balance of payments.

Test Your Understanding 7

Which of the following might cause a country's exports to fall?

A A fall in the exchange rate for that country's currency

B A reduction in other countries' tariff barriers

C A decrease in the marginal propensity to import in other countries

D A rise in that country's imports

Test Your Understanding 8

If a country has a *floating (flexible)* exchange rate, which one of the following would lead to a fall (depreciation) in the rate of exchange for its currency?

A A rise in capital inflows into the economy

B An increase in the country's exports

C An increase in the country's imports

D A fall in the country's rate of inflation

Test Your Understanding 9

Which of the following would normally result from an increase (appreciation) in a country's exchange rate?

(i) A fall in the country's rate of inflation.
(ii) A rise in the volume of its exports.
(iii) A surplus on its current account.

A (i) and (ii) only
B (ii) and (iii) only
C (i) only
D (ii) only

Test Your Understanding 10

The main advantage of a system of flexible (floating) exchange rates is that it:

A provides certainty for international traders
B provides automatic correction of balance of payments deficits
C reduces international transactions costs
D provides policy discipline for governments

5 Globalisation

5.1 The nature of globalisation

The term 'globalisation' does not have a universally agreed definition. The International Monetary Fund defines globalisation as 'the growing economic interdependence of countries worldwide through increasing volume and variety of cross-border transactions in goods and services, free international capital flows, and more rapid and widespread diffusion of technology'.

It is useful here to make a distinction between globalisation and internationalisation:

Internationalisation

Internationalisation refers to the increasing spread of economic activities across geographical boundaries. For example:

- Many firms are taking advantage of the Internet to sell to new countries overseas.
- Setting up production facilities overseas.

Globalisation

Globalisation, however, refers to a more complex form of internationalisation where much greater integration is seen. For example:

- The erosion of trade barriers is creating a single global market, rather than many different international markets.
- The homogenising of tastes across geographies. Food, once highly local in style, has become more global in many respects.
- Firms selling the same product in every world market rather than tailoring products to local preferences.
- Greater harmonisation of laws in different countries.
- The dilution of traditional cultures in some Third World countries as they are replaced by Western value systems.

5.2 The factors driving globalisation

When considering the driving forces of globalisation it can be difficult to distinguish between cause and effect. For example, does the existence of global firms drive globalisation or are they the consequence of it? Both viewpoints have validity. However, for the exam, you should consider the main drivers of globalisation as follows:

Improved communications

Advances in information and communications technology (ICT) over the past ten years have paralleled the emergence of globalisation as a concept.

- Many within developing countries see the internet as an opportunity to gain access to knowledge and services from around the world in a way that would have been unimaginable previously.

- The internet and technologies such as mobile telephony allow developing countries to leapfrog steps in their development of infrastructure. A poor land line telephone system in the Philippines, for example, is being rapidly bypassed by mobile phones with internet access.

The wider access to Hollywood and Bollywood movies has also given rise to greater multiculturalism.

Political realignments

The growth of trade agreements, free trade areas and economic unions, described above, all contribute towards the idea of single markets replacing separate ones.

In addition, political realignments have opened the huge markets of China and the old Soviet Union, both of which used to be closed to Western firms.

- The collapse of communism in the USSR in 1989 (the date of the fall of the Berlin Wall) marked the beginning of new trade opportunities in the Soviet Union.
- Political change in China led to the signing of a bilateral trade agreement with the USA in 1979. This has been further reinforced by China joining the WTO.

Growth of global industries and firms

The growth of global firms has been a key driver of globalisation.

- Some would argue that the rapid growth of corporations such as MacDonalds and Coca Cola has resulted in pressure on local cultures to accept Western tastes and values.
- Global firms can influence governments to open up markets for free trade.
- Global firms can encourage political links between countries. For example, the entry of Japanese car manufacturers into the United Kingdom fostered a stronger political dialogue between the Japanese and British governments.

Cost differentials

As discussed in chapter 2, most firms' competitive strategy is based on cost and/or quality advantages. Many firms have found that they can manufacture their products at a much lower cost in 'Third World' countries rather than in their home markets. This is usually due to much lower labour costs.

For example, most clothing sold in the United Kingdom is manufactured in factories in China, Sri Lanka and India.

A more recent development is that many firms are finding that the goods produced often have higher quality as well as lower cost than using domestic suppliers.

Trade liberalisation

The World Trade Organisation (WTO) is constantly working towards the removal of trade barriers. The role of the WTO is discussed in more detail below.

Liberalisation of international capital markets

The liberalisation of capital controls has encouraged greater freedom in international capital flows. In particular developing countries have much greater access to capital for funding growth. This has been a mixture of aid and loans, although the distinction between the two is not always clear.

5.3 The impacts of globalisation

Industrial relocation

As mentioned above, many firms have relocated their manufacturing base to countries with lower labour costs ("off-shoring").

However, this can give the impression that the only form of expansion is from 'First World' to 'Third World'. This is not always the case as illustrated by Nissan building a car factory in Sunderland in the United Kingdom to avoid EU import quotas and tariffs.

Also, the motivation is not always cost. As mentioned before some non-Western countries are developing regional areas of excellence. For example, Bangalore in India is recognised globally for its expertise in telecommunications.

Managing (often complex) global supply chains has only been made possible by the advances in ICT mentioned above.

Emergence of growth markets

As mentioned above, many previously closed markets, such as China, are opening up to Western firms.

In addition, if tastes are becoming more homogeneous, then this presents new opportunities for firms to sell their products in countries previously discounted.

Access to markets and enhanced competition

The combination of firms' global expansion plans and the relaxation of trade barriers have resulted in increased competition in many markets. This can be seen in:

- greater pressure on firms' cost bases with factories being relocated to even cheaper areas
- greater calls for protectionism.

Developments in ICT have also facilitated greater access to markets, for example by selling via the internet.

Cross-national business alliances and mergers

To exploit the opportunities global markets offer many firms have sought to obtain expertise and greater economies of scale through cross-national mergers and acquisitions.

For example:

- In 2004 American brewer Anheuser-Busch Limited purchased the Chinese company Harbin Brewery Company Ltd.
- The merger of Hoechst (a German company) and Rhone Poulenc (French) to create Aventis in 1999 created the second largest drugs manufacturer in the world at the time.

Widening economic divisions between countries

Many opponents of globalisation argue that it is creating new gaps between the rich and the poor. For example:

Rich countries have much greater access to the internet and communications services. In the current information age wealth is created by the development of information goods and services, ranging from media, to education and software. Not all poor countries are taking part in this information revolution and are falling further behind the "digital divide".

The relentless drive to liberalise trade, i.e. to remove trade barriers, promote privatisation, and reduce regulation (including legal protection for workers), has had a negative impact on the lives of millions of people around the world.

Many poor countries have been pressured to orientate their economies towards producing exports and to reduce already inadequate spending on public services such as health and education so that they can repay their foreign debt. This has forced even more people into a life of poverty and uncertainty.

5.4 Impacts of ICT on international trade and patterns of development

As discussed in chapter 2, developments in ICT have accelerated globalisation and the number of global firms. In particular improved ICT makes it much easier for firms to control long, geographically diverse, supply chains.

Test Your Understanding 11

Which of the following would hinder rather than drive globalisation?

A Improved communications

B The switch from a command to a market economy

C The growth of multi-lateral trade agreements

D Protectionism

Supplementary reading – MNCs

Definitions

A multinational corporation is one which owns or controls production or service facilities in more than one country. A corporation does not become multinational merely by trading internationally, for example, by exporting its products from its home country.

MNCs can be ranked according to the amount of foreign assets they control. When ranked in this way the United States accounts for six of the ten largest MNCs. Such MNCs are mainly found in the petroleum, automotive and electronics/computing sectors.

Alternatively MNCs can be ranked according to a transnationality index. This is a composite index that is calculated as the average of the following ratios: foreign assets/total assets; foreign sales/total sales; foreign employment/total employment. This index gives a different ranking to the one based solely on foreign assets. It is a better indicator of the extent to which a corporation operates outside its home country.

Many firms with a high ranking in this index come from smaller countries with a restricted domestic market and it is dominated by European Union countries.

Size of MNCs

The United Nations estimated that in 2002 there were approximately 64,000 MNCs with around 866,000 affiliates located abroad. Their sales revenues are equivalent to about 31% of world GDP and a third of the world's largest economic units are MNCs rather than nation states.

MNCs account for around 30% cent of GDP in the United Kingdom and almost half of manufacturing employment. Foreign MNCs operating in the United Kingdom account for 23% of output and 11% of all employment. The United Kingdom is a major recipient of inward direct foreign investment (DFI). For example, in recent years 30% of all Japanese DFI in the European Union has been in the United Kingdom. Likewise the United Kingdom is a major provider of outward DFI. United Kingdom home-based MNCs were the providers of 14% of all DFI in 2004 despite representing only 2% of all MNCs. Thus the United Kingdom is very much part of the globalisation process.

Explanation of MNC activity

There are several advantages for a corporation in establishing a production base overseas rather than trading with foreign companies.

- *Costs* can be reduced if cheaper production facilities are available in other countries. This is especially applicable in the manufacturing sector due to the abundance of cheap, high-quality labour in developing countries.
- *Expand sales* by entering new markets. MNCs have gradually switched from exporting to a foreign market to establishing sales outlet and finally a production facility. By producing overseas the MNC can avoid the costs of transporting its product and also bypass any tariffs or quotas.
- *Secure supply* by vertical integration backwards. Oil companies, such as BP and Shell, can gain access to the gas and oil resources they need.
- *An organisational structure* to manage the operations is necessary if potential advantages are to be realised. The MNC must be able to exploit those assets internal to the corporation, including human capital, financial resources, marketing and managerial skills. This process has been made possible by the use of divisional corporate structures based on product and/or geographic characteristics which have helped the management of complex global corporations.
- Advances in *new technologies* have made it easier to conduct business across national frontiers. The spread of IT-based communications systems alongside cheaper air travel have improved communications. The globalisation of consumer markets via media and popular culture have opened world markets to MNCs.

Impact of MNCs

Any assessment of the impact of MNCs on national economies will need to consider various costs and benefits.

- First, DFI by an MNC should improve economic welfare as capital is transferred to economies where the marginal rate of return on capital is highest. However, MNCs may finance overseas investment by raising the capital on the local capital market. In such cases inward investment may merely displace domestic investment that would otherwise have taken place.
- The involvement of an MNC in a foreign economy may often promote *technology transfer* which will be of benefit to the recipient economy. New technologies may be introduced without the research and development costs and the learning time which would other wise have been needed.
- Similarly local producers can copy the superior processes and organisational patterns of the MNCs. The latter may also establish direct linkages with domestic suppliers which raise the productivity of the local producers.
- However, technology transfer may only be at a low level. The MNC may only use the recipient economy as an assembly base using basic technology. Many working practices successful in an MNC's home economy may not readily transfer to another economy with different cultural traditions.
- MNCs will also impinge on the macro variables of an economy. The *balance of payments* will gain from inflows of DFI but will suffer when profits from the investment are remitted back to the home economy of the MNC. *Employment* can also be provided by MNC activity. Direct employment in the MNC's subsidiary can be supplemented by further employment in local suppliers to the MNC's operations.
- However, the employment effects can be weakened if the MNC displaces existing domestic firms. Furthermore MNCs' operations are mobile and they could well choose to locate in another economy if it proved advantageous to do so.
- Finally, MNCs can affect a government's taxation and expenditure. MNCs are notorious for being able to reduce their tax liabilities by means of *transfer pricing*. Where intra-corporation trade takes place, internal prices are set to minimise profits in economies with the highest tax rates. On the other hand, a government often has to offer grants and subsidies to MNCs in order to attract them to their economy.

Consequently the impact of the MNCs on national economies can be profound. To what extent national economies benefit from their relationships with MNCs is uncertain. The growth of globalisation seems unstoppable and with it their power to influence international trade.

6 Institutions encouraging free trade

6.1 The World Trade Organisation (WTO) and the General Agreements on Tariffs and Trade (GATT)

As trade began to recover after the Second World War attempts were made to reduce barriers to free trade around the world. The General Agreements on Tariffs and Trade (GATT) came into being in 1948. Regular rounds of talks were held to agree trading patterns around the world and to negotiate removal of trade barriers.

These negotiations have become more prolonged and complex as time has gone on.

In 1995 the World Trade Organisation based in Geneva replaced GATT. It has a number of roles:

- to ensure compliance of member countries with previous GATT agreements
- to negotiate future trade liberalisation agreements
- to resolve trading disputes between nations.

The WTO has much greater authority than GATT as it has the power to police and 'enforce' trade agreements. It faces an increasingly difficult role as the facilitator for global free trade talks.

The WTO is opposed to the development of trading blocs and customs unions such as the EU and NAFTA. Although they promote free trade between members of the union, there are normally high trade barriers for non-members, e.g. the difficulties faced by non-EU food producers when they attempt to export to the EU.

Example

There is growing tension between the developed and the developing world. The developing world regards heavy subsidy of EU and American farmers as a huge barrier to trade for their domestic farmers. At the same time, the developed world complains about export of low cost manufactured goods from the developing world that are not subject to the same health, safety and environmental regulations that they face.

Supplementary reading – The activities of the WTO

Reviewing members' trade policies

Reviews are conducted on a regular, periodic basis. The four biggest traders—the European Union, the United States, Japan and Canada—are examined approximately once every two years. The next 16 countries in terms of their share of world trade are reviewed every four years; and the remaining countries every six years, with the possibility of a longer interim period for the least-developed countries.

Anti-dumping rules

If a company exports a product at a price lower than the price it normally charges on its own home market, it is said to be "dumping" the product. Is this unfair competition? The WTO agreement does not pass judgement. Its focus is on how governments can or cannot react to dumping – it disciplines anti-dumping actions, and it is often called the "Anti-dumping Agreement".

For example, Turkey expressed concern about the Dominican Republic's decision to impose a country-wide anti-dumping duty on steel rods and bars coming from Turkey.

6.2 The European Union (EU)

The EU is an example of a single market and, within the Euro zone, an economic union (see above). It has its origins in the Treaty of Rome (1957).

The aims of the treaty were as follows:

- the elimination of customs duties and quotas on imports and exports between member states
- the establishment of a common customs tariff and a common commercial policy towards non-member states
- the abolition of obstacles to the free movement of persons, services and capital between member states
- the establishment of common policies on transport and agriculture
- the prohibition of business practices that restrict or distort competition
- the association of overseas countries in order to increase trade and development.

Supplementary reading – Further details on the EU

Harmonisation and convergence

The abolition of internal tariff barriers was achieved in 1968 but it was not until the Single European Act in1986 that the final barriers to free movement of people, goods and services were removed.

Thus member states enjoy the benefits of free trade described above while having a system of tariffs and quotas limiting exports from countries outside the EU.

There has also been a move towards greater economic and monetary union with the launch of the single European currency (the Euro) in 2002. To date 12 member states have adopted the Euro.

The danger of removing trade barriers is that domestic firms feel that the resulting competition they face is unfair. This could be because, for example, labour laws in another member state are less stringent, allowing firms there to make products at a lower labour cost.

For the EU single market to function as a level playing field, therefore, there is a need for 'harmonisation' between member states in areas such as employment legislation.

Countries who wished to use the Euro as their main currency also had to satisfy convergence criteria, including:

- Inflation:

  The inflation rate must be no more than 1.5 percentage points higher than the 3 best-performing member states of the EU (based on inflation).

- Government finance:

  The annual government deficit must not exceed 3% of the gross domestic product (GDP) and gross government debt must not exceed 60% of GDP.

- Exchange rates:

  Applicant countries should have joined the exchange-rate mechanism (ERM II) under the European Monetary System (EMS) for two consecutive years and should not have devaluated its currency during the period.

- Long-term interest rates:

  The nominal long-term interest rate must not be more than 2 percentage points higher than the 3 best-performing member states (based on inflation).

The purpose of setting the criteria was to maintain the price stability within the Euro zone even with the inclusion of new member states. However, as a result of the banking crisis and the subsequent pressure on the Euro zone countries, these criteria have had to be radically revised.

Note: This issue is discussed further when looking at exchange rate systems in chapter 8.

Future challenges

The main challenges facing the EU are as follows:

(1) Managing the current economic crisis and save the euro

While many countries have suffered economically as a result of the global banking crisis and credit crunch (see Chapter 7), four countries within the EU - Spain, Portugal, Ireland and Greece - are in particularly difficult positions. Some analysts have argued that unless these problems can be dealt with, then the viability of the euro will be in doubt.

(2) Enlargement

In 2002 member states voted to enlarge the EU from 10 to 25 members, increasing the number of consumers to over 500 million. This has brought concerns over lower labour rates in Poland, for example, that could allow Polish firms to undermine existing firms.

Enlargement has also brought into focus the need for a new European Constitution. To date this has been rejected by some member states.

(3) Reform of the Common Agricultural Policy (CAP)

The Common Agricultural Policy (CAP) is a system of agricultural subsidies which work by guaranteeing a minimum price to producers and by direct payment of a subsidy for crops planted. This provides some economic certainty for EU farmers and production of a certain quantity of agricultural goods.

Critics of the CAP argue that it increases Third World poverty by putting Third World farmers out of business. This is done by creating an oversupply of agricultural products which are then sold in the Third World and preventing the Third World from exporting its agricultural goods to the West.

6.3 The Group of Eight (G8)

The Group of Eight (G8) consists of Canada, France, Germany, Italy, Japan, Russia, the United Kingdom, and the United States. Together, these countries represent about 65% of the world economy.

The agenda of G8 meetings is usually about controversial global issues such as global warming, poverty in Africa, fair trade policies and AIDS but has implications for global trade.

The 31st G8 summit in 2005 resulted in a stated commitment to reduce subsidies and tariffs that inhibit trade.

The G8 summit has consistently dealt with:

- Macroeconomic management
- International trade
- Energy issues and climate change
- Development issues and relationships with developing countries
- Issues of international concern such as terrorism and organised crime.

The G8 does not have any formal resources or powers as is the case with other inter-national organisations such as the WTO. However, it provides a forum for the most powerful nations to discuss complex international issues and to develop the personal relations that help them respond in effective collective fashion to sudden crises or shocks. The summit also gives direction to the international community by setting priorities, defining new issues and providing guidance to established international organisations.

Test Your Understanding 12

The main objective of the WTO is:

A to raise living standards in developing countries

B to minimise barriers to international trade

C to harmonise tariffs

D to eliminate customs unions

Test Your Understanding 13

Answer the following questions based on the preceding information.

(1) International trade is based on which principle?

(2) What is the difference between absolute advantage and comparative advantage?

(3) Why are exchange rates important?

(4) What factors inhibit international trade?

(5) Give three arguments for trade protection policies.

(6) What is a VERA?

(7) What does the WTO attempt to do?

(8) Why have some companies become multinational in structure?

(9) How can multinational companies benefit national economies?

Test Your Understanding 14

Answer the following questions based on the preceding information. You can check your answers below.

(1) Name one invisible earning.

(2) What do the capital and financial accounts show?

(3) What is 'hot money'?

(4) What has caused Britain's balance of payments current account deficit?

(5) What is the difference between devaluation and depreciation of the exchange rate?

(6) How could a fall in the exchange rate help an economy?

(7) How can deflation help the balance of payments deficit?

Test Your Understanding 15

The following passage is based on a newspaper article published in February 1997, and discusses the effects of the rise in the sterling exchange rate in 1996:

'United Kingdom companies are expressing alarm at the strength of sterling after seeing the rising exchange rate choke off their exports' the CBI (Confederation of British Industry) said yesterday as the pound sterling rose to DM2.707n late trading.

The CBI said that demand for exports had levelled off for the first time since the autumn of 1993, with optimism and order books hit by the 9 per cent appreciation of sterling in the final three months of 1996. According to the CBI survey, prices were regarded as more of a constraint on exports than at any time since October 1989. The picture which emerged was of weakening export orders balanced by the strength of domestic demand for United Kingdom-produced consumer goods.

The CBI said that the decision on whether the government should raise interest rates was 'finely balanced'. Any rise in interest rates to prevent the very rapid recovery from recession leading to excessive inflation was likely to further strengthen sterling and have an adverse effect on exporters' order books.

However, the prospects of a rise in interest rates to slow inflation were lessened by the latest figures for the growth of the money supply. They showed that broad money growth fell from an annual rate of 10.er cent in November to 9.er cent in December. However, these were still well above the government's target for the growth of the money supply. In response, a Government source pointed out that the rise in sterling itself would act to reduce the rate of inflation through its effects on costs and on the level of aggregate demand.

Required:

Using *both* your knowledge of economic *theory* and *material* contained in the above passage:

(a) State whether, other things being equal, the effect of each of the following would be to raise the exchange rate for a currency, lower the exchange rate or leave the exchange rate unaffected.

- (i) A rise in interest rates in the country.
- (ii) A rise in the rate of inflation in a country.
- (iii) A surplus on the current account of the balance of payments.
- (iv) A government budget deficit.
- (v) An increase in the export of capital from the country.

(5 marks)

(b) State whether each of the following is *true* or *false*:

(i) A rise in the exchange rate tends to reduce the domestic rate of inflation.

(ii) A rise in the exchange rate tends to reduce domestic unemployment.

(iii) A rise in the exchange rate tends to worsen the terms of trade.

(iv) A rise in the exchange rate tends to worsen the balance of trade.

(v) A rise in the exchange rate tends to raise domestic living standards

(5 marks)

(Total marks = 10)

Test your understanding answers

Test Your Understanding 1

C

Test Your Understanding 2

D

International trade may result in domestic jobs being displaced by more efficient overseas competitors.

Test Your Understanding 3

B

A fixed exchange rate should bring stability but does nothing to favour domestic firms over foreign ones. All the other options are classic examples of protectionism.

Test Your Understanding 4

B

If anything, you could argue that protectionism will lead to higher inflation:

- imported goods will be more expensive due to tariffs
- the lack of competition may result in domestic goods being more expensive
- the increase in aggregate demand may result in inflationary pressure

Test Your Understanding 5

C

By definition. A single market does not have to have a single currency (that would make it an economic union)

Test Your Understanding 6

A

Exports of goods clearly appears in the balance of trade element of the current account. Interest payments and tourist expenditure appear on the invisible items section of the current account. The movement of capital by multinational companies, however, is recorded on the financial account.

Test Your Understanding 7

C

A fall in the exchange rate (depreciation or devaluation) or a fall in barriers to trade will be likely to lead to increases in a country's exports. A rise in a country's imports will have no direct effect on its exports, but may indirectly raise them, since it will have increased the level of incomes in trading partners. However, if the propensity to import in the country's trading partners falls, exports would decline.

Test Your Understanding 8

C

The exchange rate will rise if the demand for the currency increases; this will result from increased inward capital flows and increased exports, especially if lower inflation increases the demand for exports. Increased imports however will increase the supply of the currency to pay for them; the currency will therefore depreciate.

Test Your Understanding 9

C

A rise in the exchange rate will raise export prices; export volumes will fall, so statement (ii) is false, and the current account will move towards deficit, so statement (iii) is also false.

However, import prices will fall, dampening domestic inflation, so statement (i) is true

Test Your Understanding 10

B

A and B are benefits of a fixed exchange rate system since the exchange rate remains fixed and domestic economic policy is constrained by this. Response C is incorrect since transaction costs occur whenever foreign exchange is bought or sold, irrespective of the exchange rate regime. The correct solution is B since a deficit would lead to a fall in the exchange rate, which would improve the country's competitiveness and thus correct the deficit.

Test Your Understanding 11

D

Protectionism will reduce international trade and hence slow the rate of globalisation.

Test Your Understanding 12

B

The WTO is an organisation concerned with trade agreements and associated matters, and seeks a reduction in barriers to trade. The minimalisation of trade barriers is its primary aim. The WTO may see the others as desirable, but they are not its direct concerns.

Test Your Understanding 13

(1) International trade is theoretically based on the theory of comparative advantage.

(2) Absolute advantage occurs where one country is much better than another at producing one good (but much worse at producing a second good). However, a country with a comparative advantage is one which is much better at producing two (or more goods) but by different amounts.

(3) Exchange rates facilitate pricing and this enables international comparisons to be made.

(4) International trade is inhibited by transport costs, the immobility of factors, market size and protective policies.

(5) Protection is used to protect employment, help infant industries, prevent unfair competition and help the balance of payments.

(6) Voluntary export restraint agreement.

(7) The WTO tries to reduce tariff barriers and other protective measures.

(8) To reduce costs and expand markets and sales. This has been helped by the development of appropriate organisational structures and technologies.

(9) Direct foreign investment can boost: domestic capital fund; technology transfer; improvement in production processes and organisational structures; employment gains.

Test Your Understanding 14

(1) A dividend from an overseas share.

(2) The capital and financial accounts show changes in a country's external assets and liabilities.

(3) 'Hot money' refers to short-term capital movements of currencies by international financiers/speculators.

(4) Britain's current account deficit has been caused by a lack of competitiveness (for many reasons) in trade.

(5) A devaluation occurs when a fixed exchange rate is lowered, whereas depreciation refers to a floating exchange rate which is moving downwards.

(6) A fall in the exchange rate could help an economy by reducing the price of exports (and increasing the price of imports) and thereby increasing sales, which might lead to increased employment and greater export earnings (if demand is price elastic).

(7) Deflation can help the balance of payments by suppressing domestic demand for imports and by releasing goods for export (if home sales are stagnant).

Test Your Understanding 15

(a) (i) Raise
(ii) Lower
(iii) Raise
(iv) No effect
(v) Lower

(b) (i) *True*
A rise in the exchange rate reduces the domestic price of imports.

(ii) *False*
A rising exchange rate reduces exports and raises imports, thus increasing domestic unemployment.

(iii) *False*
The terms of trade are a measure of the relative prices of imports and exports; a rising exchange rate raises export prices and reduces import prices.

(iv) *True*
As export prices rise, total exports tend to fall, but the opposite occurs for imports, thus worsening the trade balance.

(v) *True*
The rise in exchange rate reduces import prices and thus raises the purchasing power of domestic incomes.

chapter

8

The Financial System II: International aspects

Chapter learning objectives

After completing this chapter you should be able to:

- explain the role of the foreign exchange market and the factors influencing it, in setting exchange rates
- explain the role of national and international governmental organisations in regulating and influencing the financial system.

1 Introduction

In this chapter we expand our discussion of the financial system to encompass international aspects, looking in particular at foreign exchange markets and the role of national, international and supranational organisations.

2 International money markets

International markets are in broadly two groups.

(1) international capital markets
(2) the foreign exchange market

2.1 International capital markets

International capital markets have greatly expanded since the 1950s. This has been the result of:

- the progressive abolition of exchange controls limiting the flow of capital in and out of economies;
- growth of multinational companies (MNCs) who often do not use capital markets in the 'home' country; by borrowing abroad in different currencies, MNCs can shop around for favourable terms and also avoid any domestic government credit restraints.

The funds available on international capital markets fall into three broad categories:

(1) short-term capital (Eurocurrency) borrowed mainly for the purposes of working capital;
(2) medium-term capital (Eurocredit) borrowed for working capital and investment purposes;
(3) long-term capital (Eurobonds) borrowed for investment purposes and for financing mergers and acquisitions. Eurobonds are bonds issued by very large companies, banks, governments and supranational institutions, such as the European Commission, to raise long-term finance (typically five years and over). These bonds are denominated in a currency other than that of the borrower, although often US dollars are used. The bonds are bought and traded by investment institutions and banks.

The international capital market is useful not only for business borrowers. It is also used for government borrowers (e.g. United Kingdom local government authorities) and provides a market for lending funds for businesses with surplus cash. Thus the market performs a useful international element to the financial asset management function of commercial enterprises.

Although these international markets operate in many financial centres they are dominated by Europe and the USA, and especially London. The term 'euromarket' had its origins in the 1970s. International trading expanded and this led to new foreign currency markets, such as the Eurodollar market. In this market, dollar balances earned by European exporters (to the USA) were held in European banks earning interest on favourable terms because they are offshore (held outside the country of origin and not subject to central bank control).

2.2 Foreign exchange markets

Foreign exchange markets are concerned with the purchase and sale of foreign exchange. This is primarily for four reasons:

(1) the finance of international trade;

(2) companies holding and managing a portfolio of currencies as part of their financial asset management function;

(3) financial institutions dealing in foreign exchange to on behalf of their customers and in order to benefit from changes in exchange rates.

(4) to manage risks associated with exchange rate movements

This market enables companies, fund managers, banks and others to buy and sell foreign currencies. Capital flows arising from trade, investment, loans and speculative dealing create a large demand for foreign currency, particularly sterling, US dollars and euros and typically deals worth £40bn are traded daily in London, the world's largest foreign exchange centre.

London benefits from its geographical location, favourable time intervals (with the United States and the Far East in particular) and the variety of business generated there – insurance, commodities, banking, Eurobonds, etc.

Foreign exchange trading may be *spot* or *forward*.

- Spot transactions are undertaken almost immediately and settled within two days.
- However, forward buying involves a future delivery date from three months onward. Banks and brokers, on behalf of their clients, operate in the forward market to protect the anticipated flows of foreign currency from exchange rate volatility.

The forward price of a currency is normally higher (at a premium) or lower (at a discount) than the spot rate. Such premiums (or discounts) reflect interest rate differentials between currencies and expectations of currency depreciations and appreciations.

As the foreign exchange market has grown, so other instruments such as futures and options have been developed to protect foreign exchange commitments. Currency futures involve the trading of forward transactions other than for currencies themselves, while currency options enable buyers (at a premium paid to the writer of the option, usually a bank) to guarantee a buying (or selling) price for a currency at a future specified date.

3 Foreign exchange risks

Firms dealing with more than one currency are exposed to risks due to exchange rate movements. There are three main aspects of this.

- Economic risk

  Long-term movements in exchange rates can undermine a firm's competitive advantage.

  For example, a strengthening currency will make an exporter's products more expensive to overseas customers. One way of managing this risk would be to set up production facilities in the markets you wish to sell into.

- Transaction risk

  In the time period between an order being agreed and payment received the exchange rate can move causing the final value of the transaction to be more or less than originally envisaged.

  Transaction risk can be hedged by buying or selling forward.

- Translation risk

  If a company has foreign assets (e.g. a factory) denoted in another currency, then their value in its home currency will depend on the exchange rate at the time. If its domestic currency strengthens, for example, then foreign assets will appear to fall in value.

  This risk, however, is not realised unless the asset is sold, so is of less commercial importance

Illustration 1 – Transaction risk

Suppose a UK Company A contracts to sell a machine to a US Company B for $300,000 payable in three months' time.

If the exchange rate now (the 'spot' rate) is £1 = $2, then the $300,000 is worth £150,000.

However, when the cash is received, suppose the exchange rate has moved to £1 = $2.10. (note: the $ has weakened compared to the £ so £1 buys more $)

The $300,000 will then be worth 300,000/2.10 = £142,857, a fall of £7,143.

Similarly an exchange gain may arise if the exchange rate moves in Company A's favour (here we would want the $ to strengthen compared to the £). The key problem lies in being able to predict future exchange rates.

Test Your Understanding 1

A Euro zone company has agreed to sell a product to a US customer for $1,200. Suppose that the Euro:$ exchange rate was €1 = $1.2 when the deal was agreed but had moved to €1 = $1.25 when the cash was received. What was the exchange gain or loss on the transaction?

A gain €40

B loss €40

C gain €60

D loss €60

Test Your Understanding 2

A UK company has agreed to sell a product to a US customer. If the dollar strengthens against sterling before the funds are received this will lead to an exchange gain.

TRUE/FALSE?

Test Your Understanding 3

A US company is struggling to compete against imported goods due to a strong dollar making imports cheaper to US consumers. What type of exchange risk is being described here?

A economic risk

B transaction risk

C translation risk

4 Exchange rate systems

4.1 Exchange rates

The exchange rate of a currency is a price. It is the external value of a currency expressed in another currency, for example,

£1 = $1.60

The exchange of currencies is vital for trade in goods and services. British firms selling abroad will require foreign buyers to exchange their currency into sterling to facilitate payment. Similarly, British importers will need to pay out in foreign currencies. Also, when funds are transferred between people in different countries, foreign exchange is required.

4.2 Exchange rate systems – floating exchange rates

Exchange rates that float are flexible and free to fluctuate in the light of changes which take place in demand and supply. Such exchange rates are examples of nearly perfect markets.

Demand

Demand for a currency, sterling say, comes from a number of sources:

- It is required to pay for UK exports – for example, a French supermarket buying English food will need to pay its suppliers in sterling.
- Overseas investors making investments in the UK will need sterling – for example, an American property company buying a factory building in the UK will have to pay in sterling.
- Speculators may buy sterling if they feel it is about to increase (appreciate) in value relative to other currencies.

- The government (strictly the central bank) may wish to buy sterling to manipulate the exchange rate.
- For some currencies there may be a demand for it to be held as an international medium of exchange as is the case with the US dollar.

Supply

- Supply of sterling is also derived from a number of sources:
- UK residents wishing to buy imports will need to sell sterling and buy foreign currency.
- UK residents making overseas investments will need to sell sterling and buy foreign currency.
- Speculators may sell sterling if they feel its value is about to decrease (depreciate) relative to other currencies.
- The UK government may sell currency on the international markets to weaken the currency to improve export performance.

Today, the sale and purchase of currencies for trading purposes is dwarfed by the *lending* and *borrowing* of funds.

Impact of different factors on the exchange rate

Putting these issues together, we can comment on how various economic factors affect exchange rates as follows:

- High inflation will weaken a currency as it makes goods more expensive thus dampening export demand and reducing the demand for the currency.
- An increase in interest rates will have a two-fold effect.

  In the short run "hot money" will be attracted to UK deposits, increasing demand for sterling and a corresponding rise in the exchange rate.

  In the long run, high interest rates will erode the competitiveness of UK businesses reducing the supply of and demand for UK goods. This will reduce the demand for sterling, reducing the exchange rate.

- A trade deficit will result in the demand for sterling to buy exports being lower than the supply of sterling to buy imports. This will result in downward pressure on the exchange rate.
- Speculation can influence the exchange rate up or down. This is usually a short-term factor.

Example using a diagram of supply and demand

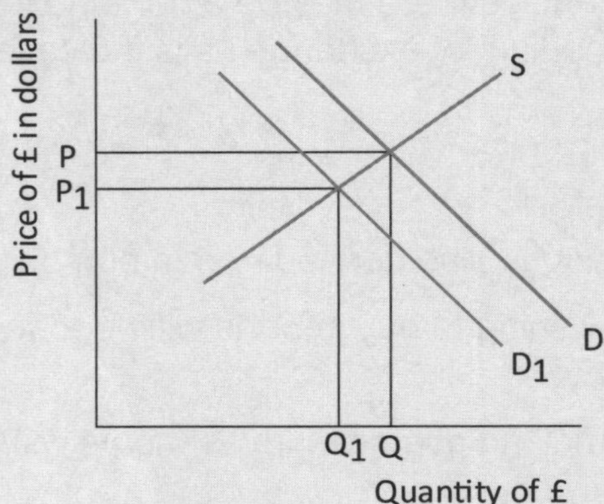

In the diagram, suppose we have a factor that causes British goods to become less competitive on world markets.

- This will result in a fall in the demand for British exports and hence a causes a shift in the demand curve for sterling to D_1.
- This shift causes a fall in the exchange rate to P_1, assuming that the demand for British imports (and hence the supply curve) remains unchanged.
- P_1 Q_1 would be a new equilibrium position at which the demand for pounds and the supply of pounds are equal.

Note: since the demand and supply of a currency for trade purposes is a tiny fraction of all demand and supply for a currency, balance of payments deficits / surpluses are unlikely to have much effect on the exchange rate.

Test Your Understanding 4

Suppose that demand for imports in the UK is inelastic. If sterling were to depreciate in value against other currencies, which of the following would happen?

	Imports would become	*Total spending by the UK on imports*
A	Cheaper in £ sterling	Would rise
B	Cheaper in £ sterling	Would fall
C	More expensive in £ sterling	Would rise
D	More expensive in £ sterling	Would fall

4.3 Exchange rate systems – dirty floating

Governments often intervene in the foreign exchange markets (either by creating demand or supply of their currency as required) in order to maintain or achieve an *exchange rate target*. The purpose of this normally is to make a country's exports more competitive, by lowering the exchange rate, or to assist in the control of inflation.

The central bank will be instructed to:

- Buy or sell the currency to raise or lower the exchange rate.
- Alter interest rates to encourage the buying or selling of the currency. For example, a raising of interest rates should encourage speculators to deposit more funds in that country. The subsequent rise in demand for the currency should cause a rise in the exchange rate.

For example, China operates a managed floating exchange rate system for the Yuan and international leaders have criticized the Chinese government for keeping the value of the Yuan artificially low, to boost exports.

4.4 Arguments for floating rates

Balance of payments

In theory, the floating rate automatically adjusts a balance of payments disequilibrium.

- Suppose a country has a balance of payments deficit due to imports being greater than exports.
- This will result in supply of the currency (to buy imports) exceeding demand (to buy exports) resulting in a fall in the value of the currency.
- The lower value of the currency will make exports seem cheaper to foreign buyers (so exports should increase) but imported goods will appear more expensive (so imports will decrease).
- The net result is that the balance of payments deficit will be reduced. This will continue until the deficit is eliminated.

The self-correcting mechanism means that policies, such as deflation, to rectify a balance of payments deficit will not need to be implemented. This gives a government greater freedom to pursue domestic policies.

Note: It can be countered that demand and supply inelasticities, the activities of speculators and the behaviour of government prevent this adjustment from occurring in the real world. In addition, it can be argued that the freedom leads to reckless *irresponsibility*. A government may assume that a floating exchange rate will solve an inflation problem and so not pursue necessary domestic policies, which maintenance of a fixed exchange rate might have forced on them, thereby worsening the inflation problem.

Speculation reduced

Less speculation will occur because a currency can appreciate or depreciate, whereas under a fixed rate regime currency changes were nearly always devaluations. This meant that speculators, who sold a currency which had been devalued, could not lose and could only gain.

For instance, someone holding £1,000 at £1 = $1.8 moves into dollars, securing $1,800 (assuming no transaction costs). If sterling is devalued to £1 = $1.4 the dollar holding is now worth £1,280 the switch back into sterling is made in order to secure a capital gain. Conversely, if sterling is not devalued, the switch back into sterling is still worth £1,000 with no loss made.

Note: If we have a fixed rate system and enough speculators sell sterling forwards (i.e contract to sell under a forward contract, even though they currently do not have any sterling), then the additional supply created could give considerable downward pressure on the value of the pound, making it even harder for the government to maintain the value within its specified band. this is what happened when the pound left the ERM , as described above. Some countries, such as China, have banned forward contracts to prevent such speculation.

Resource allocation

A more efficient allocation of resources is secured if exchange rates reflect changed economic conditions. It is argued that floating rates will reflect changes in demand and supply, and that they are more *sensitive* and respond quickly to underlying economic trends. This might enable the theory of comparative advantage to be operative.

As floating rates change daily, they are more subtle but probably at the cost of greater volatility. Fluctuations in exchange rates can cause *uncertainty*. This could deter trade, as contracts with fixed prices become more risky as exchange rate appreciation will cut profit margins. However, to some extent this problem can be offset by buying a currency in the forward market.

Reserves

A large supply of *reserves* is unnecessary in a floating system because the automatic adjustment of a balance of payments deficit (or surplus) is achieved by an exchange rate depreciation (or appreciation). In theory, reserves will be automatically maintained and so domestic policy changes such as interest rate increases will not be needed to keep the exchange rate up.

Supplementary reading – Fixed exchange rate systems

While floating/managed floating systems are currently the norm for many countries, the world economy has experienced a range of different fixed exchange rate mechanisms.

In the nineteenth and twentieth centuries, the gold standard was used, where exchange rates were fixed in terms of gold.

A managed exchange rate system was established at Bretton Woods (United States) in 1944 to encourage stability and redevelopment after the second world war. This established exchange rates between economies but allowed a 1% band either side of its parity. The rate was determined by supply and demand but governments had to manage policy to ensure that the actual rate stayed within its band. If this proved too difficult Governments were allowed to devalue their currency and move to a new but lower "peg".

For example, on 12 March 1947 the exchange rate between the Japanese yen and the US dollar was $1 = ¥50 but on the 5 July 1948 this was changed to $1 = ¥270

This system ended in 1972 when the pound sterling was allowed to float and other currencies soon followed.

In 1979 the European Exchange Rate Mechanism (ERM) was set up, partly to reduce exchange rate variability but also as a step towards monetary union and the creation of the euro in 1999. The ERM was similar to the Bretton Woods system in as much that currencies were allowed a degree of fluctuation (here 2.25%) as a result of normal supply and demand changes but governments were again expected to intervene to ensure these limits were not breached.

The pound crashed out of the ERM on 16 September 1992 ("Black Wednesday") due mainly to the efforts of speculators, notably George Soros. On that date, the UK Chancellor Norman Lamont raised interest rates from 10% to 12%, then to 15%, and authorised the spending of billions of pounds to buy sterling in order to support the value of the pound. However, the measures failed to prevent the pound falling lower than its minimum allowed level in the ERM and the decision was taken to leave the ERM.

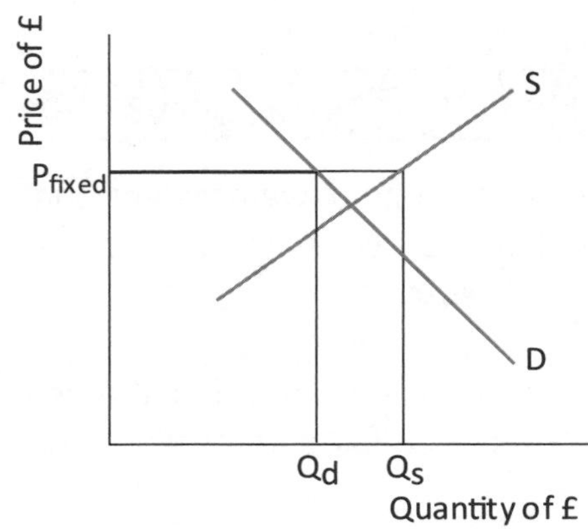

In the above diagram the exchange rate has been fixed at a level higher than would be the case if the currency were floating. As with any minimum price this results in a surplus of supply (Qs) over demand (Qd). Here the government would have to make up the gap in demand (Qs – Qd).

Supplementary reading – "Hot" money

Deposits of money can be transferred from one currency to another at short notice. This clearly affects the demand for, and supply of, currencies. The main factors influencing such transfers of what has been called 'hot money' are:

- relative interest rates – if the differential between nations changes, then capital tends to move towards the nation whose interest rate offers the most lucrative return;
- expectations – if the holders of 'hot money' expect a currency to appreciate, they will deposit money in that country, as the appreciation will raise the exchange value of the deposits;
- inflation – countries with relatively high rates will find their currency less attractive to depositors because its value is depreciating more than that of other countries.

Supplementary reading – Parity theories

Two "parity" theories claim to be able to predict future movements in exchange rates.

Purchasing power parity (PPP)

Suppose we had a product that cost the same in the UK and the US:

- Price in UK £200
- Price in US $280
- Exchange rate: £1 = $1.40

Further suppose that the inflation rates in each country are different:

- Inflation in UK of 5%, so the price of the good in one year will be £210
- Inflation in the US of 8% so the price will be $302.40

You might think that the goods are now more expensive in the US. However PPP suggests that the exchange rate will move to compensate for the differences in inflation rates, so that the good still costs the same in both countries.

The exchange rate must therefore have moved to become

- £210 = $302.40
- Therefore £1 = $1.44
- The higher inflation in the US implies a weaker economy and hence a weakening currency.

Interest rate parity (IRP)

Suppose we have £100,000 to invest for one year and are faced with the following information:

- UK interest rates 3%
- US interest rates 4%
- Exchange rate: £1 = $1.40

Given we can get a better interest rate in the US we might be tempted to convert our £100,000 into $140,000 and invest in the US.

- If we invest in the UK then we will end up with 100,000 × 1.03 = £103,000

- If we invest in the US then we will end up with 140,000 × 1.04 = $145,600

You might think that we have earned more in the US. However IRP suggests that the exchange rate will move to compensate for the differences in interest rates, so that the final amount is the same in both countries.

The exchange rate must therefore have moved to become

- £103,000 = $145,600
- Therefore £1 = $1.414
- The higher interest rate in the US implies a weaker economy and hence a weakening currency.

Test Your Understanding 5

If a country has a 'floating' (flexible) exchange rate, which one of the following would lead to a fall (depreciation) in the rate of exchange for its currency?

A a rise in capital inflows into the economy

B an increase in the country's exports

C an increase in the country's imports

D a fall in the country's rate of inflation

Test Your Understanding 6

Which one of the following would be likely to result in a rise in the value of UK sterling against the Euro?

A a rise in interest rates in the UK

B the UK central bank buying Euros in exchange for sterling

C a rise in interest rates in the Euro zone

D increased capital flows from the UK to the Euro zone

Test Your Understanding 7

All of the following would normally lead to a rise in the exchange rate for a country's currency, except which one?

A an increase in the country's exports

B an increased inflow of foreign direct investment into the country

C a short term rise in interest rates in the country

D an increase in the export of capital from the country

Test Your Understanding 8

The country of Xanadu has as its currency the Krown and for many years has fixed the exchange rate against the US dollar so

$1 = K10

Recent economic events have made this level harder and harder for the Xanadu central bank to support. A speculator has entered into a forward contract to sell 1bn Krowns at $1 = K10, on the hope that the additional pressure will force the Xanadu government to devalue the Krown.

Calculate the speculator's profit in $ if the Krown is devalued to a new level of $1 = K12.

Answer = $__________(give your answer in billions to 3 decimal places)

5 Single currency zones

One way of avoiding exchange rate risk is for each country to use the same currency. The best known example of such an arrangement is the plan for Economic and Monetary Union (EMU), which seeks to establish a single currency and monetary authority within the European Union.

Two major components of this integration are:

- A single European currency – the Euro
- The European Central bank – discussed above.

The Euro

The Euro was launched on 1 January 1999, with 11 of the then 15 members agreeing to participate. National currencies were retained until 2002 to be replaced with Euro notes and coins.

Performance of the Euro against other major world currencies has been patchy. In its first year the Euro depreciated from $1.19 a Euro to $0.80 per Euro, though it since recovered this value.

The European Central Bank (ECB)

The European Central Bank (ECB) began operations in May 1998 as the single body with the power to issue currency, draft monetary policy, and set interest rates in the Euro-zone. The Maastricht Treaty envisaged the ECB as an independent body free from day-to-day political interference, with a principal duty of price stability.

The ECB is the central bank for the Euro currency area and is based in Frankfurt. It is the sole issuer of the Euro. Its main objective, as defined by the Maastricht Treaty, is price stability. It therefore has the power to set short-term interest rates.

The main focus of its activities has been on interest rate policy rather than exchange rate policy. Like the Monetary Policy Committee of the Bank of England, the ECB pursues a policy of controlling interest rates as a means of achieving influence over the long-term rate of inflation.

Should the UK have adopted the Euro?

The arguments for and against joining a single currency zone can be illustrated by reference to whether the UK should have adopted the Euro as its currency. At the present time the UK chooses to keep its national currency and retain control over interest rate and monetary policy.

Nevertheless, debate over joining the Euro was (is) a very politically sensitive issue. Below are some of the factors that should be considered.

- Greater economic stability

  Joining the Euro could result in greater economic stability for the UK. Conversely, the UK would lose control over interest rates and monetary policy. The UK could be forced to make rate changes that are out of step with the domestic economy.

- Foreign exchange costs

  Joining the Euro would remove currency exchange costs when the UK trades with the rest of Europe.

- Exchange rate risk

  A single currency removes the risk of exchange rate fluctuations adversely affecting the profitability of trade with Europe.

- Price transparency

  If all goods and services are priced in the same currency across Europe, any price discrepancy or price discrimination is easy to detect. In reality differences in cost and taxation may mean that legitimate differences in price still occur.

- Increased volumes of trade

  Economists argue that a single currency removes a significant barrier to trade and should boost trade within Europe. The need to deal in foreign currencies can be a major disincentive for companies, particularly small businesses, to trade internationally.

Of course, given the crisis that developed in the Euro zone in 2011, there is no prospect of the UK joining the Euro in the foreseeable future. In contrast, the political debate in early 2013 is over whether the UK should have a referendum over leaving the EU altogether!

Test Your Understanding 9

All of the following are benefits which all countries will gain from the adoption of a single currency such as the Euro, except which one?

A reduced transactions costs

B increased price transparency

C lower interest rates

D reduced exchange rate uncertainty

Test Your Understanding 10

Which one of the following is not a benefit from countries forming a monetary union and adopting a single currency?

A International transactions costs are reduced

B Exchange rate uncertainty is removed

C It economises on foreign exchange reserves

D It allows each country to adopt an independent monetary policy

6 The role of major institutions in fostering international development and stability

The principal institutions encouraging world trade have been discussed above in chapter 6. Here we consider institutions more involved with international financing.

World Bank

The International Bank for Reconstruction and Development (IBRD), also known as the World Bank, was the second institution created at the Bretton Woods meeting in 1944. Its membership and decision-making processes are similar to those of the IMF. The original purpose of the IBRD was to help finance the reconstruction of economies damaged by the war. However, it soon shifted the focus of its lending to countries of the developing world.

The bank now comprises three principal constituent elements:

(1) The IBRD proper whose function is to lend long-term funds for capital projects in developing economies at a commercial rate of interest. The main source of these funds is borrowing by the IBRD itself.

(2) The International Development Association (IDA) which was established in 1960 to provide 'soft' loans to the poorest of the developing countries. The IDA:

  (a) is mainly financed by 20 donor countries providing funds every 3 years. Funding therefore depends on the generosity or otherwise of these countries.

  (b) provides loans on concessionary terms, normally interest free loans repayable over 50 years.

(3) The International Finance Corporation, which promotes the private sector in developing countries by lending or by taking equity.

The World Bank is clearly an important source of capital funds for the developing countries. However, it has been criticised in recent years over the nature of its lending conditions.

International Monetary Fund

The IMF was founded in 1944 at an international conference at Bretton Woods in the USA but did not really begin to fully function until the 1950s. The so called Bretton Woods System that the IMF was to supervise was to have two main characteristics: stable exchange rates and a multilateral system of international payments and credit.

In particular the IMF became responsible for:

- promoting international financial co-operation and establishing a system of stable exchange rates and freely convertible currencies
- providing a source of credit for members with balance of payments deficits while corrective policies were adopted
- managing the growth of international liquidity.

European Bank for Reconstruction and Development

The European Bank for Reconstruction and Development was established in 1991 when communism was crumbling in central and Eastern Europe and ex-soviet countries needed support to nurture a new private sector in a democratic environment.

Today the EBRD uses the tools of investment to help build market economies and democracies in 27 countries from central Europe to central Asia.

Test Your Understanding 11

Which of the following institutions is more commonly known as the World Bank?

A IBRD

B G8

C IMF

D EBRD

Test your understanding answers

Test Your Understanding 1

B

- When the deal was agreed, $1,200 would have been worth 1200/1.2 = €1,000
- When the cash was received, $1,200 was worth 1200/1.25 = €960
- Thus there was an exchange loss of €40.

Test Your Understanding 2

True

The UK company will be receiving dollars. If the dollar strengthens, then these dollars will become more valuable, giving rise to an exchange gain.

Test Your Understanding 3

A

By definition.

Test Your Understanding 4

C

With a depreciation in the value of sterling, import prices rise, because it costs more in sterling to obtain the foreign currency to pay foreign suppliers for the imported goods. Since demand for imports is inelastic, the fall in demand for imports resulting from an increase in their price will be relatively small, and total spending on imports will rise.

Test Your Understanding 5

C

Rising imports is the only one which will raise the supply of its currency to the foreign exchange market, depressing the exchange rate. The other three will raise demand which will push up the exchange rate.

Test Your Understanding 6

A

If interest rates in the UK rise, this attracts foreign money in to invest here. Pounds sterling are demanded in exchange for the foreign currencies in order to invest, and therefore the 'price' of the £, i.e. the exchange rate, rises.

Test Your Understanding 7

D

Capital leaving the country would increase the supply of that country's currency and reduce the exchange rate.

Test Your Understanding 8

$0.017bn

- The speculator will buy 1bn Krowns at the new exchange rate of $1 = K12, costing $0.083bn
- These can then be used to deliver on the forward contract where they can be sold at a rate of $1 = K10, thus realising $0.100bn.
- The net profit will thus be $0.100 – $0.083 = $0.017bn

Test Your Understanding 9

C

Interest rates are not directly related to the adoption of a single currency. Instead the impact would depend on the policy of the central bank administering the single currency. The others should all be benefits.

Test Your Understanding 10

D

Countries in a monetary union and adopting a single currency cannot have independent monetary policies. In the Euro zone, monetary policy is controlled by the ECB (European Central Bank).

Test Your Understanding 11

A

The international bank for reconstruction and development is also known as the World Bank.

chapter

9

Preparing for the Assessment

1 Preparing for the Assessment

This chapter is intended for use when you are ready to start revising for your assessment. It contains:

- a summary of useful revision techniques
- details of the format of the assessment
- a bank of assessment-standard revision questions and suggested solutions. These solutions are of a length and level of detail that a competent student might be expected to produce in an assessment.

Revision technique

Planning

The first thing to say about revision is that it is an addition to your initial studies, not a substitute for them. In other words, do not coast along early in your course in the hope of catching up during the revision phase. On the contrary, you should be studying and revising concurrently from the outset. At the end of each week, and at the end of each month, get into the habit of summarizing the material you have covered to refresh your memory of it.

As with your initial studies, planning is important to maximise the value of your revision work. You need to balance the demands of study, professional work, family life and other commitments. To make this work, you will need to think carefully about how to make best use of your time.

Begin as before by comparing the estimated hours you will need to devote to revision with the hours available to you in the weeks leading up to the assessment. Prepare a written schedule setting out the areas you intend to cover during particular weeks, and break that down further into topics for each day's revision. To help focus on the key areas try to establish:

- which areas you are weakest in, so that you can concentrate on the topics where effort is particularly needed
- which areas are especially significant for the assessment – the topics that are tested frequently.

Don't forget the need for relaxation, and for family commitments. Sustained intellectual effort is only possible for limited periods, and must be broken up at intervals by lighter activities. And don't continue your revision timetable right up to the moment when you enter for the assessment: you should aim to stop work a day or even two days before the assessment. Beyond this point the most you should attempt is an occasional brief look at your notes to refresh your memory.

Getting down to work

By the time you begin your revision you should already have settled into a fixed work pattern: a regular time of day for doing the work, a particular location where you sit, particular equipment that you assemble before you begin and so on. If this is not already a matter of routine for you, think carefully about it now in the last vital weeks before the exam.

You should have notes summarizing the main points of each topic you have covered. Begin each session by reading through the relevant notes and trying to commit the important points to memory.

Usually this will be just your starting point. Unless the area is one where you already feel very confident, you will need to track back from your notes to the relevant chapter(s) in the *Study System*. This will refresh your memory on points not covered by your notes and fill in the detail that inevitably gets lost in the process of summarisation.

When you think you have understood and memorised the main principles and techniques, attempt an assessment-standard question. At this stage of your studies you should normally be expecting to complete such questions in something close to the actual time allocation allowed in the exam. After completing your effort, check the solution provided and add to your notes any extra points it reveals.

Tips for the final revision phase

As the assessment looms closer, consider the following list of techniques and make use of those that work for you:

- Summarise your notes into more concise form, perhaps on index cards that you can carry with you for revision on the way to work.
- Go through your notes with a highlighter pen, marking key concepts and definitions.
- Summarise the main points in a key area by producing a wordlist, mind map or other mnemonic device.
- In areas that you find difficult, rework questions that you have already attempted, and compare your answers in detail with those provided in the Learning System.

Format of the assessment

The assessment for Economics for Business is a two hour computer-based assessment comprising 75 compulsory questions. There will be no choice and all questions should be attempted if time permits. CIMA are continuously developing the question styles within the CBA system and you are advised to try the on-line website demo, to both gain familiarity with the assessment software and examine the latest style of questions being used.

In broad terms, the entire syllabus will be covered in each assessment. Please note that the weightings of the syllabus and of the assessment are not exactly reflected in the space allocated to the various topics in this book.

The current weightings for the syllabus sections are:

- The goals and decisions of organisations – 25 per cent
- The market system and the competitive process – 25 per cent
- The financial system – 25 per cent
- The macroeconomic context of business – 25 per cent.

Test Your Understanding 1

The fall in a firm's short-run average total cost with an increase in production would be due to which of the following?

A The greater divisibility of fixed costs

B Diminishing returns to a fixed factor

C Economies of scale

D Diseconomies of scale

(2 marks)

Test Your Understanding 2

According to the traditional theory of the firm, the equilibrium position for all firms will be where:

A revenue is maximised

B output is maximised

C profits are maximised

D costs are minimised

(2 marks)

Test Your Understanding 3

The pursuit of profit will ensure that business organisations are efficient provided that:

A they operate in competitive markets

B they produce at the profit-maximizing level of output

C prices are set where demand and supply are equal

D excess profits are reinvested in the businesses

(2 marks)

Test Your Understanding 4

Other things being equal, all of the following would lead to a rise in share prices except which one?

A A rise in interest rates

B A reduction in corporation tax

C A rise in company profits

D A decline in the number of shares in issue.

(2 marks)

Test Your Understanding 5

Identify the correct word or phrase in the following to complete each of the following statements.

(i) Internal economies of scale can only be obtained when the industry/company/market increases in size.

(ii) Diseconomies of scale occur when the business becomes inefficient/technically outdated/too large and, in consequence, costs begin to rise.

(iii) External economies of scale reduce the costs of all firms when suppliers become more efficient/the industry becomes larger/social costs of production are reduced.

(iv) Technical economies of scale arise when a company is large enough to adopt new technology/invest in research and development/produce on a large scale.

(4 marks)

Test Your Understanding 6

State whether each of the following statements is *true* or *false*

Statements	True	False
(i) Economies of scale act as a barrier to entry into an industry.		
(ii) If there are significant economies of scale, the number of firms in the industry will tend to be small.		
(iii) Diseconomies of scale cause the short-run average cost curve to rise.		
(iv) If output rises at the same rate as average cost rises, this is called constant returns to scale.		

Test Your Understanding 7

Which of the following would be regarded as stakeholders in a not- for-profit organisation?

(i) Management

(ii) Employees

(iii) Suppliers

(iv) Customers

(v) Local community

A (i), and (iii) only

B (i), (ii) and (iv) only

C (iii), (iv) and (v) only

D all of them

(2 marks)

Test Your Understanding 8

All of the following have been recommended in order to improve corporate Governance except one. Which one is the exception?

A The separation of the powers of chairman and chief executive

B Limited contract for directors

C Less use should be made of non-executive directors

D Annual accounts should include a statement from auditors that the company is a 'going concern'

(2 marks)

Test Your Understanding 9

A Company is planning to invest in a new project. The information about this project is as follows:

Capital cost of project		$15,000
Expected life of the project		3 years
Scrap value of investment at end		$5,000
Expected net income streams	Year 1	$5,000
	Year 2	$5,000
	Year 3	$5,000

You are required to:

(a) Calculate the discounted cash flow of the project assuming a discount rate of 10%.

(2 marks)

(b) Calculate the discounted cash flow of the project assuming that the income stream in the third year is reduced to $3,000.

(2 marks)

(c) Calculate the net present value of the project for each case.

(2 marks)

Test Your Understanding 10

When the price of a good is held above the equilibrium price, the result will be:

A excess demand

B a shortage of the good

C a surplus of the good

D an increase in demand

(2 marks)

Test Your Understanding 11

If the price of a good fell by 10 per cent and, as a result, total expenditure on the good fell by 10 per cent, the demand for the good would be described as:

A perfectly inelastic

B perfectly elastic

C unitary elastic

D elastic

(2 marks)

Test Your Understanding 12

One of the characteristic features of oligopoly is that

A free entry of firms into the industry is always encouraged

B the pricing policy of a firm is largely determined by the state

C known consumers' preferences play no part in firms' policy decisions

D the pricing policy of firms is influenced by that of rival firms

(2 marks)

Test Your Understanding 13

Which *one* of the following would not, of itself, cause a shift of the demand curve for a product? A change in:

A consumers' preferences

B consumers' income

C the price of the product

D the prices of related products

(2 marks)

Test Your Understanding 14

A horizontal merger occurs when the merging firms are:

A in different stages of the production chain

B major firms operating in the same region

C producing different goods or services

D producing the same goods or services

(2 marks)

Test Your Understanding 15

The following diagram represents the demand and supply for a particular good over a period of time:

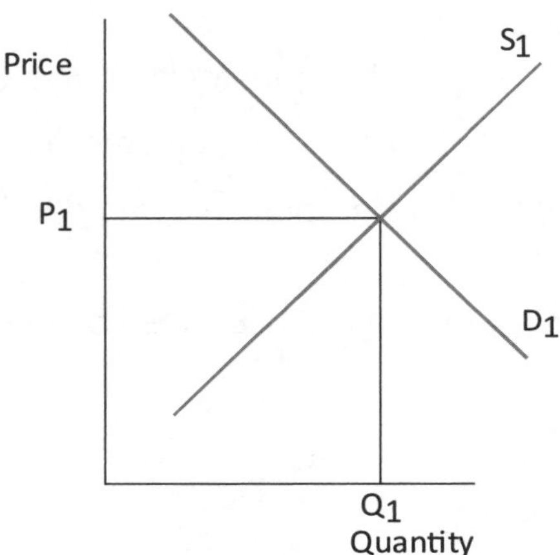

With respect to the diagram answer the following questions.

(i) Would the imposition of an indirect tax shift *the supply curve* or *the demand curve*?

(ii) Would the burden of tax be shifted most to consumers when the demand curve for the product was *price elastic* or price *inelastic*?

(iii) Would the government get the most tax revenue from imposing the tax if the demand for the product was *price elastic* or *price inelastic*?

(iv) Would the sales/output of the good fall most when the demand for the good was *price elastic* or *price inelastic*?

(4 marks)

Test Your Understanding 16

If trade unions attempt to increase the wages of their members, the result is usually that for their members:

A wages rise and employment falls

B wages and employment both rise

C wages rise without affecting employment

D wages fall but employment rises

(2 marks)

Test Your Understanding 17

The following passage is based on newspaper articles and refers to the market for coffee in the 1990s:

"Supermarkets recently ended ten years of cheap coffee when some raised the price of their own brands of instant coffee by up to 12 per cent.

Reports of severe frost damage to Brazilian coffee plantations sent the open market price of coffee beans up from $3,100 a ton to $4,000 a ton – the highest price since 1986. Even before the frost damage, the price had been rising because many coffee farmers, discouraged by the previous low price of coffee, had moved away to other crops in the search for more profit.

The current price increases will end a golden age for coffee drinkers. From 1986 to 1993, the retail price of coffee had fallen by more than 15 per cent; given that these were years of rapid inflation, the real price of coffee fell even more steeply. The result was a boom in coffee drinking, and coffee sales in the United Kingdom exceeded those of tea. Rising coffee prices may now lead to a switch back to tea drinking. This happened in the 1970s when sharp rises in coffee prices encouraged many coffee drinkers to switch their consumption to tea."

Required:

Using *both* your knowledge of economic theory *and* information in the passage:

With reference to the concept of the price elasticity of demand,

(i) which one of the following is the correct measurement of the price elasticity of demand for coffee?

(1) $$\frac{\text{\% change in price of coffee}}{\text{\% change in the demand for coffee}}$$

(2) $$\frac{\text{change in the demand for coffee}}{\text{change in the price of coffee}}$$

(3) $$\frac{\text{\% change in the demand for coffee}}{\text{\% change in the price of coffee}}$$

(ii) if the price elasticity of demand for coffee has a value of 22 would the demand be said to be
(1) price elastic or
(2) price inelastic or
(3) of unitary elasticity?

(1 mark)

(iii) if the demand for coffee was price inelastic, would the result of a shift in the supply of coffee to the left be,
(1) a large fall in price and small fall in sales or
(2) a large rise in price and large fall in sales or
(3) a large rise in price and a small fall in sales or
(4) a small rise in price and a large fall in sales or
(5) a small fall in price and a large rise in sales?

(2 marks)

Test Your Understanding 18

E-commerce generally increases the price elasticity of demand for the products of a particular supplier. Which one of the following statements does NOT describe a cause of this?

A Greater availability of substitutes from a market with more participants

B Generally lower prices due to search engines

C Lower cost of search for alternatives

D Greater focus on price due to e-commerce reducing opportunities for differentiation of service

(2 marks)

Test Your Understanding 19

Which of the following is a liquid asset, that is, one that may readily be converted into cash without loss of face value?

A Government stock

B Shares in a bank

C Fine art paintings

D Money market deposits

(2 marks)

Test Your Understanding 20

The government of D has recently introduced a minimum wage rate at a level above the existing equilibrium wage rate. If everything else remains unchanged, then:

A demand for labour will become more price elastic

B demand for labour will exceed the supply of labour in D

C there will be excess supply in the labour market in D

D the overall number of people employed in D will increase

(2 marks)

Test Your Understanding 21

State whether each of the following statements is *true* or *false*.

Statement	True	False
(i) A change in supply of a good will have the largest effect on price when the demand is price elastic.		
(ii) A change in the demand for a good will have no effect on the price if the supply of the good is perfectly price elastic.		

(2 marks)

Test Your Understanding 22

All of the following are examples of anti-competitive behaviour by manufacturing companies except which one?

A Price-fixing agreements

B Minimum price contracts with retailers

C Exclusive contracts with retailers

D The heavy use of advertising

(2 marks)

Test Your Understanding 23

The following data refers to the supply and demand for a product.

Price ($)	Quantity demanded	Quantity supplied
8	130	80
9	120	95
10	100	100
11	90	105

Using the data, calculate for this product:

(i) the price elasticity of demand for a fall in price from $10 to $9.

(ii) the price elasticity of supply for a rise in price from $10 to $11.

(iii) calculate the change in total revenue for the seller of the product if the price fell from $10 to $9.

(3 marks)

Test Your Understanding 24

All of the following would tend to increase the degree of competition in a market except one. Which one is the exception?

A An increase in the number of firms in the market

B Significant economies of scale in the industry

C An increase in consumer knowledge and awareness of the product

D A reduction in barriers to entry into the industry

(2 marks)

Test Your Understanding 25

Railway companies offering off-peak services at lower prices than for peak services must ensure that, in the short run, these lower prices cover at least

A the variable cost of providing the service

B overhead costs

C the fixed costs of production

D the average cost of providing the service

(2 marks)

Test Your Understanding 26

The marginal propensity to consume measures

A the relationship between changes in consumption and changes in consumer utility

B the proportion o household incomes spent on consumer goods

C the proportion of total national income spent on consumer goods

D the relationship between changes in income and changes in consumption

(2 marks)

Test Your Understanding 27

The running yield of a bond is defined as

A The ratio of the coupon rate to the face value of the bond

B The ratio of the coupon rate to the market value of a bond

C The coupon rate plus the capital gain from the bond

D The return from the bond when held to maturity

(2 marks)

Test Your Understanding 28

The yield from an investment is

A The redemption value of a bond
B The coupon rate payable on a bond
C The short-term interest rate
D The measure of the return on an investment

(2 marks)

Test Your Understanding 29

Assume that the current market rate of interest is 5%. The government is issuing new bonds at $100, each offering a yield at 5%.

If the market interest rate fell to 2%, what would be the maximum price a rational investor would pay for the bond?

A $40
B $100
C $200
D $250

(2 marks)

Test Your Understanding 30

Which one of the following would be associated with the money market?

A Investment trusts
B Pension funds
C Discount houses
D Unit trusts

(2 marks)

Test Your Understanding 31

State whether each of the following statements is *true* or *false*.

Statement		True	False
(i)	If the supply of a good decreases, its price will rise and the demand curve for the product will shift to the left.		
(ii)	The supply of a good is described as price inelastic if a fall in price leads to a smaller proportionate fall in the quantity supplied.		
(iii)	If a tax is imposed on a good, the burden of the tax shifted to consumers will be greatest when the demand for the good is price inelastic.		
(iv)	If the demand for a good has a price elasticity of –1 then a 10% fall in price will lead to a 10% fall in demand.		

Test Your Understanding 32

Venture capital is best described as:

A investment funds provided for established companies

B short-term investment in Eurocurrency markets

C capital funds that are highly mobile between financial centres

D equity finance in high-risk enterprises

(2 marks)

Test Your Understanding 33

Which *one* of the following can be used by governments to finance a budget deficit?

A A rise in direct taxation

B The sale of public assets

C An increase in interest rates

D An issue of government savings certificates

(2 marks)

Test Your Understanding 34

What is meant by the term 'commercial paper'?

A Another name for ordinary shares

B Another name for company cheques

C Another name for IOUs issued by companies

D Another name for the business press

(2 marks)

Test Your Understanding 35

Financial institutions are said to provide financial intermediation. This is best defined as providing:

A a means of payment by cheques

B financial advice to business customers

C an efficient means of linking net savers with net borrowers

D a service for the purchase and sale of foreign exchange

(2 marks)

Test Your Understanding 36

State whether each of the following statements is *true* or *false*.

Statement		True	False
(i)	Governments will have a financial deficit if the country's imports exceed exports.		
(ii)	Companies need financial intermediaries if their receipts exceed their payments.		
(iii)	Governments can finance their budget deficits by raising taxation.		
(iv)	An overdraft is a means for individuals to meet short-term lack of liquidity.		

(4 marks)

Test Your Understanding 37

Which one of the following distinguishes a Treasury Bond (or Gilt) from a Treasury Bill?

A A Treasury Bond is issued by the Central Bank on behalf of the government

B A Treasury Bond has a fixed rate of interest called a coupon rate

C A Treasury Bond can be traded on a secondary market

D A Treasury Bond may have a maturity date that is less than a year

(2 marks)

Test Your Understanding 38

For each of the following events, state whether the direct effect on a country with a flexible exchange rate would be to lead to a rise (appreciation) or fall (depreciation) in the country's exchange rate or to leave the exchange rate unaffected.

Event	Rise in the exchange rate	Fall in the exchange rate	Leave the exchange rate unaffected
(i) A rise in interest rates in the country.			
(ii) A rise in the demand for imports in the country.			
(iii) A significant short term fall in share prices in the country.			
(iv) Purchase of foreign exchange by the country's central bank.			

(4 marks)

Test Your Understanding 39

All of the following would result from a rise in interest rates except one. Which one is the exception?

A Business investment would tend to fall

B Share prices would tend to fall

C Sales of consumer good would tend to fall

D Government revenue would tend to rise

(2 marks)

Test Your Understanding 40

For each of the following financial instruments state whether they are money market (M) or capital market (C) instruments.

(i) Treasury bills

(ii) Certificates of deposit

(iii) Corporate bonds

(iv) Mortgages

(v) Bills of exchange

(4 marks)

Test Your Understanding 41

Which of the following would be expected to lead to a fall in the value of £ sterling against the US dollar?

(i) A rise in US interest rates

(ii) A rise in UK interest rates

(iii) Intervention by the Bank of England to buy sterling

A (i) only

B (ii) only

C (i) and (iii)

D (ii) and (iii)

(2 marks)

Test Your Understanding 42

Which *one* of the following would not result from the United Kingdom joining the single European currency (the Euro)?

A International transactions costs would rise

B Exchange rate uncertainty would be reduced

C The United Kingdom could no longer operate an independent monetary policy

D There would be increased price transparency between the United Kingdom and other EU countries

(2 marks)

Test Your Understanding 43

If in the short run a business's receipts exceed its payments it can finance this financial shortfall by all of the following except one. Which one is the exception?

A Using its cash reserves

B Issuing shares

C A bank overdraft

D A bill of exchange

(2 marks)

Test Your Understanding 44

Which one of the following is likely to result from an increase in the size of the public sector net borrowing?

A A decrease in the level of inflation

B A reduction in the level of taxation

C A rise in the price of shares

D A rise in the rate of interest

(2 marks)

Test Your Understanding 45

Which *one* of the following is a withdrawal from the circular flow of income?

A Investment

B Exports

C Taxation

D Profits

(2 marks)

Test Your Understanding 46

Last year, the government of Country A increased its budget deficit significantly. This is likely to:

A Increase the level of withdrawals from the economy

B Reduce the equilibrium level of national income

C Boost aggregate demand in the economy

D Reduce the level of employment in the economy

(2 marks)

Test Your Understanding 47

The upswing phase of the trade cycle normally leads to:

A A fall in structural unemployment

B A reduction in inflationary pressure

C The government budget moving towards a surplus

D The current account of the balance of payments moving towards a surplus

(2 marks)

Test Your Understanding 48

For the Quantity Theory of Money equation (MV = PT) to explain short-run price behaviour, it is necessary that:

A P varies inversely with M

B Interest rates remain unchanged

C Changes in V in the short run are predictable

D The number of transactions remains unchanged

(2 marks)

Test Your Understanding 49

What are the three main aims of a commercial bank which it must keep in balance?

A Profitability, liquidity, security

B Profitability, credit, security

C Prudence, liquidity, savings

D Prudence, credit, savings

(2 marks)

Test Your Understanding 50

A multinational/transnational company is one which:

A exports goods to more than one country

B buys many of its inputs from overseas countries

C has shareholders in many countries

D has production facilities in more than one country

(2 marks)

Test Your Understanding 51

The World Trade Organisation (WTO) has all of the following functions except which *one*?

A Establishing rules for the conduct of international trade

B Providing short-term capital to finance trade for low income countries

C Providing a forum negotiating reductions in trade barriers

D Settling trade disputes between member countries

(2 marks)

Test Your Understanding 52

All of the following are included as invisible items on the current account of the balance of payments except which *one* ?

A Flows of profits from assets held overseas

B Inflows of overseas investment

C Expenditure by foreign tourists within the country

D Interest payments received from bank accounts held in other countries

(2 marks)

Test Your Understanding 53

Which one of the following is always in balance?

A Balance of trade

B Balance of payments current account

C Balance of payments

D Balance of payments financial account

(2 marks)

Test Your Understanding 54

Brodeland is a country for which the demand for imports is price inelastic, and the demand for its exports is price elastic. If Brodeland's domestic currency appreciates in value, which if the following will happen?

A Exports will increase in value and imports will fall in value

B Exports will increase in value and imports will increase in value

C Exports will fall in value and imports will fall in value

D Exports will fall in value and imports will increase in value

(2 marks)

Test Your Understanding 55

The European Union has all the following features except which *one*?

A The absence of barriers to trade between all member states

B The absence of barriers to the movement of capital between member states

C Common rates of indirect taxation

D A common external tariff

(2 marks)

Test Your Understanding 56

State whether each of the following statements is *true* or *false*.

Statement	True	False
(i) The heaviest indirect taxes tend to be on goods with a high price elasticity of demand.		
(ii) An indirect tax is one where the incidence and the burden of the tax fall on different persons.		
(iii) Indirect taxes on goods are desirable since the burden of the tax falls on the foreign producer.		
(iv) Direct taxes are preferred to indirect taxes because they are always progressive.		

(4 marks)

Test Your Understanding 57

A tariff restriction imposed on the flow of imports into a country would be expected to lead to all of the following *except* which one?

A An improvement in the trade balance

B A reduction in unemployment

C Reduced competition for domestic producers

D A fall in the rate of inflation

(2 marks)

Test Your Understanding 58

Which one of the following *cannot* be used to finance a deficit on the current account of a country's balance of payments?

A Running down foreign exchange reserves

B Increased taxation

C Borrowing from foreign central banks

D Attracting inflows of short-term capital

(2 marks)

Test Your Understanding 59

Devaluation of the currency will:

A Improve the terms of trade and *not* increase the cost of living

B Improve the terms of trade but increase the cost of living

C Worsen the terms of trade but *not* increase the cost of living

D Worsen the terms of trade and increase the cost of living

(2 marks)

Test Your Understanding 60

All of the following would be likely to restrict long-term economic growth except which one?

A Increasing cost of energy as oil reserves decrease

B The scarcity of natural resources and raw materials

C Environmental damage caused by both production and consumption

D Increasing openness of economies to international trade

(2 marks)

Test Your Understanding 61

All of the following are features of globalisation except *one*. Which one is the exception?

A Rising trade ratios

B Increased international capital flows

C Improved terms of trade for all countries

D Reduced barriers to international factor movements

(2 marks)

Test Your Understanding 62

If there is a reduction in government spending, there will not necessarily be a fall in National Income if there is an increase in:

(i) Exports

(ii) Taxation

(iii) Investment

A (i) and/ or (ii)

B (i) and/ or (iii)

C (ii) and/ or (iii)

D Any of (i), (ii) and (iii)

(2 marks)

Test Your Understanding 63

Which one of the following policies would promote export-led economic growth?

A A depreciation in a country's foreign exchange rate

B An increase in a country's tariffs on imports

C An expansionary domestic monetary policy

D An increase in direct taxes

(2 marks)

Test Your Understanding 64

State whether each of the following statements is *true* or *false*.

Statement	True	False
(i) If a country imposes trade barriers on its imports, that country's economic welfare will be reduced.		
(ii) An advantage of flexible exchange rate regimes is that uncertainty is reduced for business.		
(iii) An advantage of fixed exchange rate regimes is that they make trade deficits less likely to occur.		
(iv) Free trade enables a country to re-allocate its resource to more productive uses.		

(2 marks)

Test Your Understanding 65

The following refers to the Japanese economy in the 1990s:

Table 1 Gross domestic product (1996)

		Billions Yen	**% of total**
1	Private consumption expenditure	299,440	59.8%
2	Domestic fixed capital formation	148,190	29.6
3	Government consumption expenditure	48,969	9.6
4	Stock building	1,058	0.2
5	Exports	49,589	9.9
6	Imports	246,900	–9.1
Gross domestic product		500,355	100.0

Table 2 Growth rates of GDP components (% per annum)

	GDP		**Investment**	**Government expenditure**	**Exports**
1990	4.8	4.4	8.8	4.3	5.7
1991	3.8	2.3	2.8	3.8	–0.9
1992	1.0	2.2	–2.0	2.8	–20.3
1993	0.3	1.7	–2.8	2.9	–7.3
1994	0.6	2.5	–2.4	2.0	0.3
1995	1.4	2.1	0.2	4.6	2.8
1996	3.6	3.0	8.3	2.9	9.2

(i) From Table 1 identify the three injections into the circular flow. **(3 marks)**

(ii) State whether slow GDP growth would be expected to raise, lower or be of no effect on each of the following:

- the level of employment;
- the government budget surplus;
- the level of imports. **(3 marks)**

Test your understanding answers

Test Your Understanding 1

A

Economies and diseconomies of scale refer to the long-run cost curve, hence (C) and (D) are incorrect. Diminishing returns is the short-run process which leads to rising costs. Short-run average costs thus fall initially because fixed costs are spread over a larger output.

Test Your Understanding 2

C

The theory of the firm states that firms are profit maximisers. Thus, to be in equilibrium, where the firm would have no incentive to raise or lower output, the firm would have to be at the profit maximising level of output.

Test Your Understanding 3

A

(B) and (C) are the conditions necessary for profit maximisation to take place and (D) refers to the use of profits whether the firm is efficient or not. The necessary condition for the pursuit of profits to lead to efficiency is competition; when competition is restricted firms may make profits without being efficient.

Test Your Understanding 4

A

The price of shares is determined by demand and supply. (B) and (C) would raise the demand for shares and (D) would reduce the supply. However, a rise in interest rates would reduce the demand for shares as alternative investments have become more attractive.

Test Your Understanding 5

(i) *Company*. Internal economies arise from the advantages of large scale production within the business.

(ii) *Too large*. Diseconomies of scale occur when a business becomes too big, the others can occur in a business of any size.

(iii) *The industry becomes larger*. External economies occur when the industry is large (such as specialised supporting firms), the others could occur irrespective of the size of the industry.

(iv) *Produce on a large scale*. Technical economies arise out of more efficient use of existing technology as the business becomes bigger. The others could occur at any size of business.

Test Your Understanding 6

Statement whether each of the following statements is true or false.

Statements	True	False
(i) Economies of scale act as a barrier to entry into an industry.	X	
(ii) If there are significant economies of scale, the number of firms in the industry will tend to be small.	X	
(iii) Diseconomies of scale cause the short-run average cost curve to rise.		X
(iv) If output rises at the same rate as average cost rises, this is called constant returns to scale.		X

(i) Economies of scale will give a cost advantage to existing firms thus making it difficult for new firms to enter an industry.

(ii) Economies of scale will favour large firms thus smaller firms will go out of business, reducing the number in the industry.

(iii) Diseconomies of scale affect the long-run average cost curve not the short-run cost curve.

(iv) Constant returns to scale occur when total costs and total output rise at the same rate thus keeping average costs constant

Test Your Understanding 7

D

Anyone with an interest in the behaviour of a business, whether profit seeking or not, is a stakeholder in that business. All of these may have a legitimate interest in the business.

Test Your Understanding 8

C

All of the others have been recommended by various bodies such as the Greenbury Committee. The Committee also recommended greater, not less, use of non-executive directors.

Test Your Understanding 9

(a) the calculation for the net present value is to discount each years income
Thus discounted cash flow of the project is $16,191

Year 1	$\$5,000/(1.1) = \$4,545.45$
Year 2	$\$5,000/(1.1)^2 = \$4,132.23$
Year 3	$\$10,000/(1.1)^3 = \$7,513.15$

(b) the calculation now becomes
Thus the discounted cash flow of the project is $14,688

Year 1	$\$5,000/(1.1) = \$,4545.45$
Year 2	$\$5,000/(1.1)^2 = \$4,132.23$
Year 3	$\$8,000/(1.1)^3 = \$6,010.52$

(c) The NPV of the project

First case:	$16,191 – $15,000 = $1,191
Second case:	$14,688 – $15,000 = –$312

Test Your Understanding 10

C

The equilibrium price is where demand and supply are equal. If the price is forced above this level, it will lead to an extension of supply and a contraction of demand and a surplus would exist in the market.

Test Your Understanding 11

A

If a reduction in the price of 10% resulted in a fall in total revenue of 10%, then, since revenue is equal to price multiplied by the quantity sold, the quantity sold must have stayed the same. This implies that the price has no effect on the quantity demanded: the demand is perfectly inelastic.

Test Your Understanding 12

D

The essential feature of oligopoly is that of interdependence: the effects of policy decisions are crucially affected by the reaction of rival firms. Thus pricing decisions must always take into account how rival firms are likely to react to reductions or rises in price.

Test Your Understanding 13

C

Responses (A), (B) and (D) all refer to conditions of demand which affect the position of the demand curve. Response (C) refers to the price of the good itself; a change in this would lead to a movement along the demand curve, not a shift in the curve itself.

Test Your Understanding 14

D

A horizontal merger is one between firms producing similar goods at the same stage of production. (A) is an example of vertical integration and (C) is a conglomerate merger. (B) might be a merger of any sort.

Test Your Understanding 15

(i) An indirect tax shifts *supply* curve.

(ii) The burden of tax would be shifted most to consumers when the demand curve for the product was *price inelastic*.

(iii) If the demand for the product was *price inelastic*.

(iv) Sales/output of the good would fall most when the demand for the good was *price elastic*.

Test Your Understanding 16

A

If trade unions secure a wage increase for their members, employment is likely to fall since the demand curve for labour like any other demand curve slopes downwards. A rise in price of labour (wages) will thus lead to a contraction in the demand for labour and decrease employment.

Test Your Understanding 17

(i) (3) $\frac{\text{\% change in the demand for coffee}}{\text{\% change in the price of coffee}}$

(ii) (1) price elastic.

(iii) (3) a large rise in price and a small fall in sales.

Test Your Understanding 18

B

Lower prices are not a cause of higher price elasticity in any market. They are more likely to be the effect.

Test Your Understanding 19

D

These are very short term deposits. Stocks and shares change value daily, Paintings are highly illiquid.

Test Your Understanding 20

C

The introduction of a minimum wage above the equilibrium rate will mean that more people will want to work than firms will want to employ. This will mean there is an excess of labour supplyover demand for labour.

Test Your Understanding 21

Statement	True	False
(i) A change in supply of a good will have the largest effect on price when the demand is price elastic.		X
(ii) A change in the demand for a good will have no effect on the price if the supply of the good is perfectly price elastic.	X	

Test Your Understanding 22

D

All of the first three are attempts to limit competition in one way or another. However, (D), the use of advertising, is not since advertising is one form of competition and is particularly important in some markets, especially oligopolies.

Test Your Understanding 23

(i) $$PED = \frac{\%\ \text{change in demand}}{\%\ \text{change in price}} \quad \text{thus} \quad \frac{+20\%}{-10\%} \quad \text{hence PED} = -2$$

(ii) $$PES = \frac{\%\ \text{change in supply}}{\%\ \text{change in price}} \quad \text{thus} \quad \frac{+5\%}{+10\%} \quad \text{hence PES} = +0.5$$

(iii) Revenue at $10 is $ 10 × 100 = $1000
$9 is $ 9 × 120 = $1080 thus change in revenue is +$80

Test Your Understanding 24

B

(A) and (D) would increase competition by raising the number of firms in the market. (C) would increase competition because it would raise consumer awareness of competing products. However, (B) would give a cost advantage to the larger firms and erect a barrier to entry; the number of firms will fall and competition will decrease.

Test Your Understanding 25

A

Since, in the short run, the business will have to pay fixed costs whatever the level of output, the minimum they must cover is the additional variable costs of the service. Any income above this will go towards paying the fixed cost that must be met anyway.

Test Your Understanding 26

D

Test Your Understanding 27

B

The running yield of a bond is defined as the ratio of coupon to the market value of the bond.

Test Your Understanding 28

D

Test Your Understanding 29

D

The nominal yield of the bond will be $5 (5% of $100). However, to earn $5 of interest with a market interest rate of 2%, an investor would have to pay $250 (2% of $250 = $5). Therefore, the investor would be prepared to pay up to $250 for the bond.

Test Your Understanding 30

C

Money markets are short-term market, as opposed to capital markets which are long-term markets. Investment trusts, pension funds and unit trusts all operate in long-term markets whereas discount houses operate in short-term markets.

Test Your Understanding 31

Statement		True	False
(i)	If the supply of a good decreases, its price will rise and the demand curve for the product will shift to the left.		X
(ii)	The supply of a good is described as price inelastic if a fall in price leads to a smaller proportionate fall in the quantity supplied.	X	
(iii)	If a tax is imposed on a good, the burden of the tax shifted to consumers will be greatest when the demand for the good is price inelastic.	X	
(iv)	If the demand for a good has a price elasticity of –1 then a 10% fall in price will lead to a 10% fall in demand.		X

Test Your Understanding 32

D

Venture capital is that invested in new and high-risk enterprises by buying shares in those businesses.

Test Your Understanding 33

D

A budget deficit is the difference between government expenditure and its income from taxation; this deficit must be financed by borrowing. Only (D) represents this borrowing. (A) and (B) would reduce the deficit and (C) has no direct relevance.

Test Your Understanding 34

C

Commercial paper is promissory notes issued by firms with relatively short maturity dates.

Test Your Understanding 35

C

The other three are services provided by typical commercial banks, but not by all financial institutions. But (C) is the core function of financial intermediation performed by all financial institutions.

Test Your Understanding 36

Statement		True	False
(i)	Governments will have a financial deficit if the country's imports exceed exports.		X
(ii)	Companies need financial intermediaries if their receipts exceed their payments.	X	
(iii)	Governments can finance their budget deficits by raising taxation.		X
(iv)	An overdraft is a means for individuals to meet short-term lack of liquidity.	X	

Test Your Understanding 37

B

Trerasury Bills do not have a fixed rate of interest on the face. All the remaining statements are true of both Bills and Bonds.

Test Your Understanding 38

Event		Rise in the exchange rate	Fall in the exchange rate	Leave the exchange rate unaffected
(i)	A rise in interest rates in the country.	X		
(ii)	A rise in the demand for imports in the country.		X	
(iii)	A significant short term fall in share prices in the country.			X
(iv)	Purchase of foreign exchange by the country's central bank.		X	

Test Your Understanding 39

D

Government revenue is not directly affected by interest rates. Indeed, since the government has a net debt ('the national debt') its expenditure would rise rather than its revenue. This is because with higher interest rates, the cost of servicing the national debt would increase.

Test Your Understanding 40

(i) Treasury bills	M money market
(ii) Certificates of deposit	M money market
(iii) Corporate bonds	C capital market
(iv) Mortgages	C capital market
(v) Bills of exchange	M money market

Test Your Understanding 41

A

A rise in US interest rates is likely to prompt a flow of funds from UK to US increasing the relative demand (and value) of the dollar, meaning a corresponding relative fall in value of sterling.

Test Your Understanding 42

A

The benefit of a single currency would include reduced exchange rate uncertainty (there are no exchange rates within the eurozone) and because no currency would be exchanged on intra-European trade, transactions costs would fall, not rise.

Test Your Understanding 43

B

The other three are all means of acquiring short-term liquidity to meet a short-term shortfall in finances. However, issuing shares is means of raising long-term finance typically for investment purposes.

Test Your Understanding 44

D

Increased borrowing by the government is likely to lead to a rise in interest rates. This, in turn, will normally depress share prices. Moreover, increased borrowing tends to inject expenditure into the economy, thus raising the rate of inflation.

Test Your Understanding 45

C

A withdrawal from the circular flow is a process that removes expenditure from the circular flow. Investment and exports add expenditure to the flow and are, therefore, injections. Profit is form of income and is neither an injection nor a withdrawal.

Test Your Understanding 46

C

A budget deficit (when government spending is greater than government income from tax receipts) is designed to boost aggregate demand in the economy. Government spending is an injection into the circular flow.

Test Your Understanding 47

C

In the upswing phase of the trade cycle aggregate demand rises. This increases inflationary pressure ('demand pull inflation') and pulls in extra imports worsening the balance of payments. Cyclical unemployment will tend to fall but not structural unemployment which is caused by long term not cyclic factors. However, the increase in income raises tax revenue and the fall in unemployment reduces government expenditure. The government budget moves towards surplus.

Test Your Understanding 48

D

The number of transactions (T) has to be unchanged for the equation MV = PT to be a predictor of price behaviour. Any increase in M, given no change in V in the short run, would result in a matching percentage increase in prices P.

Test Your Understanding 49

A

Test Your Understanding 50

D

Transnational companies (also known as multinational companies) may have all of the characteristics listed here. But the defining feature of such companies is that they produce their good or service in more than one country. A company producing in just one country may have all three of the other characteristics.

Test Your Understanding 51

B

The WTO's main functions are to promote free trade, resolve trade disputes and provide a framework of trade rules. However, it has no financing function. This is left to the other international bodies such as the IMF and the World Bank.

Test Your Understanding 52

B

Responses (A), (C) and (D) are all payments for economic services received. All would thus appear on the current account as invisible items. However, the flows of investment are flows of capital and therefore appear on the capital account.

Test Your Understanding 53

C

The sum of te balance of payments accounts must always balance (to zero). A surplus on the current account will be matched by a deficit on the financial and capital accounts, and vice versa.

Test Your Understanding 54

C

When a currency appreciates in value, imports become cheaper to buy but exports become more expensive for foreign buyers. Demand for imports is price inelastic, and so a fall in the price of imports will result in a fall in total spending on imports. Export prices in Brodeland's own currency will be unchanged, but prices to foreign buyers will go up. Higher exports prices to foreign buyers will result in a fall in total export volumes and total export revenue for Brodeland.

Test Your Understanding 55

C

The EU is a common market and thus has no internal barriers to the movement of either goods, services or factors of production. It also maintains a common external tariff, but indirect taxes, for example, VAT still vary from one member state to another. The Single European Market project is designed to progressively reduce these tax differences.

Test Your Understanding 56

Statement	True	False
(i) The heaviest indirect taxes tend to be on goods with a high price elasticity of demand.		X
(ii) An indirect tax is one where the incidence and the burden of the tax fall on different persons.	X	
(iii) Indirect taxes on goods are desirable since the burden of the tax falls on the foreign producer.		X
(iv) Direct taxes are preferred to indirect taxes because they are always progressive.		X

Test Your Understanding 57

D

Tarriffs allow domestic producers to raise thir prices which would generate cost-push inflation.

Test Your Understanding 58

B

Financing a deficit requires foreign currency.

Test Your Understanding 59

D

Devaluation of the currency will make imports more expensive. The price of exports should not be directly affected by the devaluation, and so the terms of trade (unit value of exports / unit value of imports) will worsen. Higher costs of imports will add to the cost of living.

Test Your Understanding 60

D

Increase output requires extra energy and raw materials. So a shortage of either would constrain the rate of economic growth. Also, environmental damage from pollution may become unacceptable (e.g. global warming) and thus places limits on output. Increased trade does none of these things and generally tend to raise productivity and hence economic growth.

Test Your Understanding 61

C

All of the others are features of globalisation but (C) cannot happen. The terms of trade measure the relationship between the prices of exports and imports. If they improve for one trading partner, they must, by definition, deteriorate for the other trading partner.

Test Your Understanding 62

B

Given that Y = C + I + G + (X - M), to avoid a fall in National Income G must be offset by an increase in C, (item (iii)) or X (item (i)).

Test Your Understanding 63

A

Depreciating the country's foreign exchange rate will make the goods it produces cheaper in foreign countries, and therefore more attractive in foreign countries. This will lead to an increase in demand for exports. Increasing tariffs will protect domestic markets and make it easier for firms to sell their goods and services at home rather than having to export them. An expansionary domestic monetary policy will boost aggregate demand in the domestic economy and will allow a firm to increase sales in its home market rather than having to increase exports to boost revenue. An increase in direct taxes is likely to make firms look to reduce the number of staff they are employing in general (rather than promoting growth at all).

Test Your Understanding 64

Statement	True	False
(i) If a country imposes trade barriers on its imports, that country's economic welfare will be reduced.	X	
(ii) An advantage of flexible exchange rate regimes is that uncertainty is reduced for business.		X
(iii) An advantage of fixed exchange rate regimes is that they make trade deficits less likely to occur.		X
(iv) Free trade enables a country to re-allocate its resource to more productive uses.	X	

Test Your Understanding 65

(i) The three injections are:

- Domestic fixed capital formation
- Government consumption expenditure
- Exports

(ii) Slow GDP growth would be expected to:

- Lower the level of employment
- Reduce the government budget surplus
- Lower the level of imports.

chapter

10

Mock Assessment 1

Chapter learning objectives

This section is intended for use when you have completed your study and initial revision. It contains a complete mock assessment.

This should be attempted as an exam conditions, timed mock. This will give you valuable experience that will assist you with your time management and examination strategy.

1 Mock Assessment 1

Paper CO4
Fundamentals of Business Economics

Instructions: attempt all 75 questions

Time allowed 2 hours

Do not turn the page until you are ready to attempt the assessment under timed conditions

Mock Assessment 1 – Questions

Test Your Understanding 1

The following financial data refers to a company (all figures are in $):

Capital employed	1.1.10	900,000
Capital employed	31.12.10	1,100,000
Gross profits for year ending	31.12.10	105,000
Interest payments year ending	31.12.10	20,000
Tax paid on profits year ending	31.12.10	15,000

What is the value of the rate of return on capital for this company?

(1 mark)

Test Your Understanding 2

Consider the following data for a proposed investment project.

Capital cost of the project	$7,000
Life of the investment	3 years
Scrap value of the capital at end of Year 3	$500
Income generated by the project	
Year 1	$2,000
Year 2	$3,000
Year 3	$2,000

From this data you are required to calculate:

(a) The discounted cash flow for the project assuming a discount rate of 10%

(1 mark)

(b) Is this project profitable for the company yes/no

(1 mark)

(c) The net present value for the project assuming a discount rate of 6% and a final scrap value of $1,000

(1 mark)

Test Your Understanding 3

Financial ratios involving profit involve a number of different profit figures, including

(i) Profit before interest and tax

(ii) Profit after interest but before tax

(iii) Profit after tax

Which profit figure is used to calculate

(a) ROCE

(b) EPS

(2 marks)

Test Your Understanding 4

What type of stakeholder would a **customer** be classified as?

A internal

B external

C connected

D disconnected

(1 mark)

Test Your Understanding 5

The principal-agent problem only occurs within profit seeking organisations

True/False

(1 mark)

Test Your Understanding 6

A UK oil company that judges that its shareholders' best interests are served by minimising its expenditure on measures to ensure that its plant and pipelines do not damage the environment is likely to be:

A applauded by all the major stakeholders in the company

B criticised by major investors in the company

C supported by the media

D supported by the UK government

(1 mark)

Test Your Understanding 7

The following is an extract from the accounts of ABC Inc.

	$000
Revenue	400
Cost of sales	200
Gross profit	200
Distribution costs	100
Admin. Expenses	10
Operating profit	90
Interest	15
Profit before tax	75
Taxation	20
Profit after tax	55
Capital employed	2,000
Share capital (Shares have a nominal value of 50c)	1,000

Calculate

(a) ROCE

(b) EPS

(2 marks)

Test Your Understanding 8

What type of ownership structure best describes a trade union?

A public

B private

C mutual

(1 mark)

Test Your Understanding 9

The 'agency problem' refers to which of the following situations?

A Shareholders acting in their own short-term interests rather than the long-term interests of the company

B A vocal minority of shareholders expecting the directors to act as their agents and pay substantial dividends

C Companies reliant upon substantial government contracts such that they are effectively agents of the government

D The directors acting in their own interests rather than the shareholders' interests

(1 mark)

Test Your Understanding 10

H Inc, a listed company, is evaluating four projects with the following details:

Project	**A**	**B**	**C**	**D**
NPV at a discount rate of 10% ($)	10,000	12,000	(5,000)	7,000
ROCE	12%	5%	13%	10%

Given the directors wish to maximise shareholder wealth, which project should be undertaken?

(1 mark)

Test Your Understanding 11

Which one of the following is not a characteristic of not-for-profit organisations?

A They need efficient and effective management

B They make financial surpluses and deficits

C They have a range of stakeholders

D The absence of any principal–agent problem

(1 mark)

Test Your Understanding 12

All of the following statements are true except which one?

A Import quotas tend to reduce prices

B Trade protection tends to reduce consumer choice

C Trade protection tends to reduce exports

D Tariffs tend to reduce competition

(2 marks)

Test Your Understanding 13

All of the following would be expected to raise share values except which one?

A An announcement of higher than expected profits

B A reduction in corporation tax

C A rise in interest rates

D A rise in share prices on overseas stock markets

(1 mark)

Test Your Understanding 14

The … (i) .... in a company are all those who have an interest in the strategy and behaviour of the … (ii) .... Their interest may not always coincide with those of the … (iii) .... who are principally interested in … (iv) .... The task of …. (v) .... is to attempt to reconcile these conflicting interests.

Read the above passage and indicate where each of the following words should be placed in the passage.

A Management

B Shareholders

C Stakeholders

D Company

E Profits

(5 marks)

Test Your Understanding 15

The principal–agent problem refers to:

A situations where a company's selling agents are not meeting the company's main sales targets

B problems arising when a principal delegates authority to an agent but cannot ensure the agent will always act in his/her interest

C cases where companies lack knowledge of particular markets and have to seek agents to act on their behalf

D the power a large company may exert over suppliers when it is the dominant buyer of that supplier's output

(1 mark)

Test Your Understanding 16

For each of the following economic processes, indicate whether the effect on the *short-run average cost* for a firm would be to raise the cost curve, lower the cost curve or to leave it unaffected.

Economic process	Raise curve	Lower curve	Leave curve unaffected
A rise in wage costs			
Increase opportunities for economies of scale.			
A fall in the price of raw materials			
A shift in the demand curve to the left			

(2 marks)

Test Your Understanding 17

Newt plc is considering the pricing of a new product, the Lavender, and has estimated the following costs and revenue figures:

Price	$5	$6	$7	$8	$9
Demand	60,000	55,000	50,000	45,000	40,000

- Fixed costs $50,000 per annum
- Variable cost $4 per unit

Required:

Calculate the maximum profit that Newt can make.

(2 marks)

Test Your Understanding 18

Economies of scale:

A can be gained only by monopoly firms

B are possible only if there is a sufficient demand for the product

C do not necessarily reduce unit costs of production

D depend on the efficiency of management

(1 mark)

Test Your Understanding 19

Which one of the following is not a factor of production?

A unskilled labour

B a machine tool

C cash reserves

D entrepreneurship

(1 mark)

Test Your Understanding 20

Indicate whether each of the following statements is *true* or *false*.

Statement	True	False
The law of diminishing returns shows how long-run cost tends to rise as if the scale of output becomes too great		
A firm's short-run cost curve is always U shaped; the long cost curve may or may not be		
For most firms technological change is one of the most important economies of scale		
Economies of scale act as barrier to entry to industries.		

(2 marks)

Test Your Understanding 21

Indicate whether each of the following are typical characteristics of an oligopoly market (yes/no).

Characteristic	Yes	No
A large number of small firms		
A preference for non-price competition over price competition		
Interdependence of decision-making		
Ease of entry and exit to and from the industry.		

(2 marks)

Test Your Understanding 22

If a business currently sells 10,000 units of its product per month at $10 per unit and the demand for its product has a price elasticity of –2.5, a rise in the price of the product to $11 will:

A raise total revenue by $7,250

B reduce total revenue by $17,500

C reduce total revenue by $25,000

D raise total revenue by $37,500

(1 mark)

Test Your Understanding 23

Which *one* of the following is a natural barrier to the entry of new firms into an industry?

A Large initial capital costs

B The issuing of patents

C A government awarded franchise

D The licensing of professions

(1 mark)

Test Your Understanding 24

If the market supply curve for a good is inelastic, an increase in demand will:

A Raise total sales proportionately more than it will raise the market price

B Raise total sales proportionately less than it will raise the market price

C Raise the market price but leave total sales unaffected

D Raise total sales but leave the market price unchanged

(1 mark)

Test Your Understanding 25

Mergers between businesses engaged in the same stage of production of a similar good or service are known as:

A Horizontal mergers

B Conglomerate mergers

C Vertical mergers

D Cross mergers

(1 mark)

Test Your Understanding 26

A good which is characterised by both rivalry and excludability is called:

A a public good

B a private good

C a government good

D an external good

(1 mark)

Test Your Understanding 27

In practice a monopoly may have its market power limited by all of the following except which *one*?

A Countervailing power from its customers

B The market may be contestable

C There may be close substitutes for the good

D The firm's long-run average cost curve may be falling

(1 mark)

Test Your Understanding 28

The following is a list of possible sources of market failure.

(i) Externalities

(ii) Monopoly power

(iii) Public goods and services

(iv) Merit goods

(v) Lack of knowledge

For each of the following cases, indicate which one of the above sources of market failure matches the case given:

A Businesses fail to properly train their employees because they fear that they will move to other firms after their training.

B There is a failure to provide efficient street cleaning services because it is impossible for the service providers to ensure that all who benefited from the services paid for them.

(2 marks)

Test Your Understanding 29

Which *one* of the following is the best example of a merit good?

A Street lighting

B A national defence force

C Company cars for top sales executives

D A system of public libraries

(1 mark)

Test Your Understanding 30

There are three types of mergers

(i) Horizontal mergers

(ii) Vertical mergers

(iii) Conglomerate mergers

Match the following reasons for a merger with the appropriate type of merger listed above.

A To increase monopoly power and control over the market

B To ensure control over supplies of raw materials and components

C To secure economies of scale

D To reduce risk by diversifying the range of products sold and the range of markets

(4 marks)

Test Your Understanding 31

State whether the following statements about the privatisation of state industries are true or false.

Statement	True	False
(i) Privatisation increases the commercial pressure on the business to make a profit.		
(ii) Privatisation ensures the business faces competition and so encourages greater efficiency.		
(iii) Privatisation is a means of solving the principal-agent problem.		
(iv) Privatisation is likely to make the business more responsive to needs of its customers.		

(4 marks)

Test Your Understanding 32

Which of the following are features of monopolistic competition?

(i) Large numbers of producers in the industry.
(ii) Choice of products for customers
(iii) High barriers to entry

A (i) and (ii) only
B (i) and (iii) only
C (ii) and (iii) only
D (i), (ii) and (iii)

(2 marks)

Test Your Understanding 33

The cobweb theorem:

A shows that, without intervention some agricultural prices will fall continuously over time

B explains why some agricultural prices are characterised by instability from one year to another

C shows that when some agricultural prices are disturbed, prices steadily return to their equilibrium level

D the imposition of minimum prices in agricultural products always lead to unsold surpluses

(1 mark)

Test Your Understanding 34

The necessary conditions for a firm to be able to practice price discrimination are:

(i) The firm must be a price setter rather than a price taker.
(ii) Barriers must exist to prevent transfer between the markets.
(iii) The price elasticity of demand must be different in each market.

A (i) and (ii) only
B (i) and (iii) only
C (ii) and (iii) only
D all of them

(2 marks)

Test Your Understanding 35

If an indirect tax is imposed on a good or service:

A The price will rise by an amount equal to the tax

B The producer decides on how much of the tax to pass on to the customer

C The price rise will be smaller the greater is the price elasticity of demand

D The price rise will be greater the smaller is the price elasticity of supply

(1 mark)

Test Your Understanding 36

All of the following are examples of where externalities are likely to occur except which *one*?

A A business providing training schemes for its employees

B Government expenditure on vaccination programmes for infectious diseases

C Attending a concert given by a government funded orchestra

D Private motorists driving cars in city centres

(1 mark)

Test Your Understanding 37

Whenever government intervention prevents prices from reaching their equilibrium level, the result will always include all of the following except which *one?*

A Shortages or surpluses

B Demand and supply not equal

C Reduced profits for producers

D Resources not allocated by price

(1 mark)

Test Your Understanding 38

A rise in the price of a good accompanied by a fall in the quantity sold would result from

A a decrease in supply

B an increase in demand

C a decrease in demand

D an increase in supply

(1 mark)

Test Your Understanding 39

If the demand curve for Good A shifts to the left when the price of Good B rises, we may conclude that

A the goods are substitutes

B Good A is an inferior good

C the goods are complements

D the demand for Good A is price elastic

(1 mark)

Test Your Understanding 40

The introduction of a national minimum wage will lead a business to reduce its number of employees most when

A the demand for its final product is price elastic

B wage costs are a small proportion of total costs

C there is a low degree of substitutability between capital and labour

D the supply of substitute factors of production is price inelastic

(2 marks)

Test Your Understanding 41

The following is a list of different types of market structure.

- Perfect competition
- Monopolistic competition
- Oligopoly
- Monopoly

Match to each of the following situations the market structure that is being described.

Situation	Market Structure
(i) In the long run, abnormal profits are competed away by the entry of new firms and for each firm output will be the optimum level of output.	
(ii) The behaviour of any one firm is conditioned by how it expects its competitors to react to its price and output decisions.	

(2 marks)

Test Your Understanding 42

A business could use all of the following to finance a lack of synchronisation in its short-term payments and receipts except which one?

A a bank overdraft

B trade credit

C its cash reserves

D a hire purchase agreement

(1 mark)

Test Your Understanding 43

A risk that an organisation may not be able to realise its assets to meet a commitment associated with financial instruments is known as:

A credit risk

B liquidity risk

C interest rate risk

D currency risk

(1 mark)

Test Your Understanding 44

Consider a bond with characteristics as follows:

- Nominal value $100
- Coupon rate 6%
- Redemption terms – to be redeemed at par in 10 years time
- Current market value – $96

Calculate the running yield.

(2 marks)

Test Your Understanding 45

A $50 nominal value share with market price of $75 and a dividend of $5 will generate a dividend yield of:

A 6.67%

B 7.5%

C 10%

D 15%

(1 mark)

Test Your Understanding 46

State whether each of the following financial instruments appearing on a commercial bank's balance sheet is an asset or liability for the bank.

Instrument	Asset	Liability
Advances		
Money at call with discount houses		
Deposit accounts		
Shareholder capital		

(4 marks)

Test Your Understanding 47

If banks are required to keep a reserve assets ratio of 10% and also wish to keep a margin of liquid reserves of 10%, by how much would deposits ultimately rise by if they acquire an additional $1000 of reserve assets?

A $10000

B $5000

C $1000

D $500

(2 marks)

Test Your Understanding 48

A bond has the following characteristics:

- Nominal value $100
- Coupon rate 7%
- Redemption terms – to be redeemed at par in 3 years time
- Current market value – $105

Calculate the bill rate.

(2 marks)

Test Your Understanding 49

If a commercial banks reallocates some of its assets from less profitable to more profitable ones,

A the bank's liquidity will be increased

B the safety of the bank's assets will be increased

C the bank's liquidity will be decreased

D the liquidity and safety of the bank's assets will be unaffected

(2 marks)

Test Your Understanding 50

Which of the following statements about the relationship between bond prices and bond yields is true?

A They vary positively

B They vary inversely

C They vary inversely or positively depending on business conditions

D They are not related

(2 marks)

Test Your Understanding 51

Under a regime of flexible exchange rates, which one of the following would lead to a rise in the exchange rate for a country's currency?

A a shift in the country's balance of payments current account towards a surplus

B a rise in interest rates in other countries

C an increasing balance of trade deficit

D the central bank buying foreign exchange on the foreign exchange market

(2 marks)

Test Your Understanding 52

Exchange rates are determined by supply and demand for currencies in the foreign exchange market. State whether each of the following would be part of the supply of a country's currency or part of the demand for that country's currency.

Statement	Supply	Demand
Payments for imports into the country.		
Inflows of capital into the country.		
Purchases of foreign currency by the country's central bank.		

(2 marks)

Test Your Understanding 53

Each of the following is a source of funds for capital investment for business except *one*. Which one is the exception?

A Commercial banks

B Internally generated funds

C The stock market

D The central bank

(2 marks)

Test Your Understanding 54

The linking of net savers with net borrowers is known as:

A the savings function

B financial intermediation

C financial regulation

D a store of value

(2 marks)

Test Your Understanding 55

If a consumer price index rises, it shows that

A the value of the currency has increased

B real consumer income has fallen

C all prices in the economy have risen

D the purchasing power of money has decreased

(2 marks)

Test Your Understanding 56

The main function of the money market is to

A enable businesses and governments to obtain liquidity

B encourage saving

C permit the efficient buying and selling of shares

D deal in credit instruments of more than one year maturity

(2 marks)

Test Your Understanding 57

After the banking crisis of 2008 and the resulting credit crunch, which of the following financial institutions was **not** bailed out by government intervention and so went into liquidation?

A AIG

B Royal Bank Of Scotland

C Northern Rock

D Lehman Brothers

(1 mark)

Test Your Understanding 58

In order to finance an excess of expenditure over taxation receipts, a government could:

A reduce its current expenditure

B issue government bonds

C raise income tax

D run an overdraft on its account with the World Bank

(2 marks)

Test Your Understanding 59

The effects of low real interest rates include all of the following except which one?

A Credit based sales will tend to be high

B Nominal costs of borrowing will always be low

C Business activity will tend to increase

D Investment will be encouraged

(2 marks)

Test Your Understanding 60

Which *one* of the following would cause the value of the multiplier to fall?

A A fall in the level of government expenditure

B A rise in the marginal propensity to consume

C A fall in business investment

D A rise in the marginal propensity to save

(2 marks)

Test Your Understanding 61

The recession phase of the trade cycle will normally be accompanied by all of the following except which one?

A A rise in the rate of inflation

B A fall in the level of national output

C An improvement in the trade balance

D A rise in the level of unemployment

(2 marks)

Test Your Understanding 62

According to the classical school, in order to manage the economy governments should:

A use active fiscal and monetary policy

B adopt a laissez faire approach and leave everything to market forces

C announce monetary rules to control inflation, and liberalise product and factor markets

D use only monetary policy to increase output and employment

(2 marks)

Test Your Understanding 63

The following is a list of types of unemployment:

- Structural unemployment
- Cyclical unemployment
- Real wage (classical) unemployment
- Frictional unemployment
- Seasonal unemployment.

Match the above types of unemployment to the following definitions.

Definition of unemployment	Type of unemployment
(i) Unemployment that occurs in particular industries and arises from long-term changes in the patterns of demand and supply.	
(ii) Unemployment associated with industries or regions where the demand for labour and wage rates regularly rise and fall over the year.	

(2 marks)

Test Your Understanding 64

All of the following will lead to a fall in the level of economic activity in an economy except which *one*?

A A rise in cyclical unemployment

B A fall in business investment

C A decrease in government expenditure

D A rise in interest rates

(2 marks)

Test Your Understanding 65

The best measure of the standard of living in a country is

A gross domestic product per capita

B the average wage

C gross national product per capita

D personal disposable income

(2 marks)

Test Your Understanding 66

Supply-side policy is designed to

A raise the level of aggregate monetary demand in the economy

B manage the money supply in the economy

C improve the ability of the economy to produce goods and services

D reduce unemployment by limiting the supply of labour

(2 marks)

Test Your Understanding 67

Indicate whether each of the following taxes are direct taxes or indirect taxes.

Type of tax	Direct	Indirect
Income tax		
Value added tax		
Corporation tax		
National insurance (social security tax)		

(4 marks)

Test Your Understanding 68

The following diagram shows the aggregate demand curve (AD) and the aggregate supply curve (AS) for an economy:

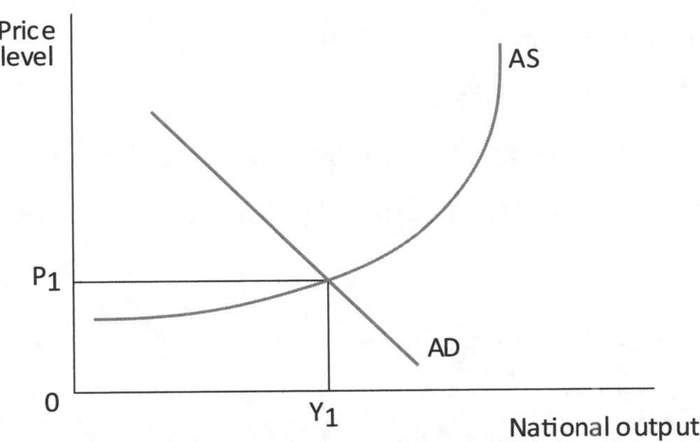

With reference to the diagram:

A .... supply shock would shift the .... curve to the left and cause the rate of inflation to increase. However the level of .... would fall. A(n) .... fiscal policy would shift the .... curve to the right leading to a .... in both the level of national output and the rate of inflation.

Use the following words and phrases to fill in the gaps in the above passage.

positive
aggregate demand
rise
expansionary
negative
deflationary
aggregate supply
inflation
national output
fall

(6 marks)

Test Your Understanding 69

All of the following will encourage the process of the globalisation of production except which *one*?

A Reductions in international transport costs

B Higher levels of tariffs

C Reduced barriers to international capital movements

D Increased similarity in demand patterns between countries

(2 marks)

Test Your Understanding 70

Which *one* of the following shows the lowest degree of international mobility?

A Unskilled labour

B Financial capital

C Technical knowledge

D Management

(2 marks)

Test Your Understanding 71

Identify which of the following statements about the balance of payments is true and which is false.

Statement	True	False
(i) A deficit on a country's balance of payments current account can be financed by a surplus of invisible earnings.		
(ii) Flows of profits and interest on capital appear in the Capital Account.		
(iii) Flexible exchange rate systems should, in principle, prevent persistent current account imbalances.		
(iv) Current account deficits tend to worsen in periods of rapid economic growth.		

(4 marks)

Test Your Understanding 72

Which of the following economic conditions is likely to lead to demand-pull inflation?

A A worsening balance of payments and a rising exchange rate

B An increase in Government spending and firms operating at full capacity

C Increased monopoly power in goods and labour markets

D An increase in interest rates and a rise in the world price of oil

(2 marks)

Test Your Understanding 73

All of the following are benefits which all countries gain when adopting a single currency such as the Euro, except which one?

A Reduced transactions costs

B Increased price transparency

C Lower interest rates

D Reduced exchange rate uncertainty

(2 marks)

Test Your Understanding 74

For each of the following events, indicate whether the direct effect of each on an economy would raise inflation, reduce inflation or leave the rate of inflation unaffected. Assume that the economy is close to full employment.

Event	Raise inflation	Lower inflation	Leave inflation unchanged
(i) A rise (appreciation) in the exchange for the country's currency.			
(ii) A significant increase in the money supply.			
(iii) The removal of house prices from the consumer price index.			
(iv) A rise in business expectations leading to an increase in investment.			

(4 marks)

Test Your Understanding 75

Compared to a fixed exchange rate system, an economy will benefit from a flexible exchange rate system because:

A it enables businesses to vary their export prices

B governments will not have to deflate the economy when balance of payments deficits occur

C it reduces the cost of acquiring foreign exchange

D it ensures that businesses never become uncompetitive in international markets

(2 marks)

Test your understanding answers

Test Your Understanding 1

10.5%

Test Your Understanding 2

(a) $(824)

(b) No

(c) $76

Test Your Understanding 3

(a) i

(b) iii

Test Your Understanding 4

C

Test Your Understanding 5

False

Test Your Understanding 6

B

The modern view is that being socially responsible can offer business benefits. This is particularly true of the oil industry where major UK and US companies have attracted very substantial criticism as a result of an apparent failure to adequately protect the environment from oil spills.

Test Your Understanding 7

(a) ROCE = operating profit / capital employed = 90/2,000 = 4.5%

(b) eps = profit after tax / number of shares = 55/2,000 = 2.75 cents per share

Test Your Understanding 8

C

Trade unions are mutual organisations for the mutual benefit of members.

Test Your Understanding 9

D

Directors, who are placed in control of resources that they do not own and are effectively agents of the shareholders, should be working in the best interests of the shareholders. However, they may be tempted to act in their own interests, for example by voting themselves huge salaries. The background to the agency problem is the separation of ownership and control – in many large companies the people who own the company (the shareholders) are not the same people as those who control the company (the board of directors).

Test Your Understanding 10

B

As it has the highest NPV

Test Your Understanding 11

D

Test Your Understanding 12

A

Test Your Understanding 13

C

Test Your Understanding 14

The *stakeholders* in a company are all those who have an interest in the strategy and behaviour of the *company*. Their interest may not always coincide with those of the *shareholders* who are principally interested in *profits*. The task of *management* is to attempt to reconcile these conflicting interests.

Test Your Understanding 15

B

Test Your Understanding 16

Economic process	**Raise curve**	**Lower curve**	**Leave curve unaffected**
A rise in wage costs	X		
Increase opportunities for economies of scale.			X
A fall in the price of raw materials		X	
A shift in the demand curve to the left			X

Test Your Understanding 17

Solution

$150,000

Price	**$5**	**$6**	**$7**	**$8**	**49**
Revenue ($000)	300	330	350	360	360
Variable costs ($000)	(240)	(220)	(200)	(180)	(160)
Fixed costs ($000)	(50)	(50)	(50)	(50)	(50)
Profit ($000)	**10**	**60**	**100**	**130**	**150**

The optimum selling price is $9 per unit, selling 40,000 units with a corresponding profit of $150,000 p.a.

Test Your Understanding 18

B

A is not true, any firm can benefit from economies of scale providing they are of sufficient size to obtain such economies. C is not true by definition. D is not true; management can generally be inefficient and still make some good decisions.

Test Your Understanding 19

C

Land, labour, capital and enterprise are the factors of production. Cash reserves are waiting to be converted into those resources.

Test Your Understanding 20

Statement	True	False
The law of diminishing returns shows how long-run cost tends to rise as if the scale of output becomes too great		X
A firm's short-run cost curve is always U shaped; the long cost curve may or may not be	X	
For most firms technological change is one of the most important economies of scale		X
Economies of scale act as barrier to entry to industries.	X	

Test Your Understanding 21

Characteristic	Yes	No
A large number of small firms		X
A preference for non-price competition over price competition	X	
Interdependence of decision-making	X	
Ease of entry and exit to and from the industry.		X

Test Your Understanding 22

B

Test Your Understanding 23

A

Test Your Understanding 24

B

Test Your Understanding 25

A

Test Your Understanding 26

B

Test Your Understanding 27

D

Test Your Understanding 28

(a) (i) Externalities

(b) (iii) Public goods and services

Test Your Understanding 29

D

Test Your Understanding 30

(a) (i) Horizontal merger

(b) (ii) Vertical merger

(c) (i) Horizontal merger

(d) (iii) Conglomerate merger

Test Your Understanding 31

Statement	True	False
(i) Privatisation increases the commercial pressure on the business to make a profit.	X	
(ii) Privatisation ensures the business faces competition and so encourages greater efficiency.		X
(iii) Privatisation is a means of solving the principal-agent problem.		X
(iv) Privatisation is likely to make the business more responsive to needs of its customers.	X	

Test Your Understanding 32

A

Test Your Understanding 33

B

Test Your Understanding 34

D

Test Your Understanding 35

C

Test Your Understanding 36

C

Test Your Understanding 37

C

Test Your Understanding 38

A

Test Your Understanding 39

C

Test Your Understanding 40

A

Test Your Understanding 41

Situation	**Market Structure**
(i) In the long run, abnormal profits are competed away by the entry of new firms and for each firm output will be the optimum level of output.	Perfect competition
(ii) The behaviour of any one firm is conditioned by how it expects its competitors to react to its price and output decisions.	Oligopoly

Test Your Understanding 42

D

Test Your Understanding 43

B

Test Your Understanding 44

The running yield, also known as the "interest yield", given by

Running yield = (annual interest/market value) × 100% = (6/96) × 100% = 6.25%

Test Your Understanding 45

A

The yield of an asset is the relationship between the income derived from it and the price that has to be paid to acquire it. In this case the market price is $75 and the income gained is $5. The yield in percentage terms is $5 divided by $75 × 100%. This is 6.67%

Test Your Understanding 46

Instrument	Asset	Liability
Advances	X	
Money at call with discount houses	X	
Deposit accounts		X
Shareholder capital		X

Test Your Understanding 47

B

Test Your Understanding 48

The bill rate is just another name for the coupon rate, here 7%.

Test Your Understanding 49

C

Test Your Understanding 50

B

Test Your Understanding 51

A

Test Your Understanding 52

Statement	Supply	Demand
Payments for imports into the country.	X	
Inflows of capital into the country.		X
Purchases of foreign currency by the country's central bank.	X	

Test Your Understanding 53

D

Test Your Understanding 54

B

Test Your Understanding 55

D

Test Your Understanding 56

A

Test Your Understanding 57

D

Lehman Brothers filed for bankruptcy in September 2008

Test Your Understanding 58

B

Test Your Understanding 59

B

Test Your Understanding 60

D

Test Your Understanding 61

A

Test Your Understanding 62

C

Test Your Understanding 63

Definition of unemployment	**Type of unemployment**
(i) Unemployment that occurs in particular industries and arises from long-term changes in the patterns of demand and supply.	structural unemployment
(ii) Unemployment associated with industries or regions where the demand for labour and wage rates regularly rise and fall over the year.	Seasonal unemployment

Test Your Understanding 64

A

Test Your Understanding 65

C

Test Your Understanding 66

C

Test Your Understanding 67

Type of tax	Direct	Indirect
Income tax	X	
Value added tax		X
Corporation tax	X	
National insurance (social security tax)	X	

Test Your Understanding 68

A *negative* supply shock would shift the *aggregate* supply curve to the left and cause the rate of inflation to increase. However the level of *national output* would fall. An *expansionary* fiscal policy would shift the *aggregate demand* curve to the right leading to a rise in both the level of national output and the rate of inflation.

Test Your Understanding 69

B

Test Your Understanding 70

A

Test Your Understanding 71

Statement	True	False
(i) A deficit on a country's balance of payments current account can be financed by a surplus of invisible earnings.		X
(ii) Flows of profits and interest on capital appear in the Capital Account.		X
(iii) Flexible exchange rate systems should, in principle, prevent persistent current account imbalances.	X	
(iv) Current account deficits tend to worsen in periods of rapid economic growth.	X	

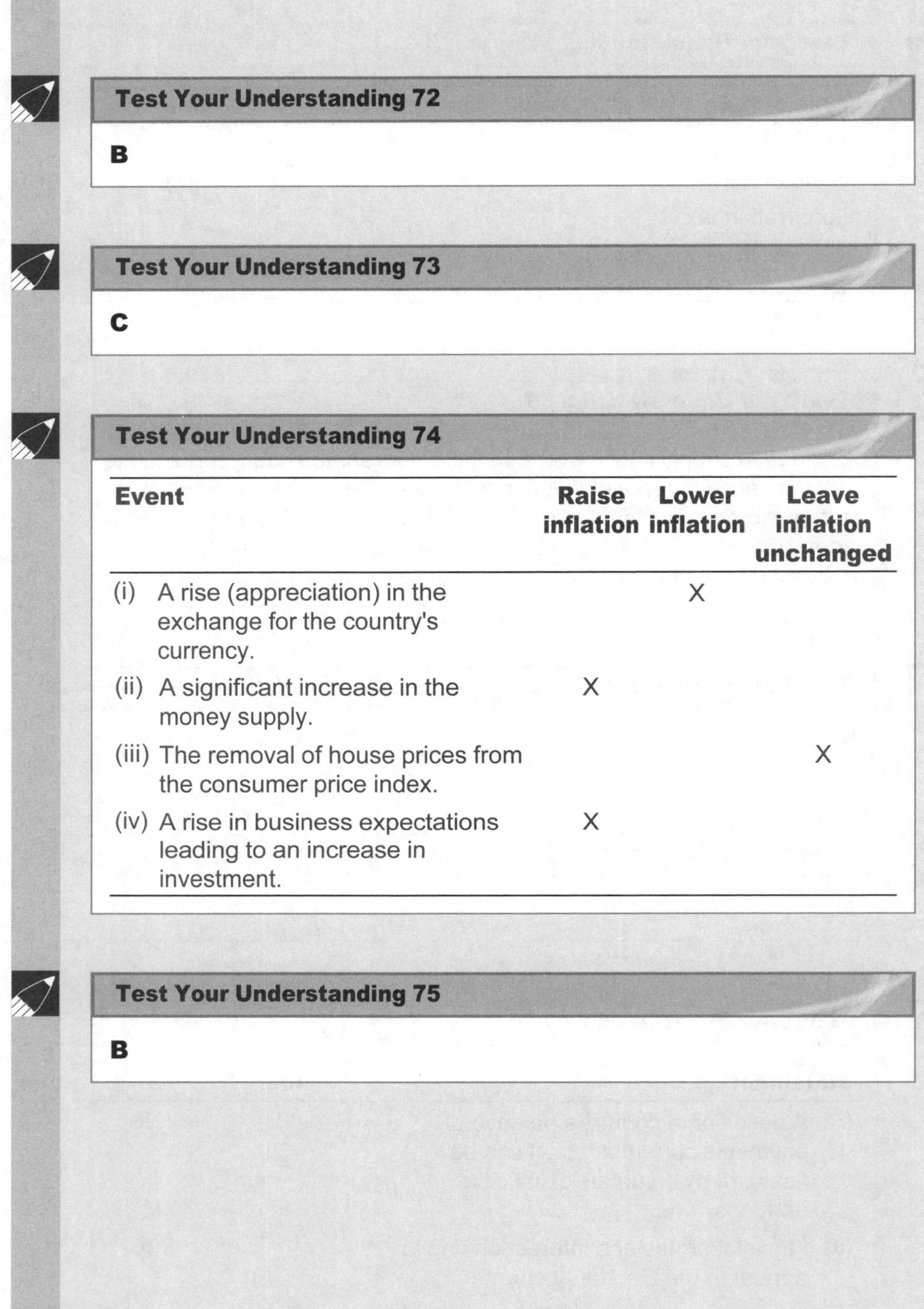

Test Your Understanding 72

B

Test Your Understanding 73

C

Test Your Understanding 74

Event	Raise inflation	Lower inflation	Leave inflation unchanged
(i) A rise (appreciation) in the exchange for the country's currency.		X	
(ii) A significant increase in the money supply.	X		
(iii) The removal of house prices from the consumer price index.			X
(iv) A rise in business expectations leading to an increase in investment.	X		

Test Your Understanding 75

B

chapter

11

Mock Assessment 2

Chapter learning objectives

This section is intended for use when you have completed your study and initial revision. It contains a complete mock assessment.

This should be attempted as an exam conditions, timed mock. This will give you valuable experience that will assist you with your time management and examination strategy.

Paper C04
Fundamentals of Business Economics

Instructions: attempt all 75 questions

Time allowed 2 hours

Do not turn the page until you are ready to attempt the assessment under timed conditions

Mock Assessment 2 – Questions

Test Your Understanding 1

Which of the following organisations is normally found in the public sector?

A Education

B Charities

C Sports Clubs

D Businesses

(1 mark)

Test Your Understanding 2

All of the following are profit-seeking except one. Which one is the exception?

A Private limited companies

B Government departments

C Partnerships

D Sole traders

(2 marks)

Test Your Understanding 3

Public goods are produced in the public sector because:

A they are characterised by non-excludability and non-exclusivity

B of the high initial capital costs their production involves

C they are examples of natural monopolies

D their production and consumption involves significant external social benefits

(2 marks)

Test Your Understanding 4

Variable cost is best defined as:

A the cost of labour and materials

B costs which change over time

C the change in total costs when output is raised by one unit

D costs which vary with the level of output

(2 marks)

Test Your Understanding 5

For each of the following events indicate whether the effect would normally be to raise a company's share price, lower its share price or leave its share price unchanged.

Events	**Raise share price**	**Lower share price**	**Leave share price unchanged**
A reduction in corporation tax			
An issue of additional shares in the company			
A fall in interest rates			

(3 marks)

Test Your Understanding 6

Indicate whether each of the following statements about not-for-profit organisations is *true* or *false*.

Statements	**True**	**False**
The absence of shareholders means that the principal-agent problem has no impact on them.		
They need to avoid losses in the long run.		
They operate in both the public and the private sectors of the economy.		

(3 marks)

Test Your Understanding 7

Consider the following data for a business:

Output/Sales	*Price*
10	$100
11	$95
12	$90
13	$85
14	$80

From this data you are required to calculate for this business:

The price elasticity of demand for a price fall from $100 to $95.

(1 marks)

Test Your Understanding 8

Consider the following data for a company's proposed investment project.

Capital cost of the project	$6,000
Life of the investment	3 years
Scrap value of the capital equipment at end of Year 3	$1,000

Income generated by the project at end of each year

Year 1	($1,000)
Year 2	$4,000
Year 3	$3,000

From this data you are required to calculate:

A The discounted cash flow for the project assuming a discount rate of 10%. **(2 marks)**

B Whether the company should undertake the project? Yes/No **(1 mark)**

C The net present value for the project if the discount rate was 5%. **(2 marks)**

Test Your Understanding 9

The following data refers to a company for a financial period.

Opening capital employed	$1.4 m
Closing capital employed	$1.8 m
Operating profit for year	$0.4 m
Corporation tax paid for year	$0.10 m
Interest payments for year	$0.05 m

What is the value of the rate of return on capital for this company?

(2 marks)

Test Your Understanding 10

State whether each of the following is an appropriate measure of the short-run performance or the long-run performance of a business.

Measures	Short run	Long run
Net present value		
Rate of return on capital employed		
Earnings per share		

(3 marks)

Test Your Understanding 11

Where there are a large number of external shareholders who play no role in the day-to-day running of a company, there is a situation that is described as:

A detached corporate ownership

B uninvolved external ownership

C dividend based shareholding

D separation of ownership and control

(1 mark)

Test Your Understanding 12

Assuming a discount rate of 5% the present value of $10,000 to be received in one year's time is:

A $10,500
B $10,050
C $9,524
D $6,667

(2 marks)

Test Your Understanding 13

An example of the principal–agent problem in business is where principals, such as ...., delegate control to agents, such as .... The problem is one of devising methods to ensure that agents act in the best interest of the principals. Managerial reward systems which link pay and bonuses to the improvement in .... is one such method.

Read the above passage and indicate which of the following words should be placed in each of the gaps in the passage.

A Management

B Stakeholders

C Shareholder wealth

D Shareholders

E Efficiency

(3 marks)

Test Your Understanding 14

Which of the following groups are stakeholders in a particular business?

(i) Employees.
(ii) Shareholders.
(iii) Management.
(iv) Customers.
(v) Suppliers.

A (i), (ii) and (iii) only
B (i), (ii), (iii) and (iv) only
C (ii) and (iii) only
D all of them

(2 marks)

Test Your Understanding 15

All of the following statements about earnings per share (EPS) are true except which *one*?

A It is relatively easy to calculate
B It is a useful measure of the change in shareholder wealth
C It is normally calculated on an annual basis
D It can be used to calculate the price-earnings ratio

(2 marks)

Test Your Understanding 16

Economies of scale could occur in the long run for all of the following reasons except *one*. Which one is the exception?

A Bulk buying by big companies
B Long-run improvements in technology in large firms
C Cheaper long-term finance for large companies
D Mass production technology adopted by large-scale producers

(2 marks)

Test Your Understanding 17

Indicate whether each of the following statements about a market economy is *true* or *false*.

Statements	True	False
The price mechanism is the only means for allocating scarce resources.		
The public sector is smaller than the private sector.		
Market prices fully reflect all production costs.		
Prices convey important information for both producers and consumers.		

(2 marks)<

Test Your Understanding 18

If a business is facing a demand for its product which is price inelastic, which one of the following would occur if that business raised the price of its product?

A Sales volume would fall and total revenue would fall

B Sales volume would stay the same and total revenue would rise

C Sales volume would fall and total revenue would stay the same

D Sales volume would fall and total revenue would rise

(2 marks)

Test Your Understanding 19

The price elasticity of supply of a good is a measure of the relationship between:

A the price of a good and the quantity supplied

B the volume of supply and changes in demand for the good

C a change in price of the good and the change in the quantity supplied

D a change in the cost of producing a good and the quantity supplied

(2 marks)

Test Your Understanding 20

A business has current sales of 10,000 units per month at a unit price of \$24. It reduces its price to \$21.60 and finds that its monthly sales rise to 11,500 units. Calculate the price elasticity of demand for this product.

(1 mark)

Test Your Understanding 21

A producer has a price inelastic supply curve for its product. State whether each of the following effects would occur (yes/no) if the firm experienced an increase in demand for its product.

Effects	Yes	No
Sales volume would increase.		
The volume of supply would increase.		
The equilibrium price would rise.		
In the short run, unit production costs would increase.		

(4 marks)

Test Your Understanding 22

If the government imposed a minimum price for a good that was above the equilibrium price, the consequence would be:

A a contraction of demand, an increase in supply and a market surplus

B a decrease in demand, an extension of supply and a market surplus

C a contraction in demand, an extension in supply and a market surplus

D a rise in supply, a fall in demand and a market shortage

(1 mark)

Test Your Understanding 23

State whether each of the following statements is *true* or *false*.

Statements	True	False
If the demand curve for Good A shifts to the right when the price of Good B falls we can conclude that A and B are substitute goods.		
If the demand for a good is price inelastic, a fall in its price will leave sales volume unchanged and total revenue reduced.		
The more price inelastic is the demand for a good, the greater is the proportion of any indirect tax levied on it that can be passed onto the consumer.		
An indirect tax imposed upon a good which has negative externalities will improve resource allocation.		

(4 marks)

Test Your Understanding 24

For firms in monopolistic competition, excess profits cannot be earned in the long run because:

A all firms are producing similar, undifferentiated goods

B there is a very large number of firms in the industry

C perfect knowledge ensures that customers always buy from the firm with the lowest price

D there are no significant barriers to entry into the industry

(2 marks)

Test Your Understanding 25

Which *one* of the following would act as a barrier to enter into an industry?

A A falling long-run average cost curve

B A U-shaped short-run average cost curve for all firms

C The existence of external economies of scale

D Constant returns to scale in the industry

(2 marks)

Test Your Understanding 26

The output of merit goods is likely to be less than the social optimum because:

A firms cannot ensure that all consumers pay the full price of the good or service

B the consumption of the good involves positive externalities

C the goods are necessities but are too expensive for some low-income groups

D the consumption of the good or service by one person does not preclude its consumption by others

(2 marks)

Test Your Understanding 27

Match the following company mergers with the merger type indicated below.

Company merger	Merger type
A steel producer merges with a producer of iron ore.	
A car producer merges with a producer of commercial vans.	
A financial services company merges with a travel company.	
A brewing company merges with a chain of inns and bars.	

A A horizontal merger

B A backward vertical merger

C A forward vertical merger

D A conglomerate merger

(4 marks)

Test Your Understanding 28

If a government imposes a maximum price for a good that is below the equilibrium price, the resulting market shortage will be greatest when:

A the demand is price elastic and the supply is price inelastic

B the demand is price elastic and the supply is price elastic

C the demand is price inelastic and the supply is price elastic

D the demand is price inelastic and the supply is price inelastic

(2 marks)

Test Your Understanding 29

In an oligopoly market, there is a heavy dependence on advertising and marketing because:

A oligopoly is characterised by product differentiation

B advertising and marketing are the only effective barriers to entry for firms

C the small number of firms ensures that price competition often leads to losses for all firms

D in oligopoly one firm's pricing policy affects the sales of other firms

(2 marks)

Test Your Understanding 30

Match the following situations to the definitions given below:

Situations	Definition
The emission of dangerous fumes from car exhausts.	
Pollution caused by the production of consumer electrical goods.	
Premature death of consumers of tobacco.	
Improved health among consumers of low fat food products.	

Definitions

A Positive externality in consumption

B Negative externality in consumption

C Negative externality in production

D None of the above

(4 marks)

Test Your Understanding 31

Evan owns $100 nominal value of irredeemable 3% government loan stock. If the required return on the loan stock increases from 5% to 6%, calculate the change in market value that will result.

A An increase of $1

B An increase of $10

C A decrease of $10

D A decrease of $1

(2 marks)

Test Your Understanding 32

All of the following would lead to a high price elasticity of demand for a good except *one*. Which one is the exception?

A The good has a large number of substitutes

B Consumers spend a large proportion of income of the good

C It refers to a long time period

D It has numerous complementary goods

(2 marks)

Test Your Understanding 33

Which one of the following would cause the supply curve for a good to shift to the left?

A The introduction of a new substitute product for the good

B A rise in wage rates for workers employed in making the good

C A fall in the price of raw materials used in its production

D The abolition of a government-imposed minimum price for the good

(2 marks)

Test Your Understanding 34

If an industry is characterised by a high concentration ratio it means that

A The industry's main customers are mainly located in one region

B Most of the output of the industry is sold to a few large customers

C The bulk of the industry's output is produced by a small number of firms

D Each firm in the industry specialises in a narrow range of products or markets

(2 marks)

Test Your Understanding 35

All of the following are conditions of demand for a good except one. Which *one* is the exception?

A The price of the good

B Consumers preferences and tastes

C The income of consumers

D The number and price of complementary goods

(2 marks)

Test Your Understanding 36

As a result of poor harvest, the .... (i) of coffee was significantly reduced and the supply curve shifted to the .... (ii). Because the demand for coffee had a .... (iii) price elasticity of demand, the result was a very steep rise in its price.

Read the above passage and indicate which of the following words should be placed in the gaps in the passage.

A supply

B demand

C high

D low

E left

F right

(3 marks)

Test Your Understanding 37

All of the following statements about a monopoly firm in the long run are correct except one. Which *one* is the exception?

A It will tend to produce less output than if the market had perfect competition

B It will earn abnormal profits

C The lack of competition will give rise to X-inefficiency

D The price set will always be higher than that under perfect competition

(2 marks)

Test Your Understanding 38

All of the following are functions of money except one. Which one is the exception?

A A store of value

B A medium of exchange

C A unit of account

D A means of financial intermediation

(2 marks)

Test Your Understanding 39

K plc orders a new machine from a foreign supplier with payment in the foreign currency. Unfortunately the domestic currency weakens during the credit period resulting in the machine costing more than originally expected.

This is an example of which kind of foreign exchange risk?

A Transaction risk

B Translation risk

C Economic risk

D Default risk

(1 mark)

Test Your Understanding 40

Indicate whether each of the following statements is *true* or *false*.

Statements	True	False
A government could finance a budget deficit by raising taxation.		
The principal function of financial institutions is financial intermediation.		
'Liquidity' refers to the ease with which assets can be converted into cash.		
The nominal value of a bond shows the amount a bond is currently worth.		

(4 marks)

Test Your Understanding 41

Which of the below is an example of fiscal policy?

A Bank of England imposing controls on commercial banks

B The removal of regulations which restrict Sunday trading

C The removal of foreign exchange controls which restrict the transfer of currencies between countries

D The creation of tax-exempt individual savings accounts

(2 marks)

Test Your Understanding 42

A debenture with a coupon rate of 8% and a nominal value of $100 was originally issued for $80 and has a market value of $120. How much interest will be paid each year?

A $8.00

B $6.40

C $9.60

D $10.00

(2 marks)

Test Your Understanding 43

The main determinant of the cost of borrowing is usually.

A maturity

B risk

C base rates

D inflation

(1 mark)

Test Your Understanding 44

Rank the following in order of risk, low to high:

(i) CDs
(ii) debentures
(iii) equity.

A i, ii, iii

B iii, ii, i

C i, iii, ii

D ii, iii, i

(2 marks)

Test Your Understanding 45

A bond has the following features.

Nominal value	£1,000
Coupon rate	4%
Current market value	£1,050

Calculate the running yield for this bond.

(2 marks)

Test Your Understanding 46

For each of the following sources of finance for a business, state whether they are appropriate to meet lack of financial synchronisation in the *short term*, the *medium* term or the *long term.*

Sources of Finance	Short term	Medium term	Long term
Trade credit for a business			
Equity capital			
Hire purchase			
Bank overdraft			

(4 marks)

Test Your Understanding 47

If a bank had total assets of $100 bn and was operating with a 10% reserve assets ratio, by how much would its total assets change in the long run if its reserve assets rose by $2 bn but the monetary authorities required banks to raise their reserve assets ratio to 12.5%?

A Rise by $4 bn

B Fall by $4 bn

C Rise by $2 bn

D Fall by $2.5 bn

(2 marks)

Test Your Understanding 48

All of the following would tend to raise the exchange rate (appreciate) for a country's currency except one. Which one is the exception?

A A fall in the volume of imports

B A rise in foreign investment in the country

C A fall in domestic interest rates

D A rise in the country's invisible earnings **(2 marks)**

Test Your Understanding 49

Which *one* of the following is an advantage for a country adopting a flexible exchange rate regime?

A It provides certainty for organisations engaging in international trade

B It eliminates transactions costs

C It reduces the need for central banks to keep reserves of foreign exchange

D Monetary policy can be used to manage the exchange rate for the currency

(2 marks)

Test Your Understanding 50

Indicate whether each of the following statements is *true* or *false*.

Statements	**True**	**False**
For a bank, its most liquid assets tend to be the least profitable.		
Certificates of deposit are tradable financial instruments.		
Bills of exchange are risky financial instruments because there is no guarantor.		
Bond prices and bond yields vary positively.		

(4 marks)

Test Your Understanding 51

All of the following are functions of a central bank except one. Which *one* is the exception?

A Acting as lender of the last resort
B Providing finance for long-term investment projects
C Acting as banker for the government
D Managing the country's foreign exchange reserves **(2 marks)**

Test Your Understanding 52

Indicate whether each of the following financial instruments is used in the *money market* or the *capital market*.

Instruments	Money market	Capital market
Mortgage		
Bill of Exchange		
Certificates of Deposit		
Gilt-edged Stock		

(4 marks)

Test Your Understanding 53

If the exchange rate for a country's currency were to rise (appreciate), would the following prices *rise*, fall or remain *unchanged* as a direct result?

Price	Rise	Fall	Remain unchanged
Domestic price of imported goods.			
Foreign price of imported goods.			
Domestic price of exported goods.			
Foreign price of exported goods.			

(4 marks)

Test Your Understanding 54

Show what you would expect to happen to the following economic indicators in the boom phase of the trade cycle in the economy.

Indicators	Rise	Fall	Remain unchanged
The rate of inflation.			
The rate of unemployment.			
A deficit on the balance of trade.			
A surplus on the government's budget.			
The underlying long-term rate of economic growth.			

(5 marks)

Test Your Understanding 55

According to the Keynesian view, the economy:

A will always tend to settle at a full employment equilibrium

B will always tend to settle at an equilibrium with high unemployment

C may settle at an equilibrium with any level of unemployment

D will not settle at any equilibrium

(2 marks)

Test Your Understanding 56

In order to calculate gross national product (GNP) for a country it is necessary to take gross domestic product (GDP) and:

A add the value of exports and subtract the value of imports

B add net property income from abroad

C add subsidies and subtract indirect taxes

D subtract the value of exports and add the value of imports

(2 marks)

Test Your Understanding 57

Indicate whether each of the following components is an *injection*, a *withdrawal (leakage)* or *neither* in the circular flow model of the economy.

Components	Injection	Withdrawal	Neither
Taxation			
Exports			
Consumption			
Investment			

(4 marks)

Test Your Understanding 58

An economy has a marginal propensity to consume of 0.8. If the government raises public expenditure by $100m, by how much will national income ultimately rise as a result?

(2 marks)

Test Your Understanding 59

The accelerator theory argues that changes in the level of investment are determined by:

A changes in the rate of interest

B the level of consumer income

C swings in business optimism and pessimism

D changes in the level of demand for goods and services

(2 marks)

Test Your Understanding 60

Inflation has all of the following effects except one. Which *one* is the exception?

A It shifts wealth from debtors to creditors

B It reduces a country's international competitiveness

C It reduces the real income of those on fixed incomes

D It raises government tax revenue

(2 marks)

Test Your Understanding 61

The following is a list of types of unemployment.

- Cyclical unemployment
- Structural unemployment
- Frictional unemployment
- Real wage unemployment

Match the above types of unemployment to the appropriate policy response below.

Policy	Type of unemployment
A policy of retraining and education.	
Adopting an expansionary monetary policy.	
Reducing the power of trade unions and professional bodies.	
Improving the information flows at job centres.	

(4 marks)

Test Your Understanding 62

The Phillips curve showed a:

A negative relationship between inflation and wage rates

B positive relationship between inflation and unemployment

C negative relationship between inflation and unemployment

D negative relationship between unemployment and economic growth

(2 marks)

Test Your Understanding 63

All of the following are direct taxes except one. Which *one* is the exception?

A Income tax

B National insurance (social security tax)

C Corporation tax

D Value added tax

(2 marks)

Test Your Understanding 64

The following diagram represents aggregate demand and supply in an economy.

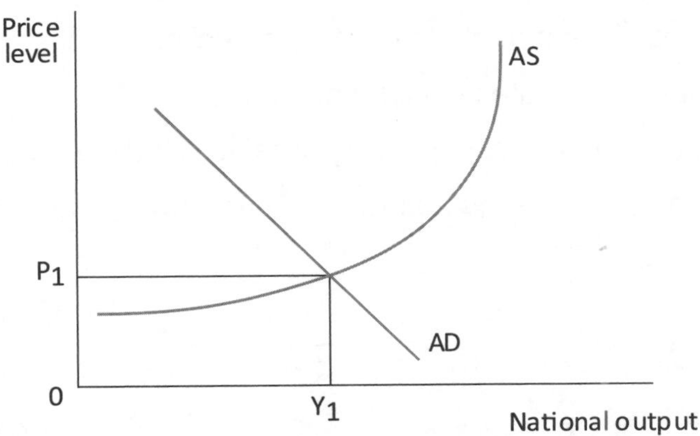

(i) From the following list, identify which one is the correct list of components of aggregate demand.

A AD = C + G + I + X + M
B AD = C + G + T + I
C AD = C + G + I + X – M
D AD = G + I + X

(2 marks)

(ii) If the government wished to shift the aggregate demand curve to the right, which of the following measures would be appropriate?

(i) A reduction in taxation.
(ii) A rise in interest rates.
(iii) A depreciation of the exchange rate.
(iv) An increase in public expenditure.

A (i), (ii) and (iii) only
B (i), (iii) and (iv) only
C (ii), (iii) and (iv) only
D (i), (ii) and (iv) only

(2 marks)

(iii) Sate which economic variable can be discussed by reference to the level P_1.

(2 marks)

Test Your Understanding 65

If the government were to adopt a restrictive monetary policy, all the following would result except one. Which *one* is the exception?

A Business investment would tend to decline

B Private saving rates would tend to rise

C Demand for goods, especially durable goods, would tend to decline

D On foreign exchange markets the currency would tend to depreciate

(2 marks)

Test Your Understanding 66

Indicate whether each of the following statements is *true* or *false*.

Statements	True	False
Supply policies are designed to shift a country's aggregate supply curve to the left.		
Monetarists believe that control of the money supply is the only effective means of preventing inflation.		
Keynesians recommend budget deficits as a means of reducing unemployment.		

(3 marks)

Test Your Understanding 67

A progressive tax is best defined as one where:

A the amount of tax paid rises as income rises

B the proportion of income paid in tax rises as income rises

C the lower the level of income, the lower the amount of tax paid

D there are higher tax bands applicable to higher income levels

(2 marks)

Test Your Understanding 68

According to Keynsian thought, economic growth is best achieved by:

A Cutting taxation

B Increasing government spending

C "Prices and incomes" policies

D Increasing labour mobility

(2 marks)

Test Your Understanding 69

If a government adopted an expansionary fiscal policy it would:

A lower taxes, lower public expenditure and maintain government borrowing

B lower taxes, raise public spending and increase government borrowing

C raise public expenditure and finance this through a rise in taxation

D reduce government borrowing in order to ease credit conditions for the private sector

(2 marks)

Test Your Understanding 70

All of the following are features of the globalisation process except one. Which *one* is the exception?

A An expanding role for multinational companies

B A reduction in artificial barriers to international trade

C Increasing international factor mobility

D A decline in the importance of international specialisation

(2 marks)

Test Your Understanding 71

Indicate for each of the following transactions whether they would be entered into the current account or the capital and financial account of the balance of payments for a country.

Transactions	Current account	Capital/Financial account
Payment for a foreign holiday taken by a resident of the country.		
A deposit of funds by a foreigner into a bank account in the country.		
Receipt of interest from a bank account in another country.		
A rise in the country's foreign exchange reserves.		

(4 marks)

Test Your Understanding 72

If a group of countries adopt free trade between themselves, establish a common external tariff and allow free movement of factors of production between member states, this is called:

A a common market

B an economic union

C a customs union

D a free trade area

(2 marks)

Test Your Understanding 73

Indicate whether each of the following statements is *true* or *false*.

Statements	True	False
Tariff barriers always reduce the economic welfare of the country imposing them.		
Taxes on expensive imports are a useful way of reducing domestic inflationary pressure.		
The main purpose of tariffs is to enable domestic producers to charge higher prices.		
The main benefit of forming a free trade area is that it encourages international specialisation between member states.		

(4 marks)

Test Your Understanding 74

Providing investment finance for development projects is the main function of:

A The International Monetary Fund

B The World Trade Organisation

C The World Bank

D The European Central Bank

(2 marks)

Test Your Understanding 75

All of the following could be used by a government attempting to reduce the country's balance of payments current account deficit except one. Which *one* is the exception?

A A deflationary fiscal policy

B An appreciation in the currency

C A rise in interest rates and restrictions on credit

D The imposition of exchange controls

(2 marks)

Test your understanding answers

Test Your Understanding 1

A

Education is the correct answer because the other organisations are normally found in the private sector.

Test Your Understanding 2

B

Test Your Understanding 3

A

Test Your Understanding 4

D

Test Your Understanding 5

Events	**Raise share price**	**Lower share price**	**Leave share price unchanged**
A reduction in corporation tax	X		
An issue of additional shares in the company		X	
A fall in interest rates	X		

Test Your Understanding 6

Statements	True	False
The absence of shareholders means that the principal-agent problem has no impact on them.		X
They need to avoid losses in the long run.	X	
They operate in both the public and the private sectors of the economy.	X	

Test Your Understanding 7

–2

Test Your Understanding 8

(a) $5,402

(b) No

(c) $131

Test Your Understanding 9

25%

- PBIT = 0.4m
- Average capital employed = (1.4 + 1.8)/2 = 1.6
- ROCE = (0.4/1.6) × 100% = 25%

Test Your Understanding 10

Measures	Short run	Long run
Net present value		X
Rate of return on capital employed	X	
Earnings per share	X	

Test Your Understanding 11

D

Test Your Understanding 12

C

Test Your Understanding 13

An example of the principal–agent problem in business is where principals, such as *shareholders*, delegate control to agents, such as *management*. The problem is one of devising methods to ensure that agents act in the best interest of the principals. Managerial reward systems which link pay and bonuses to the improvement in *shareholder value* is one such method.

Test Your Understanding 14

D

Test Your Understanding 15

B

Test Your Understanding 16

B

Test Your Understanding 17

Statements	True	False
The price mechanism is the only means for allocating scarce resources.		X
The public sector is smaller than the private sector.	X	
Market prices fully reflect all production costs.		X
Prices convey important information for both producers and consumers.	X	

Test Your Understanding 18

D

Test Your Understanding 19

C

Test Your Understanding 20

–1.5

Test Your Understanding 21

Effects	Yes	No
Sales volume would increase.	X	
The volume of supply would increase.		X
The equilibrium price would rise.	X	
In the short run, unit production costs would increase.	X	

Test Your Understanding 22

C

Test Your Understanding 23

Statements	True	False
If the demand curve for Good A shifts to the right when the price of Good B falls we can conclude that A and B are substitute goods.		X
If the demand for a good is price inelastic, a fall in its price will leave sales volume unchanged and total revenue reduced.		X
The more price inelastic is the demand for a good, the greater is the proportion of any indirect tax levied on it that can be passed onto the consumer.	X	
An indirect tax imposed upon a good which has negative externalities will improve resource allocation.	X	

Test Your Understanding 24

D

Test Your Understanding 25

A

Test Your Understanding 26

B

Test Your Understanding 27

Company merger	Merger type
A steel producer merges with a producer of iron ore.	B
A car producer merges with a producer of commercial vans.	A
A financial services company merges with a travel company.	D
A brewing company merges with a chain of inns and bars.	C

Test Your Understanding 28

B

Test Your Understanding 29

C

Test Your Understanding 30

Situations	Definition
The emission of dangerous fumes from car exhausts.	B
Pollution caused by the production of consumer electrical goods.	C
Premature death of consumers of tobacco.	D
Improved health among consumers of low fat food products.	D

Test Your Understanding 31

C

The market value = PV of future receipts, discounted at the required return.

- Annual receipt = interest of $3. The pattern of the cash flows is a perpetuity
- Current market value = 3 × 1/0.05 = $60
- New market value = 3 × 1/0.06 = $50

Test Your Understanding 32

D

Test Your Understanding 33

B

Test Your Understanding 34

C

Test Your Understanding 35

A

Test Your Understanding 36

As a result of poor harvest the supply of coffee was significantly reduced and the *supply* curve shifted to the *left*. Because the demand for coffee had a *low* price elasticity of demand, the result was a very steep rise in its price.

Test Your Understanding 37

D – economies of scale may result in a lower price

Test Your Understanding 38

D

Test Your Understanding 39

A

Test Your Understanding 40

Statements	**True**	**False**
A government could finance a budget deficit by raising taxation.		X
The principal function of financial institutions is financial intermediation.	X	
'Liquidity' refers to the ease with which assets can be converted into cash.	X	
The nominal value of a bond shows the amount a bond is currently worth.		X

Test Your Understanding 41

D

Test Your Understanding 42

A

Interest = coupon rate × nominal value = 8% × 100 = $8

Test Your Understanding 43

B

While each of the factors will affect the cost of borrowing, risk is usually the key issue e.g. an overdraft is much more expensive than a mortgage because the money is unsecured and is thus more risky for the bank concerned.

Test Your Understanding 44

A

CDs are very low risk and equity the most risky.

Test Your Understanding 45

3.81%

Test Your Understanding 46

Sources of Finance	Short term	Medium term	Long term
Trade credit for a business	X		
Equity capital			X
Hire purchase		X	
Bank overdraft	X		

Test Your Understanding 47

B

Test Your Understanding 48

C

Test Your Understanding 49

C

Test Your Understanding 50

Statements	True	False
For a bank, its most liquid assets tend to be the least profitable.	X	
Certificates of deposit are tradable financial instruments.	X	
Bills of exchange are risky financial instruments because there is no guarantor.		X
Bond prices and bond yields vary positively.		X

Test Your Understanding 51

B

Test Your Understanding 52

Instruments	Money market	Capital market
Mortgage		X
Bill of Exchange	X	
Certificates of Deposit	X	
Gilt-edged Stock		X

Test Your Understanding 53

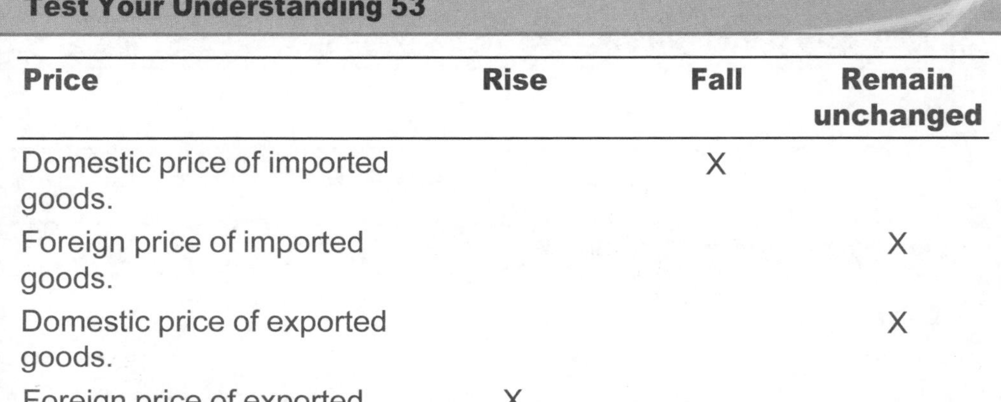

Price	Rise	Fall	Remain unchanged
Domestic price of imported goods.		X	
Foreign price of imported goods.			X
Domestic price of exported goods.			X
Foreign price of exported goods.	X		

Test Your Understanding 54

Price	Rise	Fall	Remain unchanged
The rate of inflation.	X		
The rate of unemployment.		X	
A deficit on the balance of trade.	X		
A surplus on the government's budget.	X		
A surplus on the government's budget.			X